McNAUGHTON
VOLUME 2   1939-1943

McNAUGHTON

VOLUME 2   1939-1943

John Swettenham

THE RYERSON PRESS
TORONTO WINNIPEG VANCOUVER

© THE RYERSON PRESS, 1969
PRINTED AND BOUND IN CANADA BY THE RYERSON PRESS
TORONTO WINNIPEG VANCOUVER

SBN 7700 0298 6

Library of Congress Catalog Card Number: 70-375263

Published as a Centennial of Canadian Confedera-
tion project. The preparation of the manuscript
was subsidized by the Centennial Commission.

Publié en célébration du Centenaire de la Con-
fédération Canadienne, et rédigé grâce à une
subvention de la Commission du Centenaire.

All picture credits are to the Public Archives
of Canada unless otherwise noted.

AUTHOR'S PHOTOGRAPH ON THE JACKET
BY THOMAS STUDIO, OTTAWA

Contents

Illustrations

Maps

McNAUGHTON
VOLUME 2   1939-1943

WAR LEADER
(1939-1943)

Chapter 1

~~~~~~

Recall to Arms

McNaughton, returning from England with the representatives of the Canadian Manufacturers' Association, heard over the radio the news of Hitler's attack on Poland shortly after the ship had entered the Gulf of St. Lawrence. Knowing that war was now inevitable, he at once wrote to Mackenzie King to offer himself for war service wherever he was needed. On 3 September, after the General had reached Ottawa, Britain and France honoured the pledge that they had given to Poland in an attempt to deter Hitler, and declared war on the aggressor.

In 1939 Canada was not automatically committed by Britain's act, as she had been in 1914. An autonomous nation now, Canada had the right to decide what action she would take. On 7 September Parliament assembled in emergency session and decided that George VI, as King of Canada, should proclaim the existence of a state of war between Canada and the German Reich; this was done three days later. What now seemed no more than an uneasy truce between the wars was ended; for the second time in a generation Canada was at war with Germany.

This time the pronouncement brought no scenes of wild elation. The legacy and the lessons of the First World War had penetrated too far into the hearts and minds of the people for any jubilation. Yet the decision had been Canada's own; Parliament had brought a united country into the war. Throughout the nation there was awareness of what this would mean and a calm determination to face the ordeal and whatever sacrifices it might bring.

Canada now reaped the harvest sowed by successive governments between the wars. The country was unprepared for large-scale conflict. The nucleus of an army existed (4,500 professional and some 52,000 part-time soldiers), and through McNaughton's forethought the professionals were well trained; but the arms with which they were equipped were largely the weapons of the First World War. "Had the Government carried out the scheme for an expanded Dominion Arsenal capable of producing guns and small arms which was recommended as early as 1930," the official historian of the Canadian Army in the Second World War was to write, "it would have paid a great national dividend in 1939 and 1940."[1] But McNaughton's warnings had largely gone unheeded and when war broke out Canada had, for example, only sixteen light tanks, twenty-nine Bren guns, twenty-three anti-tank rifles, and these had come from Britian. There were four modern anti-aircraft guns and the same number of two-pounder anti-tank guns in the whole country.

A carefully drafted mobilization plan was followed when the government, even before Canada's formal entry into the war, ordered the mobilization of two divisions, and ancillary troops from the militia. The confusion that had marked mobilization in 1914 was avoided. Time-honoured militia regiments were mobilized as units and brought up to strength by voluntary enlistment. Because the unanimity with which the country had entered the war was far too precious to be destroyed, conscription was avoided: every man attested into the "Canadian Active Service Force" was a volunteer. And despite the realism with which they had received the news of war, men came forward. The spirit of service was strong and in September alone some 58,000 men joined the army.

On 16 September the government decided to send one division overseas and four days later the Chief of the General Staff (Major-General T. V. Anderson) recommended that it should consist of the units mobilizing to form the 1st Division. His proposal was accepted. The question then arose: who was to command it, the selection of the commander being regarded by Mackenzie King as "one of the gravest responsibilities of the Government."[2] Of the candidates considered, however, one man stood out as the logical choice.

Ten years before McNaughton himself had attained the highest army appointment in Canada, and had held it for the unprecedented period of two terms; he was reconciled to a civilian appointment involving new challenges when, in 1935, he became president of the National Research Council. In that capacity he had immersed himself in the problems of mobilizing Canadian industry for the struggle which even then he knew to be impending, and in stimulating research and channelling it towards the developments that would be required in a highly scientific war.

His record was second to none. Not only had he proved himself to be a brave soldier, a capable and well-trained officer, a superb organizer and experienced commander; he was also a practical engineer, with wide scientific knowledge and an inventive mind, who knew intimately the equipment required by a modern army. No other military officer in Canada had these qualifications. A present-day computer, fed with the specifications for the ideal commander at that time, would have whirred, winked its flashing lights, and spelled out McNaughton's name immediately.

Mackenzie King was perfectly aware of McNaughton's suitability; he had always had, he said, "a high appreciation of his capacities." He had, however, one reservation: McNaughton was reputed to be a Conservative and had been a close associate of Bennett during the last Tory administration. "The only thing I don't like," the Prime Minister recorded, " . . . is the school from which he comes, which was the school of MacBrien, of Bennett, and Herridge." Furthermore, because McNaughton would never compromise when he felt that a course was right, he tended to organize matters to the limit and according to his lights, without regard for the personal animosities that he might provoke. King knew that there would be feeling against the appointment in the ranks of his Liberal supporters.[3]

But Mackenzie King was not seeking a politician; he was looking for the best commander he could find. And when Norman Rogers, the new Minister of National Defence, put forward McNaughton's name the Prime Minister welcomed the suggestion. The pre-eminent qualifications of McNaughton in Mackenzie King's eyes outweighed his past associations, but the Prime Minister could not resist congratulating himself on his own impartiality: "No better evidence could be given," he wrote, "of our disinterested action than in giving this command to one who comes . . . from that particular group" but there was no doubt that McNaughton was "the best equipped man for the purpose."[4]

On 6 October the appointment was formally offered to McNaughton by Mackenzie King; Ralston (Minister of Finance) and Rogers were also present. "He told me that it was the desire of himself and his colleagues that I should command the Division with the probability that a corps was in the offing. I told him that it was very pleasing to me; that I had expected that industrial mobilization would have been my job; that I was very pleased to accept."[5]

The interview, King recorded, had been "as deeply moving as any I have witnessed in my public life. One felt the enormous responsibilities that were being placed on the individual." The new commander, as he had made clear, was fully determined that the men should go into action with every possible advantage in weapons; that the major effort of the war should be made in production; and that Canada should exert itself "to arm and equip the troops to spare human lives."* This humane approach, so close to his own, struck the Prime Minister very forcibly. "From the beginning of their wartime relationship," Pickersgill wrote in *The Mackenzie King Record*, "there was a bond of sympathy between Mackenzie King and McNaughton which was never broken."[6]

The question of McNaughton's successor at the National Research Council had to be resolved in the days that followed. A view was prevalent that with the intensity of modern war—with mechanization, air power and the clash of great forces—hostilities would not be of long duration. It was a forecast that was nearly right, but with the wrong winner. Knowing that Mackenzie King shared this view, McNaughton asked him bluntly, "When the war is over, then, do you want me to go back to the National Research Council?" Mackenzie King said he did. "Well," McNaughton continued, "that makes things very easy for everybody. The Research

---

*It was a policy that McNaughton was to follow consistently, as will be seen. It brought him much criticism from those who thought he spent time on weapon development at the expense of training.

Council Act setting up the organization contains a clause whereby the Council has the authority to appoint an acting president during a president's absence on duty from the country. He said 'Is that the law?' and I assured him that it was. I recall that he looked at me very hard and he said, 'Well, whom do you want to appoint?' "[7]

McNaughton had already given some consideration to that; he had consulted his colleagues, particularly Sir Frederick Banting, and the general opinion was that Dr. C. J. Mackenzie of the University of Saskatchewan was the man for the job. He had demonstrated that as chairman of the council's Review Committee during the past summer. McNaughton, then, had his answer ready.

"Jack Mackenzie," he replied.

The Prime Minister was aghast. "But he's another Conservative!" he exclaimed.

"Does that really matter?" McNaughton fired back.

There was a lengthy pause during which King looked quizzically at the General.

"No, it does not," he finally said.[8]

As in McNaughton's case, the calibre of the man had prevailed over his personal politics. The name of Dean Mackenzie went before the council and was unanimously approved. On October 18 he arrived in Ottawa and assumed the office of acting president of NRC.[9] That same day McNaughton, still president in name, was appointed "Inspector-General of Units of the 1st Canadian Division" with effect from 5 October;[10] the prospective overseas commander would continue to enjoy an intimate association with the council.*

---

*"This was pleasing, reassuring, and useful to me and to the Canadian war effort," McNaughton commented. "I had a direct channel for my proposals to an individual who would press them forward. That, however, was not my primary thought. I considered that Jack Mackenzie was the best qualified member of NRC to lead the council and give continuity to the work in hand for all purposes. And so, with great initiative and distinction, he proved to be."[11]

In October an honour—regarded by McNaughton with great pleasure and yet with some amusement—was conferred upon the General. The Royal College of Physicians and Surgeons of Canada made him an Honorary Fellow for his distinguished services as head of the National Research Council in promoting the Department of Medical Research and for his successful efforts in putting medical research on a firm basis.

The appointment of Inspector General [McNaughton said] was just a means of giving me authority over the units, scattered from Halifax to Vancouver, that were mobilizing across the country. The season of the year didn't permit what was done in 1914—concentration at Valcartier—where they could be sorted out under myself as GOC. There was great anxiety on the part of the Government to get the Division, or a respectable part of it, moved out of Canada quickly and over into the United Kingdom both for psychological reasons and for practical reasons; we didn't want to have to try to train troops in a very cold climate, scattered in different locations and without proper facilities, when in England we would have training areas and ranges available to us in a much more moderate climate. I wanted to get these people together in a climate I could do something with, for although the British climate is raw and damp it's no worse that what we would encounter on the other side of the Channel and the environmental similarity would be useful in acclimatizing our people. So the sailing dates were arranged and I was appointed Inspector General to make sure those dates were met, to visit the units and to see that mobilization was being properly carried out. I had the authority to ask any questions I liked and, while I had no physical command over them at that stage, nevertheless I could tell the Minister directly, over the heads of all the staff officers, what I had found in the units, where there were difficulties, and what should be done although I couldn't order it. It was a very useful arrangement.[12]

McNaughton was, of course, appointed General Officer Commanding (GOC) before the division sailed from Canada in December.

On the 20th the Inspector General was given a tiny office, eight feet by six, in the Fraser Building, 53 Queen Street, in the heart of Ottawa. That day Colonel E. W. Sansom (Director of Military Training and Staff Duties) reported as McNaughton's administrative staff officer and three military clerks arrived. A few days later Major G. G. Simonds reported as General Staff Officer, Second Grade (GSO2). Such were the small beginnings of what was to grow into the headquarters of Canada's First Army.[13]

Under "Defence Scheme No. 3," a plan worked out under Mc-Naughton in 1932 and revised in 1937, the field force to be mobilized was made up of a number of units found by military districts, proportionate to their population, across Canada. The order of battle of the two divisions mobilized in 1939 included units from every part of the country. There was thus equality of opportunity for service in the various provinces, while heavy losses in battle would not bear too heavily on any one province. After his appointment as Inspector General, McNaughton, anxious to see for himself the state of the units he was to command, toured the country. He was equally anxious to be able to furnish concrete information to commanders who would, he knew, be concerned about the provision of equipment needed to put their units on a war footing.

During the last week in October McNaughton toured the East. He inspected an engineer unit at Halifax, the West Nova Scotia Regiment at Bridgewater, artillery units at Charlottetown, Moncton and Fredericton, and the Carleton and York Regiment at Woodstock. He saw artillery and service corps units in Quebec and the Royal 22e Régiment at Camp Valcartier before returning to Ottawa to report his findings.[14] Like many another inspecting officer before him, McNaughton had been impressed by Canada's manhood. He admired the "sturdy, clean-cut" men of the 22e Régiment. In the West Nova Scotias, the non-commissioned officers (NCOs) were "well qualified and intelligent" and the soldiers "of strong and sturdy physique"; he was "particularly impressed by their excellent spirit under the most adverse conditions."[15] The "adverse conditions," in fact, had shocked him.

"I discovered to my horror," he said, "that this unit was accommodated in an old curling rink. The ice had been scooped out and straw thrown down for these recruits to sleep on. They had no blankets and nobody had bought blankets for them. There were no paillasses. They had no underwear and their boots were poor. Two hundred men were without caps. Most of these things were procurable on the public market but there was an unawareness on the part of the staff down there what their responsibilities were."[16] The unit was three officers and 177 other ranks under strength, not through any shortage of volunteers, but because of a lack of accommodation and clothing. A priority message to the Master General of the Ordnance put three thousand paillasses on the way to Bridgewater immediately and the other deficiencies were made up shortly after the Inspector General's return to Ottawa.[17]

On 1 November McNaughton started out again, this time for a tour of populous Ontario and Quebec. Perhaps his visit to Toronto was the most impressive. There, on the vast Canadian National Exhibition grounds, engineer and signals units were assembled and three from the infantry—the Toronto Scottish Regiment, the 48th Highlanders and a company of the Royal Canadian Regiment. But Montreal certainly touched him most when the Canadian Officers Training Corps (COTC), of his old university, fourteen hundred strong, marched past at the half-time interval of the McGill-Queen's football game at the Molson Memorial Stadium. He gave an address that day when Lady Currie (the General's widow) laid the corner-stone of the gymnasium at the McGill Armoury.*

On these visits messages flew back to Ottawa pointing out what was wrong. They were, however, helpful and constructive. At Borden, for example, McNaughton had been appalled to find at the Armoured Fighting Vehicle Training Centre that the accommodation was both inadequate and constituted a "dangerous fire hazard involving tank equipment valued at approximately half a million dollars. This is the only equipment in Canada and cannot be replaced."[19] The thing to do, he suggested, was to separate the men from the machines:

Additional accommodation personnel urgently needed. Propose erect immediately adjacent present temporary buildings . . . three standard huts and one standard recreation for men, one standard hut sergeants' mess, two standard huts for officers, one standard hut for office and stores, all plus ablution facilities and central heating. Above to be on concrete foundations capable of encasement with tile later. Total estimated cost eighty thousand dollars. Much of material is on site already.[20]

Decisions at Ottawa, facilitated by such brief yet comprehensive reports pointing to the remedy, were not hard to make.

---

*This was built as a memorial to Sir Arthur Currie. "We go forward," said McNaughton, "in the hope that our new crusade will be worthy of our old Corps and its commander, in whose memory we dedicate this gymnasium and armoury today to the use of generations of McGill students present and future. May they long cherish the memory of him for whom it is named and remember the greatness of the contribution *he* made to Canada in war and afterwards in peace."[18]

At Toronto he had noticed some boys in the ranks. "This brings up a question of policy as to whether or not boys under 18 years of age should be allowed to proceed overseas. My view is that they should not be allowed to go. I think this matter should be decided at an early date and instructions issued."[21] Norman Rogers, the Minister, ruled a few days later that no boys under eighteen and no officers under twenty were to leave Canada; for this, Canadian mothers could thank McNaughton.[22]

On 7 November, having presented his very detailed reports covering the officers, men, accommodation, equipment, clothing and necessaries and the state of training of the units so far visited, the Inspector General left by air for a tour of the West. Sansom accompanied him, as did the newly joined General Staff Officer, (GSO1), Lieutenant-Colonel Guy Turner, who was to remain closely associated with McNaughton in mutual loyalty and respect throughout the difficult years ahead. They touched down at Fort William that day, inspected a field ambulance and then flew on to Winnipeg,[23] where at Fort Osborne Barracks, in this great prairie centre, Princess Patricia's Canadian Light Infantry and an artillery battery were drawn up for inspection. A second unit of artillery awaited inspection at the armoury. After luncheon with the commander of the 2nd Infantry Brigade (Brigadier G. R. Pearkes, who had won the V.C. at Passchendaele) McNaughton flew off on a lonely pilgrimage to his birthplace, Moosomin. He went there, not as the prospective leader of Canada's field army with a great career behind him, but as a man briefly searching for the reassuring scenes of his boyhood before facing an uncertain future. It was his last opportunity to do so before moving overseas.[24]

During the next few days the inspecting party moved west by stages: Moose Jaw; Saskatoon; Edmonton; Calgary; Vancouver; Victoria. At Calgary, on Armistice Day, McNaughton placed a wreath at the cenotaph on behalf of the garrison; all the troops in garrison marched past. On the 14th, when the Inspector General and his staff left Sea Island, Vancouver, for the two-thousand-mile return flight to Ottawa, the Saskatoon Light Infantry, the Edmonton Regiment, the Calgary Highlanders, the Seaforth Highlanders of Canada, a company of Patricias, gunners and ancillary units had all come under close scrutiny.[25]

The plane arrived in Ottawa on 15 November at the uninspiring hour of 3 A.M. On the night of the 15th McNaughton met the military members of the Defence Council and reported on his western inspection. Very little had escaped his attention. "The 6-inch howitzers allotted to medium batteries, R.C.A.," for example, "particularly those of 1 Medium Brigade, should be overhauled in preparation for despatch abroad. The guns themselves, which I inspected at various centres, are in excellent condition with little evidence of wear, but the carriages, sights and particularly the wheels, require attention."[26]

The Inspector General's comments on the state of training were particularly full and some of them were devastating. The unit that had been designated as the Tank Battalion mobilizing with the 1st Division was "not efficient as a tank unit. Consideration should be given to substituting another Tank Battalion that has reached a reasonable state of efficiency."[27] Another unit, on the other hand, was in "excellent shape with well-qualified Warrant Officers and NCOs. It was well turned-out and appeared well-trained."[28]

In general, as in the case of units inspected in eastern Canada, "the appearance and steadiness of the men on parade and their drill movements indicated that favourable progress has been made in setting-up exercises, foot and arms drill . . . in the majority of units." But it was equally obvious that units had been "handicapped through lack of funds for general training purposes."[29] Only one unit had paraded in the recently adopted battledress— "C" Battery, RCHA, at Winnipeg. McNaughton put the stamp of approval on its appearance. "It looked neat and businesslike and the men stated it was comfortable."[30]

Scores of problems which unsettled the units had been listed by McNaughton for solution. As he said, "I carried out this business across the country and filled my notebook full of notes; and each time I came back to Ottawa the members of the Defence Council were summoned to the Minister's office and I went in there and made a personal report. The telegrams that went out to the various districts to put things right were pretty multitudinous. That was what the Inspector General was for. Some people got a shaking up which didn't do them any harm."[31]

The system of drawing rations, McNaughton reported, was inflexible and unpopular. Two pounds of bread and meat per man every day was altogether too much and led to waste; but not enough alternative items, such as cornflakes and fresh milk, were issued. This often resulted in bartering activities reminiscent of a Persian market. There should be, McNaughton recommended, "a generous increase in the allowable substitutes on a value basis" and it should be introduced at once.[32] And what was the policy with regard to the wearing of the kilt by Highland regiments? Through fear of vesicant gas, the Minister ruled that battledress only would be worn.* There was a shortage of stationery and printed forms, so that commanders procured their own and sent the bills along to the headquarters of military districts for payment. Because districts had no authority to settle them they remained unpaid; and creditors were beating at the barrack gates for satisfaction. McNaughton rectified a shortage of training pamphlets, required for study by unit officers on the long Atlantic crossing, in characteristic fashion. Samples were passed to the National Research Council which, by working twenty-four-hour shifts, reproduced enough copies before the division's departure.[34]

On 16 November a most important discussion took place between the CGS and the Inspector General. It concerned the ancillary troops required to constitute, with the division proper, a balanced force. McNaughton's list differed considerably from that produced by Anderson (as, indeed, it would, for the British had asked for specific ancillary troops) "but on the insistence of the Inspector General that a balanced Canadian force is essential the Chief of the General Staff agreed to forward the proposals through

---

*"If Major-General McNaughton wants to give a display of that courage which has earned him such high esteem from one end of the Dominion to the other," one newspaper reported, "he should pay an informal visit to the Seaforth Armouries. . . . Kilts are to be laid up in mothballs to await the return of the 'Ladies From Hell'!"[33]

the High Commissioner for Canada in England[35] for consideration by the War Office."* Two days later the sanction of the Minister was obtained, and on the 20th the Defence Council approved Mc-Naughton's list.

McNaughton's insistence on a balanced force, in 1939, is interesting. For years before the war Major-General J. F. C. Fuller, one of Britain's eminent military critics and historians, had again and again advanced the concept that tank armies on their own, with little more than mop-up support from other arms ("infantry would not be needed except to garrison the country that the tanks had conquered")[38] would lead to victory. There were many who believed this, and German successes in Poland and France, and the race to the Caucasus, seemed to validate the concept of deep-thrusting armoured force. But in the final battles of the war spectacular sweeps by unaccompanied armour were no longer possible. Success required teamwork; victory was won by combined arms and not the least of these were infantry and artillery. Despite cogent arguments to the contrary, never once did McNaughton swerve from his belief in balanced force, whether division, corps or army.

On 20 November the Inspector General completed his programme with a visit to Kingston, where he inspected artillery units and the Signals centre at Barriefield; he saw the Hastings

---

*The British government had asked for technical units from Canada on 6 September, 1940, and Canada had agreed to the request before a decision had been reached to send a division. At that time, of course, McNaughton had not been consulted about the units to be sent. The original conception was that the units would be equipped at British expense and serve under War Office control "until units are absorbed into Canadian higher formation" at some future date. The decision to send a Canadian division to Britain complicated matters. McNaughton altered the list of units so that "essential arms and services for the 1st Division might be available" and he could not accept that the units should not be under his control. The CGS objected that the British would probably decline to equip the units at their expense if this stipulation were insisted upon.[36] Ralston insisted, said McNaughton, that "if these are Corps Troops and our commitment is to a division, the War Office should pay." It was, the General continued, an indication that there would be "the sharpest kind of accounting," which was distressing at a time when men were volunteering freely to spend their lives. Despite Ralston's attempts to persuade him to the contrary, Mc-Naughton remained firm that these units would be under his command in England. The financial aspect was settled some months later by Canada remaining in control of the units and footing the bill.[37]

and Prince Edward Regiment at Picton.[39] Two days later Major-General W. H. P. Elkins (Master General of the Ordnance) brought bad news of deficiencies that could not be made up. There were no flannel shirts, no battledress for officers, no field-glasses or compasses, no anti-gas capes or eyeshields; even gloves were doubtful; but the division would receive General Motors vehicles complete and in first-class order. McNaughton was curious to know if the War Office welcomed the Canadian supply of transport; he understood they did not. Elkins replied that that was not strictly true. They had no quarrel with Canada's provision of divisional transport but did not consider that Canadian sources need be developed for supplying British requirements. McNaughton considered it "certain that the War Office would later want Canadian motor vehicles" and that "supplying our own requirements now would lay the foundation for future expansion."[40] In this he proved to be a prophet. During the last seven months of 1940 the British government placed orders in Canada for 72,434 vehicles. In 1943, the peak year, the output stood "in a class by itself as a major factor not merely in British but in global war supply."[41] That year the Canadian automotive industry turned out 176,885 military trucks and by the end of the war total production had risen to 815,729.[42]

Nevertheless it was clear that the bulk of the equipment required by this division would have to be found in England. McNaughton insisted, however, that tracked carriers should be replaced by Canadian manufactures later. As for guns, he considered it "essential to initiate the manufacture of guns in Canada for the Canadian forces at the earliest possible moment." The long-term advantages would be great and there would be an immediate benefit for the troops under his command, for McNaughton could base his case for obtaining the most modern British guns, with which his men would train, on the fact that similar guns were coming from Canada.

At the end of November McNaughton journeyed to Toronto for a meeting that he was determined not to miss. It concerned experimental diamond drilling for war purposes and was attended by Lieutenant-Colonel C. S. L. Hertzberg, Commanding Royal

Engineer (CRE), 1st Division, Lieutenant-Colonel Turner, the Honourable Colin Campbell (Minister of Public Works, Province of Ontario, then serving as a subaltern in the Royal Canadian Engineers) and Oliver Hall of the Mining Association of Ontario. The question of diamond drilling in the theatre of operations had been raised by, among others, R. A. Bryce, president of the Ontario Mining Association.[43]

McNaughton's fertile mind had immediately seized on the possibilities. He was convinced that in this war the French, pinning their faith in the Maginot Line, would adopt a defensive strategy and let the Germans attack. The French had planned their line in 1930 and for almost a decade they had built and increased its strength. But McNaughton, with his experience of the breaching of the Hindenburg and Hermann Lines, felt it could be pierced. As early as 1932 he had protested against the old linear theory of defence:

I am more convinced than ever that we must move forward in our war organizations to smaller, faster, harder-hitting armies of great range of action and long endurance commanded and staffed by officers who can think in terms of combination of units and concentration of force in "areas" measured in hundreds of square miles. I use the term "areas" deliberately because the new mobility has certainly established that the old linear battle is a thing of the past. Today a marching column is just as likely, probably more likely, to be struck in rear or on its inner flank than to be attacked in front.[44]

He did think that French reserves would seal off any German penetration, and it would then be a matter of evicting the Germans from the Maginot Line, sections of which they would undoubtedly occupy. "My real thought," McNaughton said, "was that the drills would be useful for the recapture of the line." Horizontal boring, from a considerable distance away, would enable explosives to be placed under the defences or gas to be introduced through the bore holes. He was "so impressed with the possibilities of the scheme that he had devoted his last free afternoon to come to Toronto to discuss it; he said, 'We will start in a small way to see what is in the scheme and then expand if results warrant it.' "[45]

The 12th Field Company, Royal Canadian Engineers, from Winnipeg, McNaughton continued, would be going overseas with the ancillary troops. He proposed that one of its sections should be organized in Toronto and consist of Ontario "hard-rock" miners. He offered the command to Campbell, an experienced construction engineer with a knowledge of mining, who accepted. The idea appealed to Campbell; he would go to the mining districts of northern Ontario to get the right kind of men. Hall thought the Mining Association might be prepared to pay these men a bonus to make up the considerable difference in pay.[46]

McNaughton then turned to the provision of equipment; it would be expensive, and as it was not a normal military supply no funds could be expected from the government. Would the Mining Association be prepared to help with that too? Hall thought they would go a certain way in the matter and, with complete generosity, the association backed the project to the limit,[47] including the provision of extra borts (diamonds for the drills), which Hall carried in his pocket on future liaison visits to England.[48]

Before leaving Toronto McNaughton called on Mitchell Hepburn, the Premier of Ontario. The reason for the visit was to ask for the release to the army of the blankets which, the General knew, had been taken over by the provincial government on the liquidation of the relief camps in Ontario four years earlier. Hepburn readily agreed to make them available at no cost whatever. The Premier had been a pilot in the First World War and suffered some disability but, as he told McNaughton, he wished to go overseas in this war too. "He decided that he was sufficiently well to go in the capacity of A.D.C. to the G.O.C. 1st Canadian Division and as such he proposed himself to me—not only proposed himself but did everything in the world to get me to take him. But I finally convinced him that it was his duty to stay in Canada and put ginger into the mobilization. I did tell him that I wanted his Minister of Public Works in charge of a special section of tunnellers and so we finally compromised; I swapped the Premier of Ontario as an A.D.C. for the Minister of Public Works as the

nucleus of a very useful engineering organization."[49] On his
return General and Mrs. McNaughton dined with Mackenzie
King at Laurier House. "He asked for an account of what was
going on and, in a lighter vein, I gave him the story of my chat
with Hepburn and his desire to become my A.D.C. Now Hepburn
had been a thorn in his side for some time. He said, 'Andy, if
you'll only do that there's nothing that's in the gift of Canada you
can't have!' "[50]

On 2 December McNaughton, having completed the inspection
of units and done everything possible to make them ready for
Europe, became GOC 1st Canadian Division. The day before
leaving for Britain he had another interview with Mackenzie
King. They discussed conscription and the General said that he
thought the "no-conscription policy" was right.* McNaughton
was "absolutely content" with everything pertaining to the division.
"The right men had been appointed as officers. He had inspected
the different regiments; looked at almost every man. They were in
good condition—the medical examination had been very strict
because of the many seeking to enlist. . . . Everything was as complete as it could be, except the equipment which they were to
secure in England. He could not wish for a finer body of men. He
expressed his strong admiration for Rogers, who, he said, had done
excellent work as Minister; had gained the confidence of the
Army."[52] He was not so pleased, however, with the state of industry and expressed his concern to the Prime Minister that more was
not being done to gear it to the war effort. King promised to inves-
tigate. McNaughton, on parting, thanked the Prime Minister for
his support and sympathy, and was told that he would find
Mackenzie King and the government "at his back."[53]

McNaughton and his staff left Ottawa on 8 December for Halifax, the port of embarkation. A special train had been drawn up
at the Isabella siding. Alistair Fraser, vice-president of the Canadian National Railways, travelled with the train by private coach

*Dr. Robert J. Manion, the leader of the opposition, shared this view[51] and
had committed himself publicly as reported in the Toronto *Globe and Mail*, 28
March, 1939.

in which he had provided accommodation for McNaughton and his senior staff officers. The Prime Minister, the Minister of National Defence and the Adjutant General (Major-General H. H. Matthews) came to the train in the early afternoon to bid the GOC farewell.[54]

The last word I said to him [Mackenzie King recorded] was to remember that in quietness and confidence was strength, and that God was on his side. We both felt the emotion of the situation .... As I talked with McNaughton I felt a little concern about his being able to see this war through without a breakdown. I felt he was too far on in years to be taking on so great a job. Having been through the strain of a previous war he and many others like him might find they had not the endurance that they believed they had. I am even more convinced that the Canadian public would not have listened to anyone else as Commander of the Expeditionary Force.[55]

Next day, soon after dark, the train drew into Halifax where the shapes of five great liners loomed over the dockside buildings. There was no single great convoy, as in 1914; instead, the division was to be carried in two main flights. (A third, composed mainly of ancillary and technical troops, reached Scotland early in 1940.) General McNaughton and his party boarded the Cunard liner *Aquitania* and, later that evening, paid a courtesy visit to Rear-Admiral Lancelot Holland, commanding the Third Battle Squadron. Holland returned the call next day and described the protective measures. These would consist of HMS *Resolution* (battleship), close escort; two British and four Canadian destroyers, local escort; with HMS *Furious* (aircraft carrier), HMS *Repulse* (battle-cruiser) and HMS *Emerald* (cruiser) acting as a covering force. McNaughton was completely satisfied with these arrangements which were more extensive than he would have requested. There was no objection, Holland continued, to the flying of the Canadian battle flag* aboard the *Aquitania* during the voyage, as McNaughton wished.[56]

---

*This flag was white with, in the hoist, the Union Jack; the fly bore three red maple leaves on one stem and in the upper right a gold fleurs-de-lis on a blue circle. Colonel A. F. Duguid (Director of the Historical Section, General Staff) designed it. The devices used were already authorized and each was placed in accordance with the laws of heraldry to express its proper significance.

On the following morning, at a ceremony in the *Aquitania's* lounge, the flag was dedicated. Prayers were offered in English and in French; McNaughton spoke simply of the significance of the occasion; Lieutenant-Colonel Turner read the farewell telegrams sent by the Prime Minister and the Minister of National Defence and McNaughton's replies. The ceremony was recorded by the Canadian Broadcasting Corporation.[57]

The message from the Prime Minister was lengthy; no public leavetaking had been possible, but he wanted the commander, the officers and the men to know that "the hearts of the people of Canada are with you."[58] In his reply, McNaughton thanked the Prime Minister on behalf of all ranks for his sympathy and encouragement. There would be dark days ahead, "but we have faith that the efforts of the British Commonwealth, of our great Ally, of the men from Canada and of those who will follow after in a steady stream, will in the end prevail."[59]

At noon the convoy started to move when the *Duchess of Bedford* drew away from the jetty. *The Empress of Australia* followed a half-hour later, and then, at intervals, the *Monarch of Bermuda*, the *Aquitania* and the *Empress of Britain*. Once the outforts had been passed, *Aquitania* proudly unfurled the battle flag from her masthead. The weather was fine and the sky clear.

The long voyage passed without incident save on the last night out when the *Aquitania* collided with a cruiser. All the lifeboats on the port side were smashed—as well as McNaughton's motorcar which was lashed to the deck. "No ship's officer," commented McNaughton, "would admit that anything had happened!"[60] The time was used for training, lectures and exercises; ship's concerts were held in English and French. Then, on 16 December, a local escort of twelve destroyers steamed into sight; the convoy was nearing British waters.

Anthony Eden (Secretary of State for Dominion Affairs), and Canada's High Commissioner, Vincent Massey, awaited the arrival at Greenock on the morning of 17 December. They were taken by barge to HMS *Warspite*, which, with *Hood*, had gone out to greet the convoy and escort it in. From the fo'c's'le they watched the ships approach. "A number of our men-of-war were in line ahead," wrote Eden, "their convoy duty over, including H.M.S. *Hood,* the most graceful ship afloat."[61] The five great liners, *Aquitania* leading, loomed closer through a light mist that clung to the water's surface sufficiently low to reveal the snowy hills. The cheers of sailors crowding the decks of anchored warships greeted them, as did "O Canada," played by a Marine band. Answering shouts and cheers rang out from the packed troop decks. The escorting naval vessels veered off into the thinning mist.[62]

The ordinary people on shore had no idea that the arriving troops were Canadian:

Word had quickly spread on shore that something big was happening and as the convoy came to anchor thousands were making their way . . . to the water's edge.
It was when the tune of "O Canada!" came drifting across from the transports that it was realized what soldiers these were who were landing on Britain's shores and a tremendous cheer went up.[63]

"At first," wrote another reporter, "we could discern only dim, khaki-clad figures gesticulating on the crowded decks. Then we heard voices, as lone and far away as the cry of the seagulls. . . ."

The sound grew to cheers as the convoy edged cautiously to its moorings and at last one heard the authentic deep-throated martial roar as the first shipload of soldiers came alongside the quay.
Rank behind rank, line upon line, they pressed forward to the side of the ship. . . . The first coherent words to reach our ears were "Hail, hail! The gang's all here. What the hell do we care now?"
A burst of laughter sent the inquisitive gulls shrieking and circling high. Then more solemnly, with no false modesty about their patriotism, the voices intoned their anthem: "O Canada! We stand on guard for thee!"[64]

Once again, at a time of danger, Canadian troops had arrived in Britain. There they would be equipped. When that was done, it was confidently expected, the division would move to France.

The liners anchored off Greenock with the exception of the *Duchess of Bedford,* which went on to Glasgow. At noon Eden,

Massey, General Sir Charles Grant (GOC-in-C, Scottish Command), Major-General I. S. Riddell-Webster (representing the War Office), Major-General J. S. Drew (GOC 52nd [Lowland] Division), Brigadier Harry Crerar and Colonel P. J. Montague (both from Canadian Military Headquarters, London) and Lester B. Pearson (Secretary to the High Commissioner) came aboard the *Aquitania* to greet McNaughton. Luncheon was served on board.[65]

The formal welcome took place ashore during the early afternoon of a cold, fine day. The Carleton and York Regiment formed a guard of honour. "The joking, jostling throng, at a word of command, fell into flawless formation mustering fifteen deep, for the full breadth of the quay."[66] General Grant read a message of welcome from His Majesty the King, at which the assembled soldiers "put immense good will into three cheers and added a fourth for good measure."[67] The Lord Provost of Glasgow gave a local welcome on behalf of his great city; Eden expressed his gratitude for the Canadian contribution in the name of the British government. McNaughton replied to the messages of welcome and the ceremony ended.[68]

A large body of correspondents from the British, Canadian and American press besieged the GOC for interviews and McNaughton good-humouredly co-operated. One reporter wrote, "I was reminded alternately of Lord Trenchard and Charles Ruggles. He has what I can only define as a shaggy friendliness."[69] "He is slim, lean-featured and alert as a blackbird," wrote another. "His black moustache is greying but there are bushy black eyebrows over the sombre brown eyes which concentrate the frankest and most comprehending gaze as he speaks to one. His manner is natural, quite unstudied, and all the more impressive for that."[70] McNaughton's courtesy, frankness and patience won an early popularity with the press that was to continue.

Then, with Massey, Crerar, Montague, Sansom, Turner and Pearson, General McNaughton motored to Glasgow and took the night train for London.

Chapter 2

A Time of Waiting

McNaughton, Massey and Crerar spent the rattling journey in a blacked-out compartment discussing how the administration of Canadian troops in Britain would function.[1] Already in the First World War the Canadian government had insisted on the administrative control of its own troops in Britain. The principle of Canada conducting her own military business, formally expressed in the Statute of Westminster, led to the establishment of a "Canadian Military Headquarters" in this war even before the 1st Division arrived. CMHQ had been authorized by the Minister of National Defence on 26 September, 1939. Brigadier Crerar became Brigadier, General Staff, and later Senior Officer, CMHQ; Colonel the Honourable Price Montague (in civil life a Justice of the Court of King's Bench in Manitoba) was Assistant Adjutant and Quartermaster General, and Lieutenant-Colonel E. L. M. Burns GSO1. In November the headquarters moved into the Sun Life Building, next to Canada House in Cockspur Street, London. Almost the whole of these premises, as well as neighbouring buildings, were taken over as the war progressed.

Generally, the main business of CMHQ would be to arrange the accommodation, quartering and provision of the training facilities for arriving troops; to obtain equipment from the War Office and account for it; to liaise with the War Office and the GOC, Canadian Forces; and to furnish the High Commissioner for Canada with information on military questions. CMHQ would also provide the link between the GOC and the Department of National

The Canadian Commander, 1939-1943

The Canada Club entertains at the Savoy Hotel, London: McNaughton with
Lieutenant-Colonel C. C. Thompson of the Toronto Scottish, and Anthony
Eden who proposed the toast

McNaughton, with Brigadiers G. R. Turner and Harry Crerar, in Paris
en route to visit the BEF, January, 1940. At the left, Mme Georges Vanier

Associated Press

Defence. It was, of course, envisaged that, when it was equipped and trained, the division would move from the United Kingdom to take its place in France; CMHQ would then command and administer Canadian formations and units in the United Kingdom and at the base in the theatre of operations.[2]

Crerar, standing midway between McNaughton and the War Office on the one hand, and National Defence Headquarters in Ottawa on the other, was in the key position but from the start he made it clear that he recognized "the pre-eminence of General McNaughton's command in the Canadian Army Overseas and the vital necessity of close and friendly relations between CMHQ and the Canadian forces in the field."[3] The relationship between Mc-Naughton and Crerar remained consistently smooth during the latter's tenure as Senior Officer, CMHQ; the burden of both offices was adjusted with "tact, discretion and good judgment."[4] All this was very different from the chaotic administrative system established in England by Colonel Sam Hughes during the first two years of the previous war.

The train pulled into grimy Euston Station at 8 A.M. on the morning of 18 December. Burns was there to meet the Canadian group, and Dick Dewing, now Major-General, and Director of Military Operations at the War Office, who had expected Mc-Naughton's appointment to the field command. Then Mc-Naughton and Crerar motored through the grey London streets to pay a round of calls: on General Sir Edmund Ironside, Chief of the Imperial General Staff, and Winston Churchill, First Lord of the Admiralty (to thank him for the excellent naval protection on the crossing). They also saw Eden and Leslie Hore-Belisha, the Secretary of State for War. The longest visit of all, however, was with Vice-Admiral Sir Harold Brown and Lieutenant-General Sir Maurice Taylor at the Ministry of Supply. "They were delighted to have us back alongside them in this struggle," said Mc-Naughton. "The arrival of the Division had a great effect on morale."[5] But, though this was gratifying, things had not worked out so well with Taylor.

Taylor had been wounded with McNaughton at Soissons in 1918, and there had been a bond between them since. Yet it was obvious at their meeting that there was a fundamental difference in outlook concerning the equipping of the Canadians in England.

The British had calculated [McNaughton said] that they needed the exchange from the sale of British lorries and British guns to equip the Canadian Division. General Taylor, and others who were there, looked on us as customers. If we were going to produce our own equipment or weapons, that was an unfriendly act. But we *were* going to produce our own weapons and transport. I had already experimented with motor vehicles for the Army while I was Chief of the General Staff and I carried it on a bit when I was working with General Motors and Ford of Canada on industrial mobilization. It was a mighty good thing because these two principal motor car manufacturers were at least broken in to the nature of military vehicles and what was required, so that our ideas and experience could be reflected in design. But there was no end of a shindy when it was known that some of these vehicles were going to come in and displace British manufactures. It's an extraordinary thing that there are these economic considerations; the people in charge of them are not looking at it from the point of view that the life of the nation is in danger. They want to adjust balance of payments, to make financial deals about it—and this when the whole question of survival is at stake.[6]

The question of the development and supply of equipment is something which has always been very lively in my mind. You'll find address after address that I gave in the inter-war years to manufacturers' associations, engineering institutes and the rest, to arouse interest, and that was followed up and not only with vehicles. I had the conviction that the British 2-pounder anti-tank gun, since the first time I laid eyes on it in 1939, was deficient* as a weapon for handling armour and I started to work in the National Research Council on pushing up the velocity to see if we couldn't smash armour, literally by velocity, with small projectiles. We were known around the British Ministry of Supply as a pretty restless crew when it came to the development of the newer and better weapons but that didn't affect the businessmen down there; they didn't want any truck or trade with it, but we kept on. That came later but it started with the 1st Division; it really was terribly important in the end. After Dunkirk, Canada began to get into this in a very big way and, without doubt, in motor vehicles designed for the practical conditions of war, from the desert up, our

---

*"It was not only deficient," Colonel G. M. Carrie, an expert in gunnery, commented. "It was useless."

designs were best. They had been worked out by people who did everything in the way of testing and experimenting. Most of the field guns used in North Africa, though of British design, came from Canada when I couldn't even get them myself.[7]

The winter of 1939/40 was the period of the "phony war," a lull so dubbed, according to Eden, by Senator Borah. The feeling that this phrase aroused, commented Sumner Welles, was "almost sadistic." It had in it "something of the 'boos' howled out by spectators at a prize ring when the two contestants are not putting on as bloody an exhibition as they have paid to witness."[8] Nevertheless, the term was apt. The air raids on Britain which, it had been expected, would start with the opening of the war, had not materialized. Gas masks, handed out to every man, woman and child, had not been needed. Posters, depicting oil, rubber and other resources in British hands, stared from every billboard under bold black type: THESE ARE THE SINEWS OF WAR. Poland had been brutally defeated by *blitzkrieg* methods but in the West the Maginot Line, it seemed, had forced a stalemate. The British Expeditionary Force dug defensive lines along the Belgian border. An air of complacency pervaded the British Isles and people trod the blacked-out streets with confidence. Time, they were certain, was on the Allied side. "And this," said McNaughton, "was what Hitler was about. He was trying to build up a feeling of lassitude in our minds."[9]

The general trend of Allied thinking was one of exaggerated optimism. British industry had not yet rolled up its sleeves; production, though steady, was slow. And Canadian industry was still undeveloped for wartime needs, with few orders for equipment from abroad. The United Kingdom, in fact, had made no great effort to obtain supplies in North America; "so long as there was any possibility that the war might still be won on a 'business as usual' basis . . . commercial interests in Britain . . . frowned on any suggestion that . . . industrial 'know-how', and exclusive patents, should be allowed to be transmitted into North American hands, where they might prove to be industrially embarrassing to Britain in post-war competition."[10]

On the afternoon of that first day in England McNaughton and Crerar drove to Aldershot where the division was to have the quarters of the 2nd British Division, which had moved to France. "We got down to Aldershot in the late afternoon. It was dark and snowing. We had just moved into the 2nd Division's decrepit old headquarters and had got some coal. While we were standing there with our greatcoats on there was a rap at the door and a British major came in. He turned to me and said, 'His Royal Highness is here to welcome you, sir. He's a little frail but he wanted to come over himself to welcome the commander of the Canadians to England.' I went out and there was the Duke of Connaught in his car—a pretty nice gesture on the part of this old gentleman who had been Governor-General of Canada."[11] It was the start of a warm friendship between the Duke, Lady Patricia (his daughter, the former Princess Patricia), her husband (Admiral the Honourable Sir Alexander Ramsay) and the McNaughtons. The Royal Canadian Regiment, of which the Duke was Colonel-in-Chief, was with the 1st Division, and McNaughton invited the Duke to inspect it in the near future. "Psychologically," said McNaughton, "it was important to keep up the interest of the troops during this period when we were waiting for equipment. We arranged all sorts of things of a ceremonial character—things which didn't require much material but something which would keep them interested. Getting the drill up for the Duke of Connaught kept our people out of mischief. All this was not negative, it was positive."[12]

In December the first contingent of the division paraded for Leslie Hore-Belisha, Secretary of State for War. In January the King visited the division; as Colonel-in-Chief, he inspected the Royal Canadian Artillery, the Royal Canadian Engineers and the Royal 22e Régiment, and toured all the other units. On this occasion McNaughton repeated his request, which he had made at an audience with His Majesty at Buckingham Palace in late December, that Canadian units be given the privilege of mounting the palace guard.* The King and Queen, he had pointed out, were Colonels-in-Chief of Canadian regiments that were part of the 1st

---

*It had first been suggested that the Canadians should march through London; McNaughton proposed this as an alternative.

Division; these units should be chosen for the honour. King George assured him that arrangements would be made.[13] Oliver Stanley, who had by then replaced Hore-Belisha as Secretary of State for War, saw the Canadians at Aldershot in February and the same month Lady Patricia Ramsay inspected Princess Patricia's Canadian Light Infantry, a regiment that had been named for her when raised in 1914. The Princess Royal inspected units of the Royal Canadian Corps of Signals during April.

All these visitors seemed delighted with the presence of the Canadians in England. Someone who was not so pleased was the German star radio commentator, Hans Fritsche, who, in a broadcast during the last week in December, 1939, made reference to the arrival of the troops and, in particular, to McNaughton:

A few days ago a Canadian Division arrived in England, in order to take part in the fight against Germany. Their commander declared in an address that the Canadian troops came to Europe, not for adventure, but in defence of civilization. What lies must have been told to this certainly very honest Canadian soldier if he believes he is defending civilization by fighting against Germany![14]

At least, McNaughton commented, he had been recognized as an honest man.

The Canadians settled down in antiquated permanent barracks in Britain's great military centre. Though a better place to spend the winter than under canvas in the mud and wet of Salisbury Plain, as had been the lot of the first contingent in 1914, the barrack rooms were disagreeable enough. January of 1940 was to be the coldest month since 1894 and the buildings were not designed for such conditions. The single windows frosted thickly over and admitted icy draughts, which open fireplaces and the temperamental coal-burning stoves did little to relieve. Chilled to the bone, the men shivered, trained, and waited for the spring.

The 1st Division, Ironside assured McNaughton at a meeting at the War Office on 22 December, was to be given priority in the supply of training equipment. Ironside, who had been a GSO1 with a Canadian division in the First World War and who had known McNaughton well between the wars, proved extremely helpful and co-operative. McNaughton then stated that he proposed to devote the period until 28 February, 1940, to individual training; March would be used for unit collective training and April for exercises at the brigade or divisional level. Ironside found the programme sound. It fitted the War Office plans very well, as it was not expected that the division would be required on the Continent "until early May."[15]

The state of training of the division on landing in Britain was elementary, a start having been made only on the first stage—that of individual training. About half the men who joined the Canadian Active Service Force in September, 1939, had no previous military training and most of the others had had only that provided part-time in the non-permanent active militia. McNaughton issued his first divisional training instruction on 26 December, and early in January individual training though hampered by lack of clothing and equipment* began in earnest. In February, with the arrival of other convoys, the 1st Division was complete. There were then some twenty-five thousand Canadian troops in Britain. The units equipped and trained to take their place alongside the British Expeditionary Force in France. But at the end of February training was behind schedule; the period of individual training would have to be extended until the middle of March. Infantry equipment was slow in coming through and then there had been abnormal weather. The freezing of plumbing, burst pipes and a shortage of coal had brought inconvenience, discomfort and lost time.[18]

In mid-March the period of individual training ended and collective training began, first by squadrons, batteries and companies, then by regiments and battalions. "The GOC laid special emphasis

---

*"Wet boots and clothing . . . caused wasted time (a second pair of boots and a second suit of battledress were not issued until February and March, 1940.")[16] "A considerable number of artillery pieces were brought from Canada with the Second Flight but these were the 18-pounders of the last war or other obsolescent guns of heavier type. Replacing them with the 25-pounder and 5.5-inch gun howitzers proved a very slow process. The provision of transport also turned out to be difficult, but in March of 1940 the first vehicles from Canadian factories began to reach the units in England."[17]

on mobility, which he interpreted in the widest sense 'as including all those elements of quick decision, good organization and good discipline which enable a unit to move rapidly and without confusion at short notice.' "[19] On the 18th McNaughton began an inspection of the divisional units which continued until the end of April. His object was to gain "first-hand knowledge of the degree of efficiency reached by the individual man."

He selected men at random from the ranks to be examined in the various subjects in which they were supposed to be proficient. Equipment, stores, kitchens, messes and orderly rooms were all subjected to scrutiny. At the conclusion of his inspection, McNaughton expressed himself as generally satisfied that conditions were as good as could be expected . . . but warned all units that individual training did not end with the individual training period, but continued progressively throughout the soldier's service.[20]

Acting on the principle that it was "desirable to take advantage of any instruction of value,"[21] McNaughton made full use of British courses. Vacancies were taken up, for example, in artillery courses; engineer courses; signal courses; weapons courses; and courses for drill instructors, armourers, mechanics and tradesmen of a dozen sorts. For officers there were lectures, demonstrations and exercises. Selected specialist officers studied at the Military College of Science and, to train future staff officers, McNaughton made arrangements for Canadian candidates to attend war courses set up at the Staff College, Camberley.[22]

McNaughton had some difficulty in keeping the training of his division within his own hands. It was known by the middle of February that the 1st Canadian Division would come under IV Corps in France. On 23 February Major-General Claude Auchinleck, GOC-in-C IV Corps (who had been a fellow student with McNaughton at the Imperial Defence College) visited the Canadians. McNaughton made it clear that the Canadians would train separately from the corps. On 15 March Ironside sent for him and McNaughton had good reason to suspect what the meeting would be about as his staff car bowled briskly along over wet and slushy roads towards London, the Canadian battle flag snapping at its slender post.

While in Great Britain the control of all Canadian overseas forces was vested in the Minister of National Defence, with the GOC 1st Canadian Division responsible for the training and administration of both divisional and non-divisional formations and units. The War Office, however, completely ignoring the autonomous position of the Canadian troops, had already issued general instructions covering the BEF's third contingent, which automatically would have placed Canadian divisional and non-divisional troops under the GOC-in-C IV Corps, for training.[23] McNaughton, as he had already made clear to Auchinleck, regarded himself quite correctly as being completely separate from that corps on training policy while the Canadians remained in England.

Ironside, as his opening words revealed, had little knowledge of the legal grounds on which McNaughton based his position; the GOC, on the other hand, having fought so strongly for Canadian autonomy in the past, knew exactly where he stood. The present situation regarding training, the CIGS began, was causing him concern; "he expressed the thought that training policy should be laid down by the War Office, and that it should be transmitted to these troops through the Command in which they are located"[24] —all eminently reasonable, had the Canadians been British troops.

But Canada was a nation now and McNaughton could not agree. Having been one of the Canadian representatives who had drafted the Statute of Westminster at the Imperial Conference of 1930, he knew the statute inside out. "Until an Order of Detail,* under the Statute of Westminster, was signed, the British had no power to command at all. We had to keep the command in our own hands otherwise we would have had a succession of people coming in and the order and counter-order would have been similar to what we'd been through on Salisbury Plain in 1914."[25] McNaughton pointed out that the directions given him by the govern-

---

*Orders of Detail were made under the Visiting Forces Act, which the Canadian Parliament had approved in 1933 to give effect militarily to the Statute of Westminster.

ment of Canada were based on the Visiting Forces Act; these provided for the Canadian forces to "serve with" the British forces while in the United Kingdom. Canadian troops would act "in combination" with the British forces only when embarking for a theatre of war. When "serving with" British forces in England, McNaughton explained, the control of the Canadian forces was vested in the Minister of National Defence at Ottawa, who exercised that control through himself as the senior Canadian officer in Great Britain; McNaughton could not place the Canadian troops at the disposal of the British military authorities except in strict accordance with a Canadian Order in Council (P.C. 3391) in a situation that justified such a measure. McNaughton went on to say that when placed "in combination"—as on embarkation for France—the Canadian forces would then come under the command of the British C-in-C for operations though administration would remain a matter for the government of Canada. At present the Canadian division was "serving with" the British forces, and training policy remained in McNaughton's own hands.[26] This was news to Ironside; he had never seen the Order in Council. McNaughton assured him that it would be brought to his attention; the proper course was for the Canadian High Commissioner to ask the Dominions Office to brief the CIGS officially.[27]

Nevertheless, Ironside continued, he considered it reasonable that Auchinleck should have some control over the training of the division. Even here he drew a blank:

The GOC drew attention to [a War Office letter dated the week before] which instructed that "the Commander 4 Corps will no longer be responsible for the training of the Canadian Contingent." He said that the 1st Canadian Division is not yet definitely a part of the 4 Corps or of any other corps; he outlined the alternative of a self-contained Canadian formation* with its quota of ancillary troops directly under GHQ and available to be placed in any corps for tactical employment as the circumstances may demand. The GOC pointed out that due to unforeseen delay in the delivery of transport (which will prevent the despatch of the

*It was known that the 2nd Division was to be sent overseas and McNaughton had already discussed his draft of the proposed composition of a Canadian corps at the War Office.

1st Canadian Division overseas before 15 June) and the anticipated arrival of the 2nd Canadian Division, it would be infinitely better, and would cause less confusion, to have a Canadian entity in France—that could readily absorb the 2nd Canadian Division to form a Canadian Corps—than to put the 1st Canadian Division in a British Corps and the various ancillary units in other formations and subsequently withdraw them to form a Canadian Corps along with another division and additional Corps Troops. The GOC informed the CIGS that this alternative had been placed before the Canadian government but a final reply had not been received. . . .[28]

General Ironside was not put out by this stand on McNaughton's part. The two were well known to each other, since Ironside's service in the 4th Canadian Division during the First World War, and there was mutual confidence. Between these men a clash of views could take place without affecting their personal relationship. In view of these cogently presented arguments, Ironside made up his mind to substitute a British division for the Canadian Division in IV Corps; the 1st Canadian Division and ancillary units, he said, would be considered an independent formation.[29]

What then, he resumed, was the position of the senior officer at CMHQ?

The G.O.C. pointed out that, while he himself is at present the Senior Canadian Officer in the United Kingdom, he is only a transient and that, in order to ensure continuity when other formations arrive, a Senior Officer, C.M.H.Q., has been appointed to maintain liaison between the Canadian Forces in the United Kingdom and the War Office; he further emphasized that, with existing facilities, information from the War Office can reach him quicker through C.M.H.Q. than through the Aldershot Command. The C.I.G.S. then stated that he would treat C.M.H.Q. as a "Command" for the purpose of issuing War Office "Instructions" to the Canadian Forces . . . . The G.O.C. again drew attention to the fact that communications to the Canadian Forces, even though they are issued through C.M.H.Q., should be in the form of a request rather than an order so long as they are in the United Kingdom as otherwise he cannot legally comply with them under the Visiting Forces Act.[30]

Major-General Dewing subsequently instructed the various branches of the War Office, the GOC-in-C Home Forces, Aldershot Command (and other commands in which the Canadian Forces might be stationed) of the procedures to be observed when dealing with Canadian troops "serving with" their British counterparts in Great Britain.[31]

Other visits to London by McNaughton had been less challenging than this one. Apart from his call at Buckingham Palace in December, he had met Sir Frederick Banting, by arrangement, later in the month. When war was imminent Banting had joined the Medical Corps as a major for service in the field. "At my personal request," McNaughton was to write later, "he gave this up unselfishly to undertake the organization of research [chemical and bacteriological warfare] of far-reaching importance to us and which he alone could do."[32] He also acted as liaison officer between British and Canadian scientists in wartime medical research and had come to England for this late in 1939 at the request of NRC.

The main reason for Banting's visit was to discuss chemical and bacteriological warfare with McNaughton who, because of his First War experience, could not view these problems with complacency. Sir Frederick himself recorded that he had had a long talk with McNaughton and discussed with him "the one problem that I have been unable to settle in my mind,"[33] but he did not mention the subject of discussion. Seeds were sown that evening of a development that was to convert Canada into the focal centre for this research. The main need was for a testing ground large enough to contain the possible spread of contamination; McNaughton, after the British had also appreciated the need for this, was instrumental in obtaining for this purpose a thousand square miles of wasteland at Suffield, Alberta. Banting was a warm admirer of McNaughton and of his capabilities, so much so that on the outbreak of war he had advocated "putting General McNaughton in complete charge of the Canadian war effort." At that time Sir Frederick said: "I've had to deal a lot with 'Big Shots,' and I've worked here [NRC] with one really great man—General McNaughton."[34]

Mrs. McNaughton, meanwhile, was on the high seas bound for England. It was a step she had planned for some time. In this war, as in the previous struggle, she intended to be, as far as possible, at the side of her husband. In November, while McNaughton was out of Ottawa on one of his inspection tours, the Prime Minister had given a dinner at his home, Laurier House. Mrs. Joan Patteson acted as hostess, as she often did at social functions given by the bachelor Prime Minister. At dinner Mrs. McNaughton sat next to Mackenzie King, and halfway through the meal he turned to her and said, "I expect you're going?"

Not knowing whether the government's policy permitted wives to go to England, she had been careful in her reply. "I hope to," she said, with a steamship ticket already in her purse.

A few moments later Mrs. Patteson, who had not heard the quiet exchange, leaned in Mackenzie King's direction and solicitously observed that they must "look after Mrs. McNaughton when the General is gone."

"Yes," the Prime Minister replied, turning again to Mrs. McNaughton and closing one eye this time, "Yes, indeed we must."[35]

On Christmas Eve, in a heavy fog, Mrs. McNaughton arrived in London and stayed at the Carlton Hotel. McNaughton was there at the station to meet her; he stayed in town on Christmas Day. Together, over the Christmas period, they called on two former Governors-General of Canada and the widow of a third: the Earl and Countess of Bessborough, the Marquis and Marchioness of Willingdon, and Viscountess Byng of Vimy.[36] The Willingdons returned the visit six days later, when they were the guests of the McNaughtons at Wellesley House in Aldershot. The divisional staff and representatives of all Canadian formations and units in the Aldershot area were present.[37] During the first week of January Mrs. McNaughton was able to rent an unfurnished house (Crowthorne) at Farnborough.

The end of an eventful year was marked by a New Year's service conducted by the senior chaplain of the division in the lines of the Carleton and York Regiment. Accomplished musicians from Kneller Hall rang in the New Year and followed that with a musical programme interspersed with community singing. Khaki-clad chests inflated, neck cords stood out, as men in their thousands, the cold forgotten, lustily sang the songs of the day. "We're going to hang out the washing on the Siegfried Line!" was one of the more popular choruses.[38]

Dinners and other functions took up a part of McNaughton's time at this period in England and though he complained of "heavy inroads in consequence of public and semi-public functions" they could not be refused.[39] At a luncheon at the Hyde Park Hotel, London, given by the Fédération Britannique de l'Alliance Française in January McNaughton's words were singularly apt and might well be pondered in later days of dissension.

Canada [he said] derives from France and from these Islands. Our heritage from both is blended in harmony in our national life and I am happy to say is recognized in the Battle Flag which has been given to our armed forces overseas. In one canton a Union Jack of generous dimensions; in the other the lilies of Old France in a circle, the heraldic device which indicates an ancient and an honourable connection that is deeply cherished; on the fly the three maple leaves of Canada, symbolic of our own nationhood combining the heritage bequeathed to us by both our great ancestral races.[40]

Another luncheon, at the Savoy Hotel, was given by the Canada Club, under the chairmanship of Lord Mottistone,* in honour of McNaughton and senior officers of the 1st Canadian Division. The toast of "The G.O.C., the officers, N.C.Os. and men of the Division" was proposed by Anthony Eden and seconded by Oliver Stanley (Secretary of State for War). McNaughton responded, and some of his remarks about the Canadian Army may be quoted here:

Every officer is qualified for the rank he holds by reason of attendance and examination at our military schools in accordance with the rigorous requirements laid down in pre-war days. Political or private patronage does not exist: it has been stamped out by our Minister himself, and merit as judged by the responsible officers, each in their proper degree, is the sole criterion for selection and promotion.

---

*The former J. E. B. Seely, who had ably commanded the Canadian Cavalry Brigade almost throughout the 1914-18 War.

Our staff officers are products of Camberley in England, of Quetta in India and of the Imperial Defence College in London, the great post-graduate military colleges of the British Empire which Canada and the other Dominions have, for many decades, combined with the United Kingdom to support. Through them we have a uniformity in tactical doctrine which we have had a hand in forming, an asset which is of priceless value when it comes to operations in the field.

Through them, too, we have, even before we take the field, a wide range of personal friends throughout the Staffs of the British Army, Corps and Divisions, and it is no unusual experience for Canadian staff officers to go into a British Headquarters and find that between them they know everyone present . . . our relations with the British Expeditionary Force [are] in marked and pleasant contrast to 1914 when we came over practically as strangers.[41]

In February McNaughton was the guest of honour at a banquet given at the Mansion House by the Lord Mayor of London. He also attended, by invitation, church parade in the chapel of the Royal Military College, Sandhurst, and took the salute of the Cadet Battalion; he lunched with the commandant after the ceremony was over. On the 19th, with Mrs. McNaughton, he attended a luncheon at the Carlton Hotel, which had been arranged so that they might meet prominent members of the British Labour Party: Clement Attlee, Arthur Henderson, Herbert Morrison, Arthur Greenwood, A. V. Alexander, Hugh Dalton, Sir Walter Citrine and George Hicks.[42] A few days later, on the 22nd, McNaughton travelled to London again for an occasion of a different sort, when he attended the memorial service in Westminster Abbey for Lord Tweedsmuir, Governor-General of Canada since 1935, who had died in office.

Chapter 3

~~~~~~

The Illusion of Strength

Early in January, 1940, McNaughton, his three infantry brigade commanders (Brigadiers A. A. Smith, G. R. Pearkes and C. B. Price), Brigadier Crerar, five senior divisional staff officers (including Turner) and representatives of the Canadian press left Southampton for the BEF in France. They were to visit GHQ, the headquarters of the two corps and certain divisions; McNaughton also hoped to inspect the Maginot Line.[1] Next day the party arrived at Cherbourg, where McNaughton paid a call on Admiral Le Bigot, commanding the Préfecture Maritime du Nord, to thank him for the assistance that the French Navy had rendered in convoying the second flight of the 1st Division, which had at that time recently arrived in England.[2] From Cherbourg the party went on to Paris where McNaughton, Crerar and Turner remained overnight; the others went on to Arras.

A meeting had been arranged with Lieutenant-Colonel G. P. Vanier, Canadian Minister to France, at the Canadian Legation. Next day the three settled down with him to discuss the arrival of the 1st Division in France.

Colonel Vanier stated that it would be most desirable for the G.O.C. to come to Paris prior to the arrival of the Division in France in order to meet representatives of the French Government and General Gamelin; he stated that, in his opinion, it is of prime importance that when the Division arrives *it should be looked upon as a representative of a sovereign state, rather than merely another British Division** and, in consequence, that General McNaughton should be personally known to the French Government beforehand.

---

*Italics supplied.

General McNaughton and Colonel Vanier considered that, as a matter of principle, General McNaughton should have direct access to General Gamelin even though the occasion might never arise when it would be necessary for him to appeal to General Gamelin direct. It was agreed that, although the Canadian Forces would be under the Commander-in-Chief, B.E.F., for tactical operations, there might be occasions, such as happened in the last war, when the Canadian Commander would need to have access to the highest Military authority. It was agreed that general instructions in this regard should come from the Canadian Government and it was decided that Colonel Vanier should draft a message to the Department of External Affairs covering these points and forward it to General McNaughton for his comments.[3]

The 1st Division, of course, never formed part of the original BEF under overall French command; the point remained academic. Nevertheless, the similarity of the views of McNaughton and Vanier (both veterans of the earlier war) on this question is significant.

The meeting over, McNaughton, Crerar and Turner went on to I Corps Headquarters at Douai where the commander, Lieutenant-General Sir John Dill, made them welcome. (The friendship of McNaughton and Dill had lasted many years by this time.) At McNaughton's express wish to see a division in the line, Dill arranged for him to go on to Bersée where Major-General the Honourable H. R. L. G. Alexander, the future Earl Alexander of Tunis and Governor-General of Canada, explained his 1st Division's defensive system.[4]

Next day the Canadian visitors watched a tank demonstration and then called on Lord Gort at GHQ. Gort, bluff and affable, exuded confidence. Though the BEF was woefully short of tanks and guns, the French Army was good. The Maginot Line was strong, and behind its protective line and their own defences the British could build their strength. McNaughton's meeting with Gort was very friendly. There is little doubt that had the Canadian force joined the BEF there would have been smooth relationships. Gort told his visitors, before his assembled staff, that "we are happy to see the uniform of Canada back again in France where it won such honour in the Great War. It is a personal pleasure as well to renew acquaintance with my good friend General Mc-Naughton." McNaughton replied that "it will be one of the greatest pleasures of my life some day to report with the Canadian forces to Lord Gort in France: 'I am here to take your orders!' "[5] But the simple operational role which was envisaged then did not materialize for the Canadians. Instead, surrounded by complexities and difficulties, they remained in England.

On the 12th McNaughton again visited Alexander. The Canadian Division, it was visualized, would on its arrival in France perform a similar role to that of the British divisions, and he took advantage of the opportunity to check carefully Alexander's dispositions.[6] He lunched with Dill next day at Douai and talked over all he had seen and heard; in the afternoon he paid a short visit to the II Corps area where he renewed his acquaintance with the commander, a man he had seldom seen eye to eye with in the past, Lieutenant-General Alan Brooke. Then, that night, Mc-Naughton left with Crerar for a four-day visit to the Maginot Line.*[7]

His visit to the BEF had not impressed him. "They couldn't get cement, they couldn't get materials and there was no real mechanized force behind them. The tanks were limited. The 1st Armoured Division had been put together in a way that didn't work well from an organizational point of view. I was very unhappy after that visit." His actions on returning to England clearly reflected his misgivings.

"The ammunition quota that had been laid down was small. It struck me at that time as very primitive and I said so but they said, 'Oh, this is a different kind of war. We are going into a war of manoeuvre.' How did they figure they were going into a war of manoeuvre if they had no armour? God knows! They were willing to take what came to them, what the people said they could make in England and give to them. They weren't willing to go to the

---

*Once again McNaughton's sentiment—as when he visited Moosomin before going overseas—emerged. He went to Boves Castle, his headquarters for the Battle of Amiens, and picked up a three-cornered piece of white stone which he carefully preserved. On it he wrote: *Chateau Féodal, Boves; 7/8 Aug. 1918; 14 Jan. 1940.*

Government and fight with them and say, 'Look, this is not good enough!' "[8]

What he saw of the Maginot Line did nothing to reassure him.

I made an inspection, you know, of the Maginot Line. Gamelin, partly at Georges Vanier's instance and partly at my request, invited us. . . . Crerar and I went, and we sampled it in various places. We couldn't do the whole thing. We were royally entertained and fed on the best of champagne and all that kind of stuff and were shown everything. I made the usual fal-de-la speeches: what a wonderful thing it was; and I've got a button, *We hold the Line till death!* which reminds me that you can have all sorts of things on buttons but they don't work too well when it comes to the real stuff. We were met at a gate by French officers and were sent on a light railway for kilometre after kilometre underground. There were stacks of ammunition; thousands and thousands of rounds had been piled up. Everything had been done. Millions and millions of francs must have been spent on it.

I asked the commander at dinner that night, "Now, what I'm interested in is how much of the underground work is known to the Germans? Do they know what is here?" He said, "They know a great deal, because when we were building this line we had to take labour from the Saarland, which was occupied then but which is now back in Germany. A quota of labour came from there to build this Line." I said, "Let's be particular. Do they know where your tunnels are?" "Oh, yes," he said, "probably to within half a metre, horizontally and vertically." "What about the observation posts, those things we rode up to in an armoured elevator and looked through the telescopes which were already focused on salient points in German territory?" "They show up on every aeroplane photograph." I said, "What about the calibre of the guns?"— beautiful pieces of mechanism, they were; they could be laid before they came up to shoot above the ground. He said, "I don't think they know the calibre of the guns." "Does it matter very much?" I asked. "No," he said, "it doesn't matter much at all."

As I talked to them that night I got an idea of their concept of the defence of the Maginot Line. These were a series of land battleships, you see, great land battleships and if the German troops got through, in between them, they could be paralyzed. I had the impression that with a determined force, properly equipped, they could get through. The British didn't have that idea. The French had sold the British a bill of goods and they were looking at this as a real obstacle. They were terribly concerned about the gap on the left flank, up by Belgium, but not about the Line itself.

My earlier ideas on the Maginot, when it was being built, were confirmed by that visit. Far from being a defence, it was a trap. I don't think it's unfair at this stage to say that I had the same idea of the Maginot Line and the Ardennes that the Germans had acquired. They only let that period of the phony war go on to give the French morale a chance to evaporate. At the end of the last war, when I had command of the Corps Heavy Artillery, I was told to get some heavy guns to the Rhine as quickly as possible. I selected my own line of movement straight across the Ardennes and I ran troops across, and guns pulled by tractors, with no difficulty whatsoever. That's where the German mechanized forces came in 1940 and where they made their counter-offensive in 1944 and it never occurred to me that the French would think they couldn't.[9]

Before taking leave of the French, McNaughton asked for, and received, working drawings of the Maginot Line; these would be useful to his diamond drillers if the defences had to be retaken. Parts of the line, he was convinced, were bound to fall but reserves farther back, the "mass of manoeuvre," would hold the Germans as had invariably been done in the earlier war.* Then it would be a case of clearing the Germans out of the Maginot defences and in that his special section of borers would play a part.

McNaughton returned to England with his mind made up on three counts: under the defensive policy that ruled Allied military thinking he would plan on an improved engineering organization to construct the defences to help hold the Germans back; he would require better artillery methods to break up the German thrusts; and, for the same purpose, he wanted planes acting in close conformity with the ground troops under his command.

The existing organization of the divisional engineers was totally inadequate for the large amount of work required on field defences, roads and other construction tasks. He was not afraid to go back in time to a tried and trusted method of carrying out the

---

*McNaughton's first divisional indoor exercise, held on 29 January, was entitled, appropriately enough, "Approach March to fill a Gap in a Broken Front."[10]

multifarious work required. He recommended to Ottawa the "immediate adoption of the 1918 Engineer battalion organization reduced in numbers and modified to meet present day conditions."[11] Secondly, for the artillery, the method of ranging by air-bursts must be studied and practised. He had already carried out his own experiments in France, towards the end of the First World War.* At a meeting of senior British and Canadian gunners on 23 January, at which Major-General L. Browning (Inspector General Royal Field Artillery) was present, McNaughton voiced his convictions. He had, he said, discussed the importance of predicted shooting with Gort and his two corps commanders. "All agreed that accuracy must be developed in this method. Maps were now very good and it was up to the gunners themselves to better the results achieved in the last war."

The range of 13,400 yards for the 25-pounder is too long for "fall of shot" observation of percussion rounds under normal conditions and air burst ranging is the only solution; he mentioned that he had not been able to make much headway in persuading the authorities in Great Britain to adopt it but that he is determined that the Artillery of the Canadian Overseas Force will train on this method.[12]

The provision of time-fuses might be the crux of the problem, but McNaughton pointed out that he had visited the factory at Elswick where they were manufactured while on his liaison visit to British industries during August, 1939, and had been assured then that the plant would soon be in full production. General Browning agreed to do his best to get the quantity of fuses required.[13]

The third point which concerned McNaughton was the paucity of aircraft co-operating closely with British ground forces. "The Germans," he pointed out, "are using bombers as long range artillery and the stronger we can get the air component closely associated with the ground troops (and the Wing Commander close to the G.O.C.) the better."[14] He had already made arrangements for the Canadian Army Co-operation Squadron, due to arrive in

---

*Airburst-ranging methods will be described in more detail later.

February, to be stationed at Old Sarum where it would train with his troops taking part in formation exercises. Now he was not satisfied "merely with an A.C. Squadron but felt that fighters and bombers also are required; this may be possible, notwithstanding normal establishments, in the organization finally evolved for the Canadian Forces."[15]

Shortly after his return from France McNaughton arranged a meeting with senior British engineers. Major-General G. H. Addison (Inspector of Royal Engineers) and Brigadier A. Sayer (president, Royal Engineers and Signals Board) came down to Aldershot to discuss the possibilities of diamond drilling. McNaughton's CRE (Lieutenant-Colonel C. S. L. Hertzberg) was also present. The British officers warmed to the possibilities which they considered "immense" if an explosive charge of "sufficient military size" could be placed at the end of a long drill hole. Furthermore a bore seven feet below the surface for lengths of four hundred to four hundred and fifty yards would be extremely useful for rear area cable laying.

McNaughton suggested that the pipes might also be used to construct surprise obstacles in front of a German advance. This would be accomplished by *pushing* a series of pipes, fifty feet long, obliquely into the ground. The lower end of the first pipe would be about fifteen feet below the ground and the top end flush with it. The next pipe would be pushed behind the first to a similar depth so that the top end of the first overlapped the lower end of the second. The pipe could be very easily pushed by hydraulic jack* mounted on a tank transporter, numbers of which were available. By this method the pipes could be installed rapidly; and to load them with explosives was quick, convenient and safe. The drilling might also provide a means of pumping gas into an enemy-held area. The possibilities were legion, and it was cordially agreed that preliminary trials must take place as soon as Colin Campbell and his men arrived from Canada.[16]

The special section of diamond drillers arrived in February with

---

*McNaughton adopted the idea of using hydraulic jacks from the bootleggers of Windsor, Ontario, who, during prohibition, pushed pipe from the brewhouse to other premises where the drink could be safely loaded.

the third flight. Campbell had recruited men who had been working at core drilling for periods ranging from four to twenty years; they started experimental work on 18 February in a limestone quarry near Aldershot.[17] Two months later the section staged a demonstration at Bourley Hill, Aldershot, which was attended by several distinguished visitors.* Campbell (now Captain) proved conclusively the ability of the section to produce surprise tank obstacles (ditches were blown that could not be negotiated by tanks, though they tried repeatedly), communications trenches and long cable ducts for use by signallers. The drilling for these had been accomplished from a pit not more than six feet wide. Though a method of placing charges of the required size at the end of a long bore hole had not yet been developed, experiments were continuing. The spectators were well satisfied with what had been achieved so far and promised to support McNaughton's proposal to expand the section into a tunnelling company.[18]

McNaughton had travelled with the Duke of Devonshire (Under-Secretary for Dominion Affairs) to Scotland to meet the third flight bringing the ancillary units required by the division. They went out to the transports as they arrived and were guests of the Lord Provost of Glasgow on the night of 7 February.[19] Pat Dollan, the Lord Provost, had long looked forward to wining and dining McNaughton, whose forebears had come from Glasgow. That night, General McNaughton recalled, "we had a little more than 'A Wee Deoch an' Doris!'"[20]

There was also the link with James Watt. Towards the end of the dinner Dollan dispatched an assistant to the Glasgow Public Library—it was almost midnight—for every book he could find on Watt; some considerable time afterwards the harassed man returned bearing an armful of books.

---

*Besides McNaughton, these included Lieutenant-General M. G. H. Barker (GOC-in-C Aldershot Command), Lord Cadman of Silverdale (head of the Anglo-Iranian Oil Company), Mr. C. A. P. Southwell (a senior petroleum engineer of the Anglo-Iranian Oil Company), Mr. E. B. Bailey (representing the Geological Survey of Great Britain), Lieutenant-Colonel Edgar Pam (vice-president International Nickel Company), Mr. H. G. Gough (Director of Scientific Research, Ministry of Supply), Mr. Perry B. Hall (of the Ontario Mining Association), Brigadier A. Sayer (president, Royal Engineers and Signals Board) and Brigadier D. H. Pratt (commanding 1st Army Tank Brigade).

"Take your pick!" said Dollan.

"I will," returned McNaughton, "if you will undertake to clear me with the library!" He chose George Williamson's *Memorials of James Watt*, published in 1856, which was then passed round to be signed. *To our Andrew*, the Lord Provost wrote in a bold hand, *the Beloved Warrior. From Pat Dollan.* The book is still in McNaughton's library.

Early in March McNaughton learned that the 2nd Canadian Division was expected to leave Canada at the beginning of July and that it would be ready to cross to France about four months later. The arrival of this division, the Canadian government pointed out, would not hold up the dispatch to France of the 1st Division, which would join a British corps.[21] This relieved McNaughton's mind of the immediate necessity of organizing a corps headquarters; he could now focus his attention on the immediate problem of employing his division and ancillary units during the period when they would be the only Canadian formation in the field. The question of the control of the ancillary units, however, was a vexed one.

Britain, as we have seen, had offered to bear the financial responsibility for them on the undertaking that they would be under British control. McNaughton, who wanted them with his division, considered that Canada should assume the financial burden. "The more I see of the trouble over these ancillary units the more I am convinced of the wisdom of Mr. Lapointe's statement of principle in the House of Commons on 9 September last." (Lapointe, Minister of Justice, said then: "Canadians will never be mercenaries paid by any country—not even by Britain. If Canadians go to the Front Line of battle they will go voluntarily as Canadians, under the control of Canada, commanded by Canadians, and maintained by the Dominion of Canada.")[22] "Departure from it, for however good a reason," McNaughton went on, "has delayed completion of organization, caused anxiety, and distracted attention which can ill be spared from other urgent duties. Can we not set the matter at rest?"[23] Anthony Eden had suggested that the Canadian government should assume the financial cost of the ancillary troops from 1 July, 1940, and McNaughton considered that a reasonable proposition;[24] with effect from 1 September, the Canadian government did so. McNaughton saw no alternative. "If you were trying to work with the Statute of Westminster," he said, "and keep this line of political responsibility in the employment of your armed forces straight, you found it difficult enough. But if various units were under your command for one purpose and not under your command for another, I defy anybody, even a Philadelphia lawyer, to keep it so that your channels of command were clear and unambiguous. I've always insisted that the financial aspects should be a consequence, not a cause; in other words, your thought is in the lives of men, within the principles of good administration, and fair treatment. The cost is something that follows. In this case Canada had to assume the burden to cut the line of demarcation. It was the only practical thing to do."*[25]

Eden, while the controversy was still continuing, visited the division on 14 March in a blinding snowstorm. Vincent Massey was in attendance, as was Crerar (now Major-General). They saw the troops in training and Eden, in a message that he sent later to Mackenzie King, congratulated Canada "most warmly on the quality, enthusiasm, and efficiency, which is being displayed by Canadian troops here."[27] The men, in fact, remained remarkably cheerful considering the conditions.[28]

At the end of March Ironside brought General Gamelin, the Supreme Commander in France, to Aldershot to meet McNaughton, who was interested to know what this successor to Foch in war would be like. Gamelin, quick and inspiring, made a favourable impression. There might, McNaughton knew, be occasions in the future when he, the leader of a sovereign force, would

---

*Ralston, as Minister of Finance, however, had made no provision in the estimates for this (nor, in view of the circumstances, could he have done so) and it was obvious to the Canadian government at the time that the British Commonwealth Air Training Plan would place a heavy financial burden on Canada. Nevertheless, as the Canadian official historian points out, "The argument had . . . used up far more time and paper than the issue was worth," and it "reflected the importance attached to financial considerations in the days . . . of the 'phony war.'"[26]

have occasion to deal with Gamelin direct; the visit was important.[29] McNaughton showed the visitors units in training; only one unit was drawn up on parade, the Vingt-Deuxième, which Gamelin addressed. His words were recorded for transmission to Canada. The visiting party then lunched with McNaughton and his brigade commanders, and the GOC was able to convey to Gamelin something of what was in his mind. There is little doubt that the French Generalissimo grasped the point with perfect understanding. In a letter dated 1 April, Gamelin congratulated McNaughton on his *beaux régiments*; he also hoped that "this first meeting with you will renew itself in the course of months to follow. This will always be, on my part, with a great deal of pleasure."[30] In other words, the door was open.

On 8 April, a day bathed in spring sunshine, Their Majesties The King and Queen visited Aldershot when McNaughton was Acting GOC-in-C Aldershot Command. He accompanied his royal visitors to a British officer cadet training unit, and Queen Elizabeth then inspected the Toronto Scottish, of which she was Colonel-in-Chief, and the Saskatoon Light Infantry in her capacity as Colonel-in-Chief of its allied regiment (The King's Own Yorkshire Light Infantry).[31]

McNaughton spent the next week carrying out his programme of inspections of the divisional units. Though the 1st Canadian Division now had priority for the provision of equipment, and it was coming through, the units—after almost four months in England—were still not completely equipped. In addition, fuses, important for airburst-ranging, had not yet been provided.[32]

On the morning of 16 April McNaughton inspected the divisional engineers. The inspection was almost over when, at 11:45, a telephone call came through from Major-General Crerar in London. About eight hundred Canadian troops, Crerar said, would probably be required for a special operation and the need was urgent. Could McNaughton come at once to CMHQ?[33] Shortly afterwards McNaughton and Turner were on the way, driving hard, to London.[34]

Chapter 4

~~~~~~

Norway Beckons

On the way to London McNaughton turned over in his mind what the summons would be about. Was it an accelerated move to France? A good deal of planning had already been done for that. "We had got our hospital echelons over in France; our reserve stocks and our quota of ammunition of all natures; supplies of food in our own echelons and depots opposite Boulogne, and our spare vehicles were all over . . . ready for use."[1]

But a week before, the uneasy quiet of the phony war was broken when the Germans suddenly attacked Denmark and Norway. The French and British, confident that the strength of the Maginot Line had forced this move, were not alarmed at first. McNaughton considered it significant, with advantages for the Germans "like anchorages for battleships and submarine bases and the extension of air cover out over the Atlantic,"[2] and he was certain that the British assessment would eventually be the same. The British had, in fact, as McNaughton found out from Crerar on his arrival at CMHQ, decided to bolster the resistance of the small Norwegian forces and, with most of the trained British troops in France, had turned to Canada. A memorandum, setting out a War Office request for the employment of some eight hundred Canadian troops in combined operations at the Norwegian port of Trondheim, was still being typed and when it was pulled from the machine McNaughton read it through. "It seemed that, with the forces they had up there and the forces they might assemble, this was in every respect a proper operation of war and, without any hesitation, I gave the assurance that the force would be provided"[3] under Sansom, the acting commander of the 2nd Brigade.[4]

While waiting for Sansom, McNaughton, with Crerar, Burns and Turner, went over the plan with Dewing at the War Office. The Canadians would come under British command.* The intention was to seize Trondheim, with the Canadians carrying out a frontal thrust against the batteries while the British operated from the flanks. The broad outline of this confirmed McNaughton's first favourable reaction and at a later meeting with Ironside he assured the CIGS that he could count on the Canadians.[6] McNaughton then returned to CMHQ to draft the Order of Detail placing the Canadian force for Norway "in combination" with British forces. The Deputy Judge Advocate General's firm opinion† was "that the G.O.C. 1st Canadian Division could legally detail these parties for this duty" under the authority of P.C. 3391. Nevertheless, the wording of the order would require extreme care; and the units and detachments for the operation would have to be selected before they could be listed as being placed "in combination." It was not before the afternoon of the following day, 17 April, that the Order of Detail was ready for McNaughton's signature.[7]

However, by the time Sansom arrived at CMHQ on the afternoon of the 16th an operation order, spelling out his task, had been prepared. He was briefed, given a copy, and his questions dealt with. The force was to leave Aldershot for a Scottish port of embarkation on 18 April; a vast amount of business would have to be rushed through to make it ready by then, and McNaughton and Sansom returned to Aldershot. The lights burned long that night as the divisional staff dealt with the multifarious tasks required to marshal, arm, equip, feed, provide with special winter

---

*That of Major-General F. E. Hotblack. "After he had received his orders and before he got to Norway, Hotblack collapsed outside the War Office. It was a heart attack. Everybody thought he'd been murdered and there was a great ado about it all." Much to his annoyance, McNaughton himself was given police protection during his stay in London.[5]

†The opinion was that of Brigadier Montague who, as has been noted, was in civil life a Justice of the Court of King's Bench in Manitoba.

clothing* and move a force, 1,300 strong now, from Aldershot to Scotland. Two of the 2nd Brigade's battalions, having Scandinavians in their ranks, would form the bulk of the force: the Edmonton Regiment and the Princess Patricias, both in an advanced state of training.

The next afternoon Ironside visited the division at Aldershot and addressed the officers assembled in the garrison theatre on the implications of the German invasion of Norway. His appreciation proved over-optimistic. He termed it "a strategical blunder by the enemy giving us our first opening."[9] After Ironside's visit McNaughton went back to London where, in the late afternoon, he signed the Order of Detail which had by then been drawn up to Montague's satisfaction.

That done, McNaughton drafted a message for the information of Ottawa. The participation of Canadian troops, he said, was required by the military situation; "accordingly, and after full consultation with the War Office on details, I have designated [units and detachments were then listed] to act in combination." Lester B. Pearson, the Secretary to the High Commissioner, arranged for a copy to reach the Canadian Prime Minister.[10]

The Canadian contingent left Aldershot for Scotland on the evening of 18 April. It was played to the station by the pipes of the Seaforth Highlanders of Canada. McNaughton watched the men go and was struck by their readiness to be off to fight. "They were full of vigour, to put it mildly,"[11] he said. Next day the Canadians went into camp at Dunfermline to await embarkation. The only battle to come out of this, however, was a paper one between

---

*Mr. C. A. Banks, of the Canadian Munitions and Supply Office in London, was helpful here. When McNaughton had talked over supply problems with C. D. Howe (Minister of Supply) before leaving Ottawa, Howe had agreed with him that there would be occasions when the General would need to spend large sums of money, perhaps on special equipment, and that it would be just as well to have a senior representative of the Ministry of Supply available to him in London. "He sent Charles Banks, a man of parts, and through him I had a channel of communication right into the heart of the British supply system."[8] McNaughton wanted rubber boots for Norway because of snow and slush, and Banks did a sterling job in procuring them for the contingent at very short notice.

Banks had had an interesting career. In the thirties, for example, he opened up the Bulolo gold-dredging area in New Guinea; he made flying and mining history by carrying thousands of tons of equipment to the interior by air.

Ottawa and McNaughton. Mackenzie King was in the United States and in his absence Colonel Ralston (Minister of Finance) was "executing the functions" of Prime Minister.[12] Nor was the Minister of National Defence in Ottawa; Norman Rogers was on his way to London, where he arrived on 19 April.

Ralston, signing himself "Acting Minister of National Defence," while he approved sending the force, upbraided McNaughton for entering into the commitment "without prior reference to National Defence and [the] approval of [the] Canadian Government."[13] Another telegram, from the Department of External Affairs to the High Commissioner, took an even sharper tone with Vincent Massey.[14] Massey patiently explained the position: ". . . G.O.C. made full enquiries to satisfy himself that the employment of these Canadian forces was justified by the exigencies of the military situation. Having done so, the situation required, in his opinion, the immediate issue of orders on the 17th placing a portion of the Second Infantry Brigade 'in combination' with other British forces. In discharge of his responsibility in this matter the actions of the G.O.C. were based on designation of Minister under authority of P.C. 3391 dated 2 November 1939 which requires that he should act as necessitated by the military exigency of the moment."[15]

That was a correct report of the circumstances: P.C. 3391 had specifically placed the Canadian military forces in Great Britain in the position of "serving with" those of the United Kingdom and stated, furthermore, that such forces would be "in combination" with those of the United Kingdom from the time of embarkation for, and while serving on, the continent of Europe. Legally, as well as geographically, Norway was on the Continent. Again:

. . . in order to meet any situation which might demand a unified command with Britain, it provided that portions of the Canadian force might be placed 'in combination' by orders issued by Canadian service authorities designated for the purpose by the Minister of National Defence. . . . the Minister [had] designated the G.O.C. 1st Canadian Division and the Senior Combatant Officer of Canadian Military Headquarters, London, as appropriate "Canadian Service Authorities" under P.C. 3391.[16]

However, thirty hours elapsed before any information reached the government and a good deal of difficulty would doubtless have been avoided had McNaughton sent a cable warning the Canadian government of what was in the wind. As it was, he acted in good faith and placed the contingent "in combination" only after availing himself of the best legal opinion open to him. But Ralston interpreted P.C. 3391 differently and, on second thoughts, questioned McNaughton's actions; he cabled Canada House again: "Action by Canadian Service authority under paragraph III of P.C. 3391 in detailing forces to act in combination is not considered to relate to service beyond United Kingdom."[17]

Had Rogers remained in control of the Department of National Defence in Ottawa at this time it is unlikely that any controversy would have arisen.* In London he took up the cudgels on McNaughton's behalf and cabled Ralston:

Further consideration is now being given to the effect of P.C. 3391 in light of present circumstances for the purpose of arriving at a surer understanding and clearing up existing legal situation. Will advise you later of any revision that appears to be necessary but wish to emphasize that there are dynamic features in present military situation which argue against too rigid limitations upon actions taken to meet possible emergencies.[18]

Under the stand taken by Ralston, McNaughton's hands were tied in any military situation that demanded urgent action. "Regardless of the emergency," the General said, "regardless of the urgency of it, Ralston insisted that the matter should have been referred to Canada for decision. I made it clear that I had operated according to the best legal advice available . . . but that didn't satisfy Mr. Ralston. He kept this up to a point where I felt that if every time I had an operation on my hands I had to spend time on the etiquette of my association with the Department of National Defence across the Atlantic it was a pretty hopeless situation.

---

*A series of intimate discussions in London between the Minister and McNaughton gave the GOC appropriate opportunity to review the controversy that had been raised by Ralston's criticism. The matter was carefully discussed from all angles, practically as well as psychologically, with particular regard to future relations with the British.

I think, looking back at it, this broke what little trust I had in Ralston as a minister and I never regained it."[19]

It was a very poor augury for the future when, on the death of Norman Rogers in June, 1940, Colonel Ralston became Minister of National Defence. In that appointment, during the spring of 1941, Ralston ruled that troops could not be moved out of the United Kingdom without the Canadian government's consent; but McNaughton did not allow the matter to rest. He broached the subject to Mackenzie King on the Prime Minister's visit to England later that year and on 10 September the Cabinet War Committee discussed the question. It was then considered desirable to extend General McNaughton's authority to include operations *based* on the British Isles, which was the way policy ultimately developed.[20]

On 20 April, early in the afternoon, Lieutenant-Colonel Burns burst into a conference between Norman Rogers and McNaughton, at which Massey and Crerar were also present, to announce that the Norwegian operation had been cancelled. With early British successes from the flanks it seemed that Trondheim was due to fall and it had been decided that the direct Canadian assault would not be necessary. The force at Dunfermline never put to sea, and on 26 April Colonel Sansom's men were back at Aldershot.

"They were disappointed when the show was off," said McNaughton, "but none of these things are without their value. There was warm appreciation for the promptness of our action from Stanley [the British Secretary of State for War], from Ironside and from officers all along the line."[21] General Ironside, who had never quite forgotten his interview with McNaughton on training policy, had been highly gratified at the Canadian response to a real emergency.

Although the brigade has not been used [he wrote] the fact that it was so speedily made available augurs well for co-operation between British and Canadian forces in the future. I feel that it is owing to your personal interest in the matter that we were able, without getting involved in legal arguments,* to come to a swift decision.

---

*The same could not be said of the Canadian authorities.

After this example we can both feel confident of surmounting minor problems swiftly and easily.[22]

Ironside's satisfaction was matched by that of Oliver Stanley, who, in a personal letter to McNaughton, wrote in part:

I would like to convey to you my personal appreciation of the splendid way in which you yourself and the troops concerned responded to our invitation to take part in this operation. The notice was extremely short, the difficulties great and the hazards which were to be accepted were serious. Yet your own decision was immediate and the preparation of the troops was carried out with the utmost despatch and great efficiency.[23]

The rest of the division, which had jealously watched the departure of the lucky few, greeted the return with jeers, as soldiers will. "How did you find the blondes up there?" they shouted, and "Where's the reindeer you promised us for Christmas?" The humdrum round at Aldershot had been broken for only two of the remaining battalions. The King had approved McNaughton's suggestion that Canadian regiments of which he or the Queen were Colonels-in-Chief should guard the royal residence. From 17 to 24 April, first the Royal 22e Régiment and then the Toronto Scottish mounted guard at Buckingham Palace. Though Canadian troops had had this privilege before, they had always been drawn from English-speaking units. The Vingt-Deuxième were the first non-English-speaking troops of any country to perform this duty. The occasion was historic and McNaughton, who had a feeling for history, marked it by a dinner at St. James's Palace with the Captain of the King's Guard;* Anthony Eden, Norman Rogers and Vincent Massey attended.[24]

The sentries' order boards used by the King's Guard had been translated into French for the Royal 22e Régiment. McNaughton presented one set to the King, another to the Public Archives of Canada, and a third to the Historical Section (Army) at Ottawa. In May of 1940, when it was known that the Earl of Athlone was to be the new Governor-General of Canada, a fourth set was presented to him. Athlone, accompanied by his wife, Her Royal Highness The Princess Alice, visited the division on 4 May.[25]

---

*Captain Charlebois, of the Royal 22e Régiment.

At the end of March, 1940, Sir Edmund Ironside brought General Gamelin
to Aldershot to meet McNaughton: here Gamelin takes the salute at the
march past of the Vingt-Deuxième Régiment

With Lord Gort at GHQ,
France, January, 1940

Anthony Eden visits the Canadian Division in a blinding snowstorm,
14 March, 1940

Chapter 5

~~~~~~

Delusion at Dunkirk

The Western Front remained quiescent. Then, on 10 May, with the violence that had marked their irruption into Poland, the Germans struck at The Netherlands, Belgium and Luxembourg, all neutral countries. Holland was overrun in a few days of ruthless fighting. An Anglo-French army left prepared positions to assist the Belgians only to find its communications with the main French forces cut by a German thrust through Luxembourg and the "impossible" country of the Ardennes, which pierced the Maginot Line where a gap existed between it and the British defensive line along the Belgian border. German armoured divisions, in which fast tanks and mobile supporting arms worked together in swift independent thrusts, swept towards the Channel on 21 May; they moved northwards along the coast during the days that followed and so threatened to cut the communications of the BEF with England. Farther south, under the sudden assaults of aircraft and fast-moving armour, French resistance began to crumble.

On 10 May news of the German initiative came dramatically to the Canadians with the receipt of the codeword JULIUS. All troops would act "as if in contact with the enemy, maintaining constant vigilance, and standing to at dusk and dawn"; they would be ready to move at short notice.[1] On 16 May the C-in-C Home Forces (Lieutenant-General Sir Walter Kirke) summoned McNaughton to the Horse Guards to attend a conference at which the organization of Local Defence Volunteers (later the Home Guard) was discussed. A factor limiting the number of volunteers that could be recruited was the scarcity of rifles. McNaughton broke the impasse by suggesting that surplus stocks of Ross rifles might be sent from Canada. He was asked to do what he could with the Canadian authorities to get the rifles as soon as possible.*²

That afternoon McNaughton went with Kirke to another conference convened by Ironside. The commanders-in-chief of every command in Britain were there. Ironside gave a description of the German operations, based on the latest information available, and it was just as well, McNaughton thought, that the formation of Defence Volunteers had been put in hand. The news, plainly told, was unbelievably bad.

The Germans had taken The Netherlands. The attack, Ironside said, had been delivered by aircraft, mechanized troops and parachutists; "German infantry divisions had hardly been engaged." The British had been given three tasks: to remove the Dutch gold reserves; to destroy oil stored at Rotterdam and Amsterdam; and to escort the Dutch royal family to safety. All these tasks had been successfully accomplished.

He turned next to France and Belgium. German tanks, supported by waves of bombers and fighter escorts, were pouring into France. They were reported west of Sedan and as far south as Laon. There was no "mass of manoeuvre"; there were no Allied troops, Reynaud had reported to Churchill, between Sedan and Paris. The French were demoralized. The BEF was withdrawing to the line Antwerp-Malines-Brussels that night to conform with the line held by the French. It was stated, however, that the French still held Mézières and had thrown back a defensive flank to cover the rear of the Maginot Line. But the worst feature of the operation was that German success had been bought at very small cost; there had been "no real bleeding of the German Army," and German strength in the air was "four to one against us."⁴

McNaughton took in the scene: Ironside, huge and burly in front of the map, speaking gravely and holding back nothing, his

---

*The Ross rifle (an excellent rifle when it could be kept clean but a dire failure under First World War ground conditions) had been withdrawn from Canadian units in 1916 and returned to Canada. After the war, when Deputy Chief of the General Staff, McNaughton had ordered them to be repaired and overhauled and this had been done at the rate of about five thousand a year for several years. He now cabled for these reconditioned weapons which were sent by fast passenger ship. They were used to arm the Home Guard in the Canadian area and, under clean conditions, the rifles were a godsend.³

voice clear, his nerves steady; high-ranking officers, grey, most of them, or greying, brought together to hear the worst, grim-faced now, with no illusions. The long armistice was really over. This was the bitter price of the wasted years, but they were soldiers and there would be no recriminations. It had always been Mc-Naughton's fate to be a little out of step with the company in which he had found himself—a Westerner in the East, a militia officer among regulars, a soldier among politicians, an engineer among scientists, and a scientist among soldiers—but though he was a Canadian among the British that day he identified himself completely with this gathering. The army might be thrown back on the defensive but he detected no sign of weakening. The issues were clear. They were up against it but these men would fight. McNaughton sensed the resolve which united them all in a common purpose.

Ironside had not finished yet. Italy too, he warned, might declare war upon the Allies. The sailings of two liners, *Conte di Savoia* and *Rex*, were a guide. One had just passed Gibraltar on its way to Italy and the other sailed from New York on the 16th. May 21 seemed a likely date for Italy to enter the war.[5]

On the way back to Aldershot McNaughton, in his clear-headed way, turned the situation over in his mind. From Ironside's disturbing report of French demoralization it was quite obvious to him that the Maginot Line could not possibly hold out. Despite their defensive flank, if the French tried to hang onto it they would merely be playing the Germans' game; tying up in static defences troops who could be used in barring the German road to Paris and the Channel. The line would fall, and German incursions were already so deep that his diamond drillers could not possibly come to grips with it. Their role, he saw now, would be in creating quick defences, tank traps and the like, to keep the Germans out of England. A night's sleep did not change his view and on the 17th he advised the War Office that "the detachment of 1 Canadian Tunnelling Company, intended for experimental work in France, should not now be sent but should be held for more important experimental work in England."[6] The tunnellers remained.

The mobility of his troops worried him. The mobilization of the ancillary units of the division, including the artillery, depended on the provision of motor transport, and though the component parts of the Canadian transports were at Southampton and Dagenham they had not been assembled. McNaughton was convinced that the delay was due to pique at British-type vehicles having been refused.[7] On the 20th he conveyed, in the most decisive terms, his wishes regarding testing and delivery. The effect was salutary; the much needed transport began to arrive almost immediately afterwards.[8]

It was just as well. The situation in France deteriorated steadily day by day. On the 18th German armour swept into Cambrai and St. Quentin. Two days later, in a move that bewildered the French who expected a thrust on Paris, the Germans drove westwards from the old Somme battlefields, captured Amiens and Abbeville, and reached the sea. With that the communications of the northern armies with Paris and the British supply ports in Normandy were effectively cut. A panzer wedge had been driven between the northern force (a million men) and the main French armies in the south. That day, 20 May, the seventy-three-year-old Weygand replaced Gamelin as Supreme Commander. On the following day, with the British Army in Belgium still retreating, King Leopold of the Belgians made it clear to Weygand that his troops were no longer capable of offensive action. The British withdrew from the Scheldt to the defensive line along the frontier on 22 May, while behind them German armoured divisions besieged Boulogne and Calais and moved on Gravelines and Dunkirk. Nothing, it seemed, could save sixty British, French and Belgian divisions —caught between the German armour to the west and the main German forces to the east—from the closing jaws of the trap.

In this desperate situation the War Office turned to the 1st Canadian Division (now one of the few trained and equipped formations in England). The Canadians were required to restore the communications of the BEF with the Channel ports. As a first step, McNaughton was ordered across the Channel to study the state of affairs at the ports of Calais and Dunkirk. Meanwhile his troops were to move to Dover ready for embarkation. Ironside, Mc-Naughton was told, would brief him at the War Office on the morning of 23 May.

Before leaving for London, McNaughton found out from Alder-shot Command what sized force the War Office had in mind. It was to consist, he was told, of two infantry battalions, two regiments of field artillery, two batteries of anti-tank artillery and two field companies of engineers. It would thus be a small force, with plenty of firepower, which could be ready by noon that day.[9]

At the War Office McNaughton, accompanied by Turner, went straight to Ironside's office. He found the CIGS, as well as the officers holding senior War Office appointments, awaiting his arrival. Ironside came to the point at once. The situation in France, he said, was extremely grave. German armour had cut the lines of supply between the BEF and Boulogne and Calais. Only the line from Dunkirk was still open and that was not enough. Already rations were having to be flown in and the BEF was short of ammunition. Road and rail communications through Haze-brouck and Armentières would have to be restored at once and he was handing the task to McNaughton. He must do it from Calais or, failing that, from Dunkirk.

The CIGS then turned to the situation at Calais. Brigadier C. N. Nicholson (30th Infantry Brigade) was commanding there. He had one battalion of infantry, one battery of anti-tank artillery and a tank regiment, half cruisers and half light tanks. In addition, two motorized battalions were being shipped to Calais and would reach Nicholson about midday. There were some French units in Calais; just what, Ironside did not know. McNaughton would take command of all these troops; he would also take with him a Canadian force (a mixed brigade was suggested) and call forward as many more Canadian units as he wished. His command would be independent, answerable only to Lord Gort; and should that prove unworkable under the chaotic conditions on the other side, he would report directly to the CIGS.

McNaughton nodded. There had been only one interruption of Ironside's rapid flow: a brief message to advise him that Boulogne was now completely surrounded and under tank and artillery attack. Then, in conclusion, Ironside pointed out that "the most important thing of all was to get away from supposition and try to get down to brass tacks" as to what the situation actually was. "Nobody really knew for sure. He dictated an instruction which gave me *carte blanche* to take charge of the situation, French and British, and organize it on the spot. As I listened to the order being dictated I thought it was pretty far-reaching but I said nothing. I thought the drastic implication of taking over the whole Calais-Dunkirk area could be decided a little later on."[10]

The meeting broke up. In the office of the Director of Staff Duties immediately afterwards, McNaughton listed the troops he would take. From Dover there would be the Advanced Divisional Headquarters, 1st Canadian Infantry Brigade, the headquarters and two batteries of the Anti-Tank Regiment, a field company of engineers and a field ambulance. An artillery field regiment and the machine-gun battalion would sail from Southampton, arriving at their destination later. The troops would assemble at Dover and Southampton to embark for either Calais or Dunkirk. No vehicles or guns, McNaughton had been told, could be loaded at Dover; the vehicles for the complete force and the guns would have to leave from Southampton. McNaughton accepted the arrangement for the field guns and the transport but he insisted that the anti-tank guns must go with the troops. The need for them, he said, was so urgent that he would have them manhandled onto the ships at Dover and they would go as deck cargo; in that way they were eventually stowed aboard.

McNaughton and Turner left London soon after noon. A conference of the divisional staff had been convened by telephone, and McNaughton plunged into that as soon as he got back to Aldershot. The assembly of the force and the issuing of the required scales of rations and ammunition began soon after.* The units leaving from Dover, McNaughton ordered, would take

---

*Such were the shortages in England that it was very difficult to obtain even the permitted scales of explosives. These were taken away from the units on their return to Aldershot later on.

all their drivers so that any spare transport at Calais or Dunkirk could be made use of pending the arrival of the Canadian vehicles from Southampton. McNaughton also "gathered in a headquarters with a few people who were to go across with me—military police on motorcycles for despatch riding and French-speaking officers for liaison. That was done by telephone and they were waiting for me at Dover."[11]

McNaughton, accompanied by Turner and Major G. G. Simonds (his GSO2) arrived at grim Dover Castle in the early evening of 23 May. There the Adjutant General of the BEF (Lieutenant-General Sir Douglas Brownrigg) newly back from Calais, the Assistant Chief of the Imperial General Staff (Major-General A. E. Percival),* and Vice-Admiral Sir Bertram Ramsay awaited him. Lieutenant-Colonel E. L. M. Burns, from CMHQ, was also there and had brought with him the details of the Canadian sailings. The first party from Dover (the two infantry battalions and the anti-tank gunners) would be assembled ready to sail at 10 A.M. on 24 May; the rest of the force five hours later. The Southampton party would also be ready to sail on 24 May, passing up the Channel that night, if necessary, for disembarkation at either Calais or Dunkirk early on the 25th.

General Percival outlined the latest news from France: three German armoured divisions moving north towards the line St. Omer-Boulogne; two more following; strong German forces already between St. Omer and Calais, and reports of enemy tanks southwest of Calais. That done, Percival telephoned Ironside in London.

After consultation with the War Office, General Percival gave General McNaughton a copy of instructions based on the verbal instructions given General McNaughton by the C.I.G.S. earlier in the day; these were supplemented, however, by instructions to the effect that General McNaughton would visit CALAIS and DUNKERQUE, review the situation at both places, and report to the War Office as to whether any useful purpose could be served by landing his force in or near either of these two places, the War Office to decide whether the Canadian Force would be despatched,

---

*Who commanded the British garrison at Singapore when it surrendered later in the war.

and if so, to what port, following the receipt of General Mc-Naughton's report.[12]

These two sets of instructions, which were identically dated and timed, have been interpreted by Colonel C. P. Stacey, the Canadian official historian, as giving McNaughton a free choice between them.* "He could produce the first and take command in the Pas de Calais if he chose; on the other hand, if on arriving in the area he decided that the situation was not such that the original instruction remained valid, he could act on the second and simply report to the War Office. Few officers have had such wide discretion in so great a crisis."[13] McNaughton agreed with that. "I ended up by having two instructions," he said. "Percival didn't want to change the one that the Chief of the Imperial General Staff had dictated and which put me in command of the whole show. The other, the much more reasonable one, was that I should iron out the situation and report, with recommendations on what we should do. I'm very glad those two instructions have survived. My actions would have been unexplainable without them. The body of the first instruction dictated by Ironside was very good, very useful at times."[14]

McNaughton left Guy Simonds, with the Advanced Divisional Headquarters, at Dover to look after the assembly and embarkation of the troops coming down that night from Aldershot; he would also act as a vital link between McNaughton and the War Office. At about 9 P.M. McNaughton's party motored down the hill, through the town to the docks. People still walked the streets; Dover was strangely peaceful. Ten minutes later McNaughton, Turner, an intelligence officer (Lieutenant E. D. Magnus), two French-speaking officers (of the Royal 22e Régiment, who were to act as liaison officers) and ten or so military policemen clambered aboard HMS *Verity*, a destroyer provided by Admiral Ramsay. Shortly afterwards the lean shape of the vessel stalked silently out of the harbour and knifed through the gently heaving sea in the direction of Calais. A half-hour before midnight *Verity* crept into Calais. The place was in darkness but a few fires were

---

*In view of their importance, Stacey recorded both written instructions in *Six Years of War*, p. 266.

burning, throwing the dark outline of buildings into sharp relief. There was scattered sniping and rifle shots could be heard from various parts of the city.

A group of British officers was waiting at the quayside together with a French officer, Rear-Admiral Leclerc, who was Chief of Staff to the Commander, Maritime Nord. Brigadier Nicholson, however, was not there and no one knew exactly where he was. "We went into one of the transportation sheds," McNaughton said, "and I began to gather in the information that was factual."[15] No clear idea of the situation could be obtained from these officers. It seemed clear that the enemy had been established at St. Omer since 22 May. Tanks had swept into the southwestern outskirts of Calais that afternoon and there had been some shelling; there had been more in the early part of the night which had started the fires. There were only from two to three thousand refugees in the city but the population in general was very nervous.

In the small hours of 24 May, even as the discussion was going on, shells fell intermittently on Calais. McNaughton, anxious to find out more from Nicholson, went to Headquarters 30 Infantry Brigade only to discover that the Brigadier was somewhere around the perimeter; a telephone call eventually established that he was expected to be with the Tank Regiment at about 2 A.M. It was then about half-past twelve. In the meantime McNaughton elicited what he could from the brigade staff. The brigade major confirmed that the British units at Calais were as Ironside had said. All of them, with the exception of a Territorial battalion, were under Nicholson's command. That wouldn't do, McNaughton interjected. Nicholson must take the Territorial battalion over too. It was important that the defence should be effectively co-ordinated.

British troops, the brigade major continued, were disposed in close perimeter defence of the city with anti-tank guns covering all the main approaches. Their morale was good. In addition there were about two hundred French troops and a battery of seventy-five-millimetre guns on the western outskirts of the city, while on the eastern fringe there was another small French post. "I thought I'd better take a look at the Calais defences," McNaughton said, "and I did that."[16] On his way round with the brigade major he learned that provisions, about five hundred and sixty tons, had been landed the previous day but no ammunition. About half that tonnage, loaded on ten-ton trucks, would leave Calais for Dunkirk at 2 A.M. The convoy would be escorted over half the route by tanks and two companies of motorized infantry; the escort would then return to Calais. It was in connection with this that Brigadier Nicholson was out around the units; "busy marshalling the column," said McNaughton, "as I knew he would be."

It was now about 1:30 A.M. on 24th May. There seemed little point in staying longer in the hope of meeting Nicholson. The news of the convoy was what McNaughton had wanted to hear. No one he had talked to could say if communications with Dunkirk were still open, and it was essential to know beyond any doubt. The fate of the convoy would establish the point one way or the other and McNaughton wanted to be at Dunkirk to await results. "With this going on," he said, "it meant that I didn't have to reconnoitre the route to Gravelines myself. These people had to get through, to fight if necessary, so I was well satisfied with that arrangement. There was nothing more I could get in Calais. The brigade had brushed off any attacks that had come so far and it looked as if this might remain a firm base for any force we put to shore. We had left Calais high and dry of information. We had to take advantage of the night to get across to Dunkirk and have a look at the situation there."[17]

McNaughton and his party drove back to the docks. Nervous clusters of townsfolk and refugees, still in the streets, looked over their shoulders apprehensively as the cars surged past to where *Verity* was waiting. Fires were still burning and no effort was being made to put them out. Once the Canadians were aboard, the ship cleared the harbour and headed for Dunkirk with no lights showing. Nevertheless, the Germans spotted her and she was dive-bombed repeatedly just off Calais. This was a target that could hit back, however, and though it seemed at times that the destroyer was steaming through a sea that spouted water on every side, she sustained no damage and ploughed ahead. Her attackers veered off for easier game.

McNaughton had spent the time in writing a report of what he had found at Calais. "I couldn't safely telephone," he said, "because some of the Calais forts where the telephone ran across were believed to be in German hands."[18] He handed the report to the naval signals officer at 2:15 A.M. for transmission to the CIGS through Admiral Ramsay at Dover. Naval encoding took such an unconscionable time that the report had still not been completely dispatched at half-past three, when the destroyer reached Dunkirk; and, worse than that, even the first part of the message was not deciphered at Dover until 5:40 that morning, more than three hours after it had been sent.[19] McNaughton was not aware of this at the time; when he did find out it added one more fact to his store of knowledge: "They're very quick with the short messages for manoeuvring a fleet. When it comes to a reconnaissance report with landlubber's terms, all coded, it's a major operation to get the message through."[20]

The approach to Dunkirk had been even more hazardous than the departure from Calais. This time the ship was machine-gunned, as well as bombed, from low-flying aircraft. Again there was no damage, nor casualties, though bullets and bombs flayed the water all around the vessel.

Two British officers were at the jetty to meet McNaughton. He drove with them to the Bastion where Colonel Whitfield, the base commander, was waiting, as well as Brigadier R. H. R. Parminter, Lord Gort's Deputy Quartermaster General. The presence of the latter was as unexpected as it was useful; he would be able to describe the supply position of the BEF.

The force, Parminter said, had rations for about five days but the ammunition shortage was serious. Every ten-ton transport lorry in France, except those at Calais and twenty-six which had left Dunkirk via Ypres with stores for the BEF the previous afternoon, would have to be considered lost as they were either loading at Boulogne or parked near Ardres, both of which had been overrun by the Germans. An ammunition ship was expected to reach Dunkirk at 11 A.M. that morning (24 May) and he had come to improvise some sort of transport system at Dunkirk to get ammunition to the British dumps just northwest of Ypres; so far he had scraped together sixty three-ton lorries.

Hazebrouck, Parminter continued, was still in British hands. There were reports, however, that the Germans had reached Gravelines, midway between Dunkirk and Calais, on the evening of 23 May. McNaughton saw from the map that the distance from Calais to Dunkirk was only about twenty-five miles by the main coast road, so that if the reports Parminter had heard were correct the enemy was within thirteen miles of Dunkirk.

Colonel Whitfield reviewed the forces available for defence at Dunkirk. There were about a thousand "useless" French troops. The British force consisted of labour and service units only and had been strung out to man a defensive line running westwards from Wormhoudt (twelve miles south of Dunkirk on the main road to Cassel) to the Aa River in the vicinity of St. Pierre Brouck (about thirteen miles west of Wormhoudt). The defensive line was thus about thirteen miles long. It covered the major roads and railroads running from the south into Dunkirk. McNaughton saw that the line was well to the south of the Gravelines-Dunkirk coast road and could not parry a thrust from Calais. The British force was no more than a scratch one; without tanks, artillery and infantry it could impose little delay on the German armoured formations if they should thrust from the south towards Dunkirk.

Parminter then spoke of two French divisions that would start arriving at Dunkirk that same morning of 24 May. General Weygand, he said, had informed the admiral commanding at Dunkirk that the place must be held at all costs and had ordered Major-General M. de Fagalde of the XVI Corps, with two divisions, to defend it. Some French light tanks had already arrived about 9 P.M. on 23 May, and others had come in later but nothing definite was known about them.

McNaughton now had a good deal of information to pass to Ironside. What he was desperately anxious to learn, however, was whether the road was still open between Calais and Dunkirk. Were the Germans in fact across it at Gravelines, as had been reported? Gravelines was the real key to Dunkirk. He took the matter up with Parminter and Whitfield, suggesting that a reconnaissance party should be sent out at once towards Gravelines to report on the situation there. If the party met the road convoy from Calais the true state of affairs would be established beyond a doubt. But there were no British troops available for the task; reconnaissance, Parminter said, would have to await the arrival of Fagalde's men and there, for the time, McNaughton had to leave it.

By now he had come to a firm conclusion: if Canadian troops were to be sent to France at all they should be used to strengthen the situation at Calais, not Dunkirk. Two French divisions, it appeared, were on the way to Dunkirk; they would reach it long before the Canadians could; in fact some advance mechanized units were already present. The French commander, during the morning of 24 May, would then have a considerable force on the spot. Acting on the instructions of no less a person than Weygand, the commander of the Allied armies, and working closely with the Admiral du Nord, he was obviously in a better position to co-ordinate the defence of the port than any commander sent by the British. The British force in Dunkirk, as McNaughton knew, had little strength, and he himself would be in a poor position if he insisted on taking over the responsibility for the defence of Dunkirk from the French and waving Ironside's instruction in their faces.

Calais, however, was a different matter. There British troops were already manning the perimeter defences. To reinforce them and take command would be an ordinary—and orderly—operation. And there were good possibilities from that flank of operating against the rear of the enemy; of delaying, at least, his move on Dunkirk.

At 4:45 A.M. on 24 May, therefore, McNaughton telephoned Simonds, his liaison officer at Dover. He instructed him to get in touch with the CIGS immediately and to pass along the following information: that it was vital to hold Calais and the Canadians should be used to strengthen the defences there; that two French divisions were moving to the Dunkirk area with orders to hold it at all costs; that there were indications that the enemy had reached a line between Calais and Dunkirk at Gravelines; and that he was trying to arrange a reconnaissance to establish the situation at the latter place. A message from the CIGS had reached him at the Bastion, McNaughton continued, urging him to report on the situation at Calais. He had done that in detail by cipher message as soon as he had left Calais and the CIGS should have had the report at least two hours earlier. Simonds checked with the navy, found that a message had indeed come in but was still being deciphered. The first part went off to the War Office by teleprinter at 5:40 A.M., 24 May, with three parts still to follow. Meanwhile, as Simonds found out at 6 A.M., the War Office had, four hours earlier, decided to approve in principle the evacuation of Calais without having heard anything at all from McNaughton.[21]

As soon as Simonds saw the War Office message, so contrary to his General's advice, he showed a copy of McNaughton's message to the Chief Naval Staff Officer to the Vice-Admiral, Dover. "From that time on," Simonds recorded, "the C.N.S.O. continued to press Admiralty for a cancellation of evacuation orders."[22]

The matter reached Churchill through naval channels, and the views of the Prime Minister were in exact accordance with those of McNaughton.

Prime Minister to General Ismay   24.V.40

Vice-Chief of the Naval Staff informs me that [an] order was sent at 2 a.m. to Calais saying that evacuation was decided on in principle, but this is surely madness. The only effect of evacuating Calais would be to transfer the forces now blocking it to Dunkirk. Calais must be held for many reasons, but specially to hold the enemy on its front.[23]

By the 25th Churchill's views had hardened:

Prime Minister to C.I.G.S.   25.V.40

Something like this should be said to the Brigadier defending Calais. Defence of Calais to the utmost is of the highest importance to our country and our Army now. First, it occupies a large part of the enemy's armoured forces, and keeps them from attacking our line of communications. Secondly, it preserves a sally-port from which portions of the British Army may make their way home. Lord Gort has already sent troops to your aid, and the

Navy will do all possible to keep you supplied. The eyes of the Empire are upon the defence of Calais, and His Majesty's Government are confident that you and your gallant regiment will perform an exploit worthy of the British name.[24]

As will be seen, this went to the CIGS *after* Churchill had heard McNaughton's views on the evening of the 24th.

The CIGS repeated Churchill's message to Brigadier Nicholson on the afternoon of 25 May, and on the 26th it was decided not to relieve the Calais garrison. Destroyers (including HMS *Verity*), which had been standing by to evacuate the troops, were then withdrawn. "Calais was the crux," concluded Churchill. "Many other causes might have prevented the deliverance of Dunkirk, but it is certain that the three days gained by the defence of Calais enabled the *Gravelines waterline** to be held, and without this, even in spite of Hitler's vacillation and Rundstedt's orders [to halt the German armour short of Dunkirk], all would have been cut off and lost."†[25]

No sooner had McNaughton finished his telephone conversation with Simonds than he and Turner went to see Rear-Admiral Leclerc‡ at his office. He told him that he had recommended that the Canadians should be used at Calais. The road between Calais and Dunkirk must be kept open and Gravelines was the key to that. He asked that one of the French divisions coming in should push out its defences to include Gravelines and the line of the Aa River but the Admiral would make no firm commitment; they were Territorial divisions, he said, with little armament. Nevertheless, Leclerc assured McNaughton, Dunkirk would hold. Canals were being flooded to protect the port and there were two coastal batteries near the city.

---

*Italics supplied.

†This is confirmed by the British official history. The little garrisons of Boulogne and Calais "engaged two of Guderian's three armoured divisions and held them during most critical days. By the time the Germans had taken Calais and Boulogne and had 'sorted themselves out,' the divisions of the British III Corps had been moved west to face them, covering the rear of the British Expeditionary Force and guarding the routes for the final withdrawal to Dunkirk."[26]

‡Whom McNaughton had originally met at Calais and who travelled with him in the *Verity* to Dunkirk.

Admiral Abrial, commanding the Maritime du Nord, came in while the discussion continued. General Fagalde, he said, had been ordered by Weygand to defend Dunkirk, Calais and Boulogne under his (Abrial's) direction. He had been given two divisions for the task, one of which was thirty-one kilometres away, on the Yser. It would arrive during the afternoon of 24 May. It was essential, McNaughton realized, to see Fagalde. His mission would not be complete unless he could give Ironside Fagalde's plans. Could Abrial reach Fagalde? Yes, he could; the telephone line was still intact. Then would he get in touch with him, stressing the necessity of his early arrival to discuss matters with McNaughton?

Fagalde was at his headquarters. His Chief of Staff would leave immediately for Dunkirk. He himself would arrive at 10 A.M. Now there was nothing for McNaughton to do but wait. From the Bastion, Turner notified Simonds of the coming conference and was himself told of the War Office message approving in principle the evacuation of Calais. This had just reached Simonds, who, as we have seen, protested against it. From the moment McNaughton learned from Turner that Calais had heard of evacuation plans he dismissed from his mind the idea of putting the Canadians there. The situation at Calais would no longer be as he had found it. On the receipt of an evacuation warning the first thing Nicholson would do would be to pull back from the outer perimeter, to concentrate his troops behind the inner defences of the town itself. There would no longer be room for the Canadians to disembark out of reach of German guns.

The fate of the convoy that had left Calais for Dunkirk earlier that morning—as did the situation at Gravelines—became known at the Bastion shortly after 6 A.M. on 24 May. A British staff officer,* who had been at Gravelines during the night, reported at the Bastion. He had found three British tanks positioned east of the Aa River guarding the bridge at Gravelines. From the crews he had discovered that the tanks had been part of the escort for the Calais road convoy. The escorting tanks had encountered German armour between Calais and Gravelines and a battle had developed. Only these three tanks had managed to fight their way through.

---

*Captain Hill, Staff Captain "A," GHQ.

They had crossed the Aa, and had then turned beyond the swing bridge (which was now in the open position) to hold the enemy at bay should he attempt to pursue in the direction of Dunkirk.* The other tanks and the vehicles making up the convoy had got back, or at least had tried to get back, to Calais. The enemy had been at Marck, between Calais and Gravelines, and had mined the bridge there; though one mine had exploded, damaging the bridge, that had not prevented the convoy and the tank escort from crossing it. As regards the general situation, the Germans were holding all the roads south of Calais in strength. Southeast of Calais, on the St. Omer road, enemy tanks had been encountered six or seven miles from Calais. Two battalions of Guards were still holding out at Boulogne but the Germans had sealed every road leading into the port. Large numbers of refugees, without food, were reported throughout the entire area of the Channel ports.

It was clear from this report that the Calais-Dunkirk road had not yet been finally cut, although it was subject to interference and the British hold on it was precarious in the extreme. But it would not remain open for long unless troops from either Calais or Dunkirk, with artillery, kept the German armour from it; and troops for that purpose were not available at either port. Meanwhile Lieutenant Magnus, General McNaughton's Intelligence Officer, who was keeping in close touch with the French,† reported that the Calais airport at Marck was still in French hands. It had not been bombed and two runways were in use.

Turner passed all this information by telephone to Simonds at

---

*Information reached McNaughton at the Bastion that the War Office had requested the RAF to bomb Gravelines because of reported German tanks across the Aa. These were clearly British and instructions were passed to Simonds by phone to arrange to call off the bombing. This, Turner has commented, "probably had a profound effect on the course of the war. . . . Had these tanks been destroyed or damaged by the bombing planes, German armour would have had a clear run to Dunkirk as early as the morning of 24 May and, with the port in German hands, the evacuation of the BEF from there would have been impossible."[27]

†"They were quite open," said McNaughton, "about letting us have access to their information. It's really amazing how the French General Staff in war—it doesn't matter how chaotic everything else is in the armies outside—enter everything in log books by hand of the duty officer. So we got to know pretty well what the situation was."[28]

Dover who, in turn, notified General Dewing at the War Office. Dewing questioned the presence of British tanks at Gravelines; he had it from Brigadier Nicholson at Calais that they were enemy. Simonds replied that British tanks had been reported by an officer who had actually seen them and spoken with their crews.

It was now daylight on 24 May—a fine morning. Sparkling waves broke on the level beaches below the dunes to right and left of the small harbour but lights still burned in the Bastion. Under them officers waited around tables spread with maps and papers for news of Fagalde's two French divisions. Shortly after seven a telephone call from Dewing broke the suspense. Based on the information available to him, he said, nothing more was to go into Calais. McNaughton then outlined the situation at Dunkirk and spoke of the two French divisions said to be moving towards the town. It was important that he should see the French commander and assure himself of the reality, Dewing insisted. Further action would depend on his discussion with General Fagalde or his Chief of Staff. Meanwhile the Canadian troops assembled at Dover and Southampton would not put to sea.

Fagalde himself arrived at Dunkirk an hour earlier than he had said. By 9 A.M. a discussion between Fagalde, Admirals Abrial and Leclerc and McNaughton was well under way. McNaughton questioned Fagalde closely. The French general said that he had motored in from Bruges that morning. The road was clear except for refugees. He appeared tense, "in no sense of the word phlegmatic," but he gave McNaughton the impression that "he really intended to stand and fight."[29] He confirmed what the Admiral had stated earlier: that General Weygand had ordered him to take command of all land forces at Boulogne, Calais and Dunkirk under the direction of Admiral Abrial.

At Boulogne, Fagalde continued, there were two battalions of the French 21st Division with some artillery; the balance of their artillery was in Belgium but he proposed to get it to Boulogne at once, which he intended to hold at all costs. As regards command, it was essential that one man should be in charge and that would be General Lanctot, commanding the 21st Division, who would take over the two British Guards battalions at Boulogne.*

McNaughton reviewed the situation at Calais as he had found it in the early hours of 24 May. He informed Fagalde that Brigadier Nicholson was commanding the British troops there and that the men were in good heart. Fagalde seemed relieved. In that case, he stated, Nicholson would command the French troops in that area also and he would issue instructions to that effect. As for Dunkirk, Fagalde went on, two French divisions were on the way. These were the 68th, at Thourout, and the 60th, from the line north of Bruges. Both divisions were weak—they had each lost one regiment out of three in the fighting in The Netherlands—but they had plenty of horse-drawn artillery which he intended to put to use as anti-tank artillery. He hoped to get transport for the move of these divisions from the Belgians and to have them in Dunkirk that night.

The 60th, McNaughton repeated: had he understood General Fagalde to say that this division had actually been in the line? Fagalde confirmed that this was so. Then what about the gap? The division would either have been relieved by the Belgians or simply withdrawn; if the latter, the gap in the line could be covered by Belgian mechanized forces.

The significance of this statement about the 60th Division had struck McNaughton like a blow. The main body of the enemy troops was to the east of Dunkirk and this was the major threat— not the armoured scythe sweeping up from the south and west. To open a gap by withdrawing a division in contact with the enemy might well bring a torrent of German troops on the northern flank of the BEF to engulf it. "The realization of that position," he said, "was the most important piece of news I had got so far."[30] He held his peace and heard Fagalde out.

Dunkirk would be held, Fagalde continued, by defending the

---

*The Boulogne garrison, both French and British, was taken off by eight destroyers on the night of 23-24 May. McNaughton told Fagalde of Parminter's report that Boulogne had been overrun.

line of the Colme Canal from Bergues (some five miles south of Dunkirk) easterly to Furnes, thence to Nieuport and the sea. To the west, he would extend the line of defence to the River Aa, and then press on to Calais. That, McNaughton noted with satisfaction, would take in the coast road to Calais, including Gravelines on the Aa, and subsequently Marck. Who would command at Dunkirk, McNaughton asked. The commander of the 68th Division, General Beaufrère. Questioned about his own plans, McNaughton said that the employment of Canadian troops was for the War Office to decide. Fagalde urged that the most useful theatre would be Dunkirk, with as many anti-tank guns as possible; if they arrived before the French, they should at once occupy the canal positions and go into reserve as soon as the French troops could take over. Inundations would give some protection. The area to the northeast was already flooded, and that to the southwest would be flooded within a few days.

The conference, which had lasted an hour, broke up about ten o'clock; McNaughton now had all he wanted. "I had to get to the War Office with the information about that gap as soon as possible; and I made Gort's people at Dunkirk responsible for getting the information to Gort."[31] He at once phoned Dover to obtain War Office approval for leaving Dunkirk to deliver his report (which he would not entrust to the telephone), and that was given. The *Verity* lay well out at sea and the Canadian party reached her by pinnace. They arrived at Dover without incident at 1 P.M. on 24 May.

There was no one from the War Office at Dover, so McNaughton, after telephoning for instructions, went on to London and at about half past four he was with the CIGS. "I borrowed a razor and shaved in the motor car going up and I gave a personal account of what had gone on to Ironside."[32] He alerted Ironside to Fagalde's plans, emphasizing the gap that would be created by the withdrawal of the 60th Division from the line to the area of Dunkirk. He stressed his anxiety for the Calais-Dunkirk road. "He suggested that the Germans were continuing a series of interferences with the ports and that if they met opposition in those ports it seemed that they would merely mask them and proceed to interfere with communications from the next; he further suggested that the only way to stop them now is for the troops in France to get in their path with guns, as there is not time to get fully equipped troops for this role from the United Kingdom."[33]

With that statement, too, Churchill would have been in full accord. He had that day prodded Ismay with a similar assessment:

Prime Minister to General Ismay 24.V.40

... Surely Gort can spare a brigade or two to clear his communications. What else can be so important as this? Where could a reserve be better employed?
This force blockading Calais should be attacked at once by Gort, by the Canadians from Dunkirk,* and by a sortie of our boxed-up tanks [from Calais].
Apparently the Germans can go anywhere and do anything, and their tanks can act in twos and threes all over our rear, and even when they are located they are not attacked. Also our tanks recoil before their field guns, but our field guns do not like to take on their tanks. If their motorized artillery, far from base, can block us, why cannot we, with the artillery of a great army, block them? ... The responsibility for cleansing the communications with Calais and keeping them open rests primarily with the B.E.F.[34]

Ironside told McNaughton that action had been taken on Churchill's message and that Lord Gort was doing something about his communications. Three divisions would move westwards to hold the Dunkirk-Aire-Calais triangle; part of one division via Ypres to Calais and Dunkirk and the remainder on the line Aire-St. Omer; the other two divisions would deploy in the vicinity of Aire. But the group for Dunkirk would not arrive there until the afternoon of 25 May.

McNaughton's conference with Ironside had one major outcome; the War Office, not having heard from Churchill as yet, still intended to evacuate the Calais garrison and decided that no useful purpose would be served by sending the Canadian force to

---

*They were still at Dover.

Dunkirk. It was, therefore, to return to Aldershot. That conference was followed by another immediately afterwards. Ironside wished McNaughton to go with him to a meeting of the Defence Minister, his naval and air associates, and the British Chiefs of Staff.

"Dirty but shaven I marched over with the Chief of the Imperial General Staff and I was settled about halfway down the length of the table. There must have been forty or fifty persons assembled." Churchill* was there, A. V. Alexander, Anthony Eden (who had replaced Stanley as Secretary of State for War) and Sir Archibald Sinclair, attended by the service chiefs: Admiral of the Fleet Sir Dudley Pound, Air Chief Marshal Sir Cyril Newall and Ironside. Also present was Ismay (secretary, Committee of Imperial Defence), square-headed, looking more puglike than ever with his prominent eyes and pursed lips. "Churchill took over and the first order of business was that he singled me out and asked me to give an account of my mission to the continent." McNaughton had the floor while Churchill sat, relaxed but watchful.

McNaughton described the situation at Calais and Dunkirk as he knew it; he emphasized his concern over Fagalde's proposal to withdraw a division from the line near Bruges and the serious danger to the BEF that might result. That danger had, in fact, become reality on 24 May, as we shall see.

McNaughton's views on the vital importance of holding Calais were completely in harmony with Churchill's own, and it is not unlikely that the General's first-hand opinion, firmly expressed, hardened the Prime Minister's resolve. At the meeting that night it became clear that the order for evacuation had been given by some joint army-navy committee without Churchill's knowledge. By the 25th, as we have seen, there was no longer any question of evacuating Calais:

I now resolved that Calais should be fought to the death, and that no evacuation by sea could be allowed to the garrison, which consisted of one battalion of the Rifle Brigade, one of the 60th Rifles, the Queen Victoria Rifles, and a battalion of the Royal Tank

*He was Minister of Defence as well as Prime Minister.

Regiment, with twenty-one Light, and twenty-seven Cruiser tanks and an equal number of Frenchmen. It was painful thus to sacrifice these splendid trained Regular troops of which we had so few. . . .[35]

Nevertheless the decision was made. Churchill found the news of the move of the French divisions to Dunkirk reassuring; so were the details of Fagalde's defensive plan, especially with regard to flooding:

This region was lighted in my mind from the previous war, when I had maintained the mobile Marine Brigade operating from Dunkirk against the flanks and rear of the German armies marching on Paris. I did not therefore have to learn about the inundation system between Calais and Dunkirk, or the significance of the Gravelines waterline. The sluices had already been opened, and with every day the floods were spreading, thus giving southerly protection to our line of retreat.[36]

The question remained, what was to be done with the Canadian troops, still standing by at Dover and Southampton? Churchill's ardent wish to have them at Calais, or even Dunkirk, was tempered by the imperative need to preserve a trained formation for the likely contingency of the defence of Britain. The matter was discussed in all its aspects but no final decision was made. McNaughton, the Prime Minister concluded, should consider himself at two hours' notice for any eventuality.

"Then discussion went on in which I didn't take part. I've got to admit," said McNaughton, "that at about that stage of the proceedings I put my head in my hands and went to sleep. Then, through a doze, I heard in a booming voice from the head of the table Churchill giving a pep talk. That's what it was. It was a rehearsal for what later took form in his speech about fighting on the beaches, fighting on the landing grounds and in the streets. It really had a dynamic effect on the audience. It woke me up—woke everybody else up too."[37]

McNaughton remained in London that night. Next day he visited CMHQ to give Crerar and Montague his appreciation of the situation at Calais and Dunkirk. It was quite obvious from his remarks that he, at any rate, had given up any idea of his troops being employed at either place:*

. . . the main thing now is to complete the mobilization of the Division so that it may be fully mobile and able to operate effectively in the event of [the] probable attempt at invasion of this country . . .[39]

He was already thinking in terms of "mobile columns of all arms which can be moved quickly to any threatened locality."[40]

On the night of 24 May, acting on the decision which had been reached at the CIGS's conference, McNaughton ordered the bitterly disappointed Canadian troops, who were aboard ship at the southern ports, to be moved back to Aldershot. They had waited all day, expecting to get to France.

This time McNaughton had kept the Canadian government informed about the project as soon as it was proposed. The government, "deeply moved," would "look forward with deep anxiety but firm confidence to the part that will be taken by our Canadian men. . . ."[41] It seemed in London in the early hours of 26 May that this sentiment might still not be inappropriate, for on the 24th the Germans, who had been relatively quiet on this front, brought pressure to bear against the Belgian line towards Bruges in the north, against the Lys sector (centre) and in the south at either side of Courtrai. The Belgian Army broke at Courtrai, opening a gap towards Ypres and the sea. It was also pushed back

---

*The CIGS and his advisers had, the evening before, been unanimous that the Canadians should not go to Dunkirk. As for Calais, McNaughton had known since early on the 24th that the Calais garrison had received evacuation orders. Even if those orders should be countermanded—as they were—the situation there would not be as McNaughton had found it on the night 23-24 May when British troops were defending an outer perimeter giving room for the Canadians to come in behind them out of reach of the German guns. McNaughton thought it logical that Nicholson would move back from the outer perimeter on receiving evacuation orders, as indeed he did. On 24 May "a further message from the War Office confirmed the decision to evacuate, but final evacuation of the fighting troops would not take place until seven o'clock next morning [the 25th]. On this information Brigadier Nicholson shortened his front by withdrawing the infantry to the line of the Marck Canal and the Boulevard Leon Gambetta . . . and after dark the defenders were withdrawn to the old town and the quadrangle to the east, which is enclosed by the outer ramparts of the Marck and Calais canals."[32]

towards the north from the Lys, so that another gap was developing north of Menin. The main danger, as McNaughton had foreseen, had now arisen on the left of the BEF where the Germans
were pouring in from the east over the disintegrating Belgian
Army. German armour would hold the British right; the fatal
blow would be delivered from the east towards Ypres and the
coast, only thirty miles away. The main task of the BEF would be
to hold the Germans off while sealing the gap between itself and
the sea (ably done by Brooke's II Corps), and Lord Gort could no
longer entertain a thrust to the south as Weygand had ordered.
He would need all his resources to keep open the road to Dunkirk
and to evacuate his army while there was still time.

It cannot be overstressed that up to this time Gort had been acting in accordance with French orders—and the British cabinet's—to
strike southwards towards Amiens. The BEF had definite instructions to link up with the French and take station on the left of the
French Army holding the line of the Somme. Lord Gort held his
5th and 50th Divisions in reserve for this purpose, together with
what armour he had been able to scrape together. As late as 24
May, Anthony Eden was still calling for an attack to the south,[42]
and on the 25th Sir John Dill, who visited Gort briefly from London, found that the British C-in-C was endeavouring to comply
with orders. Gort was preparing an attack southwards, in conjunc-
tion with the French, for the evening of 26 May.[43]

The operation, as Churchill had it from Weygand when the
Prime Minister visited France on 22 May, called not only for an
attack by Gort to the southwest but also for a simultaneous attack
from the south—the essence of the scheme—by a new French army
group that was being former on the far side of the panzer cor-
ridor. Churchill's meeting with Weygand "ended on a note of
restrained optimism" and from that time on Lord Gort's plea for
a retreat to Dunkirk was rejected in favour of this grand counter-
assault.[44] But there was no sign of the new French army group
ever being formed. Even if Gort, with his slender resources,
managed to disengage and move southwards he would be hammering at the air. "There was no anvil," as McNaughton put it,

"against which he could strike. You couldn't join up with the French countryside."[45]

The German attacks of the 24th had brought Brooke (fearing for the safety of his left flank) to Gort on the following day, clamouring for reinforcements. By six o'clock that evening Gort had reached a decision—"to call off the 5th and 50th Divisions [his only reserve] from the attack to the south and send them over to Brookie on the left."[46] It was his own decision, taken on his own responsibility and, to his undying credit, made in the teeth of every French order and the instructions of the British government. This decision was, the British official historian writes, the "most fateful" action of the whole campaign. "Without waiting to ask authority from the French commander he ordered the 5th and 50th Divisions to abandon preparations for the attack southwards on the 26th and to move at once to the threatening gap between the British and Belgian armies. By doing so he saved the British Expeditionary Force."[47]

His decision was made just in time; had the 5th and 50th Divisions reached Brooke's corps a few hours later than they did they would have been too late to block the gap that was developing between Menin and Ypres. The Germans would have broken through.[48] As it was, when the Belgian Army surrendered on 28 May with only an hour's intimation, Gort was not faced with the overwhelming crisis that otherwise would have confronted him.

On the 25th the news reached Gort that the Canadian force would not be sent to France. Considering it would be useful to have fresh and well-trained troops in the bridgehead area, he protested and asked for a Canadian brigade at Dunkirk. The safe evacuation of the BEF was now of paramount importance, and the War Office was disposed to comply.

Shortly before 2 A.M. on 26 May a message announcing the revival of the previous scheme reached Headquarters 1st Canadian Division; the same force as before would be made ready for embarkation on the night of 26-27 May. McNaughton, roused from his bed, verified the composition and found out that it would be used "farther up" (at Dunkirk) and that the use of his force had been "fixed up by General Sir John Dill in consultation with Lord Gort."[49] (Dill had left his corps in France during April to become Vice Chief of the Imperial General Staff; he was soon to supersede Ironside as CIGS.)

Dill, it transpired, wished to see McNaughton in London at 10 A.M., but before reporting at Whitehall, McNaughton examined the log of discussions with the War Office at CMHQ. He found that arrangements had been made to move his force in two flights, the first sailing that night and the second on the following night, but that neither flight contained artillery or machine-gun units. Armed with that information, he, with Crerar and Turner, called on Dill and Dewing. Dill outlined the reason for the dispatch of the Canadian forces; the BEF was almost surrounded and facing disaster.

McNaughton made it clear that, while he was prepared "to undertake anything" he was asked to perform, he wanted to get the "best value possible" out of his troops. He did not consider the proposed expedition to Dunkirk would do so. His strong objections were based on several factors: Fagalde, by Weygand's order, had been placed in command of all troops at Dunkirk and had at least one division there; Gort, he had been told two days ago, was moving part of a British division to the port. Of what use would a Canadian brigade group be unless it was properly equipped? It would merely add to the chaos and congestion. And under the present movement scheme the force would not be properly equipped; it would have no field guns for at least twenty-four hours, and probably longer, after the arrival of the leading troops. He deplored the opportunity that had been missed at Calais. There his force might have done something against the rear of the German armoured divisions operating towards Dunkirk. Since that plan had fallen through he proposed to mobilize nine mobile groups of all arms within the division to help fulfil the primary task, as he saw it, of defending Britain.[50]

Both Dill and Dewing were convinced by McNaughton's arguments. Dill picked up the telephone and advised the GIGS that it would be useless to send the Canadians without their guns and it was apparent that the guns could not be sent that day. He suggested that Gort, who had been heartened by the news that a Canadian force would assist in the bridgehead area, should be warned in good time that it would not be there as promised. Fagalde had enough men at Dunkirk, and Dill repeated that it "would be madness" to send a Canadian brigade group unless fully equipped; he stated emphatically that they must not have a repetition of the "loss of two grand regiments," as had happened at Boulogne.* Further, he emphasized that "the defence of England itself must be given full weight" when the dispatch of any more troops to the Continent was under consideration.[51]

Ironside obviously reported this new development to Eden (Secretary of State for War); very shortly afterwards Eden, with the CIGS behind him, burst in on the discussion. Why, he demanded with some heat, was objection "now being raised to sending the Canadian Brigade Group to Dunkerque and why was it stated that this Group had no guns?" McNaughton replied that thirty-six guns were indeed available but that Movement Control had stated that they could not be sent until more than twenty-four hours after the departure of the first flight. It would be useless, he continued flatly, to send the group without its guns.[52]

No less a body than the War Cabinet, said Eden, acting on the advice of the Chiefs of Staff Committee, had on the evening of 25 May made the decision to send the Canadian brigade group to Dunkirk. He utterly failed to see that the change of conditions had been sufficient to warrant a complete reversal of the advice which had been given.[53] But there *were* difficulties about the guns. Though Movement Control by this time thought there might be a chance of arranging ships for them to leave that night from Southampton, Ironside weighed in against it. If there was any doubt at all, he said, the project should be dropped.[54]

Dewing thought it would be a difficult and slow undertaking in any case to off-load the guns at Dunkirk under existing conditions. The BEF should provide them from its own resources. "It was no more difficult to disembark them now," the Secretary of State com-

*When the facts were known it transpired that only two hundred men had been lost from the Guards battalions at Boulogne.

mented acidly, "than at the time the advice had been given." Once again Eden harked back to the War Cabinet and the members' decision. They had decided that the Canadian force would go; they alone could sanction the abandoning of the scheme. And the impression he gave was one of reluctance to recommend any change of plan.[55]

But in view of the stand taken by the assembled generals against the project, there was little Eden could do. Dewing stated coolly that a balance must be made between "a gesture to help the B.E.F." and the "bigger question" of maintaining a suitable force for the defence of England. General Percival, who had joined the discussion shortly after Eden and the CIGS, said that unless the Canadians left that night there would be no point in sending them, to which Ironside quickly retorted that the group would not go without its guns.

Ironside, it seemed, had determined to settle the matter with Eden once and for all. Before doing so he asked McNaughton, Crerar and Turner to withdraw. As he left, McNaughton told Eden that his objection to the plan was "not based on any timidity" but "on a desire to get the best possible use for the effort made" which, in his view, would be the defence of Britain. The situation was changing hourly. What might have been the right decision twenty-four hours before was not necessarily true of today.* Nevertheless, if the Prime Minister and the War Cabinet decided on the merits of the prevailing situation that the force should go, he would abide by that decision.[57]

What went on in the room after the Canadians had left can only be conjecture. Twenty minutes later, a flushed Ironside showed McNaughton the draft of a telegram to Gort informing him that the dispatch of the Canadians was now unlikely. The draft would be placed before the Prime Minister and a decision made within the hour.[58] What *is* certain, however, is that on this same day, Ironside was replaced as CIGS by Sir John Dill.[59]

---

*"It would not have been a proper operation of war to go to Dunkirk simply because the War Cabinet had approved a course of action in the light of a situation which had prevailed twenty-four hours before. If we were to go at all it had to be decided on its merits *then*."[56]

Churchill approved the message and McNaughton heard of the cancellation of the project for the second time. But the vehicles were left loaded and the troops remained on notice, which proved to be a wise precaution. Gort continued to press for Canadians at Dunkirk. He had now committed the 5th and 50th Divisions to II Corps, and had no reserve. He asked Eden late in the afternoon of the 26th for one brigade, to be followed by a second, and repeated his request that evening. McNaughton, unaware of this development, spent the afternoon at Headquarters, Home Forces, Twickenham, discussing with Brigadier A. I. Macdougall (Chief of Staff, Home Forces) the formation of mobile units in the Canadian Division for home defence.

McNaughton's visit to Home Forces at that time is the best evidence of the way his mind was working. He was convinced that the proper employment for his division was to stand ready to help defend the British coast; without a firm defence the war might well be over. "It would have been a foolish thing for us to go gallivanting across the Channel at that time. Our role was humbler, if you will, but it was a role essential to the defence of Britain."[60]

And the visit to Twickenham was useful. McNaughton wanted to ascertain what the situation in England really was. He had in mind the defence of the United Kingdom against the possibility of the Germans following up with a quickly launched invasion.

If they came across with their morale up and irrespective of casualties—in planes and glider aircraft as well as in canal boats, making full use of their submarine fleet—and got a few parties ashore it might have been the same thing that had happened in Holland; the suddenness of the blow upsetting the whole civil population, starting them on the move and making it impossible to get any real forces down the roads to meet the Germans. The first thing I found out was that arrangements for home defence lay primarily with the Lord Lieutenants of counties.* I asked to see what allocation of roads had been made so that any force available at the centre of our arc, say around Northampton, could get forward to the coast from the Humber to the Thames. Macdougall produced maps for

---

*"The Lord Lieutenants," McNaughton said, "were as the lords of creation. Military commands in England functioned by grace not by orders."

me showing the allocation of roads and I remember distinctly that those reserved for the evacuation of the civil population were coloured yellow; when you put the maps of the different counties side by side the routes coloured yellow didn't join up. There had been no co-ordination and to get the civil population dispersed in England would have caused the most infernal jam. Somebody had said that if the Germans came we must get rid of the civil population and they were going to start a movement of the civilians from the coast. I remember saying that's just about the last thing we want. That's exactly what the Germans will try to do—to start a population stampede across the country. Our mobile columns would never be able to get down the roads to reach the coast.

The first thing, I suggested, is to get an order out that everyone is to stay put, and that was done. I think that what really protected England was that nobody on Hitler's staff could have had any conception of the casualness that was around England at that time. The representation that I made on that visit was instrumental, if not decisive, in causing a change in the organization in England where the Lord Lieutenants lost their power to G.H.Q. Home Forces.[61]

Next day, at 7 A.M., McNaughton heard from Dewing:

Have had conversation with fellow on the other side [Gort]; he has made an appeal to be passed on. My recommendation is the same as yesterday, but no one should be far away as the matter will be considered by the higher ones about 1000 hrs. I have seen our new man [Dill] and his view is the same as yesterday. However, black coats [War Cabinet] may not accept and movement control has been warned.*[62]

McNaughton did not alert the troops—"Let the people rest," he said—nor were they ever told of the project's revival. Then two senior officers from GHQ in France assured Dewing that it would be "useless to send more troops into Dunkerque" and in the afternoon Crerar told McNaughton of news from the War Office that the show was "definitely off."[63]

The Dunkirk evacuation began on the night 26-27 May, when about five thousand men were brought off. The bridgehead, into which—on the 28th—Gort ordered a general withdrawal, held firm.

---

*Dewing disguised the message to some extent in case the conversation was overheard.

This was bounded roughly by the original defensive line established by Fagalde on the line Gravelines-Bergues-Furnes-Nieuport, with Fagalde's XVI Corps holding from Gravelines to Bergues, and the British the rest. By the 29th most of the BEF had arrived within the perimeter of the bridgehead, and the mustering of shipping and small craft (which had been proceeding since the 20th under the control of Admiral Ramsay at Dover) was completed; the tide of "little ships" of various kinds which had volunteered had risen, though it had not yet reached the flood.

Day after day the evacuation continued despite every effort by the German Army and Air Force to destroy the Allied troops. On 4 June, when the evacuation was declared completed, some 338,000 British and French soldiers had been successfully withdrawn, more than the most optimistic had dared predict. But to save the men, artillery, equipment and ammunition had had to be abandoned. These were the soldiers only of an expeditionary force that was practically disarmed, and of little use to defend the homeland until re-equipped.

"It is difficult to see," the Canadian official historian writes, "how sending a Canadian brigade to Dunkirk could have contributed to bringing about a better result. It would, indeed, have introduced an unnecessary complication, would almost certainly have meant the loss of more equipment, and might well have meant the loss of more men."[64]

A summary of McNaughton's role* during these anxious days is perhaps best provided by reproducing letters which passed between Dewing and McNaughton on 27 and 28 May. Dewing wrote as follows:

27 May, 1940

My dear Andy,

I am afraid your Division, or a good proportion of it, have spent a lot of time on fruitless preparations in connection with their proposed employment yesterday morning. These hurried projects

*And yet, despite his contribution, there is no mention in the British official histories of McNaughton's part in these events.

"There was agitation in the country and in Parliament to bring him back
to Canada permanently, to lead Canada's war effort."

A dinner at St. James's Palace to mark the mounting of the Buckingham Palace guard by the R. 22e R., April, 1940: Brigadier C. B. Price, Vincent Massey, Lieutenant-Colonel E. A. Blais, Anthony Eden, Captain J. G. Charlebois, Norman Rogers and McNaughton

Brigadiers Price Montague and Harry Crerar, McNaughton, H.M. King George VI, Lieutenant-Colonel Ernest Walford and Vincent Massey at the mounting of the Buckingham Palace guard by Canadian troops, April, 1940

have come your way altogether too often. I hope there will be no further question of putting troops into Dunkirk, though even tonight the question has been re-opened by a message from Gort asking for support there.

I am absolutely convinced in my mind that to put fresh troops into Dunkirk now with little or no transport would be militarily quite wrong. The most they could do would be to hold the outskirts of the town, and that would not secure the port for Lord Gort. In fact, it would be throwing good material into a quicksand which is already on the way to engulfing far too much. I don't believe it would add anything to what we should save from the quicksand.

I think, too, there is the greatest importance, as well as the greatest difficulty at the present time of seeing more than the drama that is immediately before our eyes. We must remember that we have got to win this war, first by defending England and giving the German a jolt when he attacks here; and next by building up a fresh Field Force out of the ruins of the old. Your Division and the 52nd may be vital to the first task, and with the 51st which is already in France will be the keystone on which the new Field Force will be built.

These are the reasons which have influenced me in throwing what little weight I have against the employment of your Division or any part of it in Dunkirk. The part you have been asked to play has been extraordinarily difficult. You went off on your first visit to Calais and Dunkirk full of the fire and determination to use your troops to save the B.E.F. What you thought of it as a military proposition then I don't fully know, but you were absolutely determined to do thoroughly whatever might be asked of you. Today, I think you share a good many of my feelings of the unsoundness of committing fresh troops to Dunkirk. It was much more difficult for you to express that, because you naturally had the feeling that you might be giving the impression that you and the Canadian troops were not ready to undertake a desperate adventure. I can assure you that you did not give that impression. We all know you far too well for it to be possible for any of us to entertain that suspicion for one moment; and I only mention it because I think it was in your mind.

The opportunity to use the Division will come soon enough, but it must come in circumstances in which it can play a sound military role, as dashing as you like, but militarily practicable.

Yours ever,
DICK DEWING[65]

McNaughton's reply ran thus:

28 May, 1940

My dear Dick,

On my return from Chatham this evening, I have your letter of yesterday's date and I very deeply appreciate your friendly thought in telling me of your sympathetic understanding of the position in which I found myself in the difficult circumstances of the last few days. You have clearly penetrated to the motives and considerations which governed my actions and it is a great comfort to me to know that this is so.

I was all for Calais on the first night because I thought that from that flank we might, at the least, delay the close investment of Dunkerque and with British troops in effective occupation of the perimeter there was some certainty that our deployment could be effected in an orderly and proper manner.

As for Dunkerque, from the beginning I could not see our employment there as a practical operation in war. With our small force we could not go beyond the near perimeter. De Fagalde, under his mandate from Weygand, was able to reach position much earlier than we. He, as a French general clearly in close sympathy with the Admiral du Nord and with all the local naval, military and air intelligence service at his disposal, was better placed than I, with no British troops on the spot and no staff with local knowledge, to exercise co-ordination. If I had attempted to do so and produced my instructions from Ironside, they might well have folded up!

When I heard from De Fagalde of his plan for the withdrawal of his 60th Division leaving a gap on the left, I was very anxious thinking that it might result in a torrent of German Infantry behind our lines, a far more serious matter than in our vicinity. It was to give this, in my view, vital information that I asked permission to return to Dover and later to the War Office.

As for taking the force the next day or the day after to Dunkerque, I could only see it as a gesture of no very great value and I thought it was the sort of thing the enemy would like, that is to draw some part of our not too ample reserves into the melee where they could be dealt with cheaply. For these reasons and others of like sort I could not enthuse over the project put before me.

After my visit to Macdougall of the Home Forces on the afternoon of 26 May and in the light of his explanation of the situation in the United Kingdom I knew that it would have been an act of utter folly to have sent us over and when, on the morning of 27 May, I heard from you that the project might again be on I determined to cut our force to a minimum so as not to divert any more men or resources from the defence of the United Kingdom than was absolutely necessary for the purpose of a gesture and if the War Cabinet had called on us my orders for the force, armed only with Small Arms and Anti-Tank guns and without field guns or transport, had been drafted; this force to be landed on the open beach from Dover so as to save time and perhaps avoid the dangers in the Channel from mines and air bombing.

However, thanks largely I think to the sound military judgment of yourself and of Dill, this rather theatrical sacrifice was not required of us.

Our problem now is to beat Germany and to do this we must maintain at least a toe hold on this side of the Atlantic until great friendly forces can come, and I have faith they will come, to our assistance. The coast of the United Kingdom is the perimeter of the citadel which *must* be held. All else outside is now of secondary account and even our deep affection, high regard and profound admiration for our gallant friends in France in this hour of bitterness must not overbalance judgment or prejudice the final outcome and they I think would not wish us to do otherwise.

As you know we are now going full out to organize and place our force as a highly mobile, quick acting, hard hitting reserve on which you can count for prompt action.

With best wishes and again many thanks for your note,

Very sincerely yours,
ANDREW MCNAUGHTON[66]

McNaughton's visit to France had been an interesting experience. It is obvious that he seized on the essentials in a fluid situation and did not waver; his judgment was sound. In the greatest crisis that ever faced the British Army he kept his head.

Chapter 6

~~~~~~

Fiasco in Brittany

After the last British troops left the Dunkirk beaches on 4 June all England was in suspense. What would the Germans do? No one could doubt their initiative after the overrunning of Norway, Holland, Belgium, the capture of northern France and the forced evacuation of the BEF with the loss of almost all its weapons, as well as huge stocks of ammunition and explosives which had been placed in depots along the coast.

A vast arc of coastline facing Britain had become hostile almost overnight. And behind that coast, half encircling the British Isles, the enemy could concentrate an air fleet only a few minutes' flying time away from southern England. The German Air Force greatly outnumbered the RAF, and under its shelter Hitler's victorious divisions awaited the signal to follow up the British retreat.

The Germans' alternatives were either to pounce immediately on the English coast before the hastily evacuated troops could be reorganized or to finish off the reeling French. Until it was known which way they would go the Canadian Division was held in central England to strike at enemy landings between the Humber and the Thames, which were considered imminent. The night and day after Dunkirk was the most precarious period. As we have seen, McNaughton, on his visit to Home Forces while Gort was still calling for the Canadians to come to France, had envisaged this situation, so at the end of May the 1st Canadian Division moved to the quiet country near Northampton, centrally positioned for the support of any threatened point on the "invasion coast."

McNaughton, before leaving Aldershot, formed mobile columns, taking over seven hundred vehicles of all types from British stocks to obtain the extra mobility he needed. Each mobile group was based on an infantry battalion, nine in all, and three of these were formed into an operational group under the commander of each brigade. The arms of the division—artillery, engineers and so on—were parcelled out to the three operational groups to give them the capability of independent action. The ancillary artillery regiments and machine-gun battalion remained and these McNaughton formed into a reserve group which he kept under his own hand. He was completely absorbed in this fascinating task of moulding a divisional organization to suit an unusual role; he tested the mobility of each group by night moves from Aldershot to the Northampton area.

"There weren't enough armed troops in England then to do a line of defence along the whole east coastal area. It would have taken fifty divisions. The only way was to form a highly mobile force, not necessarily very large, that could be used at the drop of a hat. If there were any landings we could get a force onto the backs of their necks before they had time to expand. We weren't trying to get a divisional action going. We'd never get a division as such deployed in time to be of use. The thing to do was to break up the division. To break it up into groups and get enough transport. The groups would be in battalion strength and through the brigades we could control them even if we were decentralized. So I broke the division up into nine rapidly moving columns."[1]

The total force was more than a division; it included the Canadian ancillary troops as well as the 1st Division. For that reason it was styled "Canadian Force." Every unit of the Canadian Force had received its complete scale of war equipment and ammunition and was at full strength. Sufficient vehicles had been obtained to transport the marching troops and a good deal of thought went into fixing up trucks and motor-cycle combinations with machine-guns for close-in air defence.

Ironside, who after vacating the appointment of CIGS had become Commander-in-Chief Home Forces, was working on a

defence plan which crystallized in June though refinement followed for many months. Canadian Force, one of only two well-
armed divisions in Britain at the time, featured prominently in
Ironside's plan, which has been described by Churchill:

There were three main elements in this early outline of a great
future plan; first, an entrenched "crust" on the probable invasion
beaches of the coast, whose defenders should fight where they
stood, supported by mobile reserves for immediate counter-attack;
secondly, a line of anti-tank obstacles, manned by the Home
Guard, running down the east centre of England and protecting
London and the great industrial centres from inroads by armoured
vehicles; thirdly, behind that line, the main reserves for major
counter-offensive action.[2]

The Canadian Force was one of "the main reserves." It would
only be committed when the enemy had actually invaded in sufficient strength to make the nature of his objective clear. The field
of operations of the force, said Ironside, would be to come to the
aid of an invaded sector in eastern England between the Humber
in the north and the Thames in the south—approximately half of
the whole eastern coast, and therefore a formidable task.[3] Mc-
Naughton, who had signed an Order of Detail placing the Canadian Force in combination with the United Kingdom forces on
1 June, ordered each of his operational groups to reconnoitre one
sector of this front and the routes leading to it, while he himself,
on 3 June, left for a three-day reconnaissance tour of the whole
area.[4]

This tour took him through fourteen English counties. The
weather, as it remained throughout that "invasion summer," was
exceptionally fine. He saw every kind of landscape: flat fenland
and the level fields of Lincolnshire studded with villages and high
church towers; the dreamy, reed-fringed Norfolk Broads; rolling
hills and woodland; and industrial and market towns. Everything
interested him: the frequency and range of tides; the means of
flooding; the defensive value of certain hills; and the ease of
passage through towns on the way to the coastal sectors. Some
towns, he found, had narrow twisting streets which would be hope-

less for rapid troop movements and these were marked down to be avoided.[5] As to the guarded concrete road blocks* going up all over the place, many of these would be "more of a hindrance than a help to British Forces operating in the area."[7]

What he feared most, as he reported to the Chief of Staff at Home Forces on his return, were the numerous "wide flat areas," which were natural landing fields, especially around Newmarket and Cambridge. Macdougall mentioned flooding, but McNaughton had looked into that possibility. The areas were above the high-tide level. Smoke, he thought, would be the answer. Smudge-pots might be made up—the navy would advise on this—so that the areas could be blotted out in case of need.[8] He had noticed that the British had denied the use of the broad main highways for landings by German aircraft by building a sandbag wall halfway out across the road, and then, a little farther along, another one out from the other side. "Any reinforcing group would have to negotiate these obstacles. We had just got our transport but we hadn't been able to do much training of our drivers in formation driving and our men were simply not trained enough to compete with them. We'd be paralyzed before we got going. With the best will in the world we'd never get there."[9]

He pointed this out to Macdougall who said, " 'Well, what do we do about it?' And I made a casual answer off the cuff. What they had in mind was the landing of light aircraft, so I said, 'Let's string some wires across and trip the brutes,' though my interest was not so much in bringing down German aircraft as in keeping the right of way open for our troops. Almost before the words were out of my mouth they accepted that suggestion. I think there was something like ten million pounds spent on trip wires in one place or another. Unoccupied aerodromes in the east of England and flat spaces were protected in the same way. They were all over the country in the end. And wires protecting defiles in the South Downs country brought German aircraft down to my certain knowledge later on."[10]

---

*The Ross rifles ordered from Canada had now arrived. "In the Kings Lynn-Ely-Huntingdon area [we] encountered several LDV men armed with Ross rifles stationed at various points along the roads."[6] (See page 56.)

Unknown to McNaughton, moves were taking place, and conversations at the highest level, which would detach him from these problems for a time. On 2 June, while the Dunkirk evacuation was still going on, Churchill had prepared a memorandum for his Chiefs of Staff. Another BEF, he insisted, should be sent at once to France, "otherwise the French will not continue in the war."

Even if Paris is lost, they must be adjured to continue a gigantic guerrilla. A scheme should be considered for a bridgehead and area of disembarkation in Brittany, where a large army can be developed. We must have plans worked out which will show the French that there is a way through if they will only be steadfast.

As soon as the BEF is reconstituted for Home Defence three divisions should be sent to join our two divisions south of the Somme, or wherever the French left may be by then. It is for consideration whether the Canadian Division should not go at once. . . .[11]

The Canadians did not, however, go at once. Prudence dictated that they should remain in Britain until it was known what the Germans were going to do. All doubt was ended when, on 5 June, the enemy, with his eye on Paris, moved against the French. That day McNaughton was placed directly under the War Office and warned of an impending operation. Between 6 and 8 June the Canadian Force moved back to Aldershot where, on the 8th, under orders now to go to France, it was visited by the King and Queen.[12]

Their Majesties were, by this time, no strangers to the troops. They passed down the ranks of successive units speaking "personally and graciously" to sun-bronzed, confident men in faded battledress who grinned warmly back. There was an air of cheerfulness, of animation at the thought of action, that was in keeping with the presence of Canada's sovereign and the sparkle of a sunny day in early June. McNaughton, as always, was much taken by this simple, good man, who invariably put his duty first, and his Scottish blood warmed to the Queen. He told the King that the troops were now battleworthy and ready to do all they could in the present Empire crisis.

That night McNaughton advised the Minister of National Defence of the visit. It was the last cable he would ever send to Norman Rogers. Two days later a news bulletin announced the death of the Minister in an air accident in Canada.[13] Rogers, as McNaughton pointed out in a message of condolence to his family, had endeared himself by his tact, patience and support.[14] Colonel J. L. Ralston succeeded Rogers. His acceptance of the vacant Defence portfolio on 5 July was disturbing. McNaughton's recollections of him in that position in the twenties were by no means pleasant and his criticism of the General's resolution of the constitutional position at the time of the abortive Norwegian expedition was far from reassuring.

Meanwhile Churchill, consistent with his anxiety to keep France fighting, had flown backwards and forwards across the Channel to imbue the French government with some of his own determination. There is no doubt that on these visits the Brittany plan was discussed.

Holding Brittany as a possible centre of resistance if Paris should fall had been considered by Paul Reynaud, the French Prime Minister, as early as 25 May.[15] Six days later Churchill discussed with him "what could be done to rebuild the British forces in France,"[16] and that day Reynaud directed Weygand to look into the setting up of "a national redoubt in the neighbourhood of a naval base" that "might be situated in the Breton peninsula."[17] On 2 June, as we have seen, Churchill's memorandum to the British Chiefs of Staff, while calling for three divisions to join the two British divisions "south of the Somme," asked that the idea of a bridgehead in Brittany should be considered. And on 11 June, during Churchill's fourth visit to France since the crisis began, he had, according to his own account, agreed with Reynaud to "try to draw a kind of 'Torres Vedras line' across the foot of the Brittany peninsula."[18]

It would appear, then, that there was general agreement between the French and British governments for the setting up of a redoubt in Brittany. In the prevailing chaos of the time, however, there is no clear record of the plans; nor were the commanders concerned with executing them fully aware of their scope and purpose. On 14 June, when Canadian troops had already landed in France, it was reported that the CIGS had still "not heard of the Brittany scheme,"[19] though he was cognizant of the attempt to form a new British Expeditionary Force.

The War Office, acting on Churchill's memorandum of 2 June, decided to reconstitute the BEF to the limits of its present resources and to build it up at a later date. There were only two divisions in England fit to move—the 52nd (Lowland) and the 1st Canadian—and these would join other British troops in France. The latter consisted of the 51st (Highland) Division, which had been in the Saar region and was now on the coastal flank of the French Army in Normandy; the 1st Armoured Division, which had lost the troops it had detached to Calais and had suffered further losses in the fighting on the Somme, together with the Beauman Force, an improvised division made up from base troops, now helping to defend Normandy. Lieutenant-General Brooke, who had returned from Dunkirk after commanding II Corps in France, was appointed to this new command.

Brooke saw Dill and the Secretary of State for War on 2 June at the War Office, where he made it clear to Eden that while the move "possibly . . . had some political value" it "promised no chances of military success and every probability of disaster,"[20] and his judgment that this was a political rather than a military act was well founded. It is corroborated by Churchill's action in refusing to throw in the fighting strength of the RAF to support the French, as they requested. Though he would send divisions to encourage the French to keep on fighting, he would not commit the metropolitan fighter force of the RAF on which the successful defence of Britain depended.

. . . in a purely military view the decision to commit every available Army division, while at the same time refusing the air support without which their operations could scarcely be effective, was a peculiar one. It emphasizes the fact, which indeed emerges clearly from Mr. Churchill's memoranda, that the formation of a new B.E.F. was a political rather than a military act; its object was to encourage the French and keep them in the war.[21]

McNaughton was warned of the impending task for his division on 5 June. At that time he too had no clear idea of what was expected of him. "After Dunkirk," he pointed out, "there was a real turmoil in the French political organization and the army. Churchill went to and fro but we didn't hear very much of the detail of what was going on because of the confusion." The impression McNaughton received was that Weygand was assembling a force of considerable magnitude to the south and west of Paris to seal off the Brittany peninsula, and that a British force would participate in this operation.[22]

He knew that of all the divisions in England at the time, his was in the highest state of fighting efficiency.

We were invited to join this force and it seemed the right thing to do. If the information which had been furnished us had been correct, it was obviously proper employment and a practical operation of war.[23]

Accordingly, on 6 June McNaughton (who since 15 May had had full authority from Ottawa to move to a "theatre of operations . . . if you consider the circumstances warrant it") informed the Canadian authorities that the division would move to France, with the first parties probably leaving on the 11th. His Order of Detail under the Visiting Forces Act placed the division in combination with the forces of the United Kingdom "until I shall otherwise direct."[24]

To prepare a division for an overseas move at short notice is a feverish business; nevertheless, by the 9th the division was ready. There was still nothing definite about what it would do in France —merely that it would operate in Brittany after landing at Brest. To find out, McNaughton invited Brooke to Aldershot to "meet the officers and have a look at the units and so that we could have an understanding about what the *modus operandi* would be."[25] The new corps commander came down on 11 June and presided at a conference at Divisional Headquarters.[26]

Brooke, at any rate, understood his task to be the creation of a redoubt in Brittany. The points he made in discussion with Mc-Naughton are entirely consistent with that idea. "Brooke and I had a long talk at which I had my senior staff officers with me. Colonel Turner kept very careful track of all this"[27] and Turner afterwards prepared a draft operation order outlining the 1st Division's part in the "reconstructed B.E.F." which is on file.[28]

The Brittany peninsula juts into the sea westwards from Pontorson (about twenty miles east of St. Malo) in the north, and from St. Nazaire in the south. Brest is at its western tip. The line from Pontorson to St. Nazaire—and thus the neck of the peninsula —is about ninety miles long; the town of Rennes, some forty miles south of Pontorson, lies along this line.

The intention of the corps commander, Turner's draft order read, was to "concentrate the whole of 2 Corps in the area to the NORTH and SOUTH of RENNES as soon as formations are assembled."[29] The corps, therefore, would be positioned across the ninety-mile neck of the Brittany peninsula.

The coasts of the peninsula projecting westwards about 150 miles from the line NAZAIRE-PONTORSON have deep water close to the shores and there are many good harbours. The average width [of the peninsula] from NORTH to SOUTH is about 70 miles. The flanks of a force operating in this area can be supported by the Navy. The country is hilly, intersected by many rivers and well wooded. From a study of the map it does not appear to be suited to the employment of large armoured formations. Apart from its extent, it is thus a favourable theatre for the operations visualized. . . .

But, because of the paucity of troops available, it was envisaged that "a division may have to hold up to fifty miles of front."[30]

McNaughton was to recall that "the general idea, which was completely agreed to by Brooke, was that under the confused circumstances we shouldn't try to plan too far ahead but that we should move as expeditiously as we possibly could to Brest. There the British staff [Brest had been a base port of the old BEF and the base staff was still there] would be available and would see to it that we got suitable areas for billeting in the vicinity in a preliminary concentration of troops. These troops would not be available for operations until the Division had concentrated. A first principle of war is concentration before you strike; and that principle would be followed."[31] His recollection is borne out by Turner's draft in which it is stated:

> *1 Canadian Division and ancillary troops* Landing at BREST . . . and assembling N.E. of the port.[32]

In these circumstances McNaughton decided not to cross to France with the leading troops. The 1st Canadian Infantry Brigade,* with the Royal Canadian Horse Artillery, would lead the move to France from Plymouth and Falmouth on 13 June. Its commander, Brigadier A. A. Smith, would take charge in the assembly area northeast of Brest, while the division was coming together pending McNaughton's own arrival.

McNaughton still had troops north of the Thames. He decided to establish an advanced divisional headquarters at Plymouth "as the most convenient place in the line of communication to Aldershot and the North. Our units were being got together and sent down to me in their embarkation areas, so I could check on their mobilization and make sure it was complete before we embarked them for the Brittany peninsula."[33]

"I've always felt a great anxiety as to whether I shouldn't have been there with the first lot," McNaughton said in 1965, "but I wasn't because I felt that the most important thing at that stage was to get my troops under my hand again."

It requires a great deal of force of character and a commander's personal attention when you are scattered like that to overcome opposition. I know that I was very, very busy on a lot of decisions to expedite that movement. I don't think we would have got half of them there at all if I hadn't been on the job. I could say things and get things done that nobody else could do.[34]

In any case there was to be no forward movement until there had been a concentration at Brest. "There was a firm understanding that they wouldn't be moved until we got there and could give the orders to move forward."[35]

---

*The mobile "group" and "column" organization against invasion had been discarded in this more conventional role.

Sir Alan Brooke* arrived at Cherbourg on 12 June, a most inauspicious day for the Second BEF, three parts of which, as we have seen, were already in France. The 51st (Highland) Division, north of the Seine, had been in action since the German offensive of 5 June. One of its battalions lost half its strength in a single day and still clung to its ground. Forbidden by Weygand to cross the Seine while there was still time, the division fought on in the Havre peninsula before becoming penned up in the little port of St. Valery-en-Caux,† where on 12 June it surrendered. Both the 1st Armoured Division and the Beauman Force suffered heavy casualties before crossing the river westwards.

On the 13th, having covered the almost two-hundred-mile journey from Cherbourg through swarms of refugees, Brooke established his headquarters at Le Mans. This might be thought an odd place to have it since it was some seventy miles forward of the defensive line he had drawn across the base of the Brittany peninsula for McNaughton two days previously. At Le Mans he met General P. de Fonblanque, who had been in command of the lines of communication troops of the original BEF, and other British officers. General de Fonblanque told him of the fate of the 51st Division. He also mentioned that the 52nd (Lowland) Division had arrived in France and that one of its brigades was already fighting with the French Tenth Army; the rest of the division was awaiting orders.[37] This division, as has been noted, was the companion division of the 1st Canadian in the Brittany venture. Brooke's instructions, as taken down by Turner on 11 June, were that the 52nd Division would disembark at St. Nazaire and assemble north of that port before moving up to take over its share of the proposed defensive line.[38] Instead of that, it was being thrown piecemeal into the battle *outside* the peninsula but Brooke, according to the records, did not demur.

---

*Awarded the K.C.B. on 11 June, 1940, for his services in France.[36]

†On 11 June, with German artillery already installed on the cliffs, two Canadian destroyers (*St. Laurent* and *Restigouche*) lay off the port in company with British ships. An officer from *Restigouche* landed but was told that the division was in no immediate need of evacuation. Some wounded were taken off by a British vessel. Later that day both Canadian ships were detached to Atlantic convoy duty.

Brooke then went on to Briare, on the Loire beyond Orleans, to visit Weygand at his headquarters. He was unable to see him until the 14th, the day on which the Germans entered an undefended Paris. The previous day Churchill had visited France for the fifth and last time before the French capitulation, when he heard Reynaud say that it was "too late to organize a redoubt in Brittany";[39] the French armies were everywhere disintegrating so that Weygand had advised his government, now at Tours, to seek an armistice. And three days earlier Italy, certain of French collapse, had entered the war on the German side. All in all, the outlook could hardly have been bleaker.

Nevertheless, three days before the French Army gave up fighting, Weygand was still actively considering establishing a redoubt in Brittany. Brooke describes the discussion he had with Weygand as follows:

We then turned to the question of the defence of Brittany, and Weygand explained that a line was to be held stretching through Rennes with its flanks resting on the sea. While he was talking I had pulled out my pocket dividers, and, setting them to 50 kilometres, I measured this line and made it out to be some 150 kilometres. I drew Weygand's attention to this and he said that it could not be as much. I therefore measured the distance again under his eyes and said that to defend a front of 150 kilometres we should require at least fifteen divisions, and that was assuming that those forces with French Tenth Army would still be available. He said that a few divisions might possibly be found from the Tenth Army. I pointed out that the plan as far as I could see had no hope of success. Weygand agreed that the idea was "fantastic". . . .[40]

Brooke then suggested that the impracticability of the scheme should be represented to the Inter-Allied Council. Weygand stated that that had been done without success. He was now putting it to Brooke as an order. An order for the defence of Brittany was then drawn up, and this was signed by Weygand, Brooke and General Georges. As Brooke had been placed under Weygand's command he had to comply but at the same time he determined to protest to the British government.

At that time we were within three days of the moment when
Pétain ordered the French Army to stop fighting. With this situation facing me, I had been told of an Inter-Allied plan to hold
Brittany, *a plan which had never been mentioned to me before
my departure**. . . . I prepared a message . . . to inform Dill of the
situation and to tell him that the only course left open was to stop
sending any further troops and to instruct me to evacuate the
rest.[41]

On his return to Le Mans in the afternoon of 14 June Brooke
telephoned the CIGS and found out that the flow of troops had
stopped. As for re-embarking the expeditionary force, Dill
"had not heard of the Brittany scheme" but would check with
Churchill.[42] Some time later the CIGS informed Brooke that "the
Brittany scheme was off and that I was to proceed with the embarkation of troops not under orders of French Tenth Army."[43]
Brooke then ordered the 1st Canadian Infantry Brigade, the only
Canadian formation that had landed, to re-embark. To clear the
52nd (Lowland) Division, one brigade of which had become em-
broiled in the fighting alongside the French Tenth Army, took a
half-hour telephone battle with Churchill; the Prime Minister
wished the division to fight on "to make the French feel we were
supporting them":

. . . without sufficient knowledge of conditions prevailing on that
front at that time, he was endeavouring to force a commander to
carry out his wishes against that commander's better judgment.
With all his wonderful qualities, interference of this nature was
one of his weaknesses. . . . The strength of his powers of persuasion
had to be experienced to realise the strength that was required to
counter it.[44]

This, then, was the background of the Brittany venture. The vicissitudes of the 1st Canadian Infantry Brigade are another story.

McNaughton, "relying in good faith on my arrangement with
Brooke," remained at Plymouth "to gather the tail of the Division

---

*Italics supplied. This statement is simply not true. When visiting the 1st
Canadian Division on 11 June, as we have seen, Brooke outlined his plan for
holding a redoubt in Brittany.

. . . in the South West. From Plymouth and Falmouth I was able to inspect each unit of the 1st Brigade and the R.C.H.A. as it went on board and I shuttled between the two ports."[45]

On 11 June the GOC received a message from the CIGS:

Personal for General McNaughton from Jack Dill, C.I.G.S. WISH YOU MY DEAR ANDY AND ALL THE SPLENDID MEN UNDER YOUR COMMAND GOOD FORTUNE AND EVERY SUCCESS IN ALL THAT LIES AHEAD OF YOU.[46]

The main body of the brigade, including headquarters, left Plymouth on 13 June and landed at Brest next morning. There Brigadier Smith fully expected to move to an adjacent assembly area, as he had been instructed would be the case, to get his brigade together and to arrange for the reception of the rest of the division. Instead he was ordered forward to Sablé-sur-Sarthe in the vicinity of Le Mans, more than two hundred miles from Brest and some seventy miles forward of the line across the base of the Brittany peninsula which Brooke had stated he would hold.

Armand Smith on arrival at Brest wasn't asked any questions about the Canadian plans. He was merely given orders with all the authority of the British Base Staff. Of course he took those orders in good faith. They were typed up with great precision. They were just as complete an order for the demolition of the fighting capability of the units as I have ever heard of![47]

Movement Control at Brest had, in fact, received instructions that the movement of divisions arriving from England was to be handled in the same way as that of the divisions of the old BEF in 1939; this had involved an assembly area around Le Mans. During the 14th, therefore, Brigadier Smith, his headquarters, three infantry battalions and attached units found themselves rolling forward in three trains towards Le Mans.

They were without their transport. That had left earlier from Falmouth and Plymouth in separate ships. On the arrival of the vehicles at Brest, Movement Control dispatched them up country in twos or threes as they were swung onto the wharf. At the collecting point fifteen miles from Brest the transport was re-sorted into groups of ten, sometimes without regard to units and with neither officer nor NCO in charge. The route was explained and, one by one, the little packets moved off on their long journey into the interior of wine-rich France.[48] The arrival of some of them, untrammelled by discipline, was rollicking; there were "some reports of drunkenness and reckless driving."[49]

Late in the afternoon of 14 June Brooke gave the order for the withdrawal of the Canadians then in France. "At the moment of reversal," said McNaughton, "the Division was some 600 miles from head to rear in a great big U, which is quite a substantial length of column for a division, to say the least."[50]

At least one unit was still at Northampton; many were in Aldershot, preparing to move; others were at Plymouth and Falmouth, embarked or preparing to embark; others again were at Brest or scattered along the roads between there and Le Mans; the 1st Field Regiment R.C.H.A was . . . at Parcé [between Sablé and Le Mans] and the headquarters of the 1st Infantry Brigade, and its three battalions and some lesser units, were steaming towards that area in trains. It was simple to reverse the move of troops in England or on shipboard at Plymouth or Brest; but to extricate the units across France was bound to be difficult.[51]

McNaughton was at Plymouth ready to leave with the Toronto Scottish when he got the message to disembark. He put through a call to CMHQ and requested confirmation from Dewing, at the War Office, which was soon obtained:

"Reports . . . indicated that organized resistance was no longer possible [and] decision had been taken NOT repeat NOT to commit First Canadian Division to France. In consequence first flight which had disembarked BREST today would re-embark tonight and return to United Kingdom."[52]

"Of course the wire was obeyed," McNaughton remarked, "and the troops were taken off, and then it became our business to find out what had become of the rest of them. We still had telephone lines into the south of England from the south of France . . . We got a certain amount of information. I don't know exactly where we got it, the Navy helped us a bit and told us what conditions were over there."[53]

What McNaughton did find out was that it was believed that the brigade was not in an assembly area near Brest, as had been agreed, and it was confirmed from London later that night by Crerar that the concentration area was near Le Mans.* "We found out what had happened—that they had been dispatched to the Le Mans area. The force was lost, the artillery and for a while the Infantry Brigade as far as I was concerned. I didn't know where they were or anything else. We were trying to trace them through naval contacts at the Loire ports . . . Can you imagine the confusion!"[55]

The brigade and the Field Regiment did not appear next day, as might have been expected from Dewing's message. The first Canadians to return were those who had not yet entrained at Brest and whose re-embarkation was a simple matter. These sailed for England on the morning of 15 June. That same morning the 1st Field Regiment got the evacuation order in the assembly area at Sablé; so did the road parties of the various units. Being mobile, they made an early start for Brest, which was reached on the morning of the 16th. Brooke and his headquarters staff travelled with them.

Brooke made de Fonblanque responsible for the evacuation. Acting on his instructions, the transport of the gunners and the vehicles of the other units were abandoned outside the port, while the guns and trailers were brought to the quay. There were no ships to take the troops off that day.

Throughout the 15th McNaughton remained at Plymouth, trying desperately but unsuccessfully to obtain definite news of the missing units. (Late that night the Embarkation Commandant, Plymouth, asked for the use of his car to "convey a personage from France to a special train"; this, he was informed next day, was "Mr. Daugalle, French Minister for War, [who] passed through

---

*"This was the first intimation received by the GOC 1 Cdn. Div. or by any member of the Staff that the original intention of making concentration in the close vicinity of Brest had been altered."[54]

Plymouth . . . to see the Prime Minister in London.")*[56] Next day he went to Falmouth but obtained no news there; in the evening he returned to Plymouth where he was told that the best hope for news would be the French liaison officer at Naval Headquarters, Plymouth, who was at present in France and who was expected back from Brest at 10 P.M. that night. This officer did not return as expected.[58] An hour later, however, there was real news: a telephone call from Canadian divisional main headquarters reporting that Brigadier Smith, his staff and the 48th Highlanders were back in Aldershot[59] and bedded down.

The eastward move of the trains carrying the infantry and Smith's headquarters had been halted some thirty miles short of the concentration area and these were turned around—the rearmost two without difficulty. These trains, carrying the Hastings and Prince Edward Regiment and the Royal Canadian Regiment, reached Brest that evening. Both battalions, re-embarked on a newly arrived ship, sailed on the afternoon of the 16th and were back in Plymouth next day, before the gunners.

Brigadier Smith's headquarters and the 48th Highlanders had been on the leading train. At Sablé the train halted, and a British transport officer walked along the carriages, found Brigadier Smith, and gave him the reversal order. Smith, who found it incredible that he should have been brought all this way only to be pulled back again without having fired a shot, looked at the officer sceptically; he was obviously a fifth columnist! Lieutenant-Colonel E. W. Haldenby of the 48th shared his opinion and questioned the newcomer closely. His name was Oates. Had he any well-known relatives of that name? The officer thought for a while, and then said yes, there was one; a member of his family had accompanied Captain Scott to the South Pole. Smith and Haldenby considered it unlikely that a German agent would know of this and decided to turn the train around.

The engineer then disputed the decision. He was bent on continuing forward into the arms of the advancing Germans. He had armed men to contend with, however, and the train was turned.

---

*General de Gaulle, Under-Secretary of State for National Defence, visited Churchill on 16 June.[57]

The train steamed west out of Sablé with 48th Highlanders riding the locomotive and others, carrying tommy-guns, on the tender, but despite these precautions the train did not reach Brest.

After Rennes the passengers had an uneasy feeling that the country was unfamiliar, which indeed it was. In the words of the official history:

In fact, a mistake had been made in routing and [the train)] was on the way not to Brest but to St. Malo. By great good fortune at that port there was a British steamer, the *Biarritz*. British troops of many regiments were already on board, but room was made for the Canadians. The overloaded vessel left harbour on the morning of the 16th and reached Southampton that afternoon.[60]

Though this belief in an error was undoubtedly the impression of the 48th (from whose diary the account was taken), it is unlikely that any mistake was made. We have noted that no ships were available at Brest that day. Early on the morning of 17 June McNaughton was in conversation with Brigadier Bissett "who had just returned from France where he was Comd Southern Area L. of C. . . . . He said that on 15 June he had seen 1 Cdn Inf Bde Group on the way back; some towards Brest, some towards St. Malo, depending on shipping,"[61] and as there were no ships at Brest for the Highlanders their move to St. Malo had probably been made under British orders.

The gunners and road parties remained at Brest throughout the 16th. On 17 June Brest garrison issued orders for the destruction of the vehicles which had been left outside the town; these were smashed and rendered useless. "Only valuable vehicles and guns already notified," the order continued, "[are] to be retained for loading."[62]

This did not include the guns of the Royal Canadian Horse Artillery, which was "under command of a very determined officer by the name of Roberts, later the 2nd Division's commander."[63] Lieutenant-Colonel J. H. Roberts stormed up to garrison headquarters where he waged a two-hour battle for his guns. Orders to destroy them were given twice—through the anxiety of General de Fonblanque and his staff that attempts to save equipment might lead to the loss of men—but Roberts determinedly saw them twice countermanded. Finally, through the intercession of the garrison commandant, Colonel W. B. Mackie (an ex-cadet of the Royal Military College of Canada), "Ham" Roberts gained de Fonblanque's reluctant permission to embark as many guns "as he could get aboard by 4 p.m."[64] That gave him an hour and three-quarters. "He said, 'Now we load the guns!' and he loaded every gun—every one of our guns—on board and got some other guns, anti-aircraft guns,* belonging to other units that were very valuable because we were short of anti-aircraft after the losses at Dunkirk."[66] The *Bellerophon,* which took this equipment, still had plenty of room, enough to have taken everything that was on the docks, had the order been given.

As it was, the RCHA left behind its tractors and limbers, which were destroyed. The regiment, sailing in three ships, reached Plymouth and Falmouth on the morning of 18 June, thoroughly disgusted at having had to abandon equipment and at quitting France without the opportunity of even seeing any Germans. "Although there was evidently no enemy within 200 miles," commented the unit's diarist "the withdrawal was conducted as a rout."[67] Small wonder that Brooke, on his arrival at the War Office after his return from France, "was greeted with an enquiry as to why he had not saved more vehicles and equipment."[68] Surely, said McNaughton, there should have been someone at Brest "able to take a grip on the situation. There were a lot of odd troops scattered about. At least they could have got patrols out around the town to give warning that the Germans were or were not attacking. There were no Germans in Brest for another 36 hours after Roberts pulled out as far as we have been able to discover."[69]

McNaughton called for complete reports on the whole fiasco. His first impressions of error hardened to conviction when the reports came in. Failure to concentrate near Brest had been a serious mistake; the dispatch of unit transport up country had been handled in slipshod fashion; and equipment had been unnecessarily destroyed—including 216 Canadian vehicles ("millions

---

*"A dozen Bofors guns, seven predictors, three Bren carriers, and several technical vehicles."[65]

of dollars worth of the finest transport an army ever had")[70] most of them recently issued and nearly new. In fact one station wagon and twelve Bren carriers (including Roberts' three) were all that remained of the transport of the brigade. More serious, on 20 June between one and two hundred men of the force had still to be accounted for, though it was soon established that only six men had been left behind. Of those, all but two motorcyclists killed and one man taken prisoner eventually returned to England, an outcome that can be considered fortunate.

McNaughton pointed out these errors in reply to a letter dated 21 June from Sir John Dill, but he did not recriminate. In that invasion summer it was more important to carry on with the job in hand. Nevertheless, despite the friendship between the two men, McNaughton found himself unable to suppress a note of dissatisfaction when writing to Dill. Here is their correspondence:

My dear Andy,

I cannot tell you how much I regret all the disappoinments you have had. It was with many misgivings that I saw you start for France, and yet while there was a hope that the French Army might still succeed we felt that they ought to have the best the Empire could give. I do hope that you won't think that it was wrong of us. Then when it was quite clear that the French Army was ceasing to offer any effective resistance we came to the conclusion that it would be a crime to let you enter the cauldron. Even you and the Canadian Division could not have saved the situation.

It is all rather a sorry tale but I am sure in the circumstances you will realize what our difficulties were and will forgive us for all the inconvenience you have been caused.

Yours ever,
JACK DILL

McNaughton replied eight days later, after he had returned to his headquarters at Aldershot:

. . . the considerations in my mind at the time this operation was ordered . . . were the same as expressed in your note, namely that it was imperative that we should go. I was under no illusion as to the probable result but I was content that we should be used for that purpose *provided we were given a chance to concentrate before going into battle and this, I was assured by Brooke, would be arranged.**

When the order for reversal was given I was at Plymouth preparatory to sailing. . . . I then thought that our troops who had landed were close in to Brest and it was not until next morning that I learned that Movement Control in France had ordered the road and rail parties forward apparently, as they arrived, to the Le Mans area. . . .

Eventually, as you know, our men saved all our guns and some other supplies as well . . . *but we lost all our transport which is very bitter medicine.*† However, we may well be thankful, as we are, to Providence, that all except a score of our men got back.

We are now squarely set for what I have long thought was the important task, the defence of these islands. Two out of three of our Brigade Groups and our reserve of Artillery, Engineers, Machine Gun Battalions etc., all on wheels are poised to go in any direction and you and the C.-in-C. can count on a quick moving, hard hitting, determined force which will be prompt to execute your orders.

There are many lessons to be learned from our experience and sometime I hope we may go over them together but, meanwhile, we have other work to do and you can be sure that we stand with you with all our hearts.[71]

In 1965, in full possession of the facts and after mature reflection, McNaughton took a sterner view. "It was in any event," he said, "risky to cross the Channel to reinforce an army, if there had been one, with at the most three or four divisions; but with no French Army the situation was impossible." As it was, under conditions prevailing at the time, the whole endeavour was "a chimera. . . . There was nothing to it at all. Literally we were moving into France to reinforce an army that didn't exist; and there wasn't the remotest chance of one being created. There weren't in the whole of France, in formed bodies, any troops to constitute an army.

"This is a really shocking state of affairs because the information that we were operating on had come primarily from Churchill

---

*Italics supplied.
†Italics supplied.

himself and must have been based on wishful thinking or something of that sort. Everybody on our side was misled. If we had any real comprehension of the political information there isn't any doubt about it that I would have put my foot down and classified this expedition as *not* a practical operation of war. I think I can say with conviction that that is what I would have done."[72] He entirely agreed, under the chaotic conditions that prevailed, with the decisions made by Brooke to evacuate the British and Canadian troops from France. He did not, however, agree with the method.

In mid-July Eden proposed that Brooke should replace Ironside as C-in-C Home Forces and Ironside accepted his retirement with "soldierly dignity."[73] One of his last acts at Home Forces was to appoint McNaughton to the command of the British VII Corps with promotion to lieutenant-general, and Brooke, as part of his new duties, visited VII Corps in early August. Brooke's visit is on record, but there are no details of his conversation with McNaughton. At that meeting, McNaughton said in 1965, "While we were riding in the motor car together, going from one place to another, Brooke referred to the fact that I had expressed to Dill, as I had, some considerable concern and anxiety that the agreed orders for Britanny had not been followed—the orders for concentration. He said in effect, 'Now you are under my orders and you are going to do as you are told in future.' " Provided they were proper orders, McNaughton returned, they would be obeyed. Brooke then stated that, in the circumstances in Brittany, he had made up his mind to "fight the Canadian battalions himself"—in other words, without a preliminary concentration he would have fed them piecemeal into the fighting, as had happened in the case of the 52nd (Lowland) Division—and that he had been "in the best position to give these battalions their orders direct."[74] McNaughton would not have it. These were Canadian troops to be kept together under their own commanders; Brooke did not press the point.

But the altercation served as a warning to McNaughton; it had great influence on his future dealings with Alan Brooke, who became CIGS some months later. After that, he never had "any real confidence that Brooke would abide by any agreement that he made" and that where he was required to discharge his responsibilities to the government of Canada for the safety and proper employment of his troops he had to be "mighty careful with Brooke." The "mutual confidence" and "kindly co-operation" that had existed between the War Office and himself became a thing of the past when Brooke succeeded to the highest post.

The relations became very difficult and I thought that I had to be exceedingly careful. We only put troops "in combination" when we had ways of getting the troops out of combination if the occasion should require. It had to be spelled out, in great detail, so that we would not run the risk that a battle-balanced organization might suddenly be broken up into splinter groups by some commander who thought he could run around as he might have done in the days of the Zulu War with little packets of troops to move.[75]

Though the attempt to reconstitute the BEF was but a minor affair in the annals of the Second World War its impact on the Canadian commander was out of all proportion to its size. He had been a close observer of Currie's stand for the integrity of the Canadian Corps in 1918; between the wars he had fought for and seen Canadian autonomy achieved. That those battles had been right and well worth waging he was now, more than ever, convinced; for otherwise Canadian troops would have been treated as British manpower, mere ciphers, subject to dispersal under British direction wherever the whim of the moment took them.

This experience in Brittany was important. It undoubtedly strengthened McNaughton in the attitude he was bound to adopt towards the British whenever, in the future, the integrity and autonomy of the Canadian force appeared to him to be in question.

Chapter 7

~~~~~~

1940: Commanding a British Corps

On 18 June, the day following McNaughton's return from Plymouth after the Brittany fiasco, the British Prime Minister announced in the House of Commons that the Battle of France was over; that of Britain, he expected, was about to begin.

Britain, strongly rallied by Churchill, was united in stubborn determination to fight to the end for her island freedom. But there was an appalling shortage of arms. "There were," the British Prime Minister said, "hardly five hundred field-guns of any sort and hardly two hundred medium or heavy tanks in the whole country," while the "armies at home were...almost unarmed except for rifles."[1] Though men and women in the factories laboured around the clock it would be months before even the equipment lost in France could be replaced. Appeals to America for weapons and ammunition met with a ready response, but the first shipments did not arrive until July.

While, at the outbreak of war, Canada had been discouraged from competing with British industry, suddenly the climate changed. Canada was asked to go ahead with everything she could produce, but manufacture would take time, precious time that might well have been conserved if the recommendations of technical officers of the Department of National Defence before the war—and, more pointedly, after it had broken out*—had been implemented by the government.

In addition, the official attitude during the period of the services' mobilization in Canada—extending into the spring of 1940

---

*Major-General W. H. P. Elkins, Master General of the Ordnance from October 1938 to July 1940, sounded repeated warnings but was largely ignored.

—had been strongly influenced by the static strategic situation in Western Europe. The phony war had lulled the government into a false sense of security that was marked by persistent efforts to economize on expenditure for defence. Financial restrictions, imposed by Ralston as Minister of Finance, prevented Canadian industry from preparing for the immense demands that would undoubtedly come when the Germans turned to the offensive; nothing had been done, for example, about ordering the twenty-five-pounder guns that McNaughton had so strongly advocated at the end of 1939. For some months after the outbreak of hostilities the service heads at Ottawa were under considerable pressure to pare their financial estimates to the bone.* There had been no comprehension in official circles of the scope and ramifications of the approaching struggle, and consequently not much had been done to gear Canadian industry to wartime needs.

The German Army, freed by the French collapse from pre-occupation with any other objective, triumphantly faced the almost defenceless British Isles with immense superiority in men, planes, tanks and guns. Most of the shipping of a large part of Western Europe was now in German hands. There was imminent danger, it seemed, of a drop by airborne troops in a chosen sector, coupled with the landing of small but powerful panzer forces to cut through the flimsy defences; then the follow-up divisions, protected by submarines and escorting planes, would be ferried over.

The British Commonwealth stood alone and the mood was exalted, ecstatic almost, and completely without fear now that the crisis had materialized. The services and the general population were keyed up for the life-and-death struggle, in which the odds were in no doubt. Of the divisions in Britain at the time, the 1st Canadian (though one brigade had been immobilized by the loss of its transport in Brittany) was by far the strongest. The twenty-eight British divisions and a number of independent brigades in the country consisted of little more than riflemen as a result of their experience in France, with three exceptions. These, the 3rd,

---

* "Careful oversight of all expenditures is an official part of our war effort."¹

43rd and the 52nd (Lowland) Divisions, were in a better state of training and equipment than the others but the first of them, although almost completely re-equipped after Dunkirk, carried many reinforcements on its strength so that its fighting value was not high; the 43rd was not fully trained nor equipped, while the 52nd, previously strong, had just returned from Brittany where, like the Canadian brigade, it had had to sacrifice its vehicles. The Canadian Division, once again converted into "Canadian Force," but with only two mobile groups instead of three (and some British tank battalions and light armour), was the "only mobile force immediately available in Great Britain,"[3] to repel a German invasion army which might be drawn from a hundred and thirty divisions, of which ten were armoured. In addition, Britain was beleaguered. Her lifelines east, south and even west, were harassed and threatened by submarines, surface ships and planes, from the North Cape of Norway to the Pyrenees. Ships bringing cargoes of food and raw materials were now vulnerable to enemy attack. Starvation was a real danger.

Threatened with invasion and under siege, Britain was now reaping the grim harvest of years of shortsightedness and neglect in both the diplomatic and armament fields between the wars. Yet the very precariousness of the present position brought a mood of exaltation to her people which would in time cool into a sober spirit of national revival as she grew stronger and a fortress emerged from almost defenceless islands.

In this period of great peril after the capitulation of France, Canadian Force assumed an importance undreamed of two months before. Placed directly under GHQ Home Forces (Ironside), McNaughton set to work to prepare his troops as "a hard-hitting mobile force ready to proceed North, South, East or West."[4]

As McNaughton saw it, Canadian Force would have to be correctly located for the fulfilment of its role; it must be appropriately organized, armed and trained; and its tactics, including the provision of obstacles, must be apt. He set about these problems with characteristic foresight and determination.

McNaughton's first concern was to move out of Aldershot, where his division had re-assembled in barracks after the Brittany distraction. Though General Bernard Paget, Ironside's CGS, had directed him on 19 June to remain where he was, the most likely areas for invasion were the south coast, as far west as Portsmouth, and the east coast stretching north to the Wash. For counter-attack, he wished to be more centrally situated than Aldershot and out of barracks. To ensure mobility, he suggested that his men and vehicles should be dispersed under cover in park areas—impossible in a barracks town—in the vicinity of Oxford.[5]

Paget, however, had the early formation of a Canadian Corps in mind and for this wished to bring the 1st and 2nd Canadian Divisions together under McNaughton's command at Aldershot. Though it would have meant promotion to lieutenant-general, McNaughton had no wish for personal aggrandizement at such a time; the job in hand came first. He urged Paget to reconsider. His present role was sufficiently demanding. This was no time to organize a corps and train a second division. He wished to be "free to fight 1 Canadian Division without the administrative and organizational problems that would arise during the period that a Corps was being formed."

Furthermore it would be wrong to remain in barracks, where it was impossible to move quickly and where an air raid in all likelihood would immobilize his force completely.[6] "What we could expect," McNaughton said, "was that the Germans would start their bombing. It was the obvious thing to do. And if they were going to invade, the thing they would go for first was where the troops were. Aldershot, a big camp, would be bombed right away. Now you can't expect to get troops out of a place that's being bombed and have them ready to fight immediately. You're going to have trouble. You're not going to be in the best shape to take on a parachute landing or anything of that sort. The thing to do was take advantage of what the English have—those lovely parks. We could put everybody under the trees and nobody would know whether we were there or not. There was a bit of trouble; some of the landowners objected that their nice beech trees would have Canadian initials carved on them, but it was nothing serious."[7]

These were cogent arguments and McNaughton's views carried conviction; on 23 June Canadian Force began the move to Oxford, though the immobilized 1st Brigade Group remained at Aldershot to be re-equipped. At Oxford, Canadian Force, suitably dispersed throughout the estates of country mansions in the area, studded with trees, bivouacked ready "to commence movement at one hour's notice in any direction as may be required to support British Divisions in meeting seaborne or airborne attacks on these islands."[8] The Canadians were, McNaughton pointed out at a conference of his senior officers, "a mobile reserve with a 360 degree front" and might have to operate "anywhere in Great Britain from the south coast, to Scotland, or in Wales. . . ." The enemy, it must be presumed, would know that the British defences were very weak:

He is now free from the French problem and will be able to turn his full attention to these islands. The initiative rests with him and he possesses freedom of action . . . We carry, together with the 4 Corps under Lieutenant-General Nosworthy,* a serious responsibility. The Canadian Force and two Tank Battalions of the 4 Corps with some Light Armoured Units comprise the only mobile force immediately available in Great Britain.[9]

The force, however, did not remain in the Oxford vicinity for very long.

On 26 June Paget again visited Canadian Force to suggest a change of plan. It was Ironside's intention, he said, to have one mobile corps under Nosworthy (IV Corps) north of the Thames. This corps would consist of the 2nd Armoured and the 43rd Divisions. Another mobile reserve would operate south of the Thames† and this would consist of a corps made up of the 1st Armoured and the 1st Canadian Divisions.

---

*Lieutenant-General (later Sir) F. P. Nosworthy.

†"Invasion was a real threat," said McNaughton, "there's no doubt about it. It wasn't something foisted out of the air to stimulate recruiting. It was a real menace and the more we studied it the more difficulties we found in dealing with any landings, particularly two moderate-sized landings, well-separated. A centralized force would be able to deal with one but it might not be able to deal with the other, particularly with the Thames Estuary cutting back into the heart of the area. The Thames in its lower reaches, the city of London and the Estuary were very serious obstacles from a communications point of view. That's why the War Office separated the central reserve and Nosworthy took one side of the Thames and I took the other."[10]

General Paget raised the question of command of the corps . . .
which is to operate south of the Thames and stated it was the C.-in-
C's. wish that General McNaughton should take command as it
would be impossible for Home Forces to control a number of
independent divisions.[11]

McNaughton had the confidence of the War Office. That he was
offered command of one of the two corps on which the life of
Britain virtually depended shows that quite clearly. Nevertheless
he fought hard to retain his present command and made an
alternative suggestion: let Lieutenant-General Andrew Thorne
(XII Corps, in position along the coast) give the general picture,
start line, and the time and direction of the attack; he would then
fight Canadian Force under Thorne's orders.

Paget, however, pointed out that a local formation would be
unable to apprehend the overall situation. That could be done
only by GHQ Home Forces which would have full intelligence and
would then be in a position to direct the mobile formations to the
point of greatest danger. Further, the formations along the coast
would in all probability be tied to the ground and so deeply
committed that the corps commander would find it impossible to
co-ordinate or control another formation coming in; they might,
in fact, be overrun, in which event the troops in mobile reserve
would have to fight a new battle under the general direction of
GHQ Home Forces. For these reasons, Paget judged it impossible
for Thorne or any other corps commander in the forward zone to
command the 1st Armoured and the 1st Canadian Divisions effectively; it was his firm opinion that these divisions should be incorporated in a new corps.[12] "Paget was right," McNaughton said.
"Thorne was a very good officer. He was at the Staff College with
me, a Guards officer and one of the most gallant men I have ever
met. But it was not really practical for him—from the middle of a
battle of that sort, a rough and tumble affair of small forces, almost
guerrilla warfare—to see the picture and to do much in the way
of organizing and controlling new forces."[13]

So McNaughton reluctantly signified his readiness to comply
with Ironside's wishes, "no matter how much he would like to
remain with 1 Canadian Division." The War Office would have to

Alan Brooke (right) visits VII Corps, August, 1940

An effective tank-trap constructed by Canadian pipe-pushing methods, August, 1940

Their Majesties visit the Canadian Division, 8 June, 1940

Canadian Corps Headquarters, Headley Court, near Leatherhead, Surrey

broach the matter to CMHQ and Paget stated he would get the War Office to act that night.[14]

During the next few days McNaughton took preliminary steps for the organization of the corps. He met the commander of the 1st Armoured Division (Major-General Roger Evans) on the 29th. This formation (a part of it had been in Calais) had lost most of its equipment in France, and now Evans was reduced to fifty infantry and thirty-four cruiser tanks though he hoped to have fifty-two cruisers within a week. It had by now been decided that the new corps would include "New Zealand Force," two brigades of the 2nd New Zealand Division and some artillery which had recently arrived in England,* and these formations, McNaughton decided, would be organized as the motorized component of the armoured division; he discussed this with the New Zealand commander (Major-General B. C. Freyberg, V.C.) and General Evans. He also had talks with General Nosworthy about their respective roles north and south of the Thames; close liaison between the two corps would be important. Then, on 2 July, Canadian Force moved into the Guildford-Reigate-Westerham area of the North Downs, centred on Leatherhead, immediately south of London.† Leatherhead had good road communications. "It was very well located for movement, with the exception of the road through Redhill which was a bottleneck of the first order."[17] That was removed by building a bypass later.

Next day Lieutenant-General Sir Guy Williams, GOC-in-C Eastern Command, expressed the view to McNaughton that "the most likely area for German seaborne attacks is between Beachy Head-North Foreland; these would probably be accompanied by airborne attacks on the North and South Downs."[18] Both these areas were in McNaughton's immediate sphere of mobile operations and, situated where he was, he was well placed for immediate counter-attack. The components of his force were dispersed;

---

*"We got the New Zealanders after a long sea voyage; we reconditioned them and got them going. They were good people. We had a happy relationship with them."[15]

†Tents, telephone lines and slit trenches were left intact at Oxford in order to confuse enemy air reconnaissance and to provide a base to which the force could return in case of need.[16]

routes to possible areas of operations were speedily reconnoitred. In these positions the units were screened from enemy observation, complete and ready for battle, with defences organized against all possible forms of attack, both air and ground, and ready for instant movement.[19] And the Canadians were well positioned not only to repulse invaders but for the continued training of all arms. They were in reach of suitable infantry and tank training areas; both Lydd and Larkhill were close for artillery, mortar and anti-aircraft practices; and so was Aldershot, with its various rifle and machine-gun ranges.

On 11 July, in reply to Ironside's request to the War Office, the Canadian government agreed to the creation of a new corps under McNaughton (this, as we have seen, was one of Ironside's last acts before turning Home Forces over to Brooke), which stipulated that the 2nd Canadian Division, when it arrived in Britain, should be included.[20] Thus McNaughton's corps, VII British, was the forerunner of the future Canadian Corps; and "the organizational experience of putting a corps together was useful to the Canadian Corps later on."[21]

On 14 July the 1st Brigade, re-equipped at last, joined Canadian Force. Seven days later VII Corps officially came into being. Its role was simple: "to counter-attack and destroy enemy forces invading the counties of Surrey-Kent-Sussex-Hampshire which are not destroyed by the troops of Eastern and Southern Commands."[22] There is virtue in simplicity; nevertheless, in execution it would be a tremendous task.

"I have learned with pride and satisfaction," Mackenzie King cabled to McNaughton on the 20th, "of your promotion to the rank of Lieutenant-General on appointment to command the new Corps. Please accept my warmest congratulations upon the enlarged opportunities of service which this more than merited recognition brings to you. I send you as always my heartfelt good wishes."[23] A wake of promotions throughout Canadian Force followed, notably that of Brigadier G. R. Pearkes to succeed McNaughton in the divisional command, and that of the faithful Turner as McNaughton's Brigadier General Staff (Canadian). It might also be noted here that changes had been made at CMHQ two weeks earlier, when Montague had replaced Crerar as Senior Officer.*

Though VII Corps was under the command of a Canadian and contained a Canadian division it was a British corps.† Its staff, therefore, consisted of both British and Canadian officers. Among those provided by the War Office was one of exceptional ability, Brigadier M. C. Dempsey who later (as Lieutenant-General Sir Miles Dempsey) commanded the British Second Army in Northwest Europe. The problem of staff duties would be particularly difficult; due to the corps commander's responsibility to two separate governments, his work would have to be conducted so that there would be no possibility of friction between them.

McNaughton was anxious to deal with the British authorities exactly as he had often wished they would deal with him. He exercised thoughtfulness and great consideration in what he regarded as a partnership. Operationally, he told his senior staff officers at his headquarters at Headley Court, near Leatherhead, VII Corps would function exactly as it would were it wholly a British corps and "Canadian administration must conform so far as might be possible with the customary British system." He did not want British staff officers "to be distracted or bothered in any way by the difficult matter of the conduct of Canadian business"; Canadian staff officers—he had Turner in mind—would "divert this business at appropriate points into Canadian channels."[26] Canadian administration procedures differed from the British and

*Crerar returned to Canada. On his departure, McNaughton informed the Prime Minister by cable that "Crerar returns to you with probably as good a knowledge of the military position of Great Britain as anyone in London." He praised Crerar's tact, discretion and good judgment and added: "He has clear ideas of the requirements to be met in Canada both present and future and if he is given sufficient authority he can now make a contribution of the very greatest importance."[24] Ralston, prompted by the Prime Minister, sought Mc-Naughton's specific recommendation by telephone and this was given by Mc-Naughton in a cable of 29 June: "Crerar to become C.G.S." Shortly after his return Crerar was appointed Chief of the General Staff, the senior military appointment in Canada.

†"There was one thing about that," McNaughton said. "I had none of this business of having to get permission from Ralston to blow my nose. This way there was no interference. You can't be put in the position of having to ask permission from across the Atlantic when somebody is going to land on the coast the day before yesterday."[25]

they would have to be brought into harmony if the fighting efficiency of the corps was not to be impaired. "Good sense," he concluded, "good liaison, and thorough frankness will prevent any difficulties."[27]

After the ground rules had been settled, a spirit of harmony and mutual confidence permeated Corps Headquarters. The spirit also extended to the various components of the corps, as indicated in a letter addressed by the GOC 1st Armoured Division to Mc-Naughton's Brigadier General Staff:

My dear Dempsey,

I went to see the Saskatoon M.G. Battalion* on the march on its way to join my Support Group, and I was very much impressed by the excellent traffic discipline they showed. Not only were the distances and speed scrupulously observed, but all the trucks were very neatly loaded and the men sitting smartly in the trucks and not lolling about.

I thought the Corps Commander would like to know this. I have not been to visit the battalion in camp yet as the C.O. said he'd like to have time to shake down first, but I had a squadron of tanks out to meet them and each company had an escort of a troop of tanks to see them into their area and the C.O. had a tank to look after him. So we did give the battalion something of a welcome to show how glad we are to have them and how much I appreciate the help the Corps Commander has given us.

Your sincerely,
R. EVANS.[28]

From the earliest days of the Battle of Britain, a month before the creation of VII Corps, McNaughton had concerned himself with the proper organization of his force for its mobile role. On 18 June (the day after he had returned to Aldershot from Plymouth) he saw Ironside at his headquarters at Kneller Hall and described his scheme of organizing the division and ancillary troops into mobile brigade and battalion groups, as had been done

---

*The Saskatoon Light Infantry (M.G.) had been placed under the orders of the Armoured Division, which then lacked infantry or machine-gun units, for support of its armour.

in the Northampton area. The C-in-C Home Forces was so convinced of the soundness of the organization that he decreed its adoption "throughout the other divisions of the forces defending Great Britain."[29]

Each column had to have a mobile unit for reconnaissance and the searching of ground. "It all depended on reconnaissance, like all war does; on proper, continuous reconnaissance; always questing for information."[30] Motorcycle combinations carrying three men, and a Bren gun mounted in the sidecar,* would be organized into reconnaissance squadrons on the basis of one squadron per brigade, with one troop for each machine-gun battalion. The matter was urgent and could not wait authority and the provision of men from Canada; men for the new squadrons would have to come from existing units, their places being filled from reinforcement drafts expected shortly. Sound reasons—to reconnoitre and protect "the movement of our several long columns ... from possible ambush"—were then presented to Canada for the formation of the new units on a temporary basis,[32] and approval was given.

Only one Canadian troop-carrying company was in the country; two more would be required to lift the marching infantrymen of the nine battalions. It was not easy to obtain vehicles in Britain at that time but the importance of the role of Canadian Force ensured priority; British vehicles were issued until they could be replaced from Canada.[33] And before June was out McNaughton had arranged for an "R.C.A.F. officer [to] form an integral part of the General Staff of the Division so that closest possible touch might be maintained between the air component and the Operations and Intelligence branches of the General Staff."[34]

In matters of organization McNaughton always championed Canadian rights. At the end of August the Bartholomew Report,

---

*"The question was, how to get reconnaissance! I bought a lot of motorcycle sidecars and put machine gunners in them—the light machine guns that we had and then we developed the Sten. We developed the Sten for mass production. That was done in Canada. We had to get a cheap gun in large quantities and I looked over various designs. I worked with the Poles on the Sten and I chose that and got it made up—a gun with low tolerance, a scatter-gun if you will, but the thing was fool-proof. So we had these motorcycle combinations to buzz ahead in, and if they came to a roadblock they could be lifted around it."[31]

approved by the War Office, suggested certain changes in unit establishments. It was agreed policy that Canadian units would deploy on the same establishments as the British but, as Mc-Naughton pointed out to Paget, "The acceptance of British War Establishments has the concomitant that Canadian representatives should be given the opportunity to express their views before any radical changes are made." Canada, he went on, was making "sizeable contributions" and it was "only reasonable that any ideas of Canadian commanders should be pooled with those of commanders in the British service." With that principle Paget agreed; he had not forgotten that the "idea of Brigade Groups had been originally developed by Canadian Force" and considered Canadian experience should be drawn upon. The Bartholomew Report would be sent to McNaughton for study before any changes were implemented.[35] As it turned out, McNaughton found himself in general agreement with the recommendations of the committee.[36]

Hand in hand with organization, it was important that the units should be appropriately armed. During the last week of June, while at Oxford, McNaughton visited a factory at Staines where he discussed the Motley anti-aircraft mounting with its designer. The mountings were of many types—for different vehicles—and some would be useful. He found out that hundred-round Bren magazines (as opposed to the standard thirty-round type) were being produced and he planned to obtain these for the guns to be mounted in the motorcycle combinations of the new reconnaissance units.[37] That evening, in a message to CMHQ, McNaughton "emphasized the value of such magazines from the standpoint of AA [anti-aircraft] defence and requested . . . the supply of approximately 2000 for 1 Cdn Div and Ancillary Troops." These were issued in November.[38] On 26 June McNaughton was able to show General Paget anti-aircraft mountings already installed in vehicles for the Boys anti-tank rifle, the Vickers machine-gun and for Bren and Lewis guns,[39] and drawings of these, at Paget's request, reached Home Forces four days later.[40]

Again in June, experiments were carried out by Captain E. H. Smith, his Staff Officer (Chemical Warfare), with various mixtures for Molotov cocktails and an approximation of "Greek fire."* It was found, for Molotov cocktails, that a mixture of coal tar (40) and gasoline (60) was the best and that a special fuse manufactured by Imperial Chemical Industries ignited them in the most successful way. Experiments showed that the use of a sling to launch them gave greater range and accuracy than any other method. Early in July each brigade group had one "30-cwt lorry loaded with one layer of 240 quart bottles and one layer of 420 pint bottles of Molotov Cocktails" and there was one "3-ton lorry in the Reserve Group loaded with 5-gallon drums of the mixture."[42] A month later various inflammable mixtures were available for use in improvised flame-throwing apparatus,[43] as were other anti-invasion devices: petrol and oil spouts (for roadside vehicle traps); and a "barrel" Molotov bomb complete with phosphorous ignition.[44]

Throughout the remainder of the summer and into autumn McNaughton concerned himself with making sure that the men would have the best weapons, the best equipment and the best vehicles it was possible to get. British designers, who appreciated his interest, sought his views. Captain Loyd (known for his Carden Loyd carrier)† discussed new-type carriers, tanks and armoured cars with him;[45] Sir Malcolm Campbell developed an armoured car and brought it for McNaughton to see;[46] the corps commander tested the Humber wheeled tank and the Daimler scout car and reported on them.[47] In August, when inspecting the RCHA, McNaughton saw for the first time a new-type thirty-hundredweight truck with four-wheel drive. He checked it over from top to bottom and then left with its driver for a short run across rough country. On his return the driver was asked by his colleagues how he had got on. "Oh, fine," he replied, "there were a few things wrong but me and Andy sorted them out."[48] War correspondents mentioned this side of McNaughton. "A picture of General McNaughton," Ross Munro wrote, "is not complete unless you see him leaning over engines on inspections, crawling

---

*"I recall the great search made through the ancient manuscripts in the Bodleian Library at Oxford," McNaughton said in 1945, "to ascertain the exact composition of Greek Fire which had last been used decisively in 1100 A.D."[41]

†See *McNaughton*, Volume 1, p. 227.

under tanks, testing gun sights, working on a breechblock";[49] while Wallace Reyburn, writing in *Maclean's,* said: "His study of weapons and equipment is not merely critical without being constructive. He has said often and at great length that he is not going to be satisfied until he knows that his men go into battle with the best weapons that it's possible for the cream of Canada's scientific, mechanical and industrial brains to produce."[50]

At every opportunity he stimulated Canada into producing the weapons and equipment he knew were needed. Fully aware of what Britain was and was not producing, he passed the details on to Ottawa. McNaughton gave general details of the latest cruiser tank (Mark VI) and promised to collect and forward manufacturing data, suggesting that "plans should be made for the production of cruiser tank Mark Six . . . War Office planning to send one . . . to U.S.A. in October. We have suggested that this be sent via Canada so you can see."[51] At the end of the year, 788 tanks were under construction in the Angus shops, Montreal, 488 for Canadian use and 300 for the British.[52]

It was the same with wireless transmitters and receivers:

British factories manufacturing these have been bombed and it is unlikely that we shall receive issues from the War Office for many months. Please advise prospects of supply from Canada.

Again, McNaughton's air squadron was experiencing difficulties with radio sets, which were unequal to the requirements for army co-operation. "From personal knowledge of our technical Signal officers, verified by Trans-Atlantic telephone today," McNaughton cabled Ralston, "the General Electric general purpose aircraft transmitter meets our need. Request your good offices with your colleague Mr. Power, Minister for Air, to send six of these sets complete. Matter is very serious as difficulties with air to ground communication is holding up our training and development of co-operation of Air Force with Infantry and Armoured Division which it is most important to perfect."[53] The sets came quickly. A month later McNaughton was able to report to Ralston:

Special aircraft wireless sets have now been received and installed in Army Co-operation aircraft of 110 Squadron. Preliminary tests have given most satisfactory results and opened the way for progress in the development of air co-operation with armoured formations and other ground troops.... In view of successful preliminary tests British authorities are considering placing orders in Canada for about 220 sets to equip eighteen Army Co-operation Squadrons. Very much appreciate the prompt help given. . . .[54]

Small wonder, with urgent British needs, that it was reported in the Canadian press that summer: "Within the last few days war orders totalling $146,863,000 have been placed with the Department of Munitions and Supply at Ottawa. That is more than the total of all war orders placed by the British, French and Canadian Governments during the first three months of the war."[55]

McNaughton seized every opportunity to stimulate research and production in Canada. In July, for example, in his capacity as president of NRC, he sent a message to mark the placing of the foundation stone of the new aeronautical laboratory and administrative building. "The Research Council," he said, "is again called upon for help and guidance and leadership in the application of science to the developing needs of our armed forces . . . ."

This act in the further advancement of the facilities required for scientific and industrial research gives confidence in Canada's will to victory and increased assurance that from her ample resources ... through her highly skilled workers and her great organization for production, we shall receive in ample measure the newer weapons which we shall need to wield in battle.[56]

From simple yet practical things, such as a night-light fitting underneath trucks which illuminated the universal gear housing* and so greatly facilitated night convoy work without being visible from the air,[57] McNaughton concerned himself with larger conceptions. In November he lunched at Air Defence Headquarters with Lieutenant-General Sir Frederick Pile, GOC-in-C Anti-Aircraft Command. After luncheon McNaughton spoke with considerable conviction of the possibility of making much longer-

---

*McNaughton picked up this idea from Montgomery's 3rd Division, then reorganizing near Southampton.

range guns than had hitherto been produced;* they would be operated electro-magnetically and to bombard Berlin might not be impossible. "Tim" Pile, who knew his man, listened carefully:

The Corps Commander laid before the C.-in-C. Dr. Thompson's papers and calculations which correspond to those already made by the Corps Commander. General Pile agreed that every possible effort should be made to construct a small preliminary working model. He agreed to obtain the services of the best experts on Turbo-Electric machinery with a view to the design of generators which would give the necessary electric power. He also agreed to take up . . . the design of the special streamlined projectile of the form indicated by General McNaughton . . . to give high stability and low resistance at high velocities. General Pile also said he would enlist the help of Professor Blackett . . . who invented the latest bomb sight. The intention was to produce the highest velocities possible.[58]

Pile, who, as Churchill attests, "was singularly free from the distaste for novel devices so often found in professional soldiers,"[59] has described this meeting, somewhat naively perhaps, and a subsequent one with McNaughton in December:

At a conference we held in December 1940 General McNaughton, the Commander of the Canadian Corps, raised the question of an electrical gun. *McNaughton was probably the best and most scientific gunner in any army in the world.*† His ideas were colossal.

---

*"In regard to guns of very long range (several hundred miles)," said General McNaughton in 1966, "calculations of the electrical method of propulsion for large-calibre weapons indicated some promise for achieving the high-muzzle velocities required. However it became evident that at these velocities the shells could have little explosive content and moreover they would be destroyed by air friction. What was required was a rocket which, starting at zero, would progressively increase in velocity as it gained altitude. The propellants then available were unable to store and release sufficient energy for this. In fact, even for guns of intermediate velocity (say of the order of 4,500 f.s. [feet-seconds] required for armour piercing) this difficulty over the propellant existed. It was suggested to two senior officers of the U.S. Chemical Warfare Corps, over on a visit, that research on this would be useful. The same suggestion was made to NRC with profitable results.

The end result (achieved by the U.S.A. in their guided missiles) gave velocities of 25,000 f.s. (17,000 m.p.h.) or so; these were reached at high altitudes when the air resistance was minute."[60]

†Italics supplied

A gun that fired a mere hundred miles was no good to him. When we talked about pushing up our muzzle velocity to four or five thousand feet per second, he laughed the idea to scorn and said we should think in terms of ten to twenty thousand feet-seconds. He had his own ways of producing these fabulous velocities. He had invented a model gun which obtained its power by shorting a dynamo, and he fired little pellets through deal boards. Now he wanted a colossal gun which would fire into Germany. Unfortunately each gun of the sort he wanted needed a vast generating station and, however we prospected the idea, we never got nearer a solution. It would have been comparatively easy to build perhaps one of these guns, but in war one of anything, unless it is a Churchill, is of very little use, and eventually we went away from ideas of this sort of gun and, as a temporary expedient, increased the velocity of our existing types . . . .[61]

The velocity of projectiles intimately concerned General Pile:

We were trying all the time to increase the efficiency of our equipment, and one of our ideas was to find methods of increasing the muzzle-velocity of our guns and reduce the time of flight of the shell. This was one of the great inherent difficulties of anti-aircraft gunnery. You could get the most efficient form of predictor, you might achieve great accuracy with your radar, and then, when you fired the gun, the enemy would see the flash, jink, and, as the time of flight of the shell was hardly ever less than ten seconds, he could be well away from the predicted spot before the shell got there.[62]

With McNaughton that day he discussed the use of a conical (tapered) barrel by the Germans to cause the projectile to emerge with increased velocity. McNaughton promised him that further investigations would be made and experiments carried out on the principles of the Gerlich conical barrel, which had been applied by the enemy to a light anti-tank gun. He looked to the construction of "a model with a bore at the breech and muzzle of about 40 mm. and 20 mm. respectively. This gun would be a smooth bore and would be adapted to fire [a] specially shaped projectile. General McNaughton gave General Pile a sketch showing his ideas as to proper form of this projectile before and after firing

and the manner in which it was fitted to the cartridge case."*[63]
But the use of a conical barrel was not the best way to achieve
increased velocity, as McNaughton came to realize later. He solved
the problem in 1942 without any specially shaped barrel—merely
a specially designed projectile—as will be seen.

McNaughton's help was also sought in defensive measures.
German bombers, apart from causing immediate destruction,
dropped bombs containing time-fuses which had the effect of
paralyzing for many hours factories vital to the war effort. In
September Professor F. A. Lindemann, Churchill's scientific
adviser, called to discuss the problem with the General.[64] Later
that month bomb disposal experiments were carried out at Redhill
Aerodrome which McNaughton attended. Some success was
obtained in locating bombs by means of a magnetic probe and
getting down to them by sinking pipe through which water was
passed under pressure.[65]

Then, on 12 November, after luncheon with Anthony Eden and
Lord Cranborne (Secretary of State for Dominion Affairs) at
General Sir John Dill's invitation, McNaughton spent an afternoon that was a distinct pleasure to him. From London he went to
Cambridge where, at the Cavendish Laboratory, this unusual
soldier discussed various measures for detecting unexploded
bombs, chief among them the use of magnetometers and ultra-
violet rays; "degaussing," which would magnetize a time-fuse clock
and so "freeze" it, seemed promising. Not much escaped Mc-
Naughton. He knew that degaussing experiments were being
conducted by Dr. Ballard† of the NRC and an interchange of
information proved fruitful.

Accompanied by Professor Inglis,‡ McNaughton arrived at the

---

*A rifled gun corresponding to these specifications was developed by Mr. Kline
of the Mechanical Division of NRC. The process of squeezing in the skirts of the
projectile, however, left the surface uneven and this—at the high velocities that
resulted—caused the energy to be dissipated in shock waves and, worse, resulted
in inaccuracy.

†Dr. Ballard had charge of the development of measures to protect Allied
shipping from the magnetic mine; in this he was highly successful.

‡The designer of the Inglis Bridge of World War I fame.

Combination Room, King's College, and later dined in Hall at the High Table; afterwards Dr. Shepherd, the Provost, received him in his rooms at King's. Later Inglis described in detail, with photographs, his latest type of "Pyramid Bridge," which was to be erected on the following morning over a tributary of the Cam. McNaughton stayed to watch it being constructed.

These visits proved useful. Inglis knew the new head of the Department of Tank Supply (in the Ministry of Supply) with whom Charles Banks (of the Canadian Department of Munitions and Supply in London) should be in touch. He also promised to bring Professor G. I. Taylor, an aeronautical expert who had unique experience in the design of streamline forms, to discuss with McNaughton the design of high-velocity projectiles.[66]

Throughout this period, as he had planned, McNaughton made use for defensive measures of Colin Campbell's "pipe-pushers," now the 1st Canadian Tunnelling Company. What was the use of tearing up unused airfields, as the British were doing, to prevent the Germans from landing? If aerodromes were heavily bombed, as was happening daily, fields that were not wanted today might well be an urgent necessity tomorrow; and these, regardless of trip wires, were being systematically destroyed. Boring machines and pipe-pushers, on the other hand, operated by the tunnellers, could quickly prepare the landing strips with pipe pushed obliquely in the ground which, when loaded with explosives, would be touched off at a moment's notice as an emergency might require; until then, the fields could be used. Generally, far too many ditches were being dug.* "A great deal of unnecessary labour and time is being expended in digging ditches," McNaughton remarked to General Evans, "and often they will serve only to block our own routes forward.[68] As early as 18 June, the Chief Engineer, Home Forces and the Inspector General of Fortifications saw the force of this and set to work to procure large quantities of pipe to

---

*"The pipe-pushers saved a lot of digging," McNaughton said. "I put on a demonstration one day from the flank of Dover Castle. A nice green sward one minute and then, with a snap of the fingers, there was a trench right from the top of the hill to the bottom. All they had to do was to send a gang of people in to straighten it out and they had an effective trench that couldn't have been dug any other way short of a month of labour; and it appeared just like that."[67]

be pushed and loaded.[69] At the end of the month, with senior officers from the War Office and Commands present, Campbell demonstrated the use of liquid explosives* for the blowing of "surprise" tank obstacles; this demonstration, staged near Shornmead Fort, Chatham, proved successful.[71]

Not only would McNaughton's surprise obstacles result in unmarred airfields and routes, unless they had to be destroyed; they also proved more effective in stopping tanks than reinforced concrete obstacles constructed with great expenditure of money and time throughout the length and breadth of England. This was demonstrated in early August before General Sir Alan Brooke,† a group of senior officers from the War Office, GHQ Home Forces, XII Corps and Chatham. An infantry tank first crushed a row of reinforced concrete "jack block" obstacles with complete ease, and then was tried against a more formidable type of obstacle:

An "I" Tank . . . was run against the new pattern standard road block consisting of two strong reinforced slotted buttresses with five 90-lb. steel rails housed in the slots and bridging the gap at a height of about 3'-6" from the ground. The tank's speed on impact was about 10 m.p.h. At the first charge the tank was brought to a stop, but the rails were heavily bowed; on repeating the run the tank easily sheared through the rails and crossed the obstacle. Next, a demonstration of "pipe-pushing" by the 1st Canadian Tunnelling Company was presented, and a trench [approximately 200 feet long, 10-12 feet deep, and 15-18 feet wide] . . . was blown. This obstacle was then attempted by two "I" Tanks both of which were trapped and unable to get out either forward or backward.[72]

---

*Though liquid explosives were used in the initial experiments, the final explosive was a solid, circular stick of cordite-like material that was specially developed by Imperial Chemical Industries to give a heaving action. These sticks were waterproof, about 2½ feet long and fitted loosely inside the pipe which had an internal diameter of 4 inches. They had a small hole down the middle to house primacord and detonators.

Much of the outstanding success achieved by the tunnellers was due to the technical proficiency of two Imperial Chemical Industries representatives, J. Hancock and J. Lorrimer, who developed the explosive. McNaughton, who knew the ICI chemists very well from his days at NRC got in touch with them and told them what was wanted. "Pretty soon," he said, "we were the biggest users of explosives in England though very little was set off, apart from demonstrations."[70]

†It was on this occasion that Brooke and McNaughton discussed the Brittany affair. (See pages 97-8.)

The demonstration impressed Brooke. He wanted "twelve companies similar to Campbell's" and asked McNaughton to find out how long it would take to equip them from Canada.[73]

McNaughton was also anxious to put certain villages in a state of all-round defence. They would then become centres of resistance and serve as pivots of manoeuvre for the mobile columns. It was important that they should not be too close to the coast because of the danger that they might be overrun in the early stages of invasion, and the Kentish village of Sarre, near Canterbury, was first selected. There, in July, the 1st Canadian Pioneer Battalion went to construct a model strongpoint.[74] Three weeks later the village bristled with defences; fifteen casemates had been installed as well as surprises in the shape of oil and petrol spouts, barrel Molotov bombs and other anti-tank devices.[75] The construction of a line of similar defended localities followed to protect the flank of VII Corps in a move towards Dover, the most likely danger area, from its position of readiness.*

On 12 August, after reconnoitring Hampshire, McNaughton visited Sarre. In the afternoon, while he was inspecting the defences, two German reconnaissance planes came over but were driven off by British fighters, which then returned to their landing ground. No sooner had they done so than twenty Messerschmitts flew immediately over the village and dropped three bombs within a hundred and fifty yards of the main road junction where McNaughton was standing. A cottage was hit, killing one adult and two or three children. An ambulance arrived within minutes of the destruction of the cottage in which the children had been

---

*"There was another thing," McNaughton recalled, "that struck me as the essence of tactics at that time. *England, I thought, is a beleaguered fortress and you've got to look at this thing as something akin to castle warfare in the Middle Ages.* I obtained, and read again, one of the best books on the defence of ground ever written, E. Viollet-le-Duc's *Annals of a Fortress.* So we built strongpoints. I turned a pioneer battalion loose to fortify Sarre in every possible way. They took ladies' boudoirs and turned them into machine-gun posts without anything showing outside; I'm sure they never got the concrete out. There was a big building inside the village that had a hoist for casks. The boys arranged a big barrel of petroleum, with phosphorus bombs inside, that was all poised ready to swing. When a tank came through the village and slowed to make the turn they would just pull a catch and the barrel would smack the tank fair and square and go off with a great gust of flame. It caused a good deal of hilarity among the troops. You're halfway through if you can get the men to laugh."[76]

playing and the bodies were removed. The German planes continued in the direction of Chatham apparently unaffected, McNaughton noted, by anti-aircraft fire.[77] It was experiences such as this that prompted him to seek a way to increase the velocities of shells.

Gas was another preoccupation. There was a need, he wrote, "to meet conditions that may quite probably arise within the next few days so that the Canadians will not be caught as they were at Second Ypres."[78] That was on 19 September. Nine days later an intelligence summary warned: "Two independent sources tell of a chemical factory in Germany producing a form of sleeping gas, the effects of which last six hours. This is said to be used to overcome coast defences."[79] But McNaughton was already doing something about the problem.

He wanted his own mobile laboratory so that gases could be identified quickly in the field—a first indispensable step to preventive measures. The British depended on civil institutions for laboratory work and on civilian gas identification officers in the field; without laboratory equipment the work of the latter could not be precise, especially if some hitherto unknown gas was used. And to wait for reports from the laboratories would result in delay that was totally unacceptable in any battle for the island's life. Most of the British laboratories, moreover, were contained in London hospitals, hazardous places to have them at this period of the war; already three hospitals had been hit by bombs.[80]

Under the capable direction of two staff officers, Rabinowitch and Smith,* a mobile chemical laboratory was built. The lorry contained "every essential convenience of the modern laboratory," so that by the first week in October the corps had "an alert and effective [means] of determining at once type and volume of gas used by the enemy and the counter-measures required."[81]

In producing this, Rabinowitch and Smith had kept close touch with the Chemical Warfare School at Porton, Wiltshire, whose

---

*Major I. M. Rabinowitch (Special Adviser on Medical Aspects of Chemical Warfare Defence, VII Corps) and Major E. H. Smith GSO2 (Chemical Warfare). Rabinowitch had been specially selected for McNaughton by Sir Frederick Banting, who had been conducting studies of gas defences at the National Research Council. (See page 33.)

facilities had been opened to them. Inevitably, through them, the British had formed a clear idea of the receptiveness and interest shown by McNaughton. Towards the end of September Davidson Pratt, Deputy Director General of Chemical Defence Research in the Ministry of Supply, came to see him. The mobile laboratory was discussed. Pratt agreed that it would be valuable; he was gratified to learn that there was no intention of reserving it for Canadian use alone and that it would be used anywhere in Britain where it would do the most good. Porton, he assured McNaughton, would co-operate to the full and would gladly interchange information.[82] Rabinowitch, towards the end of October, became a member of the Chemical Warfare Research Committee, Ministry of Supply, and acted as a liaison officer on chemical warfare matters between Britain and Canada.[83]

Pratt reviewed the broad field of chemical warfare research in Britain. Porton, he said, was far too small and the testing area formerly used by the British in French North Africa had been lost with the fall of France. No suitable area to replace it could be found in Britain. Was there a suitable place in Canada? Lord Weir, his Director General, had sanctioned the approach and had stressed its urgency.[84] McNaughton, through his conversations with Banting in late 1940, had expected this approach.

He drafted a message for Canada that day outlining the British predicament and stating that the Ministry of Supply would like to transfer this urgent work to Canada if an appropriate area could be found. The Ministry estimated the total cost at £150,000 annually and suggested financing the scheme on a fifty-fifty basis. They proposed, if the suggestion was acceptable to the government of Canada, to send over experts and submit definite proposals for consideration by both governments.[85]

The outcome was the Experimental Station at Suffield, Alberta, authorized in 1941 and operated jointly by the Department of National Defence and the British Ministry of Supply. The largest station of its kind in the British Commonwealth, it covered an area of one thousand square miles and enabled trials, comparable in size to operational chemical attacks, to be carried out under a wide range of weather conditions. Such trials were its chief function, and as a result of its work important contributions to chemical warfare theories were made. In addition, flame throwers and flame thrower fuels, so essential in the closing campaigns of the war, were assessed.

Suffield grew into an outstanding example of what co-operative effort could do. Its staff was drawn from all three services of Canada and Britain (there was also almost always at least one United States Chemical Corps Officer in residence). And in addition there were civilian scientists from both countries. The station contributed to the staff of the American Tropical Chemical Warfare Station in Panama.

In 1937 the National Research Council, under McNaughton's presidency, had instituted a programme of chemical warfare research in its own laboratories* and at a number of Canadian universities. With the setting up of Suffield, the laboratories and staff at the National Research Council were taken over by the Department of National Defence and formed the nucleus of its chemical warfare laboratories. These worked closely with the Experimental Station.

Perhaps Suffield's most important contribution was in the technical assistance given to Canadian industry in the manufacture of chemical warfare offensive and defensive equipment. A pilot plant manufactured the special chemicals required for chemical warfare purposes, including toxic gases. Apart from this lethal work, the pilot plant was the sole source in Canada of DDT and was able to meet the requirements of all three services for this valuable product at that critical period.

The location of the corps; its organization for its task; its weapons and equipment; the development of defensive measures that would preserve it and give it a fighting chance—all these were of great importance. Hand in hand with these preparations, continuing daily—often nightly—week by week, the corps trained and practised to carry out its role with precision and dispatch.

---

*See *McNaughton*, Volume 1, p. 328. As a result the 1st Canadian Division, before embarkation in 1939, was equipped with improved respirators made in Canada under its direction. Later, in association with Suffield, work continued on a more extensive scale.

To each component of his command, whether a brigade group of Canadian Force or a formation of VII Corps later on, Mc-Naughton allocated an area for reconnaissance and study in detail. Units trained in the tactics of mobile columns and studied their areas of possible operations.[86] "Through reconnaissance we knew that coast in all its aspects, how to avoid the defiles and where the defence lines would be established."[87]

The bulk of the Canadian transport had not become available until the time of the German invasion of Norway. Since then, because of the Dunkirk and Brittany emergencies, there had been no opportunity to train the drivers adequately in day and night driving or in vehicle maintenance. That drivers, through no fault of their own, were inexperienced (especially on the tricky, winding roads of England) became all too clear when Canadian Force moved to Oxford in June. It was a shabby performance, the inefficiencies of the drivers matched by the attitude of the troops who let their disappointment over not reaching France become very evident. There were complaints of "ragged spacing . . . and poor discipline. Men, not wearing steel helmets or respirators, were sleeping in the trucks . . . with feet hanging over the back. Many trucks were overloaded, swaying dangerously on the curves at even ordinary convoy speeds." When one group got itself hopelessly mixed with a British tank unit in practice run, the chaos was complete.[88] All this required hard corrective action, a measure of its success being General Evans' report of the Saskatoon Light Infantry's "excellent traffic discipline" one month later. Traffic discipline, and the ability of the corps to move rapidly to a threatened point, was the essence of success.

At the beginning of July Lieutenant-General Sir Guy Williams (GOC-in-C Eastern Command) gave his view that "8 sea borne and 2 air borne Divisions were all that the Germans could hope to maintain even for a short period." He felt that "the maximum scale of attack on the Home Counties area would be 6 Divisions by sea, 1½ by air; this would leave 2 Divisions by sea and ½ by air for a diversion North of the Thames. Diversions might be staged first in the hope of drawing troops from the areas selected for the main attack."[89]

McNaughton planned to use "the faster elements of 1 Armoured Division in a cavalry role operating against the rear and flanks of the enemy while the brigade groups used their mobility and hitting-power to drive through the enemy from different directions." The slow-moving infantry tanks (3 to 6 m.p.h.) of the Army Tank Brigade would follow up as fast as possible "to support the Infantry Brigade Groups in the event of a check."* So long as the situation was fluid, the mobile groups would push on without worrying too much about their flanks; but if the enemy established a strong bridgehead it would be necessary for him to stage "a set-piece attack utilizing all the artillery resources" at his disposal.[91]

With this general plan in mind, McNaughton trained his corps. On 6 July Churchill, Eden and Ironside (on his last visit before being replaced by Brooke), watched Pearkes' 2nd Brigade stage an attack against a supposed enemy air landing in Kent.

This was not McNaughton's day. He waited for Churchill at the rendezvous (a crossroads) for half an hour past the appointed time. He then sent out scouts who found the Prime Minister at a crossroads two miles away. McNaughton motored over. "I'm not used to being kept waiting, McNaughton," Churchill growled. "Then you must teach your aides to read a map!" the General retorted with some asperity. Churchill had expressed a wish to see the troops and McNaughton took him over to where they were lined up at the side of the road. Due to the mix-up in the crossroads, however, the officers were at the far end of the line and Churchill was annoyed when they were not introduced to him as a preliminary to his inspection. Nevertheless, he walked down the line. After going some distance, the Prime Minister got a stone in his shoe. Standing on one leg, he removed his shoe, lost his balance and brought his stockinged foot down in a pool left by a recent

---

*"The 1st Armoured Division had been pretty badly hammered in France. It had to get new tanks and the tank crews had to be trained. But we did want to use the other tanks that were operational, so we worked them in with the infantry in suitable places. Then we managed to form squadrons of tanks that were in central positions until finally the division was fully operational. We kept them back for a counter-attack role. We wouldn't have squandered them in small numbers to begin with; we held them for a heavy attack when the time came."[90]

shower. The troops laughed. The exercise began some time later, and the distinguished guests watched a battalion comb a wood in which a company of "parachutists" had been dispersed. There was a good deal of beating about in the trees and bushes but the only "enemy" the troops flushed was a single mooing cow. The last word was with Churchill. "I have wasted enough time on the Canadian Army for one day, General," he said, and turned away.*[92]

On the 17th, on ground likely to be invaded, the 3rd Canadian Brigade Group attacked the "enemy" 1st Brigade, the new reconnaissance squadrons proving very useful.[94] In August, with Evans' division growing stronger, various infantry groups co-operated with tanks in different exercises. McNaughton also took advantage of having the armoured formation by suggesting to Crerar, by then Chief of the General Staff, that this was the time to train officers and men from the Canadian Armoured Corps (which Crerar was forming at home) by attaching suitable personnel to the British division; they would then go on to British schools before returning to Canada to train armoured troops there.† Such was the nucleus of the Canadian armoured divisions.[96]

---

*The party lunched at Churchill's manor, Chartwell. During the meal Churchill heard that the 2nd Canadian Division was bound for Iceland. Next day, in a mellower mood, he wrote to Eden: "You shared my astonishment yesterday at the statement made to us by General McNaughton that the whole of the 2nd Canadian Division was destined for Iceland. It would surely be a very great mistake to allow these fine troops to be employed in so distant a theatre." The division arrived in England shortly afterwards.[93]

†"This was very useful when our men went back to Canada to help train the Armoured Divisions and the Army Tank Brigades. Willoughby Norrie succeeded Evans in command of the 1st Armoured Division and he was very helpful. I was delighted with him. Afterwards Norrie became Governor-General of New Zealand —Lord Norrie now, a very fine soldier, and one of my greatest personal friends. Norrie had a hand in another thing a little later on. I wanted somebody, a physiologist, who could say what had to be done with the innards of a tank to make it more livable for the people who had to fight in them—temperature, and living conditions in general. If the crews were more comfortable they would fight better for that. Norrie supported me. Because of NRC I was in close touch with the Medical Research Council in England and I asked them if they could find the right man for me. They said, 'You don't have to come to us. There's a young Canadian who is working over here and he's just the man you're looking for.' His name was Solandt. I'd never heard of him. First he went down to the Tank School at Bovington and then he went out to see the armour in North Africa. He wrote a report and it was very useful. What he had to say was so much common sense that it had an immediate effect on how the insides of tanks should be designed to make men comfortable. He's Chancellor of the University of Toronto now."[95]

By the end of August each brigade group had practised rapid moves, debussing and seven-mile marches to assembly areas. Every unit had also rehearsed moves by night. All battalions had completed dawn attack exercises with the co-operation of tanks and planes. By now the troops had practised their role and acquired "experience of great value,"[97] but the men were kept on their toes through continued training.*

McNaughton allowed nothing to interfere with the constant and diversified practice, by day and by night, of his mobile role. Towards the end of June, while he was still at Oxford, the Commander, South Midland Area visited him to see if he could give "any assistance in improving the accommodation of the Canadian troops in the area."[99] It was a friendly gesture, but for McNaughton the tactical considerations were "paramount at present."[100] As time passed it might be possible to increase the comfort of the men but until then they would bivouac within reach of their vehicles, ready to spring into action at a moment's notice; and in the end, he said, "We got so that we would have given a pretty damn good account of ourselves."[101] At the onset of winter, with the risk of invasion diminishing day by day, the men were housed comfortably enough; but during the "invasion summer" comfort was the last of McNaughton's considerations.

Throughout August intelligence summaries grew more and more ominous. Planes brought back reports of shipping of all types assembled in ports from Oslo to Brest; large concentrations

---

*McNaughton ordered a series of small schemes with the object of hitting the enemy hard before he could get organized. "The essence was speed. You got your reconnaissance in, and if your command is worth a damn specific orders went out to bring about co-ordination. These were not like formal operations where you have the element of time on your side. Some of those exercises were very useful because they failed. At first we hadn't had a chance to have our drivers trained; and the staff officers weren't trained in the art of handling motorized forces, particularly in the art of moving lorried formations at night. It took God knows how long to get them disentangled. It was the finest thing we ever had. It let those fellows know they had to get down to it and learn the art of movement."[98] It was at this time that Canadian Force designed and brought into use portable traffic lights which could not be observed from the air. These lanterns bore loose plastic formation devices and directional arrows that were illuminated from behind. When placed by traffic patrols, moving well ahead of the formations, they did much to remove the confusion that attends night moves. Unlit, they were also used by day.

of troops and transport were observed; and the enemy, with his usual thoroughness, carried out embarkation and landing exercises along the Channel coast. That month the scale of his air attacks upon England grew in extent and fury, pointing clearly to the main invasion. The British people fully expected one: nothing else would have prompted parents to give up their children and send them for safety to North America. This evacuation continued steadily after the fall of France until mid-September, when the *City of Benares*, carrying many children, was sunk by a U-boat. With that, the emigration stopped.

McNaughton never doubted the ability of the Germans to effect a lodgement on the British coast. A set piece attack, heavily supported by artillery, might at any time be necessary. The ability of the artillery to contribute "dead-accurate" fire in the shortest possible time would be of great importance and the corps commander laid particular emphasis on airburst-ranging.* At Larkhill, in August, McNaughton watched with Ham Roberts† a practice fired by Guy Simonds' 1st Field Regiment at which successful results were obtained[103] and at the end of the month he pointed out to General Paget that the Canadian method of airburst-ranging gave more accurate results than that described in the British artillery manuals. He suggested that a committee should be formed before which he would appear to give evidence "as it must be realized that uniformity of method is essential for the efficient co-operation of British and Dominion artillery units in battle."[104]

On 10 September a meeting took place between Colonel A.H.D. Phillips (Superintendent of Applied Ballistics, Ordnance Board), his assistant Foster (the board's mathematician) and McNaughton. In essence, McNaughton's position was this: a simple graphic solution should be substituted for the British method of airburst-ranging, which required repeated reference to tables, double interpolation, and much arithmetic (in some of which there was un-

---

*"The ranges," McNaughton said, "got to be so far out that you couldn't observe the fall of shot, and adjust from that, so we had to have precise maps. Then we had to get crossbearings on a shell burst in the air. The drill then was to determine its position with reference to the target on the map—a complicated business, but once you had it the rest was easy."[102]
†Now a brigadier and CRA 1st Division.

certainty as to whether to add or subtract).* All this was very difficult to carry out under field conditions. Not only that. The tables themselves were incomplete and, moreover, contained errors of method as well as amount. Phillips did not deny this but was prepared to accept the error. Working from the existing table, for example, at the extreme range of, say, thirteen thousand yards at a three-degree angle of sight, normal charge, he claimed that the error would not amount to much more than a hundred yards; but that was not good enough for MacNaughton. Accurate tables were essential, particularly when it was necessary to shoot close over the heads of infantry. An error of a hundred yards, even at extreme range, might make a great deal of difference in the conduct of operations. Even an error of thirty yards at shorter range was deplorable, if it could be avoided. The basic data *had* to be accurate.

There is a reluctance to change in the British character and Phillips evinced it now. If a larger-scale map was used, he suggested, the error would be proportionately reduced. He shrugged off the importance of refining the range tables to remove the cause of error.

But, McNaughton replied, the shells were good, the guns accurate; clockwork fuses, while excellent, were not essential and the easily available long-burning powder fuses could be used with good results, provided the tables were accurate. Thus the labour of preparing accurate tables was justified. It was evident that the present system was not practical, for it was not in use. Surely, when the source of error was known, it should be possible to come up with a system that would be free of complications and would not need mental arithmetic. Phillips was finally persuaded. Accurate tables of "non-rigidity corrections," which was the point at issue, would be provided.[106]

It was not, however, even a modified British method of airburst-

---

*"The War Office method," McNaughton said, "was so complicated that nobody could use it. I've seen battery commanders standing there with the sweat running down their brows trying to remember if they had to add or subtract the corrections. The airburst-ranging charts—the straight line trajectory approximations—enabled people to do it more accurately and very simply."[105]

Dr. J. Mackay Hitsman of Ottawa, who was an artillery officer in the Second World War, said: "The method outlined in British manuals was a real panic for people like me. And it took thirty minutes to carry out the procedure versus thirty seconds with the McNaughton graph."

ranging that was eventually adopted. On 4 October General Sir Alan Brooke, his Major-General Royal Artillery (Major-General S. C. M. Archibald) and the Commandant, School of Artillery watched a demonstration by the 1st Canadian Field Regiment at Larkhill. Using the McNaughton graph for airburst-ranging—a simple graphic solution which was geometrically accurate and free from the error of method contained in the British Training Supplement—the regiment, in a comprehensive series of tests, put down shell after shell with amazing accuracy. (The officer in charge of the demonstration was Lieutenant E. M. D. McNaughton, a son of the corps commander.) Brooke, a gunner himself, was profoundly impressed.[107]

McNaughton rode back from Larkhill in high heart. Despite many setbacks in the past twenty years the point had been reached where the graphic method of airburst-ranging was finally to be adopted for the whole British Army. A simple system at last would be available for accurate, comprehensive placing of fire in close support of infantry. No longer would it be necessary to rely on observers in aircraft to direct ranging onto a target invisible from the ground. It was a great achievement to have the method officially recognized in the British Artillery Training Supplement, as Brooke had promised.

The promise was kept: the method was adopted for general use throughout the British Army. But the development of methods for the control of fire is one thing; the effective use of them is another. McNaughton knew that airburst-ranging was never adequately practised and used by the British field armies in the Second World War.*

---

*"It was not used after I left. They went back to the old *laissez-faire* methods of handling artillery. But it could have been very useful. In the *bocage* country of Normandy, for example, where the villages were smothered in hills and woods, the taking of a ranging point up in the air above the target, or within a definite switch of the target area, and getting the information out of that, would have been invaluable. Having got the calibration, you could have applied it to all the batteries and guns of a whole division or a whole corps of artillery. That's what I had done experimentally in France in 1918 and I would have done it again in this war in a systematic way. In place of using the artillery as a lot of scatter-guns, shooting at hell's half-acre and not hitting anything, we'd have absolutely obliterated the enemy strongpoints and saved a lot of infantry lives. That's the way one phase of the army would have been run if I'd been there."[108]

At the time, however, everything possible was done to make artillery regiments ready for the use of airburst-ranging when required. Orders went out to modify the establishment of survey regiments to include a calibration troop with the right kind of instruments to satisfy McNaughton's insistence that regimental artillery commanders must know their individual guns if they were to achieve the accuracy of fire that he demanded.

The Number 7 directors of the regimental survey sections had to be modified, so that regiments could carry out airburst-ranging independently of the Survey Regiment. McNaughton's advice was sought by instrument experts in the design of better survey instruments to observe the airbursts. The design, once decided upon, would be sent to the Ministry of Supply in England or to Canada for manufacture.[109] Until far into the winter McNaughton conferred with the British on the finalization of airburst-ranging graphs.*

During this period samples of the new British 4.5-inch and 5.5-inch guns became available for inspection. The greater range of the 4.5 was not deemed by McNaughton to be sufficient to warrant carrying an additional type of ammunition in the field; nor did he consider the explosive content of the shell sufficient for useful effect. The 5.5 was all right; but the snag was that its shell weighed a hundred pounds, too heavy for easy handling. The answer seemed to lie in a lighter shell, which would almost match the 4.5 in range, redesigned to contain a new high-power explosive. At McNaughton's instigation, experiments took place in Canada to produce a shell with longer range and increased deadliness. An eighty-pound shell resulted, which went into full production

---

*The airburst-ranging charts were calculated and drawn by a section of 1 Canadian Survey Regiment RCA under Lieutenant P. J. Paterson who suggested useful improvements. Colonel G. M. Carrie, who was later General McNaughton's representative on the British Ordnance Board, pointed to the need for developing first-class equipment in Canada for gun calibration in the field; this was used for British and U.S. guns, as well as Canadian. Colonel Carrie also proved extremely helpful in airburst-ranging and Artillery Survey sound-ranging. Major (later Colonel) Harold Hemming, who was responsible for Field Survey flash-spotting at Larkhill, was also very useful. Hemming, a native of Prince Edward Island and a graduate of McGill, had joined the Royal Engineers and served as staff officer, Field Survey, at Sir Douglas Haig's headquarters during the First World War.

in Canadian plants. In November, 1944, when McNaughton became Minister of National Defence and automatically a member of the Canadian Mutual Aid Board, he found that the demands for medium artillery shells were, by then, practically all for the eighty-pound shell.

Meanwhile the Canadian Army had turned down the 4.5-inch guns. Later on, nevertheless, several batteries of these weapons were imposed on the Canadian Corps in Italy where, in the winter of 1943/44, they ranged more than a thousand yards short; no tables of corrections had been provided with them.[110]

Throughout August and September McNaughton attended exercises, made his own reconnaissances, and paid liaison visits to neighbouring formations. His comments on training schemes, if caustic, were constructive. On one occasion there was "little liaison between reconnaissance elements and the main body" and few attempts had been made at concealment. He drew attention to tanks starkly outlined on the skyline, and the very obvious gun positions. "The exercise had not been properly studied," he concluded, "and consequently there were a great number of men engaged . . . who would receive no benefit from it whatsoever."[111]

Many of his reconnaissances were made by air, as when he flew on 3 August in a Westland Lysander over the Southampton area (including the River Itchen) along the River Test, over Romsey, Stockbridge, Fullerton, and thence to Old Sarum, paying particular attention to the beds of rivers and the gaps in the South Downs. He would then discuss his findings with the commanders of the coastal formations concerned. On 4 August McNaughton visited V Corps at Romsey where he had an hour's talk with the corps commander (Lieutenant-General B. L. Montgomery) who had been appointed to V Corps at about the same time that he had been given VII Corps.[112] And wherever he went, he saw "McNaughton" trip wires either in place or in process of erection.

Another liaison visit, however (to Admiral Ramsay at Dover), failed to materialize as planned. Major-General C. Churchill

Mann, at that time a major on McNaughton's staff, recalls "a lovely sunny afternoon" in the General's company:

One day in early August I was instructed by the BGS to go with General McNaughton to Headquarters, Southern Command (near Salisbury). I obtained appropriate maps and had his car ready at the time ordered. I rode in front to do the map reading and the General busied himself with his brief case and papers in the back of the Buick.

An hour or so passed uneventfully when the General looked up, as we were going around a roundabout and said, "Church, where are we?" I replied, "Just by-passing Winchester, sir." To my horror, General McNaughton said, "I wanted to go to Dover."

I was aghast at this statement, and was quite sure I had been clear in receiving my orders. However, I simply said to the driver, "Continue around the roundabout, driver, we are now going to Dover."

After a silence which for me was painful the General, in a kindly way, said, "I shall be too late for my appointment with Admiral Ramsay, Church, so we will drive along the coast and have a look at the Corps responsibilities instead."

We came upon a headland where a Gatling gun (vintage 1900) could be seen. The General, a gunner himself, instructed us to stop, and we visited the position. The NCO was a British corporal. . . . He had a detachment of about eight men. General McNaughton asked him to describe his arc of fire which he did ". . . from on the right the Church Spire to on the left the Lighthouse." He gave ranges.

The General then asked if this detachment was well trained, and was assured they were. The corporal then pushed his steel helmet back a bit and said: "Sir, our new Battery Commander was in South Africa and when he first took over he remarked that he hadn't seen one of these since then. He said 'I wonder if I still remember the drill? Take Post!' We did so. He ordered 'Load!' We loaded, He took position as Number One and ordered 'Fire!' Then 'Re-load!' We did. This continued, sir, until the gun stopped firing. General, that was the end of the ammunition but we still have our rifles if the Germans land."

General McNaughton left, saying he would try to get some more ammunition, and told me to make a note of it. I am glad to recall that after our return the General told me that the error about Southern Command was not mine. Believe me, I was grateful for this news.[113]

The exoneration of Churchill Mann was not the only happy sequel to the story. The Dominion Arsenal, at McNaughton's request, manufactured a quantity of the obsolete ammunition from the old dies and some time afterwards the consignment reached the gratified corporal.

At the end of August McNaughton received word from the War Office that the operational readiness of the Canadian Division and ancillary units could be relaxed about the middle of October when weather conditions in the Channel would make invasion unlikely. At that time, he decided, he would turn his attention to "individual training and the education of all ranks." It was also important to build up a supply of potential staff officers and instructors,[114] and to have preparations for winter accommodation completed.

Already in July he had instituted planning for a Canadian OCTU (Officer Cadet Training Unit), and the school was sanctioned by the Minister of National Defence. "No one," McNaughton said, "will be allowed to attend unless recommended through the normal chain of command . . . and interviewed by an independent Board selected by me. There will be no suspicion of favouritism or patronage in selecting candidates."[115] On 23 November, 1940, McNaughton attended the closing exercises of the first course at St. Lucia Barracks, Bordon, and, following an address the keynote of which was leadership, presented certificates of qualification to thirty-eight cadets; he took the thirty-ninth to a cadet who was critically ill in hospital after a traffic accident.[116]

During September, on one of his visits to Bordon, McNaughton became convinced that a Staff School was required, as well as an OCTU. After the 2nd Canadian Division had arrived and completed training, a Canadian Corps would be formed. The British staff officers with VII Corps would then be withdrawn. The vacancies offered to Canadians for staff courses at Camberley were few; would it not be advisable then "to institute a kind of Junior Staff College, based on, and situated near, Corps Headquarters?"[117] On his way back from Bordon he weighed the idea with one part of his mind, while the other absorbed the evidence that the Battle of Britain was building to a climax. There were plane trails over Thursley. Bombs exploded on both sides of the main Leatherhead-Guildford road. White smoke poured from the woods north of Hackhurst Downs and, in the distance, a parachutist swung slowly towards the ground.[118] By the time the car had reached Headley Court, McNaughton had decided that the need for a Staff College was imperative.*

It would, he was sure, be wise to run the course in England, not in Canada. In an emergency, students would be close to their units. British staff officers, with recent experience in Norway and in France, senior Canadian staff officers and heads of services were available for instruction. Moreover VII Corps now had formations and units of all types at full war establishment, equipped for demonstrations. British staff colleges, from which help would be derived, were near, and the standards aimed at would be the same.[120]

Crerar agreed to this for the first course, though subsequently the school—the forerunner of the Canadian Army Staff College, Kingston—would be transferred to Canada. The Canadian Junior War Staff School in England was established in December with Simonds as commandant and did an excellent job in providing young staff captains and brigade majors for the new Canadian Corps.

McNaughton's preoccupation with training was broken at the end of August when he was sent for by Paget about difficulties that had arisen over a diversionary road which the Canadians wished to construct to bypass Redhill. In accordance with arrangements made with South East Command, McNaughton had already

---

*"We had lots of gallant commanding officers but very few Canadian staff officers. Having British staff officers with us had already given us a breather which we had to take advantage of. It had given us time to get the more promising young people out from units and into training at the British Staff College. When I found out the limitations on that—the British were hard put to it in the reconstitution of their forces and needed the vacancies—I had to set up a Canadian Staff College. We moved it back to Canada in due course but we broke the back of our shortage before that was done."[119]

moved the Canadian Road Construction Company to the job but, much to his annoyance, no authority had yet come through to start the work. The record tells the tale:

General Paget referred to a conversation General McNaughton had had with Sir Edward Grigg [Permanent Under-Secretary of State for War] in which . . . he blamed the War Office for the delay in getting started. The delay was due, General Paget said, not to any failure by the War Office, but in getting Treasury sanction and Ministry of Transport approval.

Wherever the obstruction lay, McNaughton was anxious to remove it. The present position, he said:

. . . was very serious for us. In the event of a move eastward as matters stood we would have to pass through the Redhill defile which was certain to be an objective for enemy bombers, that we might well experience perhaps several hundred casualties and that this loss would be inexcusable [as] we had recognized the danger in advance and knew the remedy which should be applied.

Further, while the Treasury might be making objection to the expenditure of some £10,000 for the provision of some road materials, acquisition of property and so on, the Canadian Road Construction Company was now camped at the end of the proposed diversion ready to proceed and that [I] could not assign them to other work. This unit [had] a strength of about 350 all ranks and it was probable that they were costing in pay, maintenance and interest on equipment . . . about £500 a day with nothing to show for it.[121]

Things then began to move. Sir John Reith (Minister of Transport) and Sir Edward Grigg visited the site four days later,[122] and on 5 September the CIGS, Sir John Dill, watched the power shovel and bulldozer operating and saw the Le Tourneau scraper "fill its seven yard bucket and dump its load."*[123]

The air offensive against England, which had begun on 8 August with bombing attacks on shipping and ports, switched to fighter

---

*The effectiveness of the Canadian heavy equipment made a sharp impression on the British construction companies and led to a wide programme of re-equipment.

aerodromes and aircraft factories later in the month. British fighters, though thinly stretched, still climbed from their fields to shoot the attackers out of the sky. Number 1 (Fighter) Squadron, RCAF fought with them. The Germans failed to achieve the domination of the air that they had to have before invasion. On 7 September, as though to acknowledge his defeat, the enemy concentrated his strength for a massive terror attack on London.

Bombs rained down upon the capital throughout a Saturday afternoon of perfect weather. In the evening CROMWELL, the codeword indicating the imminence of invasion, reached VII Corps. Troops occupied "alert" positions and continued to stand by at four hours' notice until the alert was relaxed at noon on 19 September. Two brigade groups of the 2nd Canadian Infantry Division, which had by now arrived in England, were ready to join the order of battle of VII Corps should they be required.[124]

Since the 7th, London had been subjected to extremely heavy air attacks. Helped by bright moonlight and patches of low cloud, unhindered by anti-aircraft fire, the enemy scored.[125] Great fires spread for miles along the river's edge; and from the Surrey hills Canadian troops could clearly see the lurid glow, pierced through by wandering searchlight beams, that marked the ordeal of London. But Londoners' morale continued high and the RAF remained in being: the enemy did not embark on the gamble of invasion. At the end of the month, though the air raids continued, the German shipping which had been collected began a reluctant move from the Channel coast.

During the standby period, McNaughton began planning for the winter. He had already started experiments on huts which, as he was not in favour of men being turned out of their beds during air raid alerts, produced "splinter proof heated dug-in shelters with canvas top and wooden ends to house twelve men"[126] which the GOC-in-C Eastern Command proposed to adopt for all corps.[127] McNaughton then turned to education.

Though Price Montague thought that educational training would be difficult with troops scattered all over the place in huts,

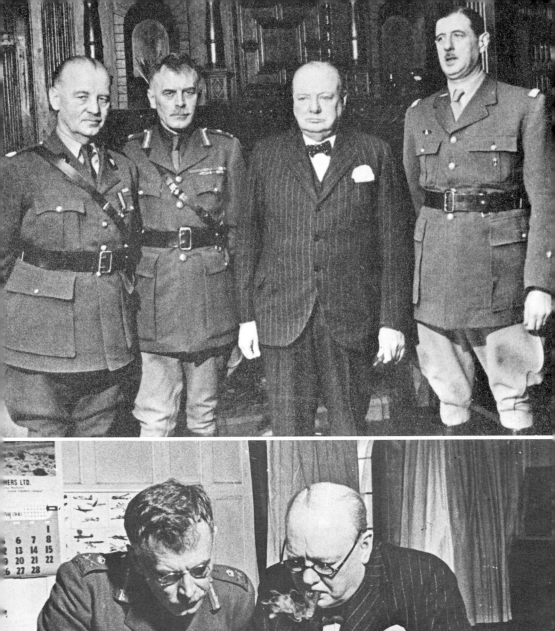

General Sikorski, Winston Churchill and General de Gaulle visit Headley
Court, February, 1941

McNaughton discusses anti-invasion plans with Churchill, February, 1941

Mackenzie King and McNaughton in pouring rain at the Canadian track and field championships, 23 August, 1941

its importance* outweighed the inconvenience. As McNaughton pointed out:

The men are now highly trained. Further intensive military training during the winter is not contemplated as it would make the troops grow stale. Under these circumstances the organization of educational training is essential to:

(a) Afford training to young Canadians that will be of benefit to them on conclusion of hostilities, and

(b) Provide a means of occupying the minds and activities of all ranks during the winter months.

Not only is there a very active demand for education but it is a matter of military expediency to provide it; in fact, I am prepared to release men from their ordinary duties for stated periods in order that they may form study groups.

He would, he went on, ask Ralston for competent persons from Canada to conduct it.[129] Eventually a Director of Educational Services (provided by the Canadian Legion) was appointed in Ottawa. This was Dr. A. E. Chatwin who arrived during November to supervise education from CMHQ.[130] Meanwhile McNaughton had found his own adviser to make a survey and start the programme going.

In the middle of September he went to London to see Colonel Vanier on his departure for Canada. (Vanier, Canadian Minister in Paris, had reached England on 22 June after a harrowing experience at sea.) Education for the troops was discussed and the name of J. Burgon Bickersteth, Warden of Hart House, University of Toronto, came up. He, it appeared, was in England performing Home Guard duties near Canterbury. McNaughton then sought the advice of Hume Wrong and Lester Pearson, counsellors at Canada House, who knew Bickersteth, and both assured him that he was the man for the job.[131]

There was a good deal of excitement in London that day. Buckingham Palace was bombed and the chapel badly hit, though

---

*"We knew we'd have an anxious time, a bad time, with the morale of the troops, when the tension of that summer was over. They were at the point already where they were *blasé* about training. It was a time to concentrate on education."[128]

Their Majesties were unharmed. A bomb fell in Swallow Street, off Piccadilly Circus, converting one building into a mound of rubble. McNaughton saw a Molotov "breadbasket" fall in Trafalgar Square—civilians calmly throwing their overcoats over the firecrackers—while fire brigades and ARP (Air Raid Precautions) workers dashed about to attend to fires "in striking contrast to civilians in French towns where minor fires were allowed to burn unhindered." He lunched with Lord McGowan (president of Imperial Chemical Industries) at Nobel House; Dill and Brooke were also present. And on the way to Headley Court that night he called on R. B. Bennett at his home at Mickleham. But he did not forget the name of Bickersteth.[132]

On 23 September McNaughton drove to the coast near Canterbury to inspect two batteries of 9.2 long-range guns which had been installed to engage German shipping close in to the French coast. The guns were manned by Canadians. He had arranged to meet Bickersteth, who had by now offered to serve "in any capacity,"[133] at a house in the precincts of Canterbury Cathedral on his way back. He arrived in the late afternoon. Bickersteth was not yet there, but at the house he had indicated McNaughton met "a dear old gentleman in gaiters" who offered him tea. McNaughton took him for a rural dean.

The clergyman proved to be an interesting companion, chatting about this and that, and tea passed pleasantly enough. When it was over McNaughton could not get away; the other was no mean conversationalist. He looked at his watch and out of the window, but there was still no sign of Bickersteth. His host, sensing his impatience, broke in: "You know, General, you've never seen Canterbury Cathedral, have you? Come along, I'll show it to you," and very reluctantly McNaughton went along.

He could not have had a better guide. Though time was passing he was fascinated despite himself. They toured the cathedral and the crypt in the half-light of an autumn evening. Then, passing a huge, ornate chair, his companion pointed to it casually, as though dismissing it as of small importance, "There," he said, "I was enthroned."[134] McNaughton then knew his companion, host and guide for what he was—no less a person than Cosmo Lang,

Archbishop of Canterbury, Primate of all England and the leader of Anglicans throughout the world.*[135]

Bickersteth finally showed up when McNaughton was putting on his coat for the journey back to Leatherhead. Home Guard duties had detained him. The General's impression was of a pleasant, capable man, and so he proved. He worked as Mc-Naughton's adviser for a year and a half and then became Head of Educational Services at the War Office.

By Mid-October Bickersteth had completed an educational survey, and study material had started to arrive.[136] At that time ninety per cent of the troops were in huts and preparations had been made for individual and educational training throughout the winter months.[137] Every advantage, of course, was taken of vacancies at British schools. In November, for example, four officers and five NCOs, Royal Canadian Engineers, left for the British Chemical Warfare School; they would then form the nucleus of a Chemical Warfare Company, RCE.[138] Twelve officers and thirty-six NCOs from the Armoured Corps from Canada—in answer to McNaughton's request—joined the 1st Armoured Division for training in October;[139] they then attended British schools before returning to Canada to disseminate this experience throughout their nascent parent corps. Here were the beginnings of Canada's magnificent armoured formations of the future.

Throughout the summer of 1940 a great deal of publicity had been centred on the Canadian commander. After the terrible humiliation of Dunkirk Britain badly needed a military hero, and the dynamic yet quiet McNaughton, commander of a force that was standing marshalled in a position of readiness, well equipped and prepared to deal quickly and effectively with invaders, caught the public imagination. The storm of publicity that came in 1941 and later, when he was the most discussed general in the British Isles, had not yet blown up, but it was beginning. McNaughton, however, had a premonition of it—and he did his best to stave it

---

*This meeting was to prove useful in the future when objections were raised to McNaughton's insistence that the prospective wives of Canadian soldiers should have their suitability assessed by regimental chaplains. He sought the Archbishop's support and obtained it.

off. In August, to the Public Relations Officer at CMHQ, he pointed to the publicity given him and suggested moderation:

I am most anxious to paint the picture of the Canadian Force in England as a *team*, each soldier playing his part willingly and wholeheartedly. It is the whole that matters, not the individual be they officers or men. I recognize the need for "human interest" stories in the press but I deplore, either for myself or the other commanders, any greater publicity than is really necessary. Apart from anything else, if it is overdone, there will be a reaction highly dangerous to the individual and the work he seeks to do.[140]

But the press would not be restrained.

In the first week in November it became known that Colonel Ralston and General Crerar would visit Britain at the end of the month. During their stay the formation of a Canadian Corps, as had been suggested by the Prime Minister, would probably be settled. McNaughton had already started to replace British staff officers and clerical staff by Canadians as vacancies occurred, so that when the time came for a Canadian formation, changes at Corps Headquarters would be as few as possible.[141]

Two large convoys, which had arrived on 2 August and 5 September, had brought the bulk of the 2nd Canadian Infantry Division, though its last battalions did not reach England until Christmas Day. There would be no other Canadian formations to consider that year. At the end of August units of the 2nd Division, which had then been in Britain for nearly a month, had still not been equipped, and on the 30th McNaughton visited the War Office to obtain a "clear picture" of the equipment situation so that he could advise his government concerning the dispatch of more troops.

The War Office, he found out, was equipping units in the Middle East at the expense of those in Britain, where there was a shortage of everything, even weapons and training ammunition. That being so, it would be pointless, McNaughton thought, to bring over more troops from Canada to winter in Britain without equipment, even at the training scale. It would be Salisbury Plain in the winter of 1914/15 all over again. Canada, he stated, was aiming at an overseas force of three infantry divisions, one armoured division and one army tank brigade, but supply was the governing factor; "the dispatch of troops who cannot be equipped makes no useful contribution to the cause of Empire." He had "grave doubts as to whether additional Canadian formations should be sent even in the spring of 1941 notwithstanding the public urge to help in Canada and the difficult question of accommodation there during the coming winter."[142] In a message to Canada, McNaughton requested that such troop movements should be deferred unless certain technical equipment for a few badly needed artillery and engineer units could be provided from Canadian or American sources.[143]

Arriving on 29 November, Ralston and Crerar were immediately admitted to Number 5 Canadian General Hospital, Taplow, one with sciatica and the other with influenza,[144] and McNaughton visited them there next day. Later, when both had recovered, conference succeeded conference on the formation of the Corps. There was some discussion of less important matters, too: whether the troops should have their clothing washed and uniforms cleaned at public expense, as the British did, or out of their own pockets as at present. McNaughton's recommendations did not convince the Minister, who on both these questions "would like to hear the views of the Divisional Commanders" before giving a decision.[145]

Nevertheless the Canadian Corps was formed within a month. McNaughton, as commander, issued a Secret Routine Order:

With effect from 0001 hrs. 25 December 1940 The Canadian Corps has been constituted to compose the 1st Canadian Division, the 2nd Canadian Division and the Canadian Non-Divisional Units presently in the United Kingdom.

The 1st Armoured Division, the 1st Army Tank Brigade, the 53rd Light A.-A. Regiment and British Non-Divisional Units previously allocated to 7th Corps came under command Canadian Corps on its formation.[146]

It was a momentous day for him. The old Corps, so ably led by Sir Arthur Currie, had now been reborn.

An eye-witness described him on that day:

I remember Christmas Day, 1940—a proud date for Canada—when the Canadian Corps was formed. I went to the commander's home in the morning to get the story. He was in high spirits, as cheerful as the season. He doesn't smile a great deal, but that morning he was literally beaming.[147]

Between Christmas and the New Year Ralston visited the units of the Corps. He saw what had been done towards shaping a modern army: the motorized infantry complete with trucks whose seats could be put out of the way in a few seconds when ordinary load-carrying was required; Canadian-designed anti-aircraft mountings; motorcycle reconnaissance units with Bren guns in the sidecar on their Motley mountings; the 1st Medium Regiment RCA with "pneumatized" guns towed by Matador tractors; and the 2nd Army Field Workshop with its workshop lorry fitted with the most up-to-date equipment and tools from Canada and the U.S.A. Here, in fact, "skill in improvization was evident throughout the entire shop."*[148]

Near Redhill, Ralston was taken to a hill from where he could obtain a panoramic view of the new bypass road. Mechanical equipment butted up and down busily, shaping it into its finished form "of four traffic lanes having a boulevard between each pair of uni-directional lanes; a twelve foot cycle path on either side of the road; and a sidewalk on the outside."[149]

That the Minister of National Defence was impressed by the organization and high state of training of the new Corps is obvious from his words:

I spent four days visiting the Canadian troops. The first day I was with the corps troops, the second day with the first division, the

---

*Already McNaughton had under consideration the amalgamation of the maintenance and repair services of the Royal Canadian Army Service Corps and Royal Canadian Ordnance Corps. The British took the lead by forming a new corps to combine these services—the Royal Electrical and Mechanical Engineers (REME). The Canadian equivalent (RCEME) was formed early in 1944.

third day with the second division, and the fourth day with the holding units. . . . Naturally it was an attractive and interesting thing to see the troops at work, in training on the roads, in billets, and elsewhere in connection with operations. I saw our mechanical transport, the reconnaissance squadrons flying past at top speed, the field park companies on the road with their bridging gear . . . the units—in one place, it may be, in the trees, in another place out on a broad field—doing their training. . . .

I watched the tunnelling company at work, and the so-called "pipe pushers" operating their special apparatus . . . I saw the Canadian Engineers, who have done such an excellent piece of work in building a by-pass road in order to relieve traffic congestion and particularly for the purpose of providing for future operational contingencies. . . . Altogether the show was one which would have gladdened the heart of any Canadian. . . .

We may well be proud of the men . . . who today are holding the front line in the battle of Britain. . . . General McNaughton, General Odlum [commanding 2nd Canadian Infantry Division] General Pearkes . . . are men we can trust and rely upon, men in whose care the honour and glory of Canada, and the cause of democracy in the world are, in my humble opinion, entirely safe.[150]

McNaughton had anticipated the role his troops would be expected to play in the defence of Britain even before the evacuation from Dunkirk. To fit them for it he had, often through sheer determination, organized, trained and given them the best weapons that were then within the capabilities of industry to supply. He had done more. Through foresight he had planted in productive ground the seeds of growth of the future Canadian Army.

Chapter 8

~~~~~~

1941 : The Canadian Corps, a Proud Inheritance

The "alarums and excursions" (as the Canadian official historian termed them) of Norway, Dunkirk, Brittany and the invasion summer were as near as the Canadian troops in Britain were to come to actual operations until August of 1942 when some of them fought at Dieppe. For that reason each of these emergencies has been examined in some detail.

The Canadian Corps inherited the GHQ Reserve role of VII Corps and remained responsible for it until the autumn when it took over the direct defence of a coastal sector. The threat of invasion still remained. "The Germans realize," a Corps intelligence commentary pointed out in January, 1941, "that the invasion of the United Kingdom is the only possible means of securing a decisive victory. Reports agree that an attempt will take place this spring."[1] And though the anti-invasion role by now was well-defined, it needed, McNaughton said, "continued thought, preparation and training."[2] Throughout the year of its existence, McNaughton perfected the organization of the Canadian Corps; he trained it, and, as he had done for VII Corps, sought to provide for the new formation the best weapons and equipment that it was possible to get.

At the beginning of 1941, after little more than a year of war, McNaughton described in broad terms the growth of the Canadian Army.* There were "two full infantry divisions in the United

---

*"Canadian Army" replaced the term "Militia" by Order in Council in November, 1940.

Kingdom and many units of Corps Troops backed by administrative and holding units. Two other divisions [were] mobilized in Canada and an Armoured Corps [was] in the making. There [were] Military Schools, Training Camps and Depots, the whole running into tens of thousands of men." The multiplication of the military power of Canada in this short period could not be arrived at precisely, but McNaughton considered that it must have increased a hundredfold.[3]

In January he informed the War Office of his plans for the shape of the Corps.* Though it would conform closely to British practice, there would be differences—"a degree of elasticity to meet special Canadian needs." Pay, dental and chaplain services would all be organized on Canadian lines and the Corps would also contain certain ancillary units which, in the British Army, were found in army or line of communications troops. The reasons for this are obvious. McNaughton intended to create a self-sufficient corps such as the Canadian Corps in the earlier war had been—"a co-ordinated organization working together rather than a collection of scattered individual units"—and within it there would be strong artillery and engineer components.[4] The British did not challenge his view; in fact, McNaughton said, he had their unfailing support while building his homogeneous Corps.[5] Thereafter, through careful planning and immense effort, he formed a Corps that was capable of operating independently, though it was never to be employed as such.

McNaughton was not interested in having troops rushed from Canada simply to get them under his command. At the end of March he came under strong pressure from the War Office to use shipping that would be available in May to move the 3rd Canadian Infantry Division and the 1st Canadian Army Tank Brigade to England. When he heard that the War Office could not provide more than a quarter of the equipment required by the infantry division, McNaughton opposed the move. He would take the tank brigade in May, and engineer units from the division, but not the division itself. He was urged to reconsider: the division could work

*Details of the 1941 programme are contained in Stacey's *Six Years of War*.

with the other Canadian divisions, carry out tactical exercises, and get acclimatized. McNaughton demurred. From May until the autumn, training facilities were better in Canada. There was more equipment there, and less congestion in the training areas. The 2nd Division, he pointed out, had been in England since August of 1940 "and is still far from being equipped."[6] Thus, while the 1st Canadian Army Tank Brigade (complete with Mark III tanks that had been made in Canada) arrived in England in June, the 3rd Division was not over in its entirety until October. The last major formation of the corps, the 1st Canadian Armoured Division* (for which units of the 4th Infantry Division had been utilized in Canada) reached the United Kingdom at the end of 1941.

The provision of a strong, independent Corps would tax Canada to the utmost in 1941. McNaughton, therefore, advised the Canadian government to take a hard look at British requests for units outside that commitment. Already there were twenty forestry companies in Great Britain—formed into the Canadian Forestry Corps—but in July the British wanted twenty more. A month earlier they had wanted no fewer than thirteen railway transportation units. Charles G. Power, Minister of National Defence for Air, who was in England at the time, cabled Ralston: "McNaughton specially stresses that before embarking on new adventures involving dispersal of our resources we should be certain that we will be in a position to carry out to the full, even in a long war, the military commitments already undertaken and supply reinforcements already pledged;"† it was also essential "to maintain Canada's production effort at the maximum." Both requests were turned down.[7]

McNaughton did, however, expand the tunnelling organization. Number 2 Tunnelling Company was formed in January and that month a detachment from Number 1 moved to Gibraltar; Number 2 joined it there in March and, during the following year, constructed Gort's Hospital in the heart of the Rock and extended

---

*Redesignated the 5th Canadian (Armoured) Division in July, 1941.

†In view of the reinforcement crisis of 1944, the note of warning struck by McNaughton here is important.

the airfield runway to accommodate heavy bombers; the latter proved extremely useful during Operation TORCH, the Anglo-American landings in North Africa in 1942.

During the next two years McNaughton's foresight in providing tunnellers paid handsome dividends, and not only in the provision of surprise obstacles. Already, at the end of January, 1941, they had used up all the available pipe in England for prepared demolitions. The need for more was still apparent and McNaughton ordered supplies of pipe from Canada; the cost of these would be recovered.[8] Apart from that, great assistance was rendered to the Ministry of Supply by developing mineral deposits of munitions value at various locations: Matlock, Derbyshire (fluorospar); Whitehaven, Cumberland (hematite); Cornwall (tin, which was especially important after the loss of Malaya); Wales (manganese); Middleton-in-Teesdale, Durham (zinc); Weardale, Cumberland, (wolfram); and the Shetland Isles (magnetite). In addition, a detachment of the 1st Canadian Tunnelling Company bored a two-mile tunnel through solid rock at Loch Laggan, Scotland. The head waters of the River Spey, instead of flowing into the North Sea, were diverted to Loch Laggan by means of the new tunnel, and thence through a dam at the west end of the loch. This operation increased the power available for the bauxite plant at Fort William by fifteen thousand horsepower; thus the supply of aluminum, required for aircraft production, could be stepped up.

The Earl of Bessborough,* who was one of McNaughton's ADCs at HQ Canadian Corps, has described the General, his difficulties, his activities and his environment at this period of his life. Without access to official documents or files, Bessborough laboured under difficulties, as he states. Nevertheless, close to the General as he was, his remarks may well be taken as the framework for a brief account of McNaughton and the Canadian Corps, and they can now be supported by the documents.

---

*Then Viscount Duncannon, eldest son of Lord Bessborough, Governor-General of Canada from 1931-35.

Life at headquarters, "a large mansion in Surrey," Bessborough said, was quite informal and "a pleasant antidote to the more orthodox service with regular or territorial units of the British Army." It was very different from the "arduous discipline of the divisional HQ" with which he had gone to France.[9]

The Canadian general considered that there were two kinds of discipline—the old and the new. The old method of enforcing discipline on uneducated soldiers he believed to be dead and no longer necessary. If only all the English generals had understood this! The new kind, thought Andy, was born of keen co-operation between officers and men and intelligent obedience of orders. Quick comprehension of orders was the *sine qua non* of present-day soldiering. He was ahead of most of his contemporaries in this respect. . . .
Moreover, his imagination and enthusiasm inspired members of his staff to serve with such energy and devotion that the dullness of army routine was unknown to them.[10]

McNaughton's office, a former bedroom, was at the end of a coir-matted hall on the second floor of the mansion. The oak panelling had been covered with fibreboard and against one wall stood an engineer's drafting table with a sloping top, only a little less primitive than the packing-crate table under which Tony the lion used to lie in the Counter-Battery Office of the old Corps Headquarters. The large window of the room overlooked woods and farmland and a long, hedge-bordered lane—a typical cross section of the pleasant Surrey countryside.

McNaughton sat behind the large desk in the plainly furnished room writing usually, or conducting interviews in "a firm, rich voice" with "an attractively rugged" Canadian accent. "His face was haggard and worn. He wore an ill-fitting battledress. A lock from his unbrushed hair fell over his forehead."[11] Other observers noted the cigarette that was usually burning on the ashtray or in his fingers and the couple of cigarette packages lying open on his desk; the speed at which he read, missing nothing of importance; and above all the high tension at which he worked, "talking man-power with one brigadier, switching to a discussion of armoured vehicles with another twenty minutes later, debating the merits of a new sound-ranging method with a gunnery officer. . . ." and somehow keeping it all in order in his mind.[12]

Training was one of his major preoccupations. "Exercise after exercise took place in different parts of the country," Bessborough continued, "and officers and men went on every conceivable course. Infantry, artillery and armoured units were all brought to a pitch of training such as few troops had achieved before."[13] These exercises were on a much larger scale than formerly. By the end of 1940 the mobile columns had mastered the art of movement and were able to reach the possible areas of operation with speed and precision. In 1941 McNaughton determined to test the ability of his Corps to reach a distant concentration area by road, to advance to make contact with the enemy supposed to have landed in East Kent and to deploy for the attack. Such was the broad outline of Exercise FOX, held early in February. The exercise rehearsed the 1st Division in a role that might well have been given to the Corps, while the 2nd Division (not actually taking part) moved up behind the 1st. At the end of February Exercise DOG tested the 2nd Division in the leading role.[14]

Traffic control, attempting to grapple with the thousands of vehicles of the Corps, broke down on both occasions and the trucks, which should have transported the troops with swift ease to the threatened sector, succeeded only in blocking the roads for other convoys. McNaughton's modest object of springing unsuspected forces upon surprised attackers had not been attained and, worse, his troops had tied themselves up in a motionless blob that would be an irresistible target for enemy aircraft. Knowing the consequences of such a tangle in actual operations he was coldly furious. One witness recalls that day: "I remember him in the winter of '40-'41 on an exercise carried out by the 1st Division in southern England. These exercises were designed to train whole formations in a moving battle . . . A number of officers from 2nd Division, of whom I was a junior one, were attached to act as umpires, being radio-linked to an exercise-control and umpire centre. I think the exercise was code-named FOX or DOG."*

---

*It was FOX.

It was a dog all right. . . . The exercise ground to a halt at some forgotten crossroads with whole battalions and assorted units and sub-units jammed nose-to-tail in those narrow, sunken lanes laughingly called roads in England. Despatch riders' motor cycles had to be hoisted over truck after truck to get them up ahead to their destinations.

A fine drizzle and a palpable air of crackling restraint was falling on a group of Canadian and British staff officers at the crossroads. It was the only time I have ever seen a person who was livid with rage. NcNaughton was livid.

It was not my division which had gotten itself into such an unholy tangle and I shared his indignation—although it was not until afterwards I understood all the reasons for his fury [when] thirty months later at Valguarnera, in Sicily, units of the same divisions did much the same sort of thing under fire.[15]

At Exercise WATERLOO in June the tangle did not recur. The Canadian Corps, a British corps and a British armoured division moved swiftly to tackle a series of landings on the east and south coasts. McNaughton's men countered a major enemy thrust against Sussex, and in a rough-and-tumble battle centred on Horsham the "Germans" were umpired out. And in BUMPER, held at the end of September, the Corps, hard, thoroughly trained and burning for action, performed equally well. This exercise, the largest ever held in Britain, involved a quarter of a million men. Two army and four corps headquarters, twelve divisions (including three armoured) two tank brigades and ancillary units all took part.

It was important that training exercises should be conducted as actual operations and equally important, even in training, that Canada's constitutional position regarding the control of her forces should be respected. This held good in all the exercises that have been mentioned but it had to be insisted upon. In an exercise conducted by GHQ Home Forces during the last week of January, 1941—Exercise VICTOR, a full-scale Home Defence scheme, without troops, designed to test all the defence organizations throughout the United Kingdom—the principle was flagrantly disregarded.

Canadian forces [Lord Bessborough wrote] were employed in a way which was in contravention of the principles laid down on the original formation of the corps as a GHQ reserve. The strength of the Canadian army had been dissipated by a policy of GHQ which involved the independent use of a Canadian infantry brigade group to stem a break-through for which a larger formation would have been needed. This meant that the brigade in question would probably have been overrun. It also meant that an accepted rule had been broken, that is to say, that the First Canadian Division should be used in battle as a whole and their contribution would thereby be greater than if used in independent groups. [The] principle that the whole is greater than the sum of the parts had been violated.

Moreover, no account had been taken of remonstrations on the part of Canadian divisional commanders at having their divisions broken up and used merely as a pool out of which GHQ considered itself at liberty to extract formations at will and place them under the command of other formations. In fact the brigade group in question had been placed under the command of another United Kingdom corps. Now it was well known that divisional *esprit de corps* was very strong in the Canadian army. . . . Therefore, any attempt to split up a Canadian division might have been disastrous. In this respect the Canadian Army differed from the British Army, in which there was often too little *esprit de division* or *esprit de corps* but very strong regimental traditions. This characteristic of the Canadian army could not be ignored in battle. It did not mean that Canadian troops were unable to fight with other Imperial Forces, but it did mean that their total contribution would be so much the greater if they fought together.[16]

Whether in training or in battle this was a principle that McNaughton would not see violated and his ADC, who was very close to the General's mind, was right to make much of it. To McNaughton it was as if Currie had never taken the stand he did when Haig split up the Canadian Corps at the time of the German offensive in 1918. On 31 January McNaughton called on Sir Alan Brooke, with whose headquarters the responsibility for the blunder rested. The prospect of further argument was uninviting after their acrimonious discussion concerning the feeding of a Canadian formation piecemeal into the projected fighting in Brittany, but McNaughton saw very clearly that the issue would have to be faced. Just as the autonomous position of Canadian troops had had to be made clear to Ironside early in 1940, he was determined to go through the business once again with Brooke. But where Ironside had been genuinely unaware of Canada's constitutional rights, and anxious to co-operate when he knew the facts, McNaughton did not have the same feeling about Brooke. "He did not sympathize with our autonomous status; it was more convenient to regard us as British troops and he would ignore it if he could."[17]

Though what passed between McNaughton and Brooke is not on record, McNaughton considered at the time that the discussion was of "great importance to the Canadian Army" and of "considerable historical and constitutional interest"; it had had "a satisfactory outcome from the Canadian point of view."[18] He could not have known then that the outcome eventually would be most unsatisfactory for himself, for, as we shall see, this issue was one of the factors that led to McNaughton's removal in 1943, when Brooke was Chief of the Imperial General Staff.

In a letter that he sent to Brooke the following day McNaughton summarized the Canadian stand. In VICTOR, McNaughton said, *elements* of the 1st Canadian Division had been committed to action in widely separated areas under a number of different commanders. This had been quite wrong. "No such situation should arise in actual operations. I have continuing responsibilities to my Government for the safety and proper employment of the Canadian troops which have been entrusted to my command."

I am naturally most anxious on grounds both of military advantage and of constitutional propriety that the Canadian Corps should be kept together; nevertheless you will recall my own recognition of the fact that in the special circumstances of the battle of Britain this might not always be best in the general interest and my agreement that for valid reasons our Divisions might be detached, *as such,** for so long as might really be necessary.

I recall your promise that before any "instruction" to make a detachment are issued that the alternatives will be carefully weighed and I confirm that under this condition I will accept

---

*Italics supplied.

your judgment at the time; it being definitely understood that a Canadian Division is not to be subdivided. . . . The fact that a Canadian Division is detached will not interfere in any way with the normal system of Canadian administration nor with my right and duty to intervene should the situation so require."[19]

Backed now by the Statute of Westminster, McNaughton's stand was even more reasonable than that taken by Currie twenty-three years earlier; and it brought equally satisfactory results for the present in so far as the employment of Canadian divisions was concerned. But, as in the previous war when Currie's stand had annoyed Haig, so McNaughton's arguments now angered Brooke.*

"Our corps commander," Lord Bessborough wrote, "was full of new ideas and did much to stimulate research among the recognized establishments. His proposed electro-magnetic gun was an especially fascinating project; and his comments on a rather ludicrous spigot-mortar, which caused a serious accident and never became a very satisfactory weapon, were lively. If some of the dugout gunners on the Ordnance Board did not always share the general's enthusiasm for a specific invention, none doubted his standing as a mathematician nor the value from the research point of view of his calculations. I do not doubt that the war might have been brought to an earlier close if some of his ideas had been more readily accepted by authority."[21]

One of McNaughton's "new ideas" was a device to illuminate military maps at night without their being visible from the air. Exercises in blacked-out England had pointed to the need for this. He first thought of using "black" light (ultra-violet light) that would be directed on maps that had been previously sprayed with a fluorescent cellulose acetate solution. It was found that an ordinary flashlight fitted with a black filter would illuminate only about

_____

*On 21 July, 1943, in discussion with McNaughton, Brooke drew attention "with some heat" to the letter McNaughton had sent him. One can feel sympathy for Brooke at that time for, as he pointed out, he had McNaughton on the one hand stressing "the military advantage of keeping the Canadian Army together" and on the other Ralston who, the year before, had insisted that "battles be found for the Canadians" even if these would involve "only a part of our force."[20]

an inch of the map and it was some time before an experimental flashlight was constructed which satisfactorily lit up an area three inches in diameter. By this time McNaughton had designed a map-reading enlarger—a magnifying glass incorporating light that was diffused downwards onto the map. This "reader" (specially designed to screen the light from above) used ordinary "white" light. It was eagerly taken up by the 1st British Armoured Division and was manufactured in quantity later.[22] The idea of using black light, however, was still not wholly dead. Representatives of the Advisory Council on Scientific and Industrial Research, the Ministry of Home Security and the British Standards Institution saw many possibilities for it, such as headlights for road vehicles and tanks and beams for the identification of troops at night, and intended to continue the experiments.[23]

Another McNaughton innovation was the conical smooth bore gun which he worked on throughout 1941, until he found a better solution which ended the experiments. On 19 February, 1941, Sir Frederick Pile invited McNaughton to a luncheon at the Dorchester Hotel to discuss the provision of new designs of anti-aircraft guns which would develop the very high velocities needed to counteract high-flying aircraft; in particular he wished to bring to the attention of the Admiralty McNaughton's proposals for a conical gun. Mr. A. V. Alexander (First Lord of the Admiralty), Admiral of the Fleet Sir Dudley Pound (First Sea Lord) Vice-Admiral B. A. Fraser (Third Sea Lord), a member of the Army Council and three Members of Parliament were at the luncheon. As a result of the meeting the navy agreed to take up the project independently of the Board of Ordnance; experimental guns of two or three different calibres would be built. A by-product of the discussion was an exchange between Pile and the navy of three hundred Bofors guns for eight 5.2-inch twin anti-aircraft guns; this came about through McNaughton who, with his finger on British gun production, advised Pile that the navy had a few spare guns of large calibre and high velocity.[24]

Both Pile and McNaughton viewed the Ordnance Board with misgivings; they expressed "extreme discontent with the opposition to new projects" which they had experienced there, as well as from the Director General of Artillery at the Ministry of Supply. And they were not alone. A fortnight earlier, when visiting the National Physical Laboratory and the Admiralty Research Laboratory, McNaughton had heard Sir William Bragg and Dr. Bernard Darwin deplore "the present state of scientific research under the Ministry of Supply" and the shortcomings of the Ordnance Board; the board tended in many cases to procrastinate and to obstruct when considering the more advanced forms of ballistics and gunnery."[25] Pile has described ways found to circumvent the Ordnance Board later when, in April, 1942, he was appointed to a committee "for the production of better weapons of war." (The first meeting had been organized "by a distinguished civilian at the Ministry of Supply" who invited various scientists, McNaughton and Pile. "The meeting was a great success and many good ideas were put forward. I found something rather humorous in the fact that no member of the War Office* was present, nor was there going to be any such person present at our future meetings."[26]

The part played by McNaughton in the development of the carrier flame thrower, the forerunner of the "Wasp," deserves special notice. It has been described by Sir Donald Banks, head of the Petroleum Warfare Department in Great Britain. The prototype, said Banks, made a successful debut at Moody Downs on 28 May, 1941, and McNaughton, who watched the demonstration, was much impressed. "Then came an exasperating lull in proceedings . . . and it was not until the latter part of July that we received any decision to go ahead."[27]

At this stage a breath of enterprise was brought in from the New World to redress some of the lethargies of the Old. Canada came into the picture. To the prescience of the Canadian Commander-in-Chief, General McNaughton, the enthusiasm of Colonel Harold Lynn, Royal Canadian Engineers, and later of Lt.-Colonels Sawyer and Arnason, and the inspiring keenness of Canadian officers and men of all ranks, much of the practical progress from this time onwards in securing the operational adoption of carrier flame-throwers was due.[28]

---

*Pile meant the Ordnance Board.

McNaughton took a hand in the design of a new carrier flame thrower which, at Canadian suggestion, was named the "Ronson." "Early in August the specification was settled and put in hand by Lagondas and in November it was careening about the Moody Downs, ridden cowboy fashion by Canadians with the governors off the engines. The *élan* of the 'Ronson Cavalry,' as they called themselves, was tremendously inspiring. Later they carried it across the Channel, emulating their fathers of the Canadian Light Cavalry [Canadian Cavalry Brigade] in 1918 in many a hard fought action in the Low Countries."[29]

There was a setback in January, 1942, when the War Office decided that any decision to proceed with the carrier flame thrower should be deferred for six months, "a virtual death-knell for a project in wartime," and at such times "the support of staunch friends is more precious than fine gold."

Among a number of such stalwart allies my mind in retrospect singles out Geoffrey Lloyd and Harold Medlicott in the [Petroleum Warfare] Department, General McNaughton and his "Ronson" cavaliers and Dick Watney and Fraser at Lagondas. McNaughton was magnificent. On his own responsibility and in the teeth of the British "official" view, he placed an order in Canada for 1,300 "Ronsons."*[31]

His foresight brought large returns. Though there was some rivalry between carrier flame throwers (Wasps, which replaced the Ronsons) and those mounted in tanks ("Crocodiles") — each at times seeming likely to displace the other—both were used in the

---

*Although Banks does not make this clear, these were not complete carriers. As McNaughton said, "The flame-thrower would need to be employed in mass on certain occasions. It would not . . . be possible to build up an organization and hold it until the right time came but if we used the universal carrier and the carrier platoon of the infantry battalions and the machine gun battalions as a basis, we could perhaps design a flame-thrower equipment which could be attached in a few hours; and if the personnel had been trained (and this training kept up), the required use either within the infantry battalion or on a much larger scale could be arranged *ad hoc* on a few days' notice when the opportunity came. With this thesis a Canadian Experimental Flame-Thrower Establishment was set up and development work pressed both in respect of flame guns, gel fuels and training. Eventually with the help of the Canadian Department of Munitions and Supply, I was able to build up a stock of some 2,000 equipments at the Depot in England ready for immediate attachment to carriers."[30] Wasps were merely better equipments than the earlier Ronsons.

final campaigns of the war with great effect. The Canadian model of the Wasp (Model 2c) "became standard for the whole Army before the end of operations"[32] and in Northwest Europe, as well as in Italy, they "fulfilled the anticipations of the visionaries. They had fought in over 500 actions, had suffered no higher casualties than the normal carrier crews and had proved themselves invaluable infantry weapons. Many a stout infanteer owes his safe return home to the flaming 'Wasps' that struck terror into the hearts of the Nazi hordes."[33]

Canadian military history [Banks concluded] . . . will record with pride the prowess of her sons in these battles . . . and it is meet that credit should also be given to them for their resource and determination in invoking these new weapons and in the early faith of a great Canadian, General McNaughton.[34]

McNaughton had organized the 1st and 2nd Canadian Reconnaissance Battalions (which replaced the reconnaissance units he had improvised for Canadian Force) as early as January of 1941. In March he sat down with Canadian technical advisers (A. S. Ellis and S. E. Swallow) to discuss the design of armoured reconnaissance vehicles to replace the old motorcycle combinations with which the battalions had been equipped; they also went into the details of a Canadian armoured car. Drawings and specifications were mailed to Canada shortly afterwards.[35]

There was good news from Canada for him that year. Canadian mechanical transport, after changes suggested by his team in Britain, would be entirely satisfactory; Canadian Bren guns and carriers had been tested and proved good; and Canadian battledress was considered superior to other issues. McNaughton felt most strongly that, until the Canadian Corps was fully equipped, it should have first call on Canadian production; in any Empire pooling arrangement, as had been suggested, he wanted the Corps to be safeguarded.[36] A Department of Development for the Canadian Ministry of Supply was to be set up, staffed by persons who would have "the widest jurisdiction in taking on new ideas and suggestions." McNaughton passed on his own ideas for the consideration of the new department, which included specific points that would improve the design of guns, ammunition and explosives; he wanted a better powder fuse for airburst-ranging. There should be a rubber track for the universal carrier and torsion rubber suspension to reduce pitching, and thus give better gunnery. Above all, he wanted landing craft for combined operations at the very earliest date and expressed the hope that these "would be manned by the Canadian Navy for the Canadian Corps."[37] And as for research in Canada, McNaughton heard in July that all three Canadian services now accepted without any question the National Research Council as a co-ordinating body.[38] The Ministry of Supply, with its new development facilities, was working in close association with Dr. C. J. Mackenzie at NRC and, as McNaughton told the Minister, C. D. Howe, would bring "fresh minds and energy" to bear on improvements and developments to meet the ever-changing needs of war.[39]

In the fall McNaughton took stock of the Canadian Corps. He was satisfied that "ceaseless training by day and by night in all the intricacies of modern mechanized warfare, through all the phases from teaching skill at arms to the individual to the combination of units, divisions and larger formations in the order of battle—and their exercise in co-operation the one with the other" had resulted in a force that was thoroughly prepared for battle. Behind the Corps stood "a united people, determined to ensure that we lack for nothing that is required—effective training in Canada for the recruits and reinforcements that will later join our ranks—factories converted to the production of munitions and new ones created to meet our needs, their output now coming forward in a rising flood—constant care for our loved ones left at home and friendly forethought for the spiritual and social welfare of those who are with us here." There had so far been little action against the enemy, and for that McNaughton thanked "Divine Providence"; otherwise "the instrument we forge might well have been destroyed in the making."[40]

The organization of the Corps, training and the design and development of proper weapons, took up a considerable part of

McNaughton's time. He was also immersed in political matters which proved as time-consuming, at any rate, as any other of his duties. Lord Bessborough, in his book, again provides the framework:

. . . here was a most remarkable man—a man of genius who was as able a commander in the field as he was a ballistician and, it might also be said, politician. For it was to a considerable extent necessary for him to be a politician too. Unlike other British corps commanders he had to deal direct with his own Prime Minister, service ministers and politicians as well as with the authorities in the United Kingdom. Members of the Royal Family, diplomats and other distinguished visitors including our own Prime Minister, and Generals de Gaulle and Sikorski* were frequent visitors to his headquarters. That he was able to perform his triple role showed an intelligence and energy of the highest order. I may say that he kept two ADCs, as well as a large corps staff, very busy indeed. As there were only twenty-four hours in the day there were inevitably moments when the troops felt that insufficient time was spent inspecting them; and no doubt there were occasions when the politicians felt that more attention should have been paid to them by the corps commander. But as others have found in high positions, it is impossible to satisfy everyone every moment of the day.[41]

The chronicle of McNaughton's hosts and guests throughout the year is indeed a large one and no attempt will be made to summarize it here. A brief indication only can be given.

In January, while Ralston was still in England, McNaughton attended a "Wolfe" luncheon at Westerham with the Duke of Devonshire, Vincent Massey, C. D. Howe and Ralston.[42] Later that month he lunched with Lieutenant-General Sir Clive Liddell, Governor and Commander-in-Chief, Gibraltar, and met Captain David Margesson, who had succeeded Eden as Secretary of State for War.[43] Another luncheon followed on the last day of January with the Lord Mayor and Lady Mayoress of London at the Mansion House.[44]

During February Winston Churchill, General Sikorski and General de Gaulle were his guests at Headley Court. They watched a

---

*Prime Minister of the Polish Government in Exile.

demonstration of armour staged by Norrie's armoured division and discussed the help the Canadians could give the Poles and French in training. After luncheon Churchill and McNaughton animatedly discussed the role of artillery under present-day conditions and McNaughton's views made a deep impression; for though it was some time before they appeared from the pen of Churchill, they are reflected in a message which he caused to be circulated throughout the army in his capacity as Minister of Defence: "Renown awaits the Commander who first, in this war, restores the artillery to its prime importance upon the battlefield from which it has been ousted by heavily armoured tanks. . . ." Churchill then set out certain rules by which this might be achieved: every field gun or mobile anti-aircraft gun should carry a proportion of solid armour-piercing tracer shot so that every such gun would become an anti-tank gun and every battery possess its own anti-tank protection;* and batteries must stand their ground and await the attack of tanks in order to destroy a proportion of them—"our guns must no more retreat on the approach of tanks than Wellington's squares at Waterloo on the approach of hostile cavalry."†[45]

Also that month Margesson lunched informally with McNaughton, as did Lord Riverdale, chairman of the Advisory Council to the Committee of the Privy Council on Scientific and Industrial Research; Major-General His Royal Highness The Duke of Gloucester was an overnight guest at the McNaughtons' home. In March Lord Cranborne, Secretary of State for Dominion Affairs, and Malcolm MacDonald, High Commissioner (Designate) to Canada for the United Kingdom, visited the Corps with Massey; Ernest Bevin, the British Minister of Labour, was a guest for dinner a few days later. Throughout the year McNaughton's visitors included the King and Queen, who inspected all units of the 2nd Canadian Division; His Majesty The King of Norway; Lady

---

*McNaughton eventually went one better than this; he invented a small-calibre solid projectile which would emerge from a field gun at a much higher velocity than the normal field gun shell. This is discussed under the year 1942.

†One of McNaughton's favourite books was *The Journal of the Waterloo Campaign* by General Cavalie Mercer. No more graphic description can exist than Mercer's account of the French cavalry charging against the British infantry—and, more to the point, into the mouths of Mercer's guns.

Patricia Ramsay; distinguished soldiers (and some who were to distinguish themselves, including Lieutenant-General B. L. Montgomery, the newly appointed C-in-C South Eastern Command); and politicians, both British and Canadian.

There were other calls on McNaughton's time which the General gave unsparingly. He would not, for example, miss a memorial service for Sir Frederick Banting* at St. Martin-in-the-Fields, Trafalgar Square. And, on a day of spring sunshine when a light breeze ruffled daffodils and tulips, he stood in Brookwood Cemetery, near Bisley, to watch Captain P. F. Seagram carried to his grave; Seagram, McNaughton's former ADC, had been killed by a bomb in London.[46] In July, out of loyalty to his old chief, McNaughton was present in the House of Lords to see R. B. Bennett take his seat as a viscount.[47]

What of McNaughton himself? War correspondents, who observed him closely, have described the General at that period of his life. He was tall—an inch short of six feet—and very thin. Almost invariably he wore battledress that never seemed quite to fit and usually some fault could be found with his appearance; though his uniform had been pressed to perfection, "the collar of his tunic got turned up as he put it on" and he would never notice. He was a man "who forgot about himself so long ago, he probably doesn't even see himself when he is shaving." His hair was unruly and "a lock of it invariably hangs down over his forehead." They saw him "standing on a hilltop on a blustery winter day in his old trench coat and the battledress that still doesn't seem to fit, quietly laying down the law about attack tactics as the troops advance over the gorse below"; they watched him, "buoyant, confident, determined," addressing "a London meeting of distinguished scientists" and "presiding at general staff meetings, interested and acquainted in detail with practically every subject touched upon." And "always you see a grave soldier whose responsibilities show in his face."[48]

He lived modestly and had no real hobby. Though Samuel

---

*Who died as a result of an air crash in Newfoundland during March.

Johnson said, "He who does not mind his belly will hardly mind anything else," McNaughton would have proved him wrong; he minded many things but would eat anything that was put in front of him and was often so engrossed in what he was doing that he sometimes forgot about mealtimes entirely. He drank little. "His favorite drink is sherry and his consumption of this is confined almost entirely to a glass before dinner." Though fond of fishing he found little time for that. "He hopefully carries a fishing rod around in his car. But it is getting rusty, for he has had only a few opportunities to cast in English streams." It was the same with chess. He read a little, not "the general run of current literature . . . It is a scientific or a military book that he would be inclined to pick up in an idle hour." At his home, Largiebeg, in the village of Tyrrell's Wood, near Leatherhead, he was a "fixer-upper." "The more appliances that go wrong in his home, the happier he is, and guests are likely to arrive of an evening and find the G.O.C., Canadian Army Overseas, down on his hands and knees behind a bureau tinkering with an electric light plug."[49] "He was a blend of kindliness and great efficiency, of modesty and full confidence. . . . Only when one has visited other corps headquarters and has noted the iron majesty of the corps commander does one appreciate the simple humility of General McNaughton."[50]

He got on well with the troops, who loved him and knew him affectionately as "Andy." "In dealing with his men he has drawn on his understanding of the psychology of handling people and getting from them the maximum of confidence and co-operation." Officers and men were moved by his frequent displays of thoughtfulness and courteousness. And his thoroughness—his mastery of detail—at first charmed, then bewildered, and finally hypnotized his hearers. The number of stories that still cluster around McNaughton's name are evidence enough of the power of his personality.

When you are in conversation with him he fixes you with his piercing, penetrating eyes as you speak. If you are asking him a question he weighs every word you say, his eyebrows will be puckered together in a frown of concentration and his whole attention is riveted on you and what you are saying. Then when he gives you his answer it will be the fullest and most easily understood answer it is in his power to give. As he speaks he works on and develops each idea, each sentence, with the same precision and exactness he would bring to a laboratory experiment. But this doesn't mean that his conversation is studied and stiff. It's merely an outcome of his inborn high regard for detail and exactness. He never talks down to you and as an officer once said, "The great thing about McNaughton is that when he's talking to you he takes it for granted he is talking to an intelligent person." There is not an ounce of sham, ostentation or pomposity in him.[51]

"As a man," one correspondent concluded, "McNaughton may definitely be rated as great. Anybody who has been in contact with him cannot help but feel he has a mind, an outstanding mind, one of the greatest Canada has produced. One comes away from seeing him at work among his troops or from a conversation with him, saying to oneself: That man's a genius."[52]

McNaughton naturally studied the overall war situation with care, for that could have a direct bearing on the employment of his troops. He had followed Wavell's campaigns in the Western Desert and East Africa with the greatest interest and had congratulated him on his success. Naval operations in the Atlantic, and their effect on Canadian convoys, he especially noted and he was gratified when, in May of 1941, Admiral Tovey (his old classmate at the Defence College) sent the *Bismarck* down; but he did not know then that his cathode ray direction finder had played a part in Tovey's triumph.

After sinking HMS *Hood* near the Denmark Strait on 24 May *Bismarck* slipped away from her British pursuers and on the morning of the 25th had broken contact; had Admiral Lütjens remained silent he might have reached St. Nazaire unscathed. Instead, wrote the British naval historian Lieutenant-Commander P. K. Kemp, he "transmitted a long wireless message to Germany giving an account of his action with the *Hood*" and this at a time when "every wireless direction-finding station in the Empire had been instructed to keep a watch on [*Bismarck's*] frequency."[53]

We have already noted the principles on which McNaughton's CRDF apparatus worked.* A thin, luminous line would point directly towards the transmitted signal. With sets, for example, installed in the south of England, the north of Scotland, and at various locations on Canada's Atlantic seaboard a number of different bearings would result. The intersection of those bearings would accurately position *Bismarck*. It was more involved than that but security regulations preclude giving a more detailed account to show how it was definitely known that the transmission came from *Bismarck;* all that can be said is that "one or two signals from the German ship were identified by Radio Fingerprint," a method whereby "the display on the Cathode Ray Tube of any particular signal" was photographed and associated with "the known characteristics of particular wireless sets and/or their operators."[54] At any rate, the bearings came in by signal and were plotted in the Admiralty where it was immediately realized that the German ship was making for a Biscay port. A British naval force (Force H) and HMS *Rodney* were at once alerted in that direction, as was the Home Fleet some time later. The chase was on. Carrier-borne planes located and crippled the German vessel. Finally, on the morning of 27 May, the *Bismarck,* pounded by gunfire into "a black, ragged ruin of a once-proud ship," was sent to the bottom by torpedoes.[55]

Two enormously significant events occurred in 1941. Anthony Eden, who was at Chequers, described the first. Early on 22 June Churchill's valet entered Eden's bedroom bearing a cigar on a silver tray. "The Prime Minister's compliments," he said, "and the German armies have invaded Russia."[56] The second occurred in December with Japan's sudden aggression against British and American interests in the Far East and the Pacific, which plunged the United States into the war against the Axis Powers. Only one aspect of the latter event immediately concerns us here. Two Canadian battalions—the first troops from Canada to fight in this war—capitulated with the rest of the garrison at Hong Kong on

---

*See *McNaughton*, Volume 1, pp. 221-2.

Christmas Day after stubborn fighting. The transport for the Canadian units, which had followed, had not reached Hong Kong when the Japanese attacked. At a subsequent inquiry, however, it was found, having regard to the rough, mountainous country over which the Canadians fought, that this had made little difference. The Conservatives, who wished to make political capital out of the dispatch of Canadian reinforcing troops, the lack of transport, and their defeat, tried hard to elicit a statement from McNaughton to the effect that the availability of vehicles would have made a difference to the outcome of the fighting. McNaughton would not say so. It must be remembered that he had studied the problem posed by the defence of Hong Kong at the Imperial Defence College; it had been accepted then that the best that could be hoped for was that Hong Kong would hold out for a time until relieved. In the circumstances at Hong Kong in December, 1941, there was no hope of relief; the troops did all that they could have been expected to do. George Drew, a leading member of the Conservative Party (who had pressed McNaughton hard), never forgave him for his refusal. His animosity towards McNaughton dates from that time.[57]

Hitler's invasion of Russia in June obviously altered the strategic picture. Although an invasion of Britain was still possible, it was hardly probable with large German land and air forces thrusting towards the East, and McNaughton began to look beyond the island citadel. At the end of June he sent Brigadier Burns (who had replaced the engaging Dempsey* as BGS, Canadian Corps) to the War Office on a fact-finding mission concerning the future employment of Canadian troops. Burns found out from Brigadier A. W. S. Mallaby (Deputy Director of Military Operations) "that it was understood in the War Office that Canadian troops were not available for employment elsewhere than in the United Kingdom." Nothing in the past could have led to that

---

*Dempsey had left the Canadian Corps, after almost a year with McNaughton, to command the British 46th Division during the first week in June. His experience with the Canadians led to excellent Anglo-Canadian relations in Second Army, which Dempsey afterwards commanded.

conclusion; McNaughton had made his troops available for Norway, Dunkirk and Brittany. The "understanding" which the War Office had could have come from Brooke, following Exercise VICTOR earlier in the year. Burns then set the record straight. The Canadian government had never taken such a stand:

. . . the position was that it would consider any proposals put forward by the Government of the United Kingdom. In considering such proposals the Canadian Government would rely, to a great extent, on advice received from the Commander of the Canadian Army Overseas, Lieutenant-General McNaughton [whose] views had always been that it was not the province of the Canadian Army Overseas to initiate suggestions for its employment, but he was always ready to advise the Canadian Government in favour of the employment of the Canadian Forces in any theatre where the need for their services could be demonstrated by the authorities responsible for strategic planning. . . . Lieutenant-General McNaughton, however, had always considered it a principle that the bulk of the Canadian Military Forces should be employed in one theatre, so that Canadian authority over our troops could be properly maintained, and would not favour any course of action that would involve splitting the Canadian Army Overseas into several packets.[58]

Mallaby, satisfied that the Canadian position had now been clarified, told Burns that he would inform Dewing of the conversation. Tentatively, Burns and Mallaby examined the Middle East as a possible theatre; the distance from Vancouver to Suez, via Singapore, was no greater than from the British Isles to Suez via the Cape, and large ships then transporting Australian and New Zealand troops might be used to carry Canadian formations still in Canada. If the Canadians were required in the Middle East, Burns suggested, the project should be studied at once and a decision taken before the 3rd Canadian Infantry Division and the armoured division started to move to Britain.[59] Mallaby saw Dewing the same day, but the outcome was disappointing. Though Dewing had been "most interested" in the possibility of using the Canadians in the Middle East he considered it "premature to raise the issue now because our requirements for home defence against the possibility of an invasion in the autumn preclude our sending further considerable forces overseas"; he would keep it in mind and bring it up "for further consideration when the invasion season can fairly be considered to be past."[60]

The ball was now in the British court and, for the time being, McNaughton was content to leave it there. With Russia under heavy German pressure, the British sought to help, not by invasion—there was no strength for that—but by raids against the enemy-held coast. McNaughton looked to raids to provide battle-indoctrination for his men, and wished the Canadian naval forces to co-operate in these enterprises. On 22 July he suggested to representatives of the RCN that not only would this be of great benefit in combined operations, but in the postwar period it would "tend to bring the Canadian Naval and Military Forces together." The naval representatives agreed that it would be a good idea, but it would be some months before they could participate because of the shortage of ships.[61]

With the chance of raids in the offing, McNaughton feared a repetition of what had happened when he had detailed troops for Norway without seeking prior approval from Canada. Indeed, it seemed that Ralston's intransigence was continuing, for he had announced in the House during April, 1941, that, in so far as the employment of Canadian troops was concerned on the Continent or anywhere else, "the position is clear, namely, that the decision would rest entirely with the Canadian Government."[62] It was obvious to McNaughton that the success of raids must depend on strict secrecy and fine timing and he asked Ian Mackenzie (Minister of Pensions and National Health), who visited England that summer, to request the War Cabinet to free his hands. Before he had heard anything from Canada, Dill asked McNaughton to carry out a raid on Spitsbergen which, the General told Ottawa, he was arranging to do unless he received instructions to the contrary. The reply, a cable from Crerar, left the decision to McNaughton's judgment.[63]

The expedition to Spitsbergen was successfully carried out at the end of August by some six hundred Canadian troops. Coal mines, stocks of coal and wireless stations useful to the enemy were destroyed; and Russian and Norwegian miners were removed from the archipelago and transported to Russia or to Britain. But no fighting had taken place, and though Dill, with his customary generosity, praised the operation in a warm personal letter of congratulations to McNaughton,[64] there was little satisfaction for the troops in that. Though others were fighting, they had been overseas for two years now and had yet to meet the Germans in battle. Because of the successful outcome of this minor operation, however, McNaughton's powers were widened; he was now permitted to take immediate action to commit his troops to raids or similar operations[65] but nothing came of this until April, 1942, when a small party of Canadians participated with the British in a raid on the French coast near Boulogne; their craft failed to put them ashore, and though the Germans fired at them the Canadians took no active part in the operation.

Despite McNaughton's willingness to fight his Corps wherever it might be needed the summer passed with his men still committed to an anti-invasion role whose significance seemed illusory. Towards the end of August Mackenzie King arrived in England and on the 23rd, with Captain David Margesson and Vincent Massey, he attended the Canadian track and field championships at Aldershot, where he delivered a short address to the troops. "At the beginning there were some vocal interruptions," wrote the correspondent of the Toronto *Globe and Mail*, but in his opinion these were "rather in the nature of a lark and symptomatic of a certain impatience to get into action." "The plain fact is," said McNaughton, who was a member of King's party, "that he was booed." And the Prime Minister knew it; he whispered to Mrs. McNaughton immediately afterwards, "Don't worry; a politician soon develops a tough hide."[66] The reason for the outburst, McNaughton thought, was that Mackenzie King had been very late in arriving and had kept the men waiting in pouring rain. But resentment of the passive role in Britain may certainly also have had something to do with it.

McNaughton had many discussions with the Prime Minister and

Mackenzie King with the McNaughtons on his visit to Canadian troops,
Aldershot, August, 1941

The senior military officers in Britain, 1941/42

Maj.-Gen. C. J. S. King, Lt.-Gen. A. G. L. McNaughton, Lt.-Gen. A. F. N. Thorne, Maj.-Gen. A. E. Percival, Lt.-Gen. L. Carr, Maj.-Gen. O. M. Lund, Maj.-Gen. C. W. M. Norrie, Maj.-Gen. R. L. McCreery, Maj.-Gen. J. T. Crocker, Maj.-Gen. J. L. I. Hawkesworth, Maj.-Gen. M. B. Beckwith Smith, Lt.-Gen. G. Le Q. Martel, Maj.-Gen. V. V. Pope, Maj.-Gen. N. M. S. Irwin, Maj.-Gen. M. B. Burrows, Maj.-Gen. R. J. Collins, Lt.-Gen. H. R. S. Massy, Air Vice Marshal P. C. Maltby, Captain J. L. Storey, R.N., Air Vice Marshal R. H. M. S. Saundby, Maj.-Gen. H. B. D. Willcox, Lt.-Gen. B. C. T. Paget, Lt.-Gen. The Hon. H. R. L. G. Alexander, Lt.-Gen. Sir Ronald Adam, Bt., Lt.-Gen. Sir Guy Williams, General The Viscount Gort, General Sir Alan Brooke, General Sir Robert Gordon-Finlayson, Lt.-Gen. Sir R. Carrington, Lt.-Gen. F. P. Nosworthy, Lt.-Gen. Sir Wilfrid Lindsell.

there was sympathy between them. Both believed that conscription, which had become an urgent topic at home, would be wrong. It would have been better, McNaughton said, if there had been no conscription in the last war; in this one it would have a harmful effect on national unity. He did, however, advocate the most careful planning for the disposition of manpower. Mackenzie King's insistence on Canada's maintaining her hard-won position was constitutionally absolutely right; his stand was of great value to McNaughton when "dealing with the Government here."[67]

All this was satisfactory. What was not so pleasing to the Prime Minister was the personality clash between McNaughton and Ralston, which the General did not trouble to hide. When informed that Ralston wished to visit Britain again, and asked whether that would be helpful, McNaughton replied: "You have asked me a straight question and I will give you a straight answer. I do not think it would." Ralston interfered in matters outside the "ministerial sphere"; he bogged himself down in detail and was difficult at the best of times. What was required was to have "the general lines of policy" defined by Ralston, leaving Mc-Naughton to work out the details himself. Mackenzie King could see "there was real feeling there" and, on his return to Canada he soon found that the hostility was mutual. Ralston was "quite antagonistic" towards McNaughton who, he said, was anxious "to get everything into his own hands." The Defence Minister, King commented, unfortunately had "the same weakness."[68] This state of affairs clearly could not last; there was bound to be a showdown sooner or later between Ralston and McNaughton.

On 26 August, still in England, the Prime Minister addressed the men of the 1st Canadian Division who had been almost two years in Britain. Churchill had told him, he said, that the Canadian Corps was being retained for the defence of Britain—the "most significant of all the factors that would ultimately determine the outcome of the war. The United Kingdom," King pointed out, "is the citadel of liberty and you have been given the honour of defending that citadel." He had made it very clear to Churchill that "the Canadian Government places no restrictions whatever upon any decision that may be made, other than that the Government itself shall have the opportunity of knowing what is contemplated and an opportunity of expressing views."[69] Should the Canadian force remain unified under Canadian command—a national ideal and the rock on which Canada's military policy had previously been founded? Or was King now beginning to veer towards considering the employment of the force in parts? The last is most unlikely, but the question was being considered by others.

In the autumn Colonel Ralston, accompanied by General Crerar, came to England. They discussed the employment of Canadian troops with McNaughton, who said that he had been repeatedly told by the British that the best service Canada could render was to remain in Britain until the time was opportune for the Corps to take part in an expeditionary force abroad. Crerar demurred; perhaps the Canadian Corps could be employed in the Middle East "either in whole or in part." McNaughton reiterated his view that the "best employment" of the Canadian Corps for the coming winter was for it to remain in Great Britain but that in the spring "it might be practicable to participate in operations elsewhere . . . as a Corps."[70] The exchange is important; it points to the fundamental difference between McNaughton and Crerar on this question of the integrity of the Canadian force. Ralston did not indicate where he stood on this occasion but it was largely at his prompting that the Canadian Army was split in 1943.

In October the Canadian Corps relieved the British IV Corps in the direct defence of the Sussex coast.[71] With growing British strength the importance of the Corps in GHQ Reserve had steadily diminished but before accepting the role of a "static corps" McNaughton made one proviso: the claims of the Canadians to lead a future offensive should not be overlooked. Brooke agreed.[72] At the end of the year the Corps, augmented by the 3rd Canadian Infantry Division, the 1st Canadian Army Tank Brigade and, finally, the 5th Canadian (Armoured) Division, guarded English beaches under Lieutenant-General B. L. Montgomery who had succeeded General Paget. Paget, in turn, had succeeded Brooke as C-in-C Home Forces and Brooke now filled Dill's shoes in the exalted position of Chief of the Imperial General Staff. McNaughton could not be enthusiastic over the last appointment.

It had been much to the joy of all of us that Dill had taken over the post of C.I.G.S. But he wasn't there very long before it became evident that he was not, and would never be, *persona grata* with Churchill who had very extraordinary ideas. So Dill left to join the Combined Chiefs of Staff in Washington and Brooke was selected by Churchill to become C.I.G.S. Then, in general policy, I was dealing direct with Brooke and with a new group of staff officers from the V.C.G.S.* downwards who were Brooke's men— this appalling business always in the British Army that each senior commander on the way up collects a number of satellites around him, a thing I tried to avoid in the Canadian army at all costs. The kindly, co-operative, mutual confidence that had existed under Dill became a thing of the past.[73]

Though the role of the Corps was static the fields of France gleamed in McNaughton's eyes. At a dramatic press conference in the fall, with the writers grouped around him, he gave a "more enlightening report" on the army, its intentions and its purpose "than he had voiced publicly up to that time. It was a masterly job."[74] What excited them most was a phrase he used for the first time: "The Canadian Army is a dagger pointed at the heart of Berlin."

The time for that was far in the future. As he told Crerar, "I have watched with interest the organization here of such special units as Commandos, Ski Battalions and Paratroops. The cycle is always the same—initial enthusiasm which is very high, drawing good officers and men from regular units, distracting and unsettling others, and upsetting the units' organization. With a prolonged period spent in awaiting the appropriate opportunity for employment, the enthusiasm evaporates. Officers and men ask to re-transfer, and return to their former units disappointed. . . . In consequence I do not advocate the establishment of any separate Paratroops in the Canadian Forces. As and when prospective operations indicate the need for landing troops by parachute . . .

---

*Vice-Chief of the General Staff.

I propose to select existing units and give them the appropriate extra specialized training."[75] He was in no hurry as yet to train troops for an invasion role, but the proper time would come. Until then he could be patient; perfecting his machine until it was ready to be launched at the peak of its power upon the enemy. The United States' entry into the war in December, he was sure, brought that day appreciably closer.

It had been a back-breaking year for McNaughton, far harder than commanding troops in battle. Problems of organization, war establishments, manpower, reinforcements, supplies and equipment, trucks, tanks and armoured cars, the design of new weapons and a thousand other matters had crossed his desk; dressed simply in battledress, like his men, his spare figure had always been present somewhere on manoeuvres, wet or fine, closely observing the progress made; he had been the host to royalty, statesmen, diplomats, scientists, industrialists and soldiers. There had been few breaks from his fifteen-hours-a-day routine—a weekend here and there, and one or two visits with Mrs. McNaughton* to the London theatres—and though he liked simple fun there had not been much of that. Once Bickersteth, in his old tweed suit, had been apprehended by a security-minded sentry who, impressed by his claim to be a member of the General's mess, had taken him there to be identified; Hertzberg, summoned to the door, looked coldly at the figure that always confronted him each morning across the breakfast table and said, "A member of the mess, is he? Never saw him in my life!" McNaughton chuckled over that for days.

He was fifty-four now, a little greyer than when he had arrived in England. He was drawn and the lines of responsibility were cut deeply into his face. For two years he had shouldered a heavy burden and though he still applied himself with absolute concentration to the task he had set himself and continued to suggest,

---

*She, at least, had one change of scene when she visited Ireland in November, 1941. At the invitation of the Admiralty, accompanied by her son Ian, she launched the aircraft carrier HMS *Unicorn* at Belfast.

urge and cajole with all the old dynamism, the strain was beginning to tell. In November he was obliged to write to Paget that he was "in the hands of our medical authorities with a low grade infection in the chest and will be away from duty for about two months when, they assure me, I will again be fully fit and able to resume command."*[76] Worn out with work, he recovered slowly, and the doctors advised recuperation until the end of February. It was a quiet period. No action for the Corps could be foreseen, and when McNaughton proposed to visit Canada to see the progress of munitions production at first hand and to discuss plans for the coming year, no difficulties arose. On 23 January, 1942, with Mrs. McNaughton, the General sailed.

---

*There was great concern in Canada. "That Lieut.-General McNaughton," read an editorial in the Ottawa *Journal* of 13 November, "will be restored speedily to complete health and strength must be the prayer of every Canadian. Few men in the war against Adolf Hitler are more vital to victory. It is doubtful whether Canadians realize fully the place that 'Andy' McNaughton has come to hold in the minds of all those who make a difference in this war. . . ." Second only to Churchill, McNaughton was "incomparably the most powerful mind, the most impressive personality, on the landscape of the war in England. . . . We know that this view of General McNaughton is shared by the people of England; shared certainly by those directing England's war effort. Here, they believe, is one of the few really commanding figures thrown up by the struggle against Hitler, one who, if God spares him, is destined to take a tremendous part in the achievement of final victory."

Chapter 9

1942: The Father of the Army

The Atlantic crossing in HMS *Ausonia,* an armed merchant cruiser, was rough. McNaughton spent the greater part of eight uncomfortable days in preparing notes on two major subjects that he intended to discuss in Canada. The first was the creation of a Canadian army of two army corps during 1942, which Prime Minister Mackenzie King announced in the House of Commons while McNaughton was on the ocean two days out from Liverpool; the second, as we have seen, concerned the Canadian production of weapons and equipment.

The First Canadian Army was, in fact, the first field army in Canadian history. McNaughton was to build it and by doing so he became widely known as "The Father of the Canadian Army." But the original suggestion that Canada should have an army had not been his; it had been made by Crerar in August, 1941. There was manpower enough, the CGS had indicated to McNaughton, for the expansion of the overseas force without prejudice to industry or other tasks.* Not only would the 4th Division be sent to Britain in 1942, but a second armoured division as well. This, Crerar concluded, would result in too large a corps but, he asked McNaughton, "Have you ever considered the pros and cons of a Canadian Army comprising 2 Corps, each of 2 Divisions and an Armoured Division?"[1] McNaughton, it is clear from his reply a month later,[2] expected the initiative to come from Canada. It was

---

*". . . our departmental studies of manpower available do not indicate that numbers will be a restrictive factor for some time yet in respect to an expansion of the Canadian Army. . . . I might say that our departmental appreciation indicates that manpower is available to maintain a Canadian Army of eight Divisions, of which two will be in Canada, for a war period of over six years from now."

188

not until much later in the year, after he had had talks with Ralston and Crerar during October, that he discussed Crerar's suggestion with the British authorities, when he found that both Paget and Brooke were not against it.

Paget considered that the expansion was "along the right lines"; the corps headquarters should be small and mobile with army headquarters performing "as much of the administration as practicable."[3] Sir Alan Brooke felt that a force or an army headquarters was required which would take over the worry of all the rear services, workshops, base organization and so on, and thus "free the Corps Commanders' hands for the job of commanding and training the fighting formations. That in itself is a full time job!"[4] McNaughton's headquarters then, in the view of no less a person than the Chief of the Imperial General Staff, would deal primarily with organization and administration; the responsibility for "commanding and training the fighting formations" would rest with Corps; and this should be remembered when allegations in 1943 that McNaughton did not concern himself sufficiently with training are discussed.

No sanction for the creation of the army had come from Ottawa as yet. On 23 December Crerar, the strongest exponent of the idea, arrived in England to command the 2nd Canadian Division,* his place as CGS being filled by Kenneth Stuart, McNaughton's old schoolmate at Bishop's College School. Ralston told McNaughton at the end of the month that he would make no decision until they had been able to explore the question fully in Ottawa, but before McNaughton arrived the policy, as the Prime Minister announced on 26 January, had been settled. It was now McNaughton's job to discuss how best the programme could be implemented, and so for the remainder of the voyage he prepared the notes he would need for his talks with Ralston.

It may be doubted if McNaughton saw the creation of an army as the most pressing need. When interviewed in the fall of 1941 by a delegation of Canadian editors—after he had been advised by Crerar to think about forming an army—he had been asked for a

---

*He acted as corps commander during McNaughton's absence in Canada.

message, pointing to the most urgent need of the moment, which could be taken back to the Canadian people. He was reported in *Hansard* to have said:

. . . put every emphasis on the production of weapons and equipment. We need technical improvements such as can be worked out under the direction of the National Research institute and others who work under Mr. Howe. Then these improvements must be put into production quickly. . . .[5]

He would not say how many should go into the army and how many into industry. "We should survey our manpower first. We want no flash in the pan. We must plan for a war of long duration and not put all our goods in the show window now."[6] And it was to stimulate production and the development of new weapons that he had wanted to get back to Canada.

On 3 February the coast of Nova Scotia, backed by snow-covered hills, was sighted during the morning of a sunny winter's day. The ship docked at Halifax and representatives of the press surged round McNaughton as soon as he stepped ashore. During the afternoon he gave an interview in the warmth and comfort of the Nova Scotian Hotel. A part of what he said was carried from coast to coast on the Canadian Broadcasting Corporation's evening programme; across the nation the morning newspapers announced his return.

The weather was still clear shortly after midnight of 4 to 5 February, when the train bringing the McNaughtons to Ottawa drew into the capital, its brightly lit streets so different from blacked-out London. The muffled figures of the Prime Minister, Defence Minister Ralston and others waited on the platform to greet the General and his wife, and the group then passed through the subway below the snowy emptiness of Rideau Street into the Chateau Laurier where the McNaughtons stayed. Mackenzie King, after a short chat with McNaughton, observed that he was "very friendly" (he was, in fact, expansive and overjoyed to be back in Canada) "and will be most helpful. He may even enable us to get over the conscription difficulty."[7]

Nearly two years before, following the fall of France in the summer of 1940, the National Resources Mobilization Act had received assent. This authorized compulsory military service but, honouring the pledges that the government had made at the outbreak of the war, limited it to home defence. In the face of mounting pressure within Canada for compulsory overseas service, which reached a crescendo after Japan's entry into the war in December, 1941, the government now sought release from the pledges it had given in 1939. This it proposed to do by plebiscite, posing to the voters the question: Are you in favour of releasing the government from any obligation arising out of any past commitments restricting the methods of raising men for military service?[8] In subsequent talks with McNaughton,* Mackenzie King obtained the reassurance that he sought. McNaughton, though wholeheartedly for the volunteer system, thought that a promise of no conscription should not have been given at the start but, once made, it should be honoured. To hold a plebiscite was right, for "if we ceased to take account of moral values, we might as well give up the cause we are fighting for . . . nothing could be more harmful than for a Government to ignore its pledges."[9] The Prime Minister was convinced that the pledge had been necessary; without it "Quebec would never have made the contribution to the unity of Canadian effort that she did" and "the highest interest had been served by the course taken." McNaughton agreed that the preservation of unity in Canada was "all-important" and should be kept "constantly in mind."[10]

---

*On the day of the McNaughtons' arrival in Ottawa, the Prime Minister wrote a letter to Mrs. McNaughton which is still in her possession:

"General McNaughton was kind enough to say that he thought you and he would find it possible to give me the pleasure of your company at Laurier House. . . .

"I have been asking myself what would be most pleasant and restful for the General and yourself. I know how many are the friends you would like to see in the course of your short stay, and it may well be that you would enjoy the company of a few of those who are particular personal friends of the General and yourself rather than company that might be quasi-official. . . . My table, unfortunately, is not large. It is intended for twelve but will seat fourteen quite comfortably.

"I was going to ask if you would be so kind and just let me know exactly what you and General McNaughton would most prefer. You see, I am treating you both as very close friends. . . ."

King then turned to the First Canadian Army, the creation of which he had announced in Parliament. Was he right in understanding that McNaughton "did not intend to ask for, and did not wish, a larger army than that for which provision has been made, except, of course, the necessary reinforcements?" McNaughton agreed emphatically; and he wanted volunteers rather than conscripts. It was desirable to get along without conscription. What he was interested in was "selective service—getting into the Army the men best qualified, and getting into industry the men that could serve there"; he stressed the need for "more in the way of war equipment." Throughout these conversations, the Prime Minister recorded with obvious satisfaction, "We were really at one in all our views."[11]

The force for which provision had been made would consist, not of six divisions as Crerar had thought possible, but of five divisions, two of them armoured, and two army tank brigades. "The next step, after the formations now contemplated have been added," McNaughton said to Stuart when discussing the army programme, "will be to provide the ancillary units required to give a thoroughly balanced and substantially self-contained formation from the front-line to the Overseas Base inclusive."[12] Here again we see the emphasis McNaughton always placed on balance and, more especially, on a national force.

McNaughton had many discussions with Ralston and Stuart on the army programme. Now that the government had settled the policy, McNaughton insisted, he should be left a free hand to work out the details. But Ralston, reluctant as always to make any concession that he feared would weaken his own authority, at first made no commitment. Nor was this the only issue between them, for an old conflict that had existed since 1941, concerning the function of Canadian Military Headquarters in England, still required to be resolved. Ralston saw CMHQ as a "forward extension of National Defence Headquarters," while McNaughton considered it "primarily a link in my communications to Canada." All this went back to the visit of the Prime Minister to Britain in 1941, when McNaughton had suggested that authority should be delegated to himself to deal on the spot with such detail as changes in establishment; that CMHQ should be considered a link in his communications to Canada and not a forward echelon of Canadian National Defence Headquarters; and that his authority as the senior combatant officer of the Canadian Army in the United Kingdom should be clearly defined to show exactly what he could deal with without reference to Ottawa. His reasoning, which did not question the need for the Minister to exercise control on policy, was simple: to refer matters of detail across the Atlantic to Canada brought delay that would be eliminated provided he were given "authority to implement established policies" which, after all, could only be decided in England, for the information and experience were available nowhere else.[13]

The clash continued—Stuart calming the contestants as best he could—until 17 March when it was resolved in McNaughton's favour. That day McNaughton was able to tell Mackenzie King that he had reached "a complete understanding" with Ralston about the freedom he was to have in the execution of policy. The understanding had been achieved with the greatest difficulty for, as the Prime Minister described it, McNaughton "had had to talk very plainly to Ralston, even to say to him that he would not continue to hold his present position unless he had the full authority he felt he should have in the matter of executing plans, once policy was settled by the Government."[14] It must have been clear to the Prime Minister that Ralston and McNaughton would never agree; "the difference between them," he acknowledged, "dated back to the time when Ralston was previously Minister of Defence"*[15] and all the indications were that it would continue. But there was no obvious replacement for the Defence Minister (apart from McNaughton), even had Mackenzie King wanted to replace him, and public opinion would certainly not allow McNaughton to be dispensed with. Ralston, as well as the Prime Minister, was quite aware of McNaughton's strong position, and that, without doubt, was why he gave in to McNaughton on this occasion.

McNaughton's return had stirred up scenes of wild enthusiasm

---

*See *McNaughton*, Volume 1, pp. 240-44.

in Canada. Wherever he appeared, usually undemonstrative people crowded forward to catch a glimpse of the soldier they trusted.* Some even tried to touch his clothes. There was agitation in the country, and in Parliament, to bring him back to Canada permanently to lead Canada's war effort (as had been suggested by Banting in 1939), which many felt was drifting under Mackenzie King. In February, 1940, before the general election in March at which Mackenzie King had increased his majority, McNaughton had been approached to lead the Conservative Party. As early as the fall of France, newspapers had contained articles, and even advertisements privately paid for, proclaiming that McNaughton could "build and drive our war machine"; he was the man for "the driver's seat."[17] Others, headed "Calling Canada," exhorted the people to "Bring McNaughton home. He will give Canada the defence we need; he will put new life into our war effort," and described him as the "best civil and military organizer in the Dominion's history." *Time* Magazine was quoted: "Soldiers of Canada and elsewhere rate him the best officer in the British Empire."[18] And in Parliament the Honourable H. A. Bruce, speaking during March, 1942, concluded a strong indictment of the government's lack of decision towards war policy with these words:

I have just one more suggestion to make, which I have saved till the last because, in my opinion, it is the most important of all. I am sure no one will gainsay the truth of my assertion when I say that we have in Canada today a man who has the knowledge and experience, and who stands out as the greatest leader this country has ever produced. I refer to Lieutenant-General A. G. L. McNaughton, whom I now suggest that the Prime Minister appoint as minister of war and deputy prime minister. It may be urged that he could not be spared from his position overseas, but I venture the opinion that after two years of effort and training and planning, someone else could now be found to carry on his duties

---

*"The Canadian people," it was reported, "are interested in this brilliant native son. . . . He has their supreme confidence for they know that they are entrusting their sons and husbands and fathers to a man of clear judgment and balanced outlook. . . . When they go into battle they will be well-equipped and well-led, having a striking power which will be irresistible."[16]

over there. I am sure that this would go a long way toward satis-
fying and relieving the anxious and much perturbed Canadian
people.[19]

The agitation was so strong that the Prime Minister did consult
McNaughton about coming back to Canada but he put it in such
a way that McNaughton would hardly accept recall:

I then said to the General, speaking quite confidentially and intimately between ourselves, that I would like to know your own
mind as respects some of the things that have been suggested, for
example I have been asked by different persons if I would not consider bringing you back to Canada instead of having you continue
in command of the Army overseas. I have replied that I felt a step
of the kind at the present juncture might only serve to break your
heart, as I thought you had before you the formation of an Army,
complete in all respects, and would wish to command it in action.
The General said that was entirely right. . . . I said I thought his
relations with the British High Command were of a character
which no one else could hope to share.[20]

Politically, Mackenzie King recorded, McNaughton's visit had
been of great value. "It has been a splendid thing, his being here
at this time."[21] McNaughton had more than once expressed his
confidence in the government, in the Prime Minister himself, and
he had stated that conscription was unnecessary; nothing more was
required than "keeping the Army at the size now provided for and
seeing that new reinforcements were provided." At a meeting of
the Cabinet War Committee, he stressed his "readiness to have
Ottawa determine the policy fully but urged the desirability of
leaving to himself and his organization the actual working out of
details." Though there was a growing agitation in Canada for a
more active role for Canadian troops, McNaughton emphasized
"the importance of the Canadian Army remaining intact in Britain to hold the heart of Britain, and to be ready when the time
came to invade the Continent." Although Mackenzie King seemed
to have convinced himself that McNaughton and Ralston had been
able to "reconcile their differences" this was far from being the
case. The Prime Minister's earlier statement that "each of them
has been greatly exercised over the possibility of not having the

final say" was shrewder and he might have surmised that Mc-Naughton's victory would only make Ralston the more determined to have the better of the argument at the next inevitable clash.[22]

Though McNaughton's visit was politically useful, that was no more than a by-product of what he had come to do. He had obtained a free hand with the detail that would attend the creation of the army and that, of course, was helpful; he now turned to the main reason for his journey: Canadian weapons production and an organization for the manufacture of better weapons in the future. On his first day in Ottawa, even before visiting the Prime Minister at his office in the House of Commons on the evening of 5 February, he had had a long talk with Dr. Mackenzie at NRC, when they had explored the ground.

Next day, with Victor Sifton (the capable Master General of the Ordnance) and Major-General Macrae (Adviser on Armaments to the Department of Munitions and Supply), McNaughton travelled to Montreal. That day and the next were spent in touring various plants: the Angus shops of the Canadian Pacific Railway where they saw Valentine tanks in process of manufacture; the Longueuil plant to see the production of six-pounder anti-tank guns; the Montreal Locomotive Works to watch the assembly of Ram tanks; and Sorel Industries where twenty-five-pounder guns and four-inch naval guns were being made. On the evening of the 6th, at the Windsor Hotel, McNaughton addressed the annual banquet of the Engineering Institute of Canada* and laid great stress on the importance for victory of the mass production of newer and better weapons. Before leaving Montreal on the evening of the 7th the McNaughtons called on the Governor-General (the Earl of Athlone) at the Ritz Carlton, where McNaughton gave an account of military affairs in England and explained what he was seeking to do in Canada.

---

*On this occasion, particularly, people surged around McNaughton, seeking to be recognized or just to touch him. Referred to in the press as "the idol of all Canada," he was described as "a very great speaker, his kindness and frankness and earnestness of speech give one the impression that the listener is having a personal conversation with him, rather than listening to a lecture on some deep subject."[23]

Shortly after his return to Ottawa, McNaughton presided over a meeting held in the Defence Council room to discuss the setting up of a Weapons Development Committee for the purpose, as McNaughton put it, "of co-ordinating and forwarding the development of new weapons and technical equipment." Briefly, McNaughton felt that the weapons and equipment of the British Army were not of a sufficiently modern standard. Those of the enemy were noticeably better. For two years he had had to be patient while Canadian industry was changing over from a peacetime to a wartime footing. This, as he had seen in Montreal, was now well advanced and one of the primary reasons for his present visit was to propose ways and means of ensuring that the Canadian forces should, in future, be equipped with the newest and most efficient weapons.

British industry, he said, was based on a corps of highly skilled tradesmen and there were none better in any country in the world. This expert skill was the foundation of British armament design, which, as a result, was not generally of a type suited to the methods of modern American mass production. Thus, while certain weapons were excellent, they were not produced in sufficient quantity. North American manufacturing methods, on the other hand, had been reduced to the utmost simplicity, so that mass production processes could be used to turn out quantities of almost every type of equipment with less highly skilled all-round workmen.

The chief fault with the British system, however, apart from its lower yield of weapons, was that the complacent Ordnance Board often overrode the officials responsible for design. Its members failed to take heed of what the user stated was required in battle. Instead, they produced what *they* felt was needed and, in fact, their attitude often appeared to be that the army must take what it was given and, moreover, like it.

McNaughton was not prepared to accept that. Over the past year and more he had built up the Staff Duties section at CMHQ in London with specialist officers so that a constant flow of the latest technical information and "user" information was available to the committee, whose function would be to examine proposals from the Canadian Army Overseas concerning developments and to set up research and design groups to execute such projects as might be found to be practicable.[24]

The soundness of McNaughton's proposals was appreciated and the government accepted them. A committee was set up consisting of Victor Sifton, chairman, and with Dr. Mackenzie (NRC), H. J. Carmichael and R. E. Jamieson (Department of Munitions and Supply) and Colonel G. P. Morrison (Director of Technical Research) as members. It began to function while McNaughton was still in Canada.[25]

Towards the end of February McNaughton, accompanied by Dr. Mackenzie, saw what industry was doing in western Ontario. They visited Research Enterprises (largely Mackenzie's creation) in Toronto where they saw G.L. III sets—directional radar for gun-laying—being made. These were the sets which, in the words of General Sir Frederick Pile, "proved such a godsend to us when the enemy resumed his heavy night raids in the winter of 1943" and were, he went on, "indeed a triumph for Canadian scientists and Canadian production."[26] At various factories in Toronto, the "steel city" of Hamilton, and Windsor they saw guns, small arms (including Sten sub-machine-guns), munitions and vehicles being turned out in quantity. McNaughton addressed the assembled representatives of these industries at luncheons and dinners and also talked to the workers as they came off shift. His theme was always the same: that Canadian industry had done a magnificent job in converting from a peace to a war footing; and to urge the radical improvement of old weapons, the development of new ones,* and the design of all of them for North American mass production methods.[27]

He also had many opportunities to discuss the work of NRC with Mackenzie, the acting president. McNaughton was preoccupied with the problem of obtaining higher velocities for projectiles for use against tanks and aircraft. Mackenzie agreed to experiment with a high-powered rifle to discover the critical velocity for the greatest penetration of armour while keeping a

---

*At the gun shop of the John Inglis factory, for example, McNaughton urged the development of a twenty-millimetre rapid fire gun for anti-aircraft purposes; at St. Catharines Foundry Products he wanted development work started with high-velocity projectiles and new types of armour.

constant striking energy; in other words, a progressively lighter bullet would be used with a steadily increasing muzzle velocity. Their discussions ranged over plastic armour, powder metallurgy and other technical matters.

On 27 February, in Toronto, McNaughton was invited to attend a luncheon at the Royal York Hotel in honour of a Chinese delegation visiting Canada from Washington. The luncheon had a sequel. Lachlan Currie, one of President Roosevelt's executive assistants, accompanied the delegation and over the meal he had a short talk with McNaughton. Their brief chat so impressed him that as soon as dessert was over he telephoned Roosevelt, which resulted in a request by the President to Mackenzie King for McNaughton to visit him at the White House. McNaughton heard of this from the Prime Minister when he got back to Ottawa, and in consequence his return to Britain was postponed from 12 to 19 March to enable him to make the trip.[28]

McNaughton and his wife flew to Washington on the morning of 8 March in an aircraft provided by the RCAF. They were met by Major-General Maurice Pope (the Canadian Military Representative) and had tea at the Canadian Legation, where Field-Marshal Sir John Dill and Lieutenant-General H. C. B. Wemyss (head of the British Army Staff in Washington) came to meet them. McNaughton, in a talk with Dill, could only speculate about what the President would wish to discuss with him but he thought it would be the setting up of the Weapons Development Committee in Canada and chemical warfare developments at Suffield in Alberta. He gave the reasons for setting up the committee and Dill, as the Canadian government had done, saw their force. He too, he said, had been most unhappy at times with the attitude of those controlling British designers, and Wemyss (an engineer) agreed that the army had suffered from the unco-operative attitude on the part of officials of the British Ministry of Supply. Both felt that the British Army, as well as the Canadian, would eventually benefit from McNaughton's initiative.[29]

Next morning McNaughton met General George C. Marshall

(Chief of Staff, United States Army) at the War Department. He outlined the Canadian Army programme for the year: "an Army of two Corps complete with Corps, Army, Line of Communications and Base Units down to and including the fourth echelon of maintenance." The army would have an air force component of six squadrons completely under its operational command. The immediate task of the army was to take part in the direct defence of Great Britain with an ultimate role of an offensive character— "a landing and an attack on Western Europe." Marshall agreed that sooner or later that would have to be done but, meanwhile, what about morale? The American soldier, he said, was first-rate when he could clearly see the task ahead; it was another matter when the objective was too far distant for that. A close study, McNaughton replied, was being made of morale. He anticipated no difficulties for some time to come.[30]

McNaughton went directly from Marshall to the President and was with him for about an hour. Roosevelt was direct, affable and informal and his straightforwardness appealed at once to McNaughton. Contrary to all his expectations, McNaughton soon found that Roosevelt had brought him there to discuss neither weapons nor chemical warfare, but strategy in its broadest sense.

The world, Roosevelt began, could be divided into three general areas for strategical operations: the Pacific (including Australasia, the Dutch East Indies and the Malay States); the Mediterranean Basin, the Middle East, the Persian Gulf, India and the Indian Ocean; and the North Atlantic lines of communication, the United Kingdom and Northwestern Europe. He then considered each area in turn.

In the first he thought that strategical direction should rest with the United States in consultation with Australia and New Zealand. American soldiers were about to be sent to reinforce those countries. He spoke of a step-by-step advance from the coast of California southwesterly through the various archipelagos to secure the control of various bases along the route from Honolulu to Australia and New Zealand; these bases would be put to use for the transfer of bombing aircraft. Strength developed in these various archipelagos, he pointed out, flanked the main Japanese thrust southwestward from Japan through Thailand, Borneo and Malaya. He was confident that the resources available to the United States were quite adequate for the purpose he had in mind. His reason for sending United States forces to Australia and New Zealand, Roosevelt continued, was to compensate them for their troops then in Egypt, Palestine and Syria and he hoped that both countries would recognize the advantage to themselves of direct American support. Shipping, moreover, would not be wasted in moving Australian and New Zealand troops from the Middle East back to their own countries. As to the northern approaches to the North American continent, along the line of the Aleutians and Alaska, Japanese penetration there would be most unlikely because of the lack of vital objectives and the great distances involved. Nevertheless, though he could see no immediate danger, the occupation of Dutch Harbor, or even an attack there or elsewhere in the Aleutians, would have a strong effect on American public opinion compelling in all likelihood the holding of large forces—of more use somewhere else—on the west coast. Reaction in Canada, McNaughton said, would be the same.

Turning to the second area, the President thought that strategical direction in that zone should rest exclusively with the British. He wondered if that would not be just about the limit of what would be immediately possible for them after the reverses they had suffered. The United States, he went on, would continue to supply aircraft and material on the present scale but did not expect to have to send troops.

Strategical direction in the third area, in his opinion, was a matter for the United States, the United Kingdom and Canada in co-operation. Three American divisions were just arriving in Northern Ireland. What troops did Canada have in Britain? McNaughton, as he had done with Marshall, gave the strength and described the programme for expansion. "We are part," he said, "of a strategical reserve which sooner or later will be employed against Hitler. In the meantime our very presence in England will continue to tie down German forces, perhaps in greater strength." The President echoed Marshall's concern about morale. How did it go with the Canadians who had been denied action against the enemy now for quite a while? McNaughton repeated that he had no particular anxiety on that score. The men had been worked very hard; they had facilities for education; and with an expanding force there was ample opportunity for promotion. "They are just as well aware as I am of the wisdom of deferring action until a proper opportunity arises. . . . What we wish to do is not to fight for the sake of fighting, but to bring the maximum possible continuing effect against the enemy."

Roosevelt wanted to know from McNaughton how he thought these proposals for the strategical direction of the war would be received in London; he intended to communicate the substance of them to Churchill that night. McNaughton answered that the British were realists. They knew the United Kingdom to be a potential theatre of operations and he expected they would welcome relief from responsibility for the Pacific zone.

What about the efficaciousness of bombing, using Britain as a base? General Arnold,* Roosevelt went on, thought a great deal might be accomplished by repeated bombing, particularly if this were spread over a tremendous number of targets. Arnold would aim at damaging civilian morale in every hamlet containing more than a hundred houses. His theory was that widespread harassing bombardment, if conducted on a scale that could now be developed, might well prove decisive; the present policy of attacking important but relatively few objectives was not proving to be of very great value. The President then cited a personal experience from his boyhood when he had had a succession of fights with a schoolmate bigger than himself. One day, unexpectedly but completely, the other boy had caved in. He thought that German morale would crack under repeated attacks and that when the end came it would be sudden and complete. General Marshall, however, had different ideas; he thought that an attack by ground forces would also be required.

McNaughton, much as Roosevelt's story had amused him, agreed with Marshall. He described his own experiences in France, especially in 1916, when it had been thought that a tremendous

---

*General Henry H. Arnold, Commanding General of the United States Army Air Corps.

volume of artillery fire alone could win battles. This was a fallacy. Infantry and firepower in intimate co-operation had proved the answer. As for bombing, "We are not within sight by decimal points of sufficient bombers to expect decisions by them alone." The Germans had aimed at the paralysis of Britain, rather than out-and-out destruction, but his observations had convinced him that the effects of bombing soon wore off; people grew accustomed to it, ignored it, and went about their business in the usual way. It would be essential to plan for the employment of ground forces on the Continent at the proper time.

It was important that something should be done, the President said. He was under considerable pressure from Stalin to open another front against Germany, and soon. He stressed the political importance of doing so in order to encourage the Russians and keep them in the war. Hitler might make favourable offers of peace to Russia—perhaps all lands up to the old frontier—which could be very tempting. He did not put too much faith in the Russians. It was quite possible that "military considerations might well have to give way to the overriding broad political factors."

They then talked of other matters. Roosevelt mentioned the Alaska Highway and how grateful he was that "Mackenzie" had agreed to its construction through Canada. He revealed a full comprehension of the engineering difficulties that would be encountered and the reasons for the selection of a route that would reduce them and speed up the work. He pointed out the value of the road for the movement of troops and stores required for the defence of Alaska. Weapons were discussed and McNaughton expressed the hope that the new development committee in Canada might be a suitable means to bring Canadian industry into co-operation with the United States.[31]

Both men were completely absorbed and time passed quickly. Roosevelt's quick mind made a fine impression and McNaughton was sorry when the interview was terminated by the announcement of another visitor, who, in fact, had been kept waiting for half an hour. As they shook hands, Roosevelt laughed and said McNaughton must be sure to see his service chiefs before he left for Ottawa.

McNaughton saw some of them that day over luncheon at the Canadian Legation: the Chief of the Air Staff (Major-General Millard F. Harmon), the Commander of the Service of Supply (Major-General Brehon Somervell), the Assistant Chief of Staff (Brigadier-General J. H. Hilldring), as well as Dr. Vannevar Bush of the Carnegie Institute.* The talk centred almost entirely on the design and development of weapons and McNaughton became so engrossed that he was loath to leave the legation drawing room where the conversation continued after luncheon. Next day Hilldring went out of his way to tell McNaughton that he had not heard "such a frank expression of opinion for a very long time"; many of McNaughton's "crisp remarks" would echo around the War Department for months to come. That night McNaughton and his wife dined with Sir John Dill, for whom McNaughton recounted the gist of what Roosevelt had said.

On 10 March McNaughton visited Vice-Admiral Horne (Acting Chief of Naval Operations) at Roosevelt's request. Horne wanted McNaughton's views on the place the air force should occupy in the organization of the fighting services. The United States Navy had its own air service. So had the the army, but there the air corps was moving more and more towards a separate identity. A movement was afoot in Congress for the establishment of a Ministry of Defence with a separate department for each of the three services and with one Chief of Staff over all three. What did McNaughton think?

McNaughton said he had been closely concerned with the problem over the past twenty-five years. He was sure that air power alone could not win battles either on land or at sea. He was convinced, if success was to be achieved, that both the army and the navy must retain, or obtain, complete operational command of the air forces they required to carry out their tasks. That was why he himself had lately pressed, and obtained approval, for

---

*Something came out of the talk with Vannevar Bush. Dr. Mackenzie of NRC wrote to McNaughton on 14 July, 1942: "I was down to Washington two weeks ago and had a very interesting conference with Dr. Vannevar Bush. They have followed the suggestion which you made on your recent visit and now have a three-man committee, operating on a very high level, that is reporting directly to the President. It is called the Joint Committee on New Weapons."

squadrons of the Royal Canadian Air Force to be formed and allotted for service with the Canadian Army. These squadrons, while they would continue to be RCAF, would be entirely under his operational command; an army co-operation wing headquarters would be formed to administer them. When the time came for the Canadian Army to operate on the continent of Europe he envisaged having not less than five squadrons for each division. He had thus no hesitation in advising Horne to resist the move that was afoot. As for the establishment of a Ministry of Defence with a Chief of Staff over all three services, to his mind the idea was not desirable. He doubted the possibility of finding the superman such an appointment would demand. He favoured the British idea of the close, intimate and effective co-operation of the several Chiefs of Staff concerned. The United States, he felt sure, would do well to avoid such a step which, however attractive it might appear on paper, or in logic, was unlikely to work out well in practice. Horne was delighted with these remarks which were "exactly what he had hoped to hear." His only regret was that he could not conscript McNaughton to appear before the Congressional Naval Committee so that he might give the politicians who composed it the "wholesome benefit" of his knowledge.[32]

McNaughton called on one other officer that day—Brigadier-General Dwight D. Eisenhower, then Acting Chief of the War Plans Division of the War Department. It was the first time he had encountered that famous grin. Eisenhower admitted that he had problems. During the three months he had been in his present division he had been tortured with the conundrum of presenting the Germans with a second front; the only right way to do it, he was now convinced, would be to attack Western Europe from the British Isles. What did McNaughton think about that?

McNaughton agreed with him—very definitely. Hitler must be defeated and the best way to bring about his downfall was to attack him from the west. He himself had to think constantly in terms of the defence of the United Kingdom but he had never lost sight of that. The Canadian Army programme for 1942 provided for the completion of a force which, for its size, would have considerable striking power and would be ready for an eventual offensive in

Western Europe. He had always been certain that an offensive would "sooner or later have to be launched from the United Kingdom across the narrow seas" and it was gratifying to know that the United States War Plans Division was thinking along the same lines.[33]

Later in the afternoon McNaughton faced a battery of some thirty to forty American press representatives who had gathered at the Canadian Legation. He and Mrs. McNaughton dined with the British ambassador before leaving for Ottawa next day. The visit, in the words of the Canadian minister, "had the effect of putting Canada on the map so far as Washington was concerned."[34]

McNaughton remained in Canada for another week and his schedule was exhausting. His talk with Eisenhower had convinced him that some day there would be a pressing need for landing craft and it would certainly be many months before these could be put into mass production. With Victor Sifton and D. A. Clarke (Director General of Shipbuilding), he explored the prospects of building them in Canada.[35] The purpose, McNaughton said, was to provide assault, motor and other landing craft for the movement of land forces, on the scale of two or three armies, onto the continent of Europe. He would obtain drawings and specifications on his return to Britain; meanwhile Canada should keep an eye on American developments. He also examined the tank production schedule and arranged for Bailey bridges to be made in Canada.[36] With Norman Robertson of the Department of External Affairs, he called on Graham Towers, the Governor of the Bank of Canada, to discuss financing Canada's war effort. He lunched with the Governor-General at Government House.

The Prime Minister wanted to know what had gone on in Washington. Dr. Charles Camsell, the Deputy Minister of Mines and Resources, telephoned to ask McNaughton if a metallurgical laboratory for his department should be built; it certainly should and on NRC property to be near the council's facilities. What about uranium? Would future needs justify the re-opening of the Eldorado Mines at Great Bear Lake? The use of uranium, McNaughton said, was the subject of speculation; in any case, the growing need for radium would be sufficient warrant for the re-opening of the mines.[37]

He visited the NRC laboratories again; he sat for a painting to be used in a recruiting campaign; he was photographed by Karsh. With his daughter he saw a film; he recorded a speech for Canada's second Victory Loan. And, on 17 March, the McNaughtons went to Montreal to visit their younger daughter Leslie at the convent at Sault au Recollet. Mrs. McNaughton chose a painting at the Watson Picture Galleries for presentation to the aircraft carrier *Unicorn,* which she had launched at the end of 1941.[38]

On 19 March the McNaughtons left Ottawa to return to England. They broke their journey at Quebec where they were received by Sir Eugène Fiset, the Lieutenant-Governor. Accompanied by Brigadier Georges Vanier, they called on the Premier (Adélard Godbout) and Cardinal Villeneuve. McNaughton toured the filling plant at the Valcartier Arsenal and the St. Malo shops in Quebec.[39]

Next day the McNaughtons sailed in the *Capetown Castle.* A farewell message from Mackenzie King, and another from the CGS (Stuart), in which he reported progress on the preliminaries for constructing landing craft, were brought on board just before the gangway was pulled up. One from Ralston missed the boat and was taken out by RCAF tender, which overhauled the ship. The flurry of McNaughton's Canadian visit was over; he could rest for a few days until the ship arrived at Liverpool on 28 March and he was back in the gloom of bomb-torn Britain where the task of building an army awaited him.[40]

To build an army is among the most intricate operations known to man. There must be no failure through lack of foresight. Every unit is the component of a vast machine designed to fulfil its purpose efficiently and economically, with the right numbers of men, weapons and vehicles and all the equipment required in modern war, and each component must mesh with the next to give the necessary battle-winning power. No army can be allowed to stall for want of some essential service such as the provision of reinforcements, ammunition, bridging, "petrol, oil and lubricants" or food; there must be facilities for the reconditioning of tanks and vehicles, even of men. And so an elaborate organization must be set up to keep the machine in motion from the factories to the front-line soldier. Throughout the remainder of 1942 and for many months in 1943 McNaughton was absorbed in this detailed, time-consuming, yet to him fascinating, procedure. It was a continuous process that will be referred to now and again but for a more comprehensive account the reader must look elsewhere.*

At the end of March McNaughton discussed his proposals for the organization of the First Canadian Army with both General Paget and General Montgomery. In the middle of April, at His Majesty's request, he spent an hour at Buckingham Palace where he again described what would be done, emphasizing that the army would not be dispersed but concentrated in Britain for future decisive operations. The King was eager to know about McNaughton's talk with Roosevelt and the attitude in Canada towards the war.[41]

The new Canadian Army would take shape by stages. The Canadian Corps (now 1st Canadian Corps) under Crerar would be "in combination" with the British for operations in any emergency; everything else came directly under McNaughton while the new force was being built. An army headquarters, little more than a nucleus, was to be created first and this would then be expanded to about half its final strength (including the units required to work with army headquarters and ancillary units as required) during a second phase that would end about the middle of June. It was anticipated that the last phase, the organization of 2nd Canadian Corps, could be completed by July but, mainly because of a shortage of trained staff officers, its headquarters was not set up until the middle of January, 1943. Headquarters First Canadian Army came into being at Headley Court on Easter Monday, 6 April, 1942, and that day McNaughton watched its first guard mounting—the guard, as might be expected, coming from the artillery.[42]

The selection of men who would be required as leaders and specialists in the new units, and the rejection of others, was carried out by scientific methods. McNaughton made use of the Directorate of Personnel Selection which had been established at

*See Stacey, *Six Years of War*, pp. 98-104.

CMHQ, largely at his instigation, in the fall of 1941. Mc-Naughton's interest in the use of psychological methods for personnel selection dated from 1939 when, as president of the National Research Council, he had attended a conference of service representatives and members of the Canadian Psychological Association, under the chairmanship of Sir Frederick Banting, to discuss the application of psychological tests in wartime. McNaughton strongly advocated such methods and thus placed the stamp of approval of Canada's senior scientific body on the project. The scheme came to fruition in 1941, through the General's urging from England, at a time when "his own picturesque statement that the Canadian Army was to be a dagger pointed at the heart of Berlin expressed the intention to reorganize and re-train the Canadian units so that the Army would be sharpened into a highly trained, highly mobile and highly mechanized operational force". To implement such a plan it became a matter of immediate urgency to withdraw from units "those men who were suitable as leaders and specialists," and as the army contained "a dangerous proportion of men . . . of mental incapacity and emotional instability," these would have to be weeded out.[43]

What McNaughton required was an inventory of the human material at his disposal and, through the application of psychological tests, that was what he hoped to get. The army did not accept Personnel Selection easily ("It was looked upon at first with a good deal of suspicion as the brain-child of bespectacled professors and inquisitive psychologists") but its value as an efficiency measure was incontrovertible, for "however *willing* a man might be to learn a new skill, if he could not absorb the training in the limited time available, he was of little use."[44] Personnel Selection played an increasingly important role while the war lasted and in the postwar years. "In this," wrote Colonel W. R. N. Blair, the president of the Canadian Psychological Association, in 1966, "as in other areas of our national life, it can be said that the General's influence was significant and lasting."[45]

McNaughton was concerned not only with army matters, but with having an air component as well. On 21 April he talked this over with Sir Charles Portal (Chief of the Air Staff), whom he had known since they had flown together in the previous war:

I said that we recognized that the full number of R.C.A.F. Squadrons could not be formed at once; that I advocated a programme spread over the next three or four months; that I would like to prepare this programme with . . . Army Co-operation Command R.A.F.; that I was quite prepared to leave over the organization of the Second Army Co-operation Squadron until late summer as I knew something of the difficulties as regards provision of machines.
I understood also that another limiting factor was the provision of aerodromes. . . .[46]

From two army co-operation squadrons the force would be built up to an army wing headquarters and six squadrons. McNaughton was prepared to help by constructing an aerodrome if the ground and the materials could be placed at his disposal. Not only would that give an additional airfield; it would also test the abilities of the Canadian engineers to do this kind of work. It was a good offer and Portal seized it. If the Canadian Army would build an aerodrome, he said, they should have the use of it, or an equivalent. The result was Dunsfold.[47]

Work on Dunsfold Aerodrome, south of Guildford, in Surrey, started on 4 May. It was to have a concrete runway six thousand feet long and a hundred and fifty feet wide, smaller runways of more than four thousand feet in total length, a perimeter track, fifty parking areas for planes and six miles of access and camp roads. Previously work on similar airfields had taken a year, and that at Dunsfold was complicated by two hundred acres of woodland that first had to be cleared and the moving of one hundred thousand cubic yards of soil.

The Canadian sappers had advantages, however. Though giant earth-moving equipment, obtained from the United States under "lend-lease" arrangements, was strange to the British it was quite familiar to them; and the stumps of trees were rapidly blasted out of the ground by pipe-pushing methods. The laying of a hundred and thirty thousand linear feet of drainpipe and the pouring of concrete went quickly so that the first plane was able to land as early as 20 June. By the middle of August the field could be used in an emergency, and on 3 October the first bomber touched down. The aerodrome was officially opened two weeks later when McNaughton handed it over to Air Marshal Harold Edwards, AOC-in-C of the RCAF in Great Britain. McNaughton was proud of Dunsfold.

Prime Minister King had, meanwhile, sought release from the pledge he had given at the outbreak of war (that there would be no compulsory overseas service) by means of the plebiscite that he had discussed with McNaughton. On 27 April the voters gave Mackenzie King the release he sought and on 1 August the National Resources Mobilization Act was amended to give the government full powers to order general conscription. The Prime Minister, who saw no need for conscription yet, adopted the formula "not necessarily conscription but conscription if necessary." Despite his new powers, King said, he must seek an expression of confidence from Parliament before sending any conscripts overseas. Ralston wanted no hesitation of that kind if the men were needed, but King insisted that his proposition was the right one and on 7 July Ralston submitted his resignation. The Prime Minister, who had no wish to advertise any split between the Minister of Defence and himself at such a time, required him to continue "though, knowing his tenacity, I felt that he might hold tight to his resignation, particularly as I can see that, through . . . opposing his views, he was becoming somewhat antagonistic towards myself."[48] Ralston did not withdraw his resignation; King did not accept it, and so agreed that Ralston would continue in office even if the resignation was not formally withdrawn. The Defence Minister, therefore, remained with his resignation sitting in the Prime Minister's pocket to be used at an appropriate time.

Throughout 1942 training in Britain continued. The great exercise of the year was TIGER, which General Montgomery directed during May, and in which Crerar's 1st Corps played a major part. The exercise clearly demonstrated the hardiness of the men, for during the eleven days it lasted "some units marched on foot as much as 250 miles, which is about the life of army boots on English roads." Because the Canadians fought as they would if they were the advanced element of a cross-Channel invading force, transport was cut to a minimum "and troops lived hard under conditions approximating active service." Nevertheless, McNaughton's report continued, "they have come through these strenuous tests with enhanced morale and confidence in themselves. Staff work, road discipline and supply arrangements were on the whole excellent."[49]

"Battle drill" was common that year. A British idea, it consisted of minor exercises in which the basic principles of tactics were taught and the importance of team play stressed. To accustom the men to the conditions of actual battle, live ammunition was fired over their heads or close to them, and artillery, grenades and mines were used. Realizing the value of this type of training, McNaughton approved the establishment of a Canadian Battle Drill School on 15 April and he saw to it that large-scale field exercises were conducted in which the gunners put down concentrations as close as was safely possible in front of the advancing infantry; through "field-firing" exercises, as much vividness as possible was injected into the training of the Canadian troops for battle.

Nevertheless, there was a limit to the realism of such training. In battle, bullets are aimed to kill, not to miss; and there are times in war when it seems that the inferno of blasting explosions will never cease. Sometimes on exercises in England even the simulated noise of battle was never heard. Consider a platoon, positioned behind a village church, its members listening to the raucous strains of "South of the Border" or "Sweet Adeline" filtering through the blacked-out windows of the pub down the road; it became hard for them to take the business seriously. That morning, at the map-board briefing, they could visualize from the pointing stick the attack on the Downs in the middle of the night; now here they were on the Downs in the middle of the night, and it was quite impossible to do so. It is unfortunately true that no amount of training makes up for the actual experience of battle, and McNaughton knew this. In November, 1942, he arranged with the War Office for selected officers and NCOs to gain battle experience by attaching them to the First British Army in Tunisia. They were then exchanged for others, to give experience to as many Canadians as possible.

He thus put training into its right perspective, more so than orthodox soldiers of the regular school who, in his position, would not have looked beyond it. A good many of the Canadian troops in England had trained for almost three years and were now at a pitch that certainly their predecessors in the earlier war had not achieved; only the shock of actual battle was needed to drive the lessons home. Training was essential—his record between the wars shows that he was convinced of that—but McNaughton did not elevate it into a fetish that would only have made the troops stale. He was commander enough to bestir himself to see that essential training was carried out; that it was properly given; and to impart the necessary ginger (as, for example, when he attended the battle drill school in November and was very critical of its supervision);[50] and always to keep his finger on the training pulse. It came as no surprise to him when, in December, General Sir Bernard Paget inspected the Canadian troops in training and remarked on the high standard of their efficiency. "Looking to the possibilities of 1943," Paget said, "I derive high hopes from all I see and know of the Canadian Army. When the great day comes it will play a decisive part in the decisive battle...."[51]

Troops require more than training if they are to win battles. They must be armed with the right weapons. All the training in the world would have been without value if there had been insufficient landing craft to deliver troops and weapons on the shores of Hitler's Europe. McNaughton had good news of landing craft in April; he heard from Canada that delivery would start in June at the rate of four hundred a month[52] and he kept Vice-Admiral Lord Louis Mountbatten (Chief of Combined Operations) informed. His interest in the development and production of better weapons continued; he laboured in this field throughout the year.

On 27 April, at his request, McNaughton visited Oliver Lyttelton, the British Minister of Production, in London. Lyttelton wanted him to study an outline of the proposed British organization for the control of production and give his comments; he also wanted him to suggest how Canadian production could be linked to it. McNaughton, as a first step, said there should be a full exchange of information and mutual planning.[53] Mountbatten also consulted him, the most fantastic meeting perhaps being that between Mountbatten, McNaughton and a Mr. Geoffrey Pyke, who had advanced the theory that airfields could be made out of floating islands of ice.* Churchill was behind the scheme. As it appeared that Canada's North was the logical place to form these islands of more than two million tons of flat-topped ice, McNaughton facilitated Pyke's mission to North America. At McNaughton's instigation NRC carried out experiments to see if there was anything in the idea; it proved to be too expensive and therefore impracticable.[54]

In guns, the search for higher velocities continued The advantages of increased velocity are many: the chance of hitting a moving target is greatly enhanced; range increases with velocity, as does the penetration of armour; and the weight of the equipment required to penetrate a given thickness of armour can be greatly reduced. This last is very important for airborne operations, and in ordinary ground warfare a smaller gun is easier to conceal.

At the beginning of April a standard two-pounder anti-tank gun, fitted with a "muzzle-squeeze" attachment, pierced a hundred-millimetre armour plate at a striking velocity corresponding to a range of two hundred yards and damaged a sixteen-millimetre plate placed behind it. This was a far better performance than ever before. A muzzle velocity of about forty-five hundred feet per second was achieved with a light (fourteen-ounce) projectile. Had this modification been available in Libya, the whole campaign might have turned out differently. McNaughton considered the hyper-velocity attachment "a step forward" but only as "an interim measure pending the completion of new designs of guns

---

*The details of this project (HABAKKUK) will be found in Wilfrid Eggleston, *Scientists at War* (Oxford University Press, 1950).

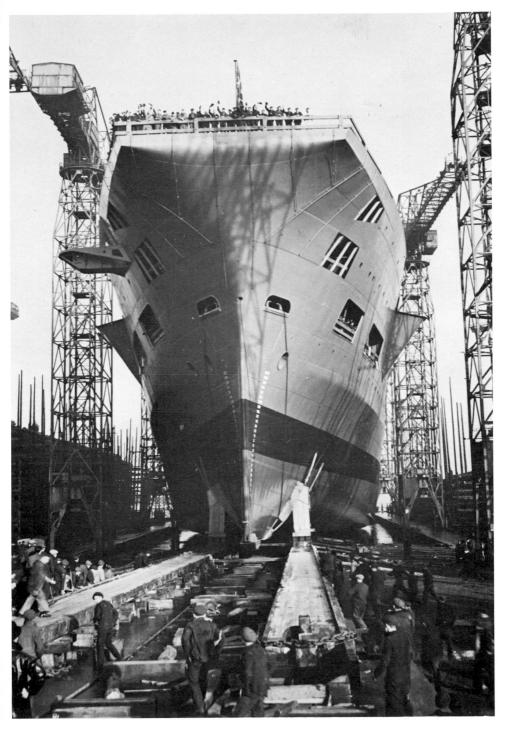

HMS *Unicorn*, launched by Mrs. McNaughton, 1941

After the launching ceremony

With Dr. C. J. Mackenzie of the National Research Council at the annual
banquet of the Engineering Institute of Canada, Montreal, February, 1942

incorporating these or other principles on a fundamental basis rather than as an afterthought."[55]

He had, as has been noted, advocated the design of a conical or "squeeze" gun, a gun with a tapering barrel to squeeze the projectile, thus causing it to emerge with increased velocity and a decreased cross section that would reduce resistance to the air. He had thought about this for many years, and during his presidency of NRC before the war had obtained an anti-tank rifle which employed this principle to study the relationship between velocity and armour penetration.* Since then the Germans had developed a squeeze gun that had been used against tanks to some effect. One of these had been captured in North Africa and McNaughton had studied it; he had a model made up for trials. In April, however, when attending a meeting with the British Director-General of Weapon Production and other experts in research and gun design (and with General Pile an interested spectator) he came up with a radically new conception.

He now proposed an ingenious solution to the problem of obtaining increased velocity, one that would require the design of no new guns. Trials of the gun modelled on the German pattern had convinced him that, though increased velocity could undoubtedly be produced, dangerous muzzle squeeze resulted which caused excessive barrel wear, could damage the gun, and might injure the gun crew as well. And there was a further disadvantage when the shell was squeezed; it emerged from the gun deformed and without the fine surface finish that would permit it to maintain its velocity. "At the super-velocities contemplated, every scratch would develop a shock wave that would dissipate energy," said McNaughton.[56] There was no point, therefore, in developing a tapered gun. All that needed to be done was to develop a new form of hyper-velocity projectile to be used in existing guns.

This could be done, he said, by firing a small shell from a gun

---

*Dr. D. C. Rose of the Physics Department, who carried out the study, made a notable contribution in this field at the Canadian Army Research and Development Establishment during the war.

of larger calibre. It would be accomplished by carrying a two-pounder anti-tank projectile, for example, in a light metal or plastic "shoe" that would exactly fit the barrel of a twenty-five-pounder. The shoe would take the place of the driving band of a twenty-five-pounder shell, sealing off the gases and transmitting the propellant and rotational forces to the small projectile. Then, after the shoe had carried the projectiles up the bore of the gun it could be blown off at the muzzle by a small pellet of powder, leaving the projectile to travel on to its target in perfect ballistic shape with little resistance from the air. A much larger charge could be used in the twenty-five-pounder gun than would be the case in the two-pounder; thus the small projectile would have the benefit of greater thrust than if fired from its own gun and this would result in increased velocity. Furthermore, with this method a gun could be used in a dual role; a field gun, having a quota of this new ammuntion, could fire its normal shell or it could be used as an anti-tank weapon simply by inserting a shoe projectile.

The simplicity of the proposal appealed to the assembly. It was agreed that the Ammunition Design Board should be asked to work on some experimental shoe ammunition. The shot, McNaughton said, should have a tungsten-carbide core because of the remarkable armour-piercing properties of this compound.* As to the availability of tungsten, which was questioned, McNaughton believed that sufficient would be found in Canada; he had already asked the government of Canada to give high priority to finding and developing new sources of supply.[57]

Experimental ammunition was made up but it was not at first successful due to the failure of the type of plastic used for the shoe; it was even then apparent, however, that increased muzzle velocity had been achieved. Tests continued on the covered-in range at Woolwich Arsenal, while parallel developments proceeded in Canada. The British confined themselves to designs for six-pounder and seventeen-pounder guns and the Canadians concentrated on those for the seventy-five-millimetre tank gun and the twenty-five-pounder.[58] The "Sabot" projectile eventually resulted — the

---

*Chiefly as a result of its high density.

"Kettle" design (British) and the "Pot" design (Canadian)—and was used with excellent results on enemy armour in the final battles of the war.[59]

The story of the Sabot has a modern ending. On the island of Barbados, at the present time, The Space Research Institute of McGill University is using a gun to carry out its high altitude research project. The vehicles that are sent soaring into the upper atmosphere—sophisticated projectiles—are known as Martlets* and are a development of McNaughton's anti-tank ammunition of 1942.

Early in May, using the 5th Canadian Armoured Division, McNaughton staged a demonstration of the "Snake," flame-throwing carriers, the Canadian Number 19 wireless set and certain types of Canadian vehicles for the CIGS and other visitors. The Snake, a device that enabled tanks to pass safely through enemy minefields, is worth more than passing mention. Its origins dated from the fall of 1941 when Brigadier F. F. Worthington, who at that time commanded the 1st Canadian Army Tank Brigade, sought a method of crossing minefields and talked the matter over with Lieutenant-Colonel A. T. MacLean, CRE 2nd Canadian Infantry Division. MacLean experimented with Bangalore torpedoes (pipes packed with explosives) and determined that they were effective against mines. Worthington then suggested that tanks might push loaded pipes into the sides of ditches to blow the lip away and make it possible for tanks to cross. Colin Campbell and his pipe-pushers tried that. It was found that the pipes buckled but that a tank could push pipe quite easily over the surface of the ground. As a result, the tank-pushed Snake, which could be initiated safely from inside the tank, was developed. When fired in a minefield it detonated the mines ahead of the tank, which then passed through.[61] Information on all the equipment demonstrated that day was passed to Washington by Wemyss, who was visiting England at the time.[62]

---

*These vehicles have reached altitudes of ninety miles. Fitted with rocket-boost motors that will cut in "once the projectile has passed through the region of high atmospheric drag," they should be able to place a satellite into orbit at far less cost than a purely rocket system.[60]

Towards the end of the month a meeting was arranged at the Institute of Electrical Engineers to give McNaughton the opportunity of meeting the members of the Engineering Advisory Committee of the War Cabinet, who wished to discuss with him "technical developments and the means of improving arrangements for . . . research and development." The talk, it was reported, was frank and "covered a wide range of subjects."[63] Again during May McNaughton attended a reception given by Lord Hankey (chairman of the committee), where British, Dominion and United States scientists were present.[64] On 16 June General Weeks, the Deputy Chief of the Imperial General Staff (DCIGS), was his dinner guest at Headley Court. After dinner McNaughton, in private conversation with Weeks, deplored the "lack of real progress" in weapon development. There was a need for a light twenty-millimetre automatic gun—power operated and on a self-propelled mounting—with a course-and-speed sight designed for the combined anti-aircraft and anti-tank role; also for a heavier gun of similar design. He foresaw the need for a heavy anti-aircraft gun able to fire, at high velocity, a hundred-and-fifty-pound shell fitted with a radio-impulse fuse. Weeks agreed, and promised to press for them.[65]

Major-General A. E. Macrae* (Military Technical Adviser, Department of Munitions and Supply in Canada) was a frequent visitor. On 25 June he gave some interesting figures to the General. Experiments had confirmed McNaughton's contention that, for a particular thickness of armour, there were three critical velocities for projectiles. At a relatively low velocity (2,500 foot-seconds) the projectile did not penetrate the armour; from 2,500-2,700 f.s. the armour was penetrated; at velocities between 2,700-3,500 f.s. the projectile broke up and did not penetrate the armour; and above 3,500 f.s. the projectile again penetrated the armour. At this higher velocity it was found that the hardness of the projectile made no difference to the result; lead penetrated as well as steel. Above the critical velocity, density rather than hard-

---

*A Canadian in the British Army who had made a name for himself in gun design. He had been "borrowed" by Canada early in the war to advise the Minister of Munitions and Supply.

ness was what counted. A copper-sheathed missile gave better results than steel-sheathed (the copper seeming to serve as some kind of lubricant) and the ideal high-velocity projectile might be composed of a lead core with a tungsten-carbide tip inside a light alloy or copper case of ballistic shape.[66] Canada was experimenting with multiple-plate armour. A fifteen-to-twenty-millimetre air space between a thin outer plate and the main armour gave almost as good protection as homogeneous armour; at the same time it saved steel—equivalent to the air space—and weight.

Thus through the liaison visits of members of NRC and officials of the Department of Munitions and Supply, McNaughton kept in close touch with Canada.* C. D. Howe, the dynamic Minister of Supply, visited McNaughton in October. Together they reviewed the production field and discussed the deficiencies in vehicles and armament of the Canadian Army Overseas. Howe's production figures were reassuring; five to six thousand Stens every month; two hundred and fifty tanks; Number 19 wireless sets, binoculars, G.L. III directional radar sets, small arms and munitions in ample quantity. By now twenty-millimetre Hispano-Suiza guns on Inglis mountings and forty-millimetre Bofors light anti-aircraft guns were in production, as were Mosquito aircraft for the British. Production of tanks, McNaughton thought, should turn to the Mark IV with seventy-five- or seventy-six-millimetre guns, thus putting the production on a standard North American basis. The provision of landing craft, especially support landing craft mounting twenty-five-pounder guns for use close in to the open beaches, should be stepped up; and additional vehicle trailers, which would increase the carrying capacity in the rear echelons, were required.[67]

All in all, by the end of the year McNaughton could be satisfied with the progress made. On 17 December he reviewed the

---

*One visit is not without interest. In July Professor Shenstone (the NRC liaison officer in England) brought Professor G. T. R. Hill to meet McNaughton. Hill, who had been professor of aeronautical engineering at the University of London, was on the way to be Shenstone's "opposite number" in Canada. McNaughton told Hill about the NRC Aeronautical Museum in Ottawa and how much he would like to obtain for it the first variable pitch propeller (invented by W. R. Turnbull, a Canadian) in the possession of the Imperial Museum in London. Hill succeeded in obtaining its release and return to Canada.

units of the Canadian Army as they drove slowly past him on a stretch of the Crawley bypass road to celebrate the third anniversary of the arrival of the first Canadian contingent in Britain. It was a superb exhibition of mechanized strength, a fulfilment of his maxim that machines and weapons should be provided "to multiply the strength and mobility of man."*[68] The army, and Canadian production, had come a long way since the late thirties when McNaughton had taken the first steps at NRC to gear the country to the coming war:

When we were at peace we had made no preparation for war industry, but Canadian manufacturers sent a delegation to this country . . . to be ready for anything that might be required in the way of production. . . . It takes time to train staffs on the particular machines required, and it takes time to get together machine tools. . . . To begin with there was only one thing to do: to take existing types and to get manufacture under way; then to develop better types of equipment, artillery weapons and various kinds of armoured fighting vehicles and motor transport. In due course prototypes of improvements on existing types were turned out and production began on these. A comparatively short space of time elapsed from the time the prototypes were produced until the articles were in mass production . . . and they have stood up in a most satisfactory manner. We know that Canada can produce the weapons of war that will be the best. That is not enough, though, because there is nothing static in war or weapons. Weapons are continually changing and new ones must be produced. When I went back to Canada last winter I carried that message to the manufacturers. I knew there was no use in pressing for improved types earlier because we then urgently needed supplies of existing types. Reports now reaching me from the other side show that Canadian industry is going to be heard from before long in the race for better weapons. The German has got ahead of us and we must catch up and get ahead of him.[69]

---

*Next day Hannen Swaffer devoted his whole column in the British *Daily Herald* to the Canadian Army which he described as "probably the finest fighting force in the world." Britons would be grateful to the Canadians for their guardianship of the island, for "it was on the Canadians—unknown then to the British people—that we relied." He referred to McNaughton as a "superb soldier . . . a really magnificent artillery officer." Charles Rawlings, writing in the American *Saturday Evening Post*, referred to "the motorized hell on wheels that is the Canadian mechanized army."

Not only was McNaughton's driving energy in design and production of use to Canada; it was also useful to the British whose Ministry of Supply, on hearing about McNaughton's Weapons Development Committee in Canada, decided to set up a similar board in England and persuaded both General McNaughton and General Pile to attend its meetings.*[70] McNaughton's advice was sought on all aspects of this important field. In fact Beverley Baxter, a member of the British House of Commons, went so far as to suggest a "supreme directorate" for the Empire to "provide the sword that would carve the way to a triumphant ending of the war." He wanted four men together in council: Churchill, Smuts of South Africa, Menzies of Australia and McNaughton of Canada. Writing in the *Sunday Graphic* on 8 June, Baxter described McNaughton as having "those qualities of unusual penetrating thought which lift him completely from the groove which is the course of our war effort so far."

In June Tobruk, despite its earlier gallant stand, capitulated to the Germans with surprising ease. "This was one of the heaviest blows I can recall during the war," wrote Churchill. "Not only were its military effects grievous, but it had affected the reputation of the British armies. At Singapore 85,000 men had surrendered to inferior numbers of Japanese. Now in Tobruk a garrison of 25,000 [actually 33,000] seasoned soldiers had laid down their arms to perhaps one-half of their number."[71] On 24 June a motion of censure of Churchill's government was tabled and Sir Stafford Cripps (Lord Privy Seal) busied himself with the points of criticism to be met. On 1 July Cripps sent for McNaughton and talked with him for more than an hour. Cripps then passed his findings to Churchill in the form of a report dated 2 July, and two of them were as follows:

(4) *Weapons.* Perhaps the strongest line of criticism is that after nearly three years of war we still find ourselves inferior in

---

*McNaughton attended the first meeting of the British Weapon Development Committee in July. One of the members was Sir Charles Darwin (Scientific Adviser to the Army Council), whom he originally encountered as a sound-ranger in the First World War.

vital weapons such as tanks and anti-tank guns, and that this inferiority has been largely responsible for the débâcle.

(5) *Research and Invention.* There is a considerable feeling that although we have in this country very skilled research workers, scientists, and inventors we have somehow or other failed to make good use of their abilities in the race for efficient equipment, and that there is room for some improvement in the method or organization in order to get the full benefit from this important branch of war effort.[72]

These recorded views represented the convictions of Mc-Naughton.[73]

McNaughton had arrived at these convictions largely through his experiences with the Ordnance Board. We have seen some of his work towards the production of better weapons throughout this narrative; it is now time to pull some of the scattered threads together.

It was noted that in September, 1941, McNaughton met the Superintendent of Applied Ballistics and finally persuaded him to accept a simplified system of airburst-ranging. Phillips was so impressed that he arranged a full meeting of the Ordnance Board to hear McNaughton. Commander R. H. Stokes-Rees, the Superintendent of Armament Design (Guns) at the Ministry of Supply, attended that meeting in an *ex officio* capacity and heard Mc-Naughton put forward suggestions for more battleworthy weapons; he was surprised and delighted to hear that they were what he had pressed for, and had had turned down flat by the board, for the past two years. After McNaughton had left, Stokes-Rees stayed on to hear the board's reaction, which amounted to this: "A brilliant man, of course, but quite mad!"*

Here, to Stokes-Rees, was "a supporter in the wilderness," and two days later he arranged a meeting with McNaughton. They worked together closely after that. Both watched trials of weapons, whether British or Canadian, and Stokes-Rees often arranged for

---

*This and other quotations which follow (unless referenced) are from a report sent to the writer in February, 1969, by Commander R. H. Stokes-Rees.

Sir Albert Stern (chairman of the Special Vehicles Committee) to be there too.

McNaughton appointed a Canadian liaison officer to Stokes-Rees' staff at Gun Design Headquarters, Knockholt; on McNaughton's instructions one of his senior officers, Brigadier F. F. Worthington (a man of long experience with tanks), worked closely with Stern and Stokes-Rees in the field of armoured fighting vehicles. Some progress was made—notably the development of the "muzzle-squeeze" attachment, which gave the two-pounder the ability to penetrate German armour, pressed for by Stokes-Rees during the past two years,* and which McNaughton saw for the first time during April, 1942. For any real progress, however, it seemed that the Director General of Artillery (at the Ministry of Supply) and the Ordnance Board would have to be bypassed; this could be done by McNaughton in Canada to some extent, as in the case of the carrier-borne flame thrower. Then McNaughton left for Canada early in 1942 and during this visit was provided with every valuable document of progress, in the hope that Canada would take over where the outdated Ordnance Board had stultified development and production. The setting up of the Canadian Weapons Development Committee resulted.

McNaughton returned to England where Stokes-Rees informed him that a technical meeting in London, without representatives of the Ordnance Board, had been approved by the Director General of Weapons Production—Claude (later Sir Claude) Gibb, and that it had been suggested that McNaughton should set the agenda and rough out the preamble, which the General was to give. This was done by McNaughton and Stokes-Rees at Headley Court on 3 April, 1942. They compiled a list of guests, including, from the services, Pile (Anti-Aircraft), Browning (Airborne), Mountbatten (Combined Operations) and Teasdale-Buckell (Admiralty), as well as their technical chiefs; Gibb would invite certain technical civilians "and at this point McNaughton was his

---

*The "Littlejohn" attachment and special projectiles had been invented by a Czech arms manufacturer (Frantisek Janecek), who placed his secret at the disposal of the British after the Czechoslovakian crisis of 1938. It had still not been made available to the British troops in Libya at the time of Rommel's victories of 1942.

usual delightfully naive self, suggesting Gibb be asked to include
Oliver Lyttelton, Minister of Production, on his list."

This "most irregular meeting"—so labelled by the Ordnance
Board—took place on 11 April. All those invited were present, or
sent their deputies with messages of support. This was the meeting
("organized by a distinguished civilian at the Ministry of Supply"
at which no member of the Ordnance Board was present) which
was noted by General Pile, as we have seen. It was important.
News of the meeting prompted Lyttelton to seek out McNaughton
on 27 April, as has been recorded, with the object of setting up
a better British organization; and it had other consequences,
apart from the British Weapon Development Committee, as we
shall see.

McNaughton, as arranged, was invited to address the sixteen
present and excelled himself. Having outlined the urgent requirements, he injected the role Canada could now play, stressed the
vital liaison essential between the users and the producers, laid
down the immediacy of experimental work without obstruction
and then went, as he was bound, into the detailed technical story
of the successes of the past few months. It was here, for the first
time, that he expressed the thought that a sabot or shoe to carry
a light, tough, sub-calibre projectile at hyper-velocity would be
better than taper bore or muzzle-squeeze. This was sheer brilliance
—both Design and Production instantly concurred.

Finally, a Committee was formed of Gibb and his ammunition
deputy; McLay (Production); Stokes-Rees and Dr. Guy (Design);
with Dr. Gough (Research) as Chairman. As *ex-officio* members
(Users), McNaughton, Pile, Teasdale-Buckell and the nominees
of Browning and Mountbatten. [There would be] immediate
implementation.

Though scant recognition has been accorded McNaughton for
his outstanding armament development in the war years he did,
according to Stokes-Rees, inspire "universal admiration." So much
so that Sir Albert Stern,* "the multi-millionaire banker, donating
his services free and with no axe to grind, felt instinctively that
McNaughton was the only person of stature who could save the

---

*Who had done much to develop the tank in World War I.

Allies in the armament field"; he suggested that Canada should be approached for McNaughton's services. It was obvious to Stern that Professor Lindemann, Churchill's scientific adviser who supported the Ordnance Board, would have to go if McNaughton's services were to be effective; and Lindemann obviously would not go as long as Churchill remained Minister of Defence. Here, Stokes-Rees asserts, was the reason for the vote of censure of July, 1942.

McNaughton played no part in this; it would have been completely alien to his forthright nature. He knew nothing of Sunday meetings at Stern's country house, attended by worried Members of Parliament (including Earl Winterton, Clement Davies, Aneurin Bevan, R. R. Stokes and E. H. Keeling) who had been hammering away in the House for better weapons to no effect.

Defeat in Libya and the loss of Tobruk brought things to a head. As late as 6 May, 1942, the commander of the 18th Armoured Division had felt it necessary to warn his tank crews, armed with the two-pounder gun, that their weapons would not penetrate German armour at any range or from any angle. Stern, it is said by Stokes-Rees who was present at the weekend meetings, set about staging a vote of censure, a first step being to select a spokesman who commanded trust and respect in the House.

Stern found such a man in Sir John Wardlaw-Milne, who was sufficiently impressed with what was laid before him to agree to act. In fact, in proposing the House's lack of confidence in the conduct of the war, Wardlaw-Milne did extremely well. Then, at the conclusion of his motion, he begged leave to suggest that Major-General H.R.H. The Duke of Gloucester be asked to accept the appointment of Commander-in-Chief. . . . Before those fateful words, Wardlaw-Milne had the Vote of Censure won; at their conclusion it was irretrievably lost.

Churchill, who had been sitting head bowed like a beaten man throughout Wardlaw-Milne's lengthy and considered motion, had only raised his eyes once and that when the proposer came to this suggestion. Then he faced him and looked straight in his eyes. . . . Churchill rose, bowed to the Speaker and left the Chamber. Those within earshot said he mumbled, *"Lèse-majesté!"*. . . .

To Stern and his devoted team, who had but the single aim to

see the fighting men better armed, the whole fiasco was inexplic-
able—that is, until Wardlaw-Milne explained. Churchill had
invited "his friend Johnny" into his office for a chat immediately
before the motion. He agreed that probably "both hats" were a
bit much for him; that he should probably delegate Defence.
Wardlaw-Milne said he had never had any difficult job made so
easy for him. In conclusion Churchill hinted that an old friend
could let him down lightly. The British loved their royalty; why
not propose the Duke of Gloucester? It was as simple, if that is
the right word for it, as that.

The censure debate began on 1 July. Wardlaw-Milne, in moving "that this House . . . has no confidence in the central direction
of the war," pointed to the "vital mistake" that had been made
in combining the offices of Prime Minister and Minister of
Defence. Churchill had enormous responsibilities as Prime Minister; he could not exercise proper direction over Defence as well.
What was required was "a strong and independent man . . . in
charge of all three branches of the Armed Forces"; one strong
enough "to demand all the weapons which are necessary for
victory."[74]

He made no recommendation concerning Churchill's successor
in Defence but there had been speculation in the press. Ten days
before, for example, Wilson Broadbent, political commentator
of the *Daily Mail,* had predicted a shake-up in the British War
Cabinet; Churchill would be relieved as Defence Minister by
McNaughton whose "decisive practical mind" already exerted
considerable influence in defence planning. The rumours were so
persistent then that an official statement came from 10 Downing
Street in which it was denied that "any change in the structure
of the War Cabinet or in the office of Minister of Defence is
contemplated."[75]

It is true, as Stokes-Rees states, that Wardlaw-Milne put forward
the name of the Duke of Gloucester as Commander-in-Chief of
the British Army. That suggestion brought bitter condemnation
from members of different political persuasions. John McGovern
pointed to a long line of disasters: on the Continent in 1940; at
Hong Kong; Malaya; Singapore; Burma; and now in Libya "with

no information given." There was ample justification for an attack on Churchill.

The hon. Member moving the Motion made out a good case for a Vote of No Confidence in the Government, but he destroyed the whole of his case when he suggested that we wanted a strong man as Commander-in-Chief and that we should have the Duke of Gloucester. I said to myself, "Good heavens! Is it as bad as that?" I would like to ask the hon. gentleman what was the basis of that suggestion because it did not seem to me mentally suitable to the individual who suggested it. . . . I was very wrapped up in the hon. gentleman's speech, but he destroyed the whole value of it by this stupid suggestion.[76]

"What is the solution that has been offered to the House?" Robert Boothby asked.

I yield to no hon. Member in my admiration, affection and loyalty for the Royal Family; but I cannot believe that the final solution of our present problems, in our great fight for democracy, is to be found in the appointment as Commander-in-Chief of His Royal Highness the Duke of Gloucester.[77]

The British had fought with inferior weapons in Libya. The German Mark IV tank had mounted a seventy-five-millimetre gun. The British, in a tank armed with a two-pounder gun of an effective range of, it was said, six hundred yards, were hardly a match for an enemy tank firing a fourteen-pound projectile with a range of two thousand yards. Not only that. The Germans tanks had better armour. If a British tank was lucky enough to get close to a German tank without being destroyed, its projectile bounced off the heavy armour. A small army, if equipped with superior weapons, can outfight larger numbers of the enemy; the reverse had applied in Libya. The question which the government was required to answer was whether they had designed new weapons fit to win the war, and the answer to that was no.

"Strategy," Aneurin Bevan pointed out, "dictates the weapon, and tactics . . . the use of the weapon." Churchill's misconception of modern war had led to the wrong strategy; and "the strategy being wrong, the wrong weapons were produced."[78]

Oliver Lyttelton attempted a lame defence. Clement Davies referred to him—the Minister of Production—as "Ethelred the Unready." "Never during my period in this House have I heard anything so tragic as the confessions which were made in that speech."[79] There were obstructions and delay from top to bottom. "Whether it is the Civil Service, whether it is the top, I do not know; but right through Production, in every sphere . . . you get this delay."[80]

Lindemann, by then Lord Cherwell, came under strong attack. "Another criticism," said Wing Commander A. W. H. James, "relates to the activities of Professor Lindeman [*sic*]. If the Prime Minister's estimate of Lord Cherwell is correct, the opinion of every scientist and industrial or business man I have ever met is wrong."[81] Some scientific direction was wanted, to advise the War Cabinet what to do, but not, stated Morgan Price, "a certain scientist who up to now has had a sort of roving commission to go about interfering in the various Departments. That is not the way to run a modern war." Churchill was wanted as "the political head" but he must "call to his aid the very best opinion in the world of science and design."[82] Churchill's attempts to control scientific development through his scientific adviser, Lord Cherwell, said Dr. Haden Guest, was an abuse of his powers and authority; he should not do "that kind of thing which his training does not equip him to do."[83] The fact that there was "no scientific control of the processes of production in respect of military equipment [was] very much the central direction of the war, and the lack of scientific direction one of the chief difficulties."[84]

Where did the solution lie? There must be "a qualified, scientific, technical staff above the Ministry of Supply and the War Office," S. S. Hammersley suggested.[85] Sir George Schuster was more specific:

All the time we want to be sure that the very best scientific brains, the best brains for practical mechanical problems of production, and the best brains on the military side are working together on this matter. If we have not the right kind of brains in our Army— because I think the Army should take a lead—then let us get them from somewhere else. The need is for *fighting knowledge*,

mechanical knowledge and scientific vision all combined.* I wonder whether it might not be advisable to get a man like General
McNaughton of the Canadian Forces and put him at the head
of the Ministry's [Production] Joint Production Staff. Possibly
Canadian production could be worked in with ours. The combination ought to give him a big enough job.[86]

And in the Lords, on the same day, it was suggested that
Churchill had not the time to be Prime Minister as well as Minister of Defence. "Let us find our Milner or our Smuts," said Lord
Mottistone, "call him Minister of Warfare or Captain-General,
and put him in charge of the jarring elements to be the deciding
voice."[87]

In the closing speech of the debate Churchill dwelt, with the
irony of which he was master, on the proposed appointments of
this "all-powerful potentate" and this "Royal Duke."

The Mover of this Vote of Censure has proposed that I should be
stripped of my responsibilities for Defence in order that some
military figure or that some other unnamed personage should
assume the general conduct of the war as Chief of the Chiefs
of Staff and that he should have under him a Royal Duke as
Commander-in-Chief of the Army, and finally, I presume, though
this was not mentioned, that this unnamed personage should find
an appendage in the Prime Minister to make the necessary ex-
planations, excuses and apologize to Parliament when things go
wrong, as they often do and often will. . . .[88]

Though the motion of censure was heavily defeated the battle
for better weapons was won. Victory did not come at once but
this was the turning point. The inferiority of British weapons had
been exposed and there was recognition, from Churchill down,
that they must be improved. Up-to-date and even advanced weapons
were given a chance at last, and in most cases the armed forces were
well served.

Throughout July the indictment of British design and the hunt
for a solution continued. An editorial in the *Times* of 9 July

---

*Italics supplied.

pointed to the evidence that "British design was in certain respects demonstrably inferior and that quantity failed to make up for quality.... In general, it is evident that science has never yet been given its proper function and status in this war except perhaps in relation to air defence.... This is the more unfortunate since the man of science is a natural innovator and this war will be won by innovators or not at all. The time has come to give science and research their due at a higher level of responsibility." Schuster, in a letter to the editor of the same newspaper dated 14 July, spelled out what was required:

> ... at the head of a Joint Production Staff,
>
> (1) ... a fighting service man with vision and drive who knows the urgency of battle.
>
> (2) Quick decision and clean responsibility for settling what is wanted within the limits of what can be supplied.
>
> (3) Close personal contact, at the top and lower levels, from the beginning and at all stages of design and production, between scientists and technicians, practical manufacturers and production engineers, and between all these and fighting service men.

Production was debated in the House of Commons in the middle of the month when "Mr. Lyttelton was not so fortunate in the encounter with Professor Hill, whose demonstration of the neglect of scientific and technical advice at what may be called the strategic level of production was only too convincing."[89] Hill pressed for the appointment of a soldier-scientist:

The man who knows about weapons and tactics should be able to have some influence upon strategy; because it is certain that those who deal with strategy know nothing whatever about weapons .... The three subjects of production, strategy and technique are inevitably mixed together.[90]

On the night of the 16th "an influential deputation of scientists, M.Ps. and peers" asked the government to set up "a full-time scientific and technical joint board which would have as its aim the fullest strategic use of scientific man-power and resources and the proper organization and exchange of scientific and technical information relating to the war effort."[91] Lord Strabolgi pressed for "the most effective use of the scientific and inventive talent of the nation for war purposes." While there were "eminent scientists" attached to the various ministries their work was "departmentalised." His suggestion was that there should be "a scientific general staff, consisting of a team of the best brains available, to work whole time, and with prestige and influence equal to that of the Chiefs of Staff Committee. The chairman should sit on the Defence Committee and should attend the War Cabinet in an advisory capacity when necessary—and that should be nearly always." Viscount Samuel agreed that there should be such a body. It should have "a chairman of sufficient status and authority to give it prestige and influence; if he could be a member of the War Cabinet so much the better; and he must be someone with a knowledge of science in relation to industry."[92]

There certainly was something wrong; a Select Committee of National Expenditure reported on the Royal Ordnance Factories and found them "guilty of considerable lack of foresight in planning," and this at a time when "Canadian production of munitions in the second quarter of the current year was almost three times that of the same period last year."[93]

The right weapons were vital. Ellis Smith quoted the German panzer expert, Guderian, in the House of Commons:

Four weeks' drum fire, a four months' pitched battle and 400,000 casualties gained for the British in 1917 a strip of land nine miles by five miles. At Cambrai with 400 tanks and the loss of 400 men they obtained the same results in 12 hours.

The British had forgotten that, said Smith. "For 20 years they have preferred to strut about with spurs on instead of encouraging mechanical engineering."

This is an engineers' war and a war of machines. Is there an engineer in the War Cabinet? Is there an engineer among the supply Ministers? Is there an engineer on the General Staff? Do the General Staff accept the advice tendered by the engineers? I have documentary evidence to prove that they do not.[94]

A man of ingenuity and restlessness of mind was required, a man "of sufficient status and authority" and one "with knowledge of science in relation to industry." The British, as Mackenzie King had done when seeking a leader at the outbreak of the war, turned to McNaughton. It will have been noted that the "influential deputation" that had put its proposals before the government on 16 July had requested the setting up of a "scientific and technical joint board" and it was to head such a body that Churchill sought McNaughton.*

Churchill asked Australia's High Commissioner, S. M. Bruce (later Viscount Bruce of Melbourne), to sound McNaughton out, which he did on 9 July. Bruce, a lawyer and businessman from Victoria who had been educated in England, was a former prime minister of his country; he attended meetings of the British War Cabinet on behalf of Australia. McNaughton, who was in London to attend a meeting of the Chiefs of Staff Committee, called on Bruce at the War Cabinet offices at his request, and there Bruce asked him whether he would take over the direction of technical development for all three services as a member of the British government. Whether a formal approach would have followed is not known, for McNaughton did not hesitate to put his country ahead of whatever personal ambitions he might have had. He refused to consider it, explaining that he was "responsible to the people of Canada for the Canadian Army overseas" and felt that he should remain with it. He believed that the main trouble lay, not with the navy or the air force, but with the army; and here the able General Weeks, as DCIGS, could improve matters were he given support for drastic measures.[96]

It is idle to speculate on what General McNaughton's personal fortunes in the Second World War might have been had he shown interest in the proposed appointment to chair a board "with prestige and influence equal to that of the Chiefs of Staff Committee." But it may be assumed that if Lord Beaverbrook (as Minister of Aircraft Production) made a name for his work for one service,

---

*At the time of McNaughton's leaving the Canadian government in August, 1945, he referred to Churchill's invitation to come into the British government, "which," Mackenzie King recorded, "I recall."[95]

McNaughton, had he been appointed, would have done no less for three. It can, however, be said that the approach, informal though it was, justified McNaughton's policies on weapon development. In equipment, the First Canadian Army was still far from being complete. At the end of July, for example, one of the armoured divisions (the 5th) had, against an establishment of 332 tanks, only 84 outmoded models, of which 44 had no armament whatsoever. The other armoured division in Canada fared even worse.[97] Tanks and guns, then, were the crying need of the Army at that time, and McNaughton concentrated on the problems throughout 1942. But not only that. He wanted to be sure that his men had the best weapons, in every field, that could be devised. "In history," he wrote when Chief of the General Staff in 1932, "we are not long concerned with nations unable or unwilling to keep pace with armament development."

However notable their civilization, however brave their warriors, and however adept their statesmen in the art of treaty-drafting, they soon pass off the stage before the onward march of those well able to forge and wield the newer weapons.[98]

McNaughton's was the correct policy and the British recognized it as such; hence their overtures. His acceptance could only have benefited both the British and Canadian forces. Canada, it is plain, had produced a soldier of whom she could be proud, a recognized expert in this field, on whom various branches of the British government depended for advice.*

July, which opened impressively with a Dominion Day service at Westminster Abbey, was busy for McNaughton. That month he had two main occupations other than building the Army and

---

*And in 1944 Norman Robertson (Under-Secretary of State) told McNaughton the gist of a conversation he had had with Colonel Zabotin, Soviet Military Attaché:

"In referring to his studies at the Red Army Staff College, Colonel Zabotin said that careful attention was devoted to the military theory of contemporary foreign writers such as General de Gaulle. In this connection he said that General Mc-Naughton's technical study [published in the *Canadian Defence Quarterly*] on questions of artillery fire was regarded as a classic."[99]

weapon development: the championship of Canadian autonomy and the review of a Chiefs of Staff decision which he undertook at Churchill's bidding.

The commemoration service at the Abbey was moving; Canada's ensign flew red from the Abbey staff while another, given to the dean by three representatives of the fighting services, lay on the altar. The notes of "O Canada," played on the organ, soared through Edward the Confessor's great church and thanks were given in prayer for the great men in Canada's history. Canadians, both servicemen and civilians, filled the pews. It was rendered doubly poignant for General and Mrs. McNaughton by a personal tragedy—the loss of their son Ian, a squadron leader in the RAF, who had failed to return from a raid over Germany on the night of 22 June, 1942. On the 23rd Mrs. McNaughton had motored to London, where the General was recording a message for Canada to mark the opening of Army Week, to break the news; as always, in bad moments and in good, she was at his side.

The question of the constitutional position of the Canadian Army in the United Kingdom and, more particularly in an expeditionary force that might be formed, had arisen at the end of May. The War Office had asked the Dominions Office, in the event of operations outside the United Kingdom, for the Canadian Army to be placed under full control of the commander-in-chief of the expeditionary force, to be employed whenever and wherever required by him.[100] That, for McNaughton, was far too comprehensive. He discussed it with Paget on 2 June, after which Paget informed the War Office:

From the practical point of view I do not anticipate difficulties over the question of operational control and I suggest that it is best to leave it to McNaughton and me to carry on as we are now doing in close co-operation and not attempt further to define our position by means of legal definitions.[101]

Ten days later the Secretary of State for Dominion Affairs addressed a more reasonable request to the Canadian High Commissioner. He asked the Canadian government to approve the inclusion of Canadian forces in the prospective expeditionary force and their being under the operational control of the British Commander-in-Chief; and that those Canadian forces remaining in the United Kingdom, which were available for operational duties, should be regarded as being under the operational control of the C-in-C Home Forces.[102] McNaughton, however, objected to the High Commissioner's message notifying the Canadian government of this and suggesting its acceptance. He considered that the message, as it stood, lent itself to misinterpretation by "elements" in the War Office and Home Forces as "a surrender by the Canadian Government of effective control over the Canadian Army." He anticipated "a series of small encroachments on our autonomy" —none of which by itself would justify reference to the Canadian government—but which, in the aggregate, would "impose subordination."[103] There must, argued McNaughton, be a provision for Canadian troops, in the last resort, to be taken out of combination with the British. This power, and "the knowledge that I would not hesitate to use it in an extreme case in the discharge of my duty to the Government of Canada," would ensure the retention by the Canadian forces of their present autonomous position.[104] But Massey demurred. Relationship with the British, he felt, were such that disagreements would smooth themselves out in a friendly way.

"It must be remembered," McNaughton recalled, "that the High Commissioner had never had experience of battle even on the lowest level of command. In conversation he showed a lack of awareness of the confusion that an uncertain wording in a military policy directive could cause. He had no understanding of the difficulties the Canadian Corps Commander had experienced with the British in 1918. A Contingent Directive of the grave character under contemplation was no place for the slightest ambiguity of any sort and Massey's attempts to placate the British, if acted upon, might well bring disaster to Canada's forces."[105] It was not 1918 now. Canada, a nation in her own right (though McNaughton described autonomy as "often depending—with many an anxious moment—on the force of military character of the Canadian Commander"),[106] could guard against the employment of her troops

in unsound operations by the insertion of a clause, clearly understood, before commitment. To do otherwise would be to provoke
a situation which would or would not be smoothed out by the
personalities of the British and Canadian commanders concerned
—they might well be Brooke and McNaughton. Whoever would
be involved, McNaughton felt that essential precautions must be
taken. He therefore remained firm. As Massey had previously
discovered, the head of the Canadian Army "generally has his
mind made up on the matters he wishes to discuss, and co-operation with him is a bit like co-operation with an Act of Parliament."[107]

McNaughton put before the High Commissioner a revised
wording which Massey finally adopted. It boiled down to this:
Canadian troops would be under the operational control of a
commander-in-chief of a British expeditionary force but such
direction would be exercised through the Canadian commander
who, unless otherwise specified by him, would have the right to
approve or not any task or plan of operation assigned the Canadian troops.[108] The War Office, anxious to retain as free a hand
as possible for its commander-in-chief, objected, politely but very
strongly, that its existing formula was adequate.[109] Nevertheless, in
September the War Office accepted the position and McNaughton
thought he could be satisfied that Canadian autonomy, having thus
been emphasized, would have to be respected.[110]

On 9 July McNaughton appeared before the Chiefs of Staff at
their invitation. Churchill and the War Cabinet, he was told,
wished him to review an operation known as JUPITER.

This operation, planned for not earlier than October when the
hours of daylight would have dwindled, had been pushed by
Churchill during the late spring and early summer as a means of
bringing effective and immediate aid to the Russians. On 2 June
he had drawn up a memorandum for consideration by the Chiefs
of Staff Committee, advocating the seizure and retention of two
aerodromes in Northern Norway from which Allied convoys to
Russia were being attacked with consequent heavy loss. The

British Prime Minister wanted JUPITER as an alternative to SLEDGEHAMMER—an "emergency" cross-Channel attack on Brest or Cherbourg proposed for 1942—which was strongly backed by Roosevelt, but which the British considered far too precipitate.[111] Churchill urged that about seventy bombers and a hundred fighters based on two airfields guarded by ten to twelve thousand German troops were all that prevented entry into Norway. As he himself said: "If we could gain possession of these airfields and establish an equal force there, not only would the northern sea route to Russia be kept open, but we should have set up a second front on a small scale from which it would be most difficult to eject us. If the going was good we could advance gradually southward, unrolling the Nazi map of Europe from the top. All that has to be done is to oust the enemy from the airfields and destroy their garrisons."[112]

"Unrolling the Nazi map of Europe from the top": the grandly rolling cadences of this Churchillian phrase, beating sonorously with the insistence of a tom-tom, became a nightmare to the Chiefs of Staff—and to McNaughton—in the weeks that followed.

Until the last moment, insisted Churchill, the Germans would not know whether JUPITER was an expedition or another convoy; and once SLEDGEHAMMER was definitely off, the Russians would support such an operation and there might also be important repercussions in Sweden and Finland. Describing the actual landing, Churchill wrote: "This is a fierce and hazardous operation, but small beer compared with what we are talking about in 'Sledgehammer.' "[113] It would, moreover, be possible to bring superior forces to bear at the point of attack.

It was in fact an "Arctic Gallipoli" (though strategically not so well founded as its 1915 predecessor), designed to satisfy to some extent the importunate demands of the Russians and the clamour of public opinion in North America and Britain for a second front. This alone was not a sound objective but there was, at that time, an apparent danger of Germany inflicting such defeats on Russia that she would be forced out of the war. This must not be forgotten in assessing the discussions of strategy which took place that summer. If successful, the action would eliminate the risks the Arctic convoys had to run, thereby saving hundreds of lives, many precious ships and thousands of tons of equipment and supplies; and it would help to keep the Russians fighting. However, after study by the Chiefs of Staff, Churchill's proposal was rejected. They reported that, apart from the hazards of the operation, the country had insufficient resources to undertake it at that time.[114]

Ismay, Chief Staff Officer to Churchill in his other capacity as Minister of Defence, has reported that "not once during the whole war" did Churchill "overrule his military advisers on a purely military question."[115] But he came close to it on this occasion. Not content with the adamant "No" with which the Chiefs of Staff had pronounced judgment on JUPITER, the Prime Minister requested that the project be reviewed by a new and unprejudiced mind. Attlee, the Deputy Prime Minister, thereupon proposed McNaughton as the person best fitted to carry out the investigation. Churchill warmed to the suggestion:

I thought that this operation would give a glorious opportunity to the Canadian Army, which had now for two years been eating its heart out in Britain awaiting the invader. I therefore had a long talk on this subject in the garden at Chequers with General McNaughton, of whom I had a high opinion, and whose influence with the Canadian Government was powerful. I explained the whole position to him in all its bearings, and asked him whether he would conduct a personal inquiry into the scheme and make a plan, for which all aid would be given him by our technical departments.[116]

The meeting at Chequers took place on 12 July. On the 8th, however, before he discussed the operation with McNaughton at Chequers, Churchill had directed Brooke to entrust McNaughton with the preliminary study and planning of JUPITER and to give him all the necessary assistance from the British Chiefs of Staff organization. While dubious about the need for a review —(evidently smarting a little, Brooke commented in his diary: "It having been suggested . . . that, with his more flexible and fertile brain, McNaughton would find a way out when the Chiefs of Staff had failed . . .")[117]—the Chief of the Imperial General Staff could do no other than bring the Canadian commander in. The Chiefs of Staff withheld their previous criticism from McNaughton so that he could enter the study with an open mind. After he had been given the task, however, he soon found out from Brooke what this attitude really was. "After lunch I [Brooke] sent for him to my office and informed him privately how matters stood, as I did not want him afterwards to imagine that we were suggesting that the Canadians should undertake an operation which we considered impracticable."[118]

Decidedly "unusual constitutional arrangements" had been made (as the Chief of the Air Staff was to report later),[119] to permit the review by the Canadian leader of a decision made by the British Chiefs of Staff, "the supreme battle headquarters of the Armed Forces of Great Britain, the Commonwealth and Empire, and of the Allied Forces in exile."[120] The position in which Mc-Naughton found himself was extremely awkward. If he arrived at the same conclusion as the Chiefs of Staff he was bound to arouse Churchill's ire; and if he agreed with Churchill that the operation was feasible, over the heads of the Chiefs of Staff, the resignation of all the members of that august body was not unlikely. In fact Brooke told him later that he would have resigned. One thing, however, was quite certain. McNaughton would call the shots as he saw them, impartially and with no regard to self. He would do what he had to with integrity and common sense. The decision to entrust the review to him had been wise.

On 10 July McNaughton set to work on the review. He spent the morning studying the papers, and then sent for Brigadier Guy Simonds, a man gifted with cool intelligence, to head the staff who would undertake the detailed work. He also notified Canada by cable of what was in the wind. At midday a telephone call requested McNaughton to lunch with Churchill at Chequers on Sunday, 12 July.

McNaughton remembered the meeting as a pleasant one, "a privileged interview during which Churchill covered nearly all the ramifications of the war in a most intimate fashion," and, knowing how vital the information would be to the Canadian government, he made a synopsis of what was discussed immediately after the meeting and sent it on to Ottawa.

Those present at the luncheon were the Prime Minister and Mrs. Churchill; Lord Cherwell [the former Frederick Lindemann, Churchill's scientific adviser]; Sir Archibald Sinclair [Secretary of State for Air] and Lady Sinclair; the Prime Minister's daughter, Mrs. Sandys and her husband; Major-General Ismay; Commander Thompson; and a secretary and young lady whose names I did not know.[121]

Before lunch McNaughton had an animated conversation with Lord Cherwell which continued — the two sat side by side — at the luncheon table:

I had a very intimate talk with him on some of the newer weapons of war that I had conceived. Though I was never too convinced of the fundamental soundness of Lindemann* we had a very interesting talk. Churchill in those days never moved without him and always called him in as the "Prof." He would say, "Here, Prof, come along"—and this, that or the other thing. As I recollect, I was very much concerned at that time with the question of the flame throwers—Churchill had backed the chap who put the flame thrower into the Churchill tank. If you put his name on it he got mesmerized and so there was a proposal to build the "Crocodile," the flame thrower based on the tank that bore his name. I had taken the opposite view and that was that if flame was to be of any use—a weapon of special but limited usefulness—the thing that was most important was mobility and the Canadian carrier seemed to be the most promising vehicle.[122]

"At the luncheon . . . the conversation ranged over a wide variety of subjects. . . . A disposition map of Libya giving the situation at about 0700 hours this morning was brought in and the Prime Minister and General Ismay expressed satisfaction; they thought that Auchinleck appeared to have opened the door of a trap."[123]

After lunch was over, Churchill, dressed in a dark grey siren suit, his zip-up "rompers," conducted McNaughton into the garden. "We went out into the orchard and he sat me down

*He questioned his judgment.

alongside him on the bench under an apple tree. Everyone else was excluded from the garden. In the course of the discussion he got up and marched up and down in front of me, to and fro, giving out his ponderous thoughts. And I was answering—when questions were asked I gave him the answer—and I gave him quite a lot of information about Canada he never had before."[124]

Had McNaughton been a collector of Churchilliana he would have garnered at first hand some handsome gems for his collection. He was not but, even so, he noted every word with a fine exactness.

The Prime Minister referred to a possible German attack on Murmansk. He said one new German division was reported moving up. He referred also to a possible Russian attack from Murmansk which might draw off forces from Norway and elsewhere. He mentioned the growing importance of Murmansk as the season advanced towards winter when Archangel is closed. He mentioned the snowmobile which is under development in Canada. He said that even fifty of these machines in which men could live and fight under snow conditions might have a significant effect on the course of operations in North Norway. I said that I knew the Canadian General Staff had taken up this project energetically and that already there were reports of a pilot model having been produced by General Motors. I also knew that the Ford car had been adapted as a snowmobile. I said that I would cable Canada for early reports and sample machines.[125]

The conversation then turned, as McNaughton had expected, to the review of Operation JUPITER:

In referring to his difficulties with corporate advice from the three Services, Churchill said, "Soldier, sailor and airman are each by themselves bold fellows but together they become filled with doubts and inhibitions."

In reference to the Home Fleet he described the attitude of Admiral Tovey towards distractions from the important task of protection of the North Atlantic convoy route.

The Prime Minister referred to the Russian convoy: the difficulties which had to be faced, the losses which had been incurred and the reasons why this effort to help our allies should be maintained. He gave a short appreciation of the effect any failure in this convoy might have on Stalin and on Roosevelt. The Prime Minister referred to the German air and land forces in North

Norway which I described as "probably the most remunerative detachment in all history."

Churchill referred to the possible use of British sea mobility to cause dispersion of German Forces in Norway and along the coast of the Low Countries and France. He referred to our slight margin of sea superiority and the far-reaching effect which might result if it were lost by any mischance. If the *Tirpitz* and the German heavy cruisers with her were not contained, then the flow on the North Atlantic would cease until they were rounded up again. He spoke of the effect of the losses in the Russian convoy; on the morale of the merchant marine and said that beyond a certain point or percentage this effort could clearly not go on.

The Prime Minister spoke about the fundamental differences between climatic conditions in the North in October and in December after snow was on the ground. We spoke of the importance of having expert knowledge of the precautions to be taken in winter flying.

He next spoke of the defect inherent in the German character whereby they found difficulty in improvising to meet a thrust which had deranged one of their methodical plans.

Churchill emphasized that the present task is a study, without commitment to employ Canadian Troops, but he remarked that our people naturally knew about cold climates.

The Prime Minister expressed a wish to visit the Canadian Armoured Division at an early date. He had never seen a Ram tank. In talking about the size of the Canadian Forces now in the United Kingdom, Churchill expressed surprise at the numbers we now have here. In his estimate he spoke of some fifty or sixty thousand!!*

In response to a question from the Prime Minister I gave an outline of the development to date in respect to the setting up of the special staff. I referred to my meeting with C. of S. Committee on Thursday, 9 July; to the receipt of the papers on the subject on 10 July, and to the meeting yesterday, Saturday, 11 July, with Major-General Kennedy and others when it had been agreed that the "I" [Intelligence] and "G" [Operations] staffs would be named today and that we would be careful to base our analysis on facts and not on opinions and I said I proposed to buttress myself against any pre-conceived opinions being interjected into the argument. I told him also of the procedure I intended to follow, namely, as a first step, the assessment of the enemy's land forces and of those needed to meet them. This would give a measure of

---

*Canada had more than three times that number of soldiers in Great Britain at the time.

the Naval and Air requirements. The Prime Minister remarked on the importance of obtaining Norwegian information and the co-operation of their staff in London.

In reference to various possible operations the Prime Minister spoke of the importance of having plans worked out in great detail and placed away for ready use when the proper opportunity came.[126]

They discussed other subjects. Churchill recounted at length, in a pugnacious yet humorous way, some of his experiences in the South African War and particularly his associations with General Buller. He criticized the War Office then and now and said: "We dislike armies and so we are content to have the worst War Office in the world to point to as an example."[127]

He was particularly bitter about British failure to produce prototype tanks before the war and for this he blamed Hore-Belisha. He criticized the army for an over-use of motor transport and the air force for its large ground staff. He said that one fighting airman protected two hundred and fifty draft evaders.[128] "So few," McNaughton wryly interjected, "to cover so many?" The Canadian leader then observed that he understood the Germans devoted a higher proportion of their troops to repair and maintenance than the British.[129]

The gearing of industry to the war machine was next reviewed. McNaughton felt that though much had been done, Britain's industry was still far from being efficient. The country was not using men or machines as economically, as imaginatively, in fact as well, as it needed to do. The result was that Britain was not producing enough to justify the amount of manpower committed to factories up and down the country. He saw no reason why this should not be pointed out to Churchill; it would be foolish to ignore reality:

The question of North American industry came up and I referred to the importance of standardizing; and to the fundamental difference between an industry based on mass production and one based on the skill of the individual craftsman. I quoted as examples the Bofors guns and the 25-pounder breech blocks in which savings of from 50% to 80% of machine manhours had been effected in Canada by the introduction of special-purpose machines and the breaking of the job into single operations. I referred to the new M.4 American tank, to the advantages of cast steel, and to the U.S.A. 75-mm. gun. The discussion then shifted to the 25-pounder and the possibility that the U.S. will adopt this weapon, which the Prime Minister said was now in plentiful supply.

I made reference to the increased importance of British industry undertaking maintenance and the urgent need that research and development of new weapons and equipment should take place in the environment of mass production that is on the North American continent.

From that the conversation again turned to tanks, a subject dear to Churchill's heart since he had done so much to bring about their development in the First World War.

The Prime Minister again expressed resentment against those who failed to prepare in 1936 even a prototype of the new tanks, and therefore of their criticism now. He expressed regret that he had ever had a hand in starting the tank because the British race had failed to keep the advantage. He referred to the deplorable complacency in British political and public affairs of 1938.

Just before I left, Lord Cherwell asked if, in infantry anti-tank weapons, the suppression of flash and bang are worth the sacrifice of 10% of range and I replied, "Yes, most certainly."[130]

It had, McNaughton concluded, been an interesting experience. It was to be followed by another meeting at Chequers, perhaps more interesting still, when the outcome of the JUPITER review at last became clear in September.

McNaughton was left pretty much in the dark by the British planners as to what operations they intended against the enemy in 1942. Since the end of April he had known that a large-scale raid against Dieppe (RUTTER) was contemplated and on 20 May the 2nd Canadian Division had assembled in the Isle of Wight to practise its part in the operation. RUTTER had come to a halt with bad weather on 8 July, the day set for the assault, but the plan had been revived a week later under the code name JUBILEE and was to be carried out in August.

McNaughton knew that General Marshall was over in London (he had met him in Paget's mess on 24 July) but he had no idea that he was there with Admiral King and Harry Hopkins for momentous, perhaps the most momentous, strategic discussions of the war. On the instructions of Roosevelt, Marshall had first come to England in April to press for a main cross-Channel invasion in 1943 and a more limited operation by about the middle of September, 1942, if a critical situation warranted it, or if the German situation in the West was sufficiently weakened. As we have seen, the British also had plans for this (SLEDGEHAMMER), but by the end of July, considering the operation premature at that time—and therefore foolhardy—they had managed to substitute for it Operation TORCH, an Anglo-American occupation of French North Africa. Canadian participation in TORCH was not contemplated; the British, in fact, had "a very definite reason for not caring to send them to Africa."

During 1941 malicious criticism had represented the British as pursuing a policy of fighting the war with Dominion soldiers. "I have long feared the dangerous reactions on Australian and world opinion," wrote Mr. Churchill, "of our seeming to fight all our battles in the Middle East only with Dominion troops." He accordingly exerted himself actively to get additional *British* divisions from the United Kingdom into action in the Desert with a view to "freeing ourselves from the imputation, however injust, of always using other people's troops and blood." To have sent Canadian formations to Africa would have played into the hands of the hostile propagandists.[131]

Though McNaughton would have welcomed fighting his Army as such in North Africa, he did not even hear about the operation until September. General Anderson's First British Army, while it lacked the cohesion of its Canadian equivalent, formed the British force. McNaughton, however, considered there was another motive, though it was not expressed by Churchill, for preferring a British force. Canadian ideas of independence were already too strong to suit the British taste; a close liaison in North Africa between Canadian and United States troops, coming as they did from neighbouring countries, would undoubtedly strengthen that independence.[132] He said much the same to Ralston:

I spoke of the attitude of the War Office before TORCH. Brooke had kept me apart from Eisenhower as far as he could. He said he did not want the complication of another nationality. He had given us a subsidiary task, to prepare an operation which might probably be required.* This he knew, and so did I, was a very remote contingency.[133]

McNaughton did hear from Lieutenant-General Sir Archibald Nye, the Acting Chief of the Imperial General Staff in the absence of Brooke (who was in the Middle East), that ROUNDUP, the full-scale invasion of France, would be later than had been thought; that was on 3 August. But he was not told that it was TORCH that would make the postponement inevitable. Nye wished to know if the Canadians would be ready for the invasion by May, 1943. By then, McNaughton said, the Army, together with the reinforcements required to cover wastage at the predicted rates, would be deficient by thirty-nine thousand all ranks of those required. He wondered if it was reasonable to set the target date at 1 May, 1943, or should it be another date some months later. Nye could not say; it all depended on the situation on the Russian front. If the Germans were able to move even a part of their armies in Russia to the West, a cross-Channel invasion would be possible "only if there should take place a definite and pro- nounced crack in morale in Germany itself as a consequence of bombing, hunger or hardship. If this occurred we should have been guilty of unpardonable lack of preparation if we were not in a position to take advantage of the situation to launch an attack in Northwest Europe."[134]

So McNaughton determined to prepare his Army, *as an army*, as far as possible. His reasoning, reminiscent of Currie's at the time of the German offensives of 1918, is best given in his own words:

Any reduction from this composition would mean that the Cana- dian force proceeding abroad would, from necessity, be allotted a less important role and probably would be decentralized under

---

*This was TONIC, which is examined later.

At the Quebec Arsenal, 1942

Lieutenant-General Crerar and Major-Generals Turner and Montague at Headley Court, April, 1942

British command. This could only result in acceptance by Canada of an inferior role in the total Allied war effort which would reflect adversely upon public opinion generally at home and abroad; [moreover] such splitting up would result in a very marked decrease in the effect we could have on the enemy.[135]

August nineteenth, a lovely summer's day, saw the raid on Dieppe, largely executed, as we have noted, by the 2nd Canadian Division. The story of it has been admirably and comprehensively told by Colonel C. P. Stacey,* and a detailed account is no part of this book; certain points, however, do deserve emphasis.

The plan for the Dieppe operation was a British plan which was endorsed by McNaughton and also by Crerar in whom the military responsibility was vested. Of it, Montgomery said, "I am satisfied that the operation as planned is a possible one and has good prospects of success, given:

(a) Favourable weather.

(b) Average luck.

(c) That the Navy put us ashore roughly in the right places, and at the right times. . . ."[136]

Crerar agreed that "the plan is sound, and most carefully worked out" and pointed out that the commander of the 2nd Division, Roberts, and his brigade commanders had "expressed full confidence in their tasks—given a break in luck."[137] McNaughton was "satisfied that all arrangements . . . are in order and this operation may now proceed."[138] As for the troops, in Montgomery's words, "The Canadians are 1st Class chaps; if anyone can pull it off, they will."[139]

But plans, no matter how meticulously made, can usually be counted on only as far as the point of first contact with the enemy. "Thereafter," as General Sir Frederick Morgan, who planned the Normandy landings of 1944, points out, "the god of battles takes the matter into both hands, one side of the scale goes up, the other down."[140] In other words, there is a factor of luck which cannot be accurately assessed before the operation goes in and so the outcome is a gamble, as war has always been.

---

*See *Six Years of War*, pp. 325-408.

On 19 August luck did not favour the raiding forces. The intention was to capture Dieppe by means of simultaneous flank attacks delivered "at the beginning of nautical twilight" (while it was still dark enough for the landing craft to touch down in safety) to be followed, half an hour later, by the main attacks directly on the port itself. Once captured, a perimeter would be established around Dieppe while the port installations and other targets were destroyed.* The force would then withdraw. The timings, especially of the flank attacks, sought to achieve surprise, a major principle of war. Though all seemed well at first—the weather was good and the invasion fleet crept across the dark Channel on smooth water—surprise was far from complete. At 3:47 A.M., at a time when the assault craft had been offloaded from their mother ships and had been on their way to the beaches for nearly an hour, the most easterly group of the seaborne force ran into an enemy convoy and a sharp fight ensued. This had unfortunate consequences: the sound of gunfire out at sea alerted the enemy in the eastern part of the area to be attacked; and the landing craft carrying men to that area were scattered so that only seven out of twenty-three of them succeeded in landing their troops.[141] The attack in the extreme eastern sector, therefore, failed.

Though there was no general alarm along the whole front to be attacked—in the west the first wave of infantry landed without a shot being fired at them—it was McNaughton's conviction that bad luck in the east eventually ruined the whole enterprise. Failure on the extreme left (east) extended to the unit closest to it and so, slowly but progressively, misfortune crept from east to west until at last the units on the western flank, which had at first been successful, were also affected and forced to withdraw.[142] But for that chance encounter at sea, McNaughton believed the operation would probably have been successful.[143]

---

*For these demolitions, McNaughton had taken the lead in developing, with explosives experts, shaped hollow charges. These would demolish reinforced-concrete walls up to a thickness of six feet. "Beehives," "hayricks" and "cones," as they became known, proved especially useful on D-Day, 1944, and in subsequent operations. Further details will be found in A. J. Kerry and W. A. McDill, *The History of the Corps of Royal Canadian Engineers*, II (Ottawa: Military Engineers Association of Canada, 1962-1966).

McNaughton had been in his office all day on the 19th to receive reports of JUBILEE; he motored to Portsmouth that evening to meet General Roberts and the troops returning from Dieppe and his heart was heavy. Though the casualties had not yet been assessed,* it was quite apparent that this first battle had been very costly for Canada. Next day, at Mountbatten's headquarters, he heard the reports of officers and men and three days later he stood in Brookwood Cemetery while forty soldiers, who had died of wounds sustained at Dieppe, were buried. Already, however, he was looking beyond the immediate tragic result. "These lessons," he said, "should facilitate to a very great degree the carrying out of operations of similar and larger scale whenever necessary,"[144] and that proved to be the case; they saved countless lives in the grand-scale invasion of Normandy during 1944.

Many inaccurate or misleading accounts of Dieppe were published. One book by an American correspondent, which appeared some months later, wrongly stated that Canadian troops were used at McNaughton's insistence, and implied that the Canadians had altered the British plan of attack to include the frontal assault against the port. McNaughton, though invited to do so, characteristically declined to refute the statements; such action would, he considered, be interpreted as seeking "to shift responsibility" onto the British. (The reader of Colonel Stacey's account will note the attendance of Brooke on 30 June at a private conference on the subject of Dieppe at 10 Downing Street and his obvious responsibility for the operation;[145] he will also note, from the complete absence of any reference to the conference in *The Turn of the Tide,* Brooke's equally obvious reluctance to shoulder any part of it.) This decision, as Stacey pointed out, was "one which in the end probably did General McNaughton himself considerable harm," for the Canadian press continued to dwell on Dieppe for many months and repeated a good deal of ill-formed criticism. "Although, as has been made apparent," the official historian continued, "the responsibility for the tactical plan was widely distributed and the Canadian share was limited, it was declared in

*They totalled 3,367 all ranks.

at least one respectable publication* that the project of a raid on Dieppe and the plan for it were almost exclusively the work of Canadian officers and proved the bankruptcy of Canadian generalship; and there can be little doubt that such criticism did something to undermine the hitherto unassailable prestige of General McNaughton with the public.[146] The criticism would also, we may be sure, strengthen the hand of Ralston when he placed the question of McNaughton's military judgment before the Prime Minister in the summer of 1943.

Although the JUPITER review had been completed and passed to the Chiefs of Staff Committee on 6 August, it was not until September that McNaughton heard how it had been received. The Chiefs of Staff praised it highly; it was "one of the clearest and most ably worked out appreciations which they had ever had before them"—but then it did support the position they had taken (that an invasion of Northern Norway was impracticable) against that of Churchill.[147]

The review pointed out that there was "little possibility of surprise, and that success would depend on a combination of weather conditions against which the odds would be about six to one in December," the month proposed for the attack. The general conclusion was: "The operation is an extremely hazardous one. With good fortune quick and decisive successes might be gained—on the contrary, the result might be a military disaster of the first magnitude. In view of the sizes of the forces involved it is considered that the risks would only be acceptable if politically the results to be achieved were judged to be of the highest importance."[148]

On 17 September McNaughton had a long talk with Brooke in London. He had now heard in a roundabout way of TORCH and that this would postpone ROUNDUP until a later date, and he told Brooke, quite flatly, that "the lack of stability in planning for operations was a source of considerable embarrassment to him." The Canadian Army had been invited to take part in

---

*Saturday Night, 12 June, 1943.

ROUNDUP (the cross-Channel invasion) with a target date of 1 May, 1943. Did Brooke now know what that meant? To complete the Army by that date manpower resources would have to be stretched to the limit, encroaching to some extent upon industrial production. There would be in England, after the next convoy had arrived, 167,000 men for the Army programme; there must be 250,000 and that would require a flow of 8,000 to 10,000 men every month for the next nine or ten months. Staffs and units would have to be organized. All this had been explained to Ottawa and early approval was expected when now, through a chance conversation with Paget, he understood there had been a change of plan. Such changes, unless he was informed of them, might have grave effects on the Canadian war effort and could seriously damage McNaughton's relations with his own government.

Brooke confirmed that TORCH (the occupation of French North Africa) would probably take place; ROUNDUP was still under consideration but the target date had been postponed. It was not that he did not want to give McNaughton information; his difficulty too was that planning was continually shifting and there was no stability. The JUPITER review was very much to the fore and only with difficulty had he stopped Churchill from sending cables to Stalin. Regular meetings were the only way of keeping McNaughton informed and Brooke suggested they should meet every two or three weeks. The CIGS was one of many in England at that time who felt that McNaughton should be at their disposal.

Brooke then turned to the review of JUPITER which McNaughton told him he was to discuss with Churchill. He emphasized that the Chiefs of Staff agreed fully with the Canadian appreciation; and if TORCH went on there would be by no means enough shipping for Norway. But McNaughton would have a hard job convincing Churchill that an invasion of Northern Norway was impracticable. The Prime Minister was set on using three Canadian divisions out of five initially required for JUPITER; McNaughton was in for a "stormy session." It would be well to make no reference to this conversation or to infer that they shared the same views, as otherwise they might expect to face

Churchill's charge that they had "ganged up against him." Churchill was a difficult man to deal with, Brooke continued. He talked of his recent visit to Moscow with the Prime Minister, of Churchill's great energy and of his habit of appearing in Brooke's bedroom in the early hours of the morning to discuss strategy. Brooke deplored "the constant flow of proposals for operations and changes in operations with which he deluged his military advisers" and his "constant suggestions of particular individuals for particular responsibilities." He had great difficulty in convincing Churchill that these matters should be left to his military advisers. Brooke had had to tell him firmly that "he could not play a pawn on the chess-board of war and expect it to be a queen for he had not the particular knowledge to know a queen from a pawn." It seemed, the CIGS added, that Churchill regarded himself as a reincarnation of his great ancestor Marlborough.

McNaughton replied that, in his judgment, JUPITER was not a practical operation of war; he had so informed the Canadian government and they knew that his opinion had been endorsed by the Chiefs of Staff Committee. It was most unlikely, therefore, that the use of Canadian troops in Norway would be approved and he would never proceed without that sanction.[149]

Churchill invited McNaughton to meet him at Chequers on Saturday, 19 September. He arrived shortly before half past one and was met by Commander Thompson with whom he chatted for a short while in the large reception room. Then the Prime Minister and Mrs. Churchill came downstairs and the four went in to lunch. After luncheon Churchill led McNaughton to what he called the "circular seat" in the orchard, where they talked all afternoon. Then they went in for tea with Thompson, Lord Cherwell and Churchill's son Randolph, after which McNaughton drove back to Headley Court.

"My discussion with the Prime Minister," McNaughton recorded, "commenced on going into lunch and continued with few breaks until I left at 1740 hours [5:40 P.M.]. It covered a very wide range of subjects. . . ." The first major topic, as may be imagined, was the invasion of Northern Norway.

The Canadians, Churchill began, were no doubt busily preparing for "Arctic war." McNaughton parried the thrust. That was far from being the case; their attention had not been deflected from ROUNDUP, though he believed there was now talk of postponing the operation. Churchill would not be drawn. His attention remained focused on Norway and McNaughton's JUPITER review which, he said, was open to criticism. "I replied," McNaughton wrote, "that I liked opinions out in the open and, where I disagreed, he could be sure I would say so." Then, Churchill continued, as a start the opinion expressed that aircraft carriers could not operate successfully within the range of shore-based aircraft could be discounted. The navy had tried out a new method of using carriers; they had used them in threes to seaward, beyond the range of shore-based aircraft, but within reach of the convoy they had to cover. The air defence of a recent convoy to Malta had been successful, as had that of another to Archangel. Carrier-borne aircraft, he assured McNaughton, could now beat off air attacks coming from the coast without putting their parent ship in jeopardy. McNaughton was glad to hear it. The opinion he had expressed had been based on the best technical advice available at the time; but he knew very well that nothing was static in war. New technical equipment and methods could quite easily alter the delicate balance between attack and defence, sometimes in favour of one, sometimes of the other. He would review his appreciation in the light of this latest experience.

There was another matter, Churchill continued. A much greater power of moving troops by road and effecting air concentrations had been conceded to the Germans than had been allowed the Allied forces; this disparity was surely wrong. McNaughton did not think so. The figures for road movement had been worked out in a most careful way. The Germans had improved the Arctic Highway and other roads and their ability to concentrate and maintain their formations had not been overstated. As for air, his figures rested "on the factual basis of what the German Air Force had actually achieved when it had concentrated to cover the move of the *Tirpitz* along the Norwegian coast." The estimate of German mobility was certainly impressive but it would be dangerous to underrate the enemy's achievements.

Churchill, as Roosevelt had done earlier in the year, then stressed the importance of keeping Russia in the war: ". . . the very great political importance of forwarding supplies to Russia . . . where the principal fighting was taking place; there was no more useful business for us than to make arms and give them to Russia. If Russia were to cease active fighting, Germany would have [the divisions] now on the Eastern Front available for essays through the Caucasus, through Turkey, through Spain and Morocco into West Africa, or even for an attack on England." The very fact that the recent convoy to North Russia had got through in substantial measure made it impossible for him not to continue to send supplies by that route. "If this one had had the same losses as the last it might have been possible . . . to say to Stalin, 'Look, it is not worth while!' " Now the convoys would continue and the risks must be reduced. The naval escorts had proved costly in ships, oil and effort but the mechant sailors deserved protection. How much easier it would be if the Germans were driven out of Northern Norway. "The German investment in troops and aircraft in northern Norway," he continued, using the words McNaughton had used to him in July, "is one of the most remunerative in history. It must be eliminated!"

Stalin, Churchill felt sure, would provide some divisions in the North for an offensive from Murmansk. The position farther south would stabilize and the Russians would want to have their men fighting somewhere. Why not the North, where in winter they would have a great advantage? Churchill, in Moscow, had indicated possible co-operation by the British to the extent of two divisions. Stalin had then agreed to let his bombers smash the light huts that the Germans used, so that they would freeze to death. What better preparation could there be than that for turning the enemy out?

The Prime Minister then went on to commend that part of McNaughton's appreciation which stated that plans, to be of any use, must be translated from paper into action. That was it exactly. While he did not agree with all the statements, nevertheless it was an admirable paper and would form the basis for further action.* He reviewed the various projects then in contemplation. ROUNDUP would have to be postponed if TORCH materialized because of the few American troops in Britain. And TORCH, of which he had told Stalin, was important. It would give American troops an opportunity to fight at an early date; it might remove the menace of Rommel and free the sea route to Suez and beyond; it would encourage Turkey; and it would open the way for an attack on Italy. As already mentioned, SLEDGE-HAMMER, the "emergency" plan for an attack on Brest or Cherbourg in 1942, would not go in. JUPITER might be carried out in January of 1943 or, if it should not but was well prepared, it would at least have given good cover for TORCH and be ready to go in later. Security precautions for JUPITER need not be observed too closely; it would be a good thing for the Germans to have to consider an attack on Norway. This to McNaughton, the commander of a possible Canadian force bound for Northern Norway, could only be alarming in view of the paramount importance, in war, of surprise.

An argument then developed about the correct strategy to be adopted. Should it be ROUNDUP, a direct attack on the enemy's strong centre, or should it be TORCH and JUPITER? Churchill declared that the right thing to do was to *contain* the centre and then carry out sorties on the flanks. McNaughton disagreed. He pointed to the long vulnerable lines of communication required for outflanking and observed that with these sorties "we fought geography—not the enemy." Churchill countered by saying that the enemy had only so many submarines; they might as well attack in one place as another. He did agree, however, that each new line of communication created an additional and heavy commitment for escorting craft. What McNaughton described as "this interchange of views" continued until Churchill pulled himself up short and looked quizzically at McNaughton over the top of his spectacles. "I sometimes envy Stalin," he said: he could shoot

---

*McNaughton, as he stated in his record of their conversation, judged that the Prime Minister had leapt "straight to the plan set forth in the later part." He had "ignored the earlier part wherein the hazards of weather, the lack of protection against the air, difficulties of transport and the possibilities of containment by smaller enemy forces are indicated."

those who disagreed with him and had already expended a great deal of ammunition for that purpose. Perhaps so, said Mc-Naughton with a straight face, but "democracy had some advantages too." Masters, as well as servants, could give up office without being shot. Churchill conceded that there was something in that; he went on to speculate on the number of personal enemies he had. He thought there were only five: Hitler, Tojo, Mussolini, De Valera and Gandhi. Perhaps he should not include Mussolini; that would accord him a dignity he did not deserve.

Churchill's mind was set on JUPITER. Talks with Stalin had been suggested in McNaughton's paper. The Prime Minister thought it would be a good idea to send three or four staff officers to Moscow but—as in July, pacing up and down in his siren suit in front of McNaughton—he began to think aloud. Staff officers from the War Office would penetrate no farther than the lower levels of Soviet planning and that would be a waste of time; it was necessary in Moscow to go to the very top; the present ambassador, Clark-Kerr,* had no access to Stalin; Stafford Cripps had never seen him; Mason-MacFarlane† had only once got forward of Kuybyshev.‡ But if McNaughton would go—and he stopped his perambulation, faced the General directly, and then came over to sit by him—he would certainly see Stalin. He could be sure of that. Churchill continued to speak persuasively. McNaughton could go out on the plane to Cairo, which touched down at Gibraltar, and once in Egypt he would fly on to Moscow; it was fairly comfortable; the RAF would provide a fighter escort. A plane was going to Cairo at the end of the week, in any case, to bring Smuts to London; McNaughton could go in that. The journey to Moscow would take only three or four days and he need not be away for more than three weeks altogether. He could visit the front in Libya and see some of the fighting on the way back. Yes, that was it. He would approach Mackenzie King for his consent to McNaughton's undertaking this important mission.[150]

---

*Sir Archibald Clark-Kerr.

†General F. N. Mason-MacFarlane, Head of the British Military Mission to Russia.

‡The Soviet government had been moved to Kuybyshev in October, 1941, when Moscow was seriously threatened.

Throughout this confidential conversation, McNaughton wrote:

The Prime Minister's tone was most friendly. I felt he was seeking to persuade—perhaps flatter—me into a course of action concerning JUPITER on which he had set his heart, knowing full well that as originally conceived it did not command the minds of his Chiefs of Staff. He repeatedly disclaimed interference with them only to go on and indicate that it was he who put forward the thoughts for operations. They were the ones to work out the details but it was he who indicated what was to be done and the details had to match up to what he thought desirable.

As to the mission to Moscow, McNaughton's only comment was that he was anxious to do whatever he could to help win the war, but that he could make no move without the consent of the Canadian government. Privately, as he admitted more than twenty years later, he would have "given my eye-teeth to have gone" provided his visit did not commit the Canadian government to a military course of action in which he had no faith.[151]

Churchill must have sensed what was in McNaughton's mind: "He said that my going would involve no commitment for the use of Canadian troops in JUPITER," though he went on to say quite frankly that "he personally wished to employ them there .... " Whether JUPITER came off early in 1943 or later, preparations should be made. The effort would be useful and was justified. Preparations made so far, McNaughton said, pointing to his part in the JUPITER review, had caused "some acidity" in his relations with the Chiefs of Staff; he was most concerned that good relations should be maintained between Canadian and British forces. Churchill reassured him about the Chiefs of Staff; he would see to that. Any action the Prime Minister might require would be put to McNaughton through the Chiefs of Staff and he could therefore count on their full co-operation and assent.[152]

The afternoon's discussion included other topics. Over luncheon Dieppe was mentioned. McNaughton described the "chance encounter" which had affected the Canadian left and the "consequent heavy casualties." Churchill spoke of his statement to the Commons and his belief that the operation had been "necessary and worthwhile." In the orchard, as well as JUPITER, they spoke of PLOUGH, a force designed to operate in the Norwegian winter, which would depend on small airborne tanks for movement, fighting and shelter. McNaughton said that six hundred of these vehicles, manufactured by Studebaker in North America, would be ready in December, 1942; three thousand United States and Canadian troops would be trained to use them. What did McNaughton think about the Churchill tank? His name had been tagged onto it, the Prime Minister growled, although he believed it had defects. McNaughton said he did not think much of it, though the reworked model might be useful. As he had done with Brooke, McNaughton mentioned his difficulties in obtaining information about operations; news of the postponement of ROUNDUP should have been given him as soon as it was known. In future, Churchill said, McNaughton should have the use of the Cabinet War Room where he would have access to a mass of up-to-date information.[153]

McNaughton, as we have noted, left Chequers shortly after tea on Saturday, 19 September. "On the following Monday," Sir Alan Brooke recorded:

A limp-looking McNaughton walked into my room and literally poured himself into my armchair. I asked him how he had got on. He informed me that he had had a ghastly week-end. He had been kept up *till all hours of the morning** until he did not know which way he was facing. Winston's control of the English language . . . had left him dumbfounded![154]

That statement in Sir Arthur Bryant's *Turn of the Tide* was not in accordance with the facts; more than any other, it prompted McNaughton to condemn the book as "egocentric bunk"; his forthright statement was prominently displayed in the London *Times*[155] but he did not give all the reasons for his anger to the *Times* reporter.

On the morning of the supposed conversation, Brooke was not even in London. On Monday, 21 September, at 9:15 A.M., McNaughton's Personal Assistant (Major Dan Spry) recorded: "General McNaughton spoke on the telephone to General Kennedy,

---

*Italics supplied.

D.M.O. [Director of Military Operations] War Office, and advised him that he had met the Prime Minister at Chequers on Saturday. General Kennedy said he knew of this and that the Chiefs of Staff Committee were meeting at Chequers that morning. General Nye (V.C.I.G.S.) would be representing the C.I.G.S., *who was away in the north of England until about Wednesday, 23 Sep 42.** General Kennedy said that General Nye would return to the War Office about lunch time and that he thought it would be well for General McNaughton to see General Nye early in the afternoon ...." which, accompanied by Simonds, McNaughton did.[156]

McNaughton's meeting with Nye on the afternoon of 21 September was thoroughly practical. At Chequers that morning Churchill had announced to the assembled Chiefs of Staff his intention of sending McNaughton to Moscow. Staff talks there "were to imply no commitment on the part of the Governments of Great Britain, Canada or the U.S.S.R." and any plan arrived at would be "subject to the approval of all the Governments concerned...." A draft cable from Churchill to Stalin had been drawn up, which McNaughton read. Both he and Nye agreed that a sentence, stating that McNaughton was being sent, could not be included without the acquiescence of the Canadian government, and Nye agreed to bring that to Churchill's attention. McNaughton, after his talk with Churchill, wanted full details of the operation of the last Malta and Archangel convoys, particularly those concerning air protection, and Nye agreed to obtain them from Sir Dudley Pound that evening.[157] There is no record whatever of any meeting between McNaughton and Brooke during September after that interview with Churchill.

Nothing came of Churchill's proposal that McNaughton should go to Moscow though much came of the inquiry with Sir Dudley Pound. The latter, approached by Nye, expressed a wish to see McNaughton who visited the Admiralty late on 22 September. McNaughton wanted to have at first hand confirmation of the new carrier tactics which Churchill had said had proved effective

---

*Italics supplied.

and which, therefore, cancelled out the objections that McNaughton had expressed in the JUPITER review. He was shocked to learn from Pound that, "contrary to the Prime Minister's views, the experience of the Malta and Archangel convoys had borne out, and shown the soundness of" the Canadian conclusions.[158]

McNaughton left the Admiralty in some heat. Suppose he had accepted Churchill's assurances without checking them and that three Canadian divisions, already mentioned by Brooke, had been embarked for this enterprise under the false assumption that all danger to the convoy from shore-based enemy air attack had been removed? To say that it was not a proper operation of war was too mild a term for it; it would have been no less than an act of criminal folly. And yet this man, as Defence Minister, was playing a real part in the strategic direction of the war; seeking to persuade his advisers to undertake operations against their better judgment. The sooner Churchill was removed from the post of Defence Minister the better.

Mackenzie King viewed both the operation and the Moscow mission with horror; he thought it clear from McNaughton's message that the General wished to undertake neither task, not realizing that McNaughton would have welcomed the trip to Moscow. King felt "we would be drawn into a difficult situation, if once McNaughton went at the head of a mission" and that if he were to do so it would give rise to comment in Britain, Canada and the United States where he would be discussed in terms of "a Generalissimo for a second front."[159] Accordingly, on 25 September, he cabled Churchill* to the effect that the importance of doing everything practicable to encourage and sustain Russia was very much in his mind; but to send McNaughton to Stalin "without a realistic plan in which he himself has confidence" would be to risk failure as well as McNaughton's own future usefulness.[161] Churchill's reply expressed "disappointment," though in conversation with Ralston during October the British Prime Minister said that once he realized McNaughton was against the project he himself "thought no more of it."[162]

---

*Who, he feared, was "more of a Commander in Chief than a Prime Minister and will not accept the advice of his own advisers."[160]

For McNaughton, however, the matter did not end there. During the visit of Stuart and Ralston in October, he discussed the JUPITER review with them. He pointed to Churchill's "new" carrier tactics, Pound's denial of their effectiveness and the danger of taking Churchill's statements at face value. He also told them of his conversation with Brooke in September. As a result of all this, he said, he now lacked faith in the higher direction of the war. Stuart—whether at McNaughton's instigation is not stated—had already had a confidential talk with Sir Stafford Cripps in which the Leader of the House of Commons "had spoken freely of the characters and abilities of the Prime Minister and the members of the Chiefs of Staff Committee and of the views and policies which each advocated." It was clear, McNaughton recorded, that "General Stuart's account of Sir Stafford's statements shows that his views and mine are in close accord on these matters."[163]

Cripps had suggested to Stuart that he should next approach Field-Marshal Smuts to persuade Churchill to give up the Ministry of Defence but Stuart had indicated that the right man for that would be McNaughton. On the evening of 30 October, therefore, McNaughton went to Sir Stafford Cripps's flat to meet Smuts, as had been arranged. Smuts asked McNaughton where they had met before and McNaughton reminded him of their talks in Ottawa a dozen years earlier when he had been CGS. They talked cordially for an hour on many subjects. Cripps then intervened, requesting that McNaughton give his views on "the higher organization for the direction of the war." McNaughton did so.

I said that the greatest need was for stability and that there was no room for improvisation, however brilliant. The preparations required were vast and a long time element was inherent; in consequence I did not see why Dominion political chiefs should not be able to participate in forming the basic plans. The Chiefs of Staff should not have departmental responsibilities—they should be free to plan; they should report to the War Cabinet, not an individual, however gifted. There should be Dominion military representation in the War Cabinet and then the Dominion military commanders could turn their minds to their own job without having to look back over their shoulders. . . .[164]

McNaughton, above all, emphasized the need for firm offensive planning. Cripps then alluded to dwindling British manpower. Smuts referred most sympathetically to the British difficulties in the war so far, mentioning the short-term decisions which had had to be taken. He stressed "the British genius" for improvisation, of which, he said, the present Prime Minister was a typical example of his race. At the end of their conversation McNaughton invited Smuts to visit the Canadian troops. Smuts said he would very much like to do so and to spend an evening with McNaughton in further discussions about the higher organization for war; he also said that Churchill might like to be with him.[165]

"Stripped of all cover," ran McNaughton's summary of the meeting,

and apart from the great value of the discussion on many matters of general interest, the net result of this interview is that I let Field Marshal Smuts, in the presence of [the Leader of the House of Commons], know my anxiety over the present situation with regard to the higher direction of the war. Although I never mentioned the Prime Minister by name or office he evidently took my remarks as indicating where my criticism lay. He was obviously nervous at the trend the conversation had taken. His reference to the British genius for improvisation and to the Prime Minister as a master of this technique; also his suggestion that Churchill should be with him when he visited Canadian troops; these were defensive and left me with the conviction that he had no intention whatever of undertaking any action that would bring him into the least conflict with the Prime Minister.

Field Marshal Smuts is an old man, older I think even than his years, and tired, as well he may be after all his struggles and accomplishments.

Rather than take any action of aggressive leadership he will counsel patience—as I heard him do to Sir Stafford as we said goodbye—and hope that somehow things may work out.[166]

Smuts—without Churchill—visited the Canadian Army on 5 November and, although he and McNaughton had a long conversation, the "higher direction of the war" was not discussed. Smuts did not raise it and McNaughton did not press him. McNaughton had pointed to a situation which he saw as dangerously wrong and, with integrity and without fear of the consequences to himself, he had described it to one who enjoyed a special relationship with Churchill. More than that he could not do.*

The JUPITER review, McNaughton found out at his first meeting with the CIGS since he had been at Chequers, still rankled in Brooke. On 17 October he criticized McNaughton "very forcibly" for not having been more emphatic against it when he was with Churchill.

I said I did not think I could have been more so; that in the flood of Mr. Churchill's talk I had had little opportunity to say anything at all; that my views were clearly given in my paper; that these had been brushed aside; that I had never accepted the Moscow assignment; that I had made it clear that I could do so only with the consent of my Government and in harmony with the Chiefs of Staff Committee and on a realistic basis; that when it was clear that the basis proposed was unrealistic then I had felt that I could not meet the Chiefs of Staff Committee. This view had been endorsed by the Government of Canada.[168]

---

*November fifth, 1942, was a most unpropitious day to question the higher direction of the war. On the previous day the Battle of Alamein had ended in victory and the Germans were in full flight along the North African shore. Churchill had survived the motion of censure in July when British fortunes were low; with Alamein and TORCH successful in November he was not likely to be assailed again. Though nothing was done about them, McNaughton's views did become known in the War Cabinet. L. S. Amery (Secretary of State for India), whose relations with McNaughton were close, tackled him about them at a private meeting on 8 November. McNaughton repeated what he had said to Smuts. Canada, with a large army "170,000 strong, fully trained, and as yet uncommitted," required a voice in policy-making. If Canada were to be given a hand in framing policy, the military commanders could then concentrate on their "proper task" of carrying it out without having to worry about its "soundness and propriety." Amery said that he thought part of the trouble lay in the attitude of the Canadian government which had been very averse to joining any formal body in London. He hoped that Mackenzie King, now that air travel was so easy, might find it possible to come to London every few months for the meetings of an Imperial Conference or War Cabinet and he spoke of the great value which had come from Sir Robert Borden's attendance at these in 1917 and 1918. McNaughton said he judged that the War Cabinet had very little to do with the formulation of policy. Amery agreed; of TORCH "he had heard the code name [and] knew vaguely that it was related to somewhere in North Africa but the War Cabinet had not been given any details or even an idea of the magnitude and scope of what had been intended." Amery said that the Prime Minister's character was such that he used the War Cabinet as something to which he gave his own views, not from which he drew advice; its members were not encouraged to enquire beyond what he saw fit to tell them or to interject themselves into matters outside the scope of their own departments.[167]

Brooke, somewhat mollified, went on to discuss the Prime Minister and his powerful art of persuasion. McNaughton said that he had felt, during the interview at Chequers, that he was "wheedling." It was then that Brooke said that he had felt "so strongly about the impracticability of JUPITER . . . that if McNaughton had been forced to undertake it he would have resigned." Both men agreed that there should be a frank exchange with each other and that "if any cloud should seem to arise we would meet at once to clear the air." Brooke then, in a superb display of mimicry, played the part of Churchill, "using the Prime Minister's words in the first person"; he was "so intense and dramatic" that McNaughton left fully convinced that he was "overwrought and very tired and harassed." It would appear that he was not himself for, McNaughton recorded, "he seemed very loath to let me go."[169]

Ralston, during his visit to the United Kingdom in October, visited the Prime Minister, Sir James Grigg (Secretary of State for War) and Alan Brooke. Stuart told McNaughton that Ralston's conversation with Grigg had confirmed what he had already told them: ROUNDUP would be delayed. He himself now hoped that the target date for the completion of the First Canadian Army would be set back to 1 October, 1943.[170] At his meeting with Churchill, Stuart continued, the substance of what Ralston had said was this: that there were "no strings" attached to the employment of the Canadian Army, either in whole or in part; that the government of Canada wished it to be used where it would make the greatest contribution; that any proposal for employment would be considered; that McNaughton's advice would be sought before a decision on any specific project was reached; and, that being so, the British authorities should keep McNaughton more closely informed than had hitherto been the case.[171]

On 17 October, at his meeting with Brooke when the JUPITER review had been discussed, McNaughton heard of another project. Brooke had spoken of TORCH for which, he said, the use of Gibraltar was absolutely necessary or an alternative would have to be provided. The Germans might enter Spain or persuade the

Spaniards to close the aerodrome in the neutral zone at Gibraltar. Should the aerodrome be threatened there were two possibilities: to seize Spanish Morocco for which a force (the Northern Task Force of two infantry divisions and an armoured brigade) would be required; or to seize the Canary Islands (code name TONIC) for which they had in mind a corps of two divisions.

General Brooke then referred to his talks with Colonel Ralston . . . who had expressed a wish for the more active employment of the Canadian Army and . . . to meet this wish he proposed to invite us to undertake one or other of the two projects. He was against Canadian participation in the "Northern Task Force" which would be [in] close association with U.K. and U.S. troops because of the administrative difficulties in maintaining a self-contained Canadian organization, the necessity for which he accepted; further he was anxious that any Canadian force employed might be so used that it could be returned to the Canadian Army at an early date as he attached great importance to keeping them as a well-balanced, self-contained organization for Home Defence and eventual employment on the Continent.[172]

For these reasons Brooke thought that the Northern Task Force should be found by Paget and the troops for TONIC by McNaughton. Brooke, it seemed, had now come to accept McNaughton's views that the paramount task of a self-contained Canadian Army was an eventual invasion of Western Europe. McNaughton, therefore, welcomed TONIC as an intermediate task for the experience it would bring, and he told the CIGS that he would study the plan. If it were a practicable military operation, "as he had no doubt it would be," he would seek the permission of his government to undertake it.[173]

Immediately afterwards McNaughton met Ralston at the Dorchester Hotel and told him what had happened. "I judge," he wrote, "that the suggestion that the Canadian Army should undertake TONIC was no surprise to the Minister of National Defence,"[174] and at the end of the year McNaughton was still complaining that "the Army Commander had been placed in the embarrassing position of having to discover at second-hand" the theme of the Minister's discussions.[175]

The Canadian government having given permission, Mc-Naughton saw Paget on 4 November. The 1st Corps would prepare for TONIC and McNaughton planned, therefore, to organize the 2nd Corps to take its place in the defence of Britain. He discussed with Paget the commander he proposed to appoint for the new corps (Major General E. W. Sansom) and there was complete agreement.[176] McNaughton set up a planning staff to work closely with the British authorities in London, and throughout the next two months he grappled with the problem of reorganizing his Army, both to make ready a part of it for TONIC and to bring it into conformity with British establishments, as we shall see.

What McNaughton did find out during this period was that National Defence Headquarters in Ottawa was extremely slow in sanctioning the reorganization he had proposed, and in December he complained to Massey. He described his plans and expressed his "dissatisfaction" with the delays caused by National Defence Headquarters' slowness in replying to his cables. He told the High Commissioner that he was "not entirely satisfied with the attitude that was apparently being taken by the Minister of National Defence." He said that "if the situation did not improve in the near future he might have to ask Mr. Massey to cable the Prime Minister" to tell him of his uneasiness because of the possibility of Canadian participation in operations during 1943.[177]

TONIC, however, had been given its death blow three days before this conversation with Massey. The North African landings had been successful; there had been no hostile move in Spain. On 28 December McNaughton called on Major-General J. N. Kennedy (Director of Military Operations) at the War Office and told him that to continue to entertain thoughts of taking the Canary Islands was now "fantastic." Kennedy agreed: it had already been decided that the operation was no longer required. That was the first McNaughton had heard about the cancellation and he can hardly be blamed for his remark that "there was obviously something wrong with the machinery which had failed to keep him informed of the progress of the planning," especially as he had gone to the trouble to set up a planning group to work closely with the British authorities in London.[178]

The delays and seeming inaction in Ottawa were largely caused through manpower and shipping difficulties. In November, 1942, after his return from England, Stuart sent a despondent cable to McNaughton. The limitations imposed by these difficulties led him to the conclusion that a First Canadian Army, able to operate wholly independently, could not be formed.[179] McNaughton, who since his return from Canada in the spring had been preoccupied with the creation of a self-contained army on the lines of established policy, accepted the news with remarkable patience. It seemed, he recorded, "that it may not be possible to operate as a Canadian Army" and undertook to place the situation before the CIGS. The exchange with Brooke is significant, in the light of future events:

I told General Brooke that while I, perhaps naturally, thought Canada's contribution could be most effective if given in the form of a Canadian Army substantially self-contained, yet the thing which weighed most with me was that the contribution should be the maximum towards winning the war and that if this, having regard to time and place, required the use of individual divisions separately or even the breaking up of divisions, then I was prepared to consider any proposition on its merits and report thereon to Canada. I said that what I would like to know was the time and place and extent of the possible operation which might be foreseen requiring the participation of Canadian troops and some idea of the probabilities so that we could determine the course to be followed.[180]

This, for McNaughton, was the maximum concession he could make. It loyally reflected the policy of the government of Canada as Stuart had reported it to McNaughton a month before; but it is doubtful if McNaughton would have remained to carry out a policy of dispersal to which he himself was unalterably opposed.

The Canadian Army, Brooke said, should remain in being ready to cross to the Continent by 1 August, 1943; there was "a definite possibility of a German crack after the winter" and, in his view, that possibility would increase throughout the summer, becoming "very definite in the autumn." He envisaged the First Canadian

Army "holding a bridgehead of limited depth . . . should a definite crack in German morale be evident." In those circumstances it would not be necessary to have the full Army; line of communication troops might be extemporized. Nor would the lack of reinforcements at full scale be of much significance. He spoke of the importance of keeping the objective of a self-contained Canadian Army alive, as this would give the best results, and by the beginning of October he would like to see the full structure of the Canadian Army completed.[181]

"All through," McNaughton recorded, ". . . a note of high optimism was evident. . . . We must be ready to put in the finishing blows when the opportunity came." An invasion of Britain need no longer be contemplated. Equally evident was British "high regard for Canadian troops and for the way in which we had accepted any task proposed, shown no resentment at the constant changes, and gone ahead with our preparations without complaint. . . ." When summarizing this conversation with Brooke for Stuart, McNaughton ended with the statement that it was "very definitely General Brooke's opinion that the project for a Cdn Army should be maintained. . . ."[182]

McNaughton, in consultation with the CGS in Ottawa, worked out a programme for the completion of the Army. He was now alive to the fact that a completely self-contained army might be unattainable and on 21 December he reported that the War Office had agreed to provide nine thousand men per Canadian division to complete the rearward services "to back the Canadian Army in an operational role." This would mean a saving of forty-five thousand Canadian troops, "thus relieving Canada of tremendous problems of shipping." That seemed to him "ample proof that the British authorities deem it wise and expedient to keep the Canadian Army together as a unified fighting force" and he reiterated his view that "the Canadians will do much better working together than to be split up under other commands."[183]

A week later he decided to organize the Army as far as possible on British war establishments; hitherto he had had his own ideas on points of detail. This would make it very easy to incorporate

Canadian corps or divisions in a British force—or vice versa—should it be necessary. He had some doubts about reorganizing his armoured divisions and before doing so he consulted Dempsey, his old Brigadier General Staff, who was now commanding the 42nd Armoured Division. Before that he had spent two days at the Tank School at Bovington, where he had studied the detailed organization of British armoured divisions and the latest type of thinking on what types of tanks were required for various roles.[184] On this visit, as always, he had revealed his appalling appetite for facts and he had a clear picture of the British organization in his mind. What he wanted to know from Dempsey was how useful the organization had proved in battle. Dempsey said "the combination of armoured, infantry and reconnaissance elements seemed to be in a reasonable proportion." His own personal opinion, as the commander of a British armoured division for the past year, was that the organization was "the closest to the ideal which had yet been drawn up." In that case, said McNaughton, he would accept it.[185]

In January, 1943, the Cabinet War Committee approved the general scheme of reorganization and announced that 64,000 men would be sent overseas by the end of August, 1943, as well as 5,000 reinforcements each month from September onward. In March a "manpower ceiling" of 232,100 by 1 September, 1943, was approved.* Planning could go ahead with these figures to complete the composition of the First Canadian Army and its reinforcements. General McNaughton was left free to mould his force within those limits and he felt that "the total manpower now allotted . . . was sufficient to develop the balanced army he had proposed."

Nineteen hundred and forty-two had been a trying year. Yet, for all its vicissitudes, McNaughton was confident that the idea of a Canadian Army had survived both in Canada and in the highest

---

*It was assumed that First Canadian Army would be in action by that date. The flow of 5,000 reinforcements per month thereafter would be to replace battle casualties, not to increase the manpower ceiling.

echelons of British military thought. As "further evidence of the British view that Canada's Army should be retained as a fighting whole," he told his Public Relations Officer on Christmas Eve, 1942, the forces representing the "British" in the manoeuvres to be held in March, 1943, had been turned over to his command. "It will be," McNaughton said, "a dress rehearsal for the full-scale invasion of the Continent."[186]

Chapter 10

1943: The Shoals of Politics

The exercise to which McNaughton had referred was indeed a rehearsal for the invasion of the Continent and he fully appreciated its special significance for the First Canadian Army. In his complaint to Vincent Massey about the slowness of National Defence Headquarters in acting on his proposals for the reorganization of the Army, McNaughton had stressed that these measures should be urgently approved "in view of the pending G.H.Q. manoeuvres."[1]

On 2 January, 1943, McNaughton cabled Stuart:

GHQ manoeuvres (code name SPARTAN) scheduled for early March to study attack on the Continent from an established bridgehead which is role contemplated for Cdn Army. British side to be under my command using Cdn Army Headquarters, 1 Cdn Corps of two Inf Divs, 5 Cdn Armd Div in British Guards Armoured Corps, 12 Corps with three British Divs etc. The preparations for this very large scale exercise will absorb my attention from about middle of January onward and accordingly I am most anxious to clear up our organizational problems at earliest date.[2]

One week later authority reached McNaughton from Stuart to reorganize the 4th and 5th Canadian Armoured Divisions on British lines, and his other proposals for the development of corps, army, GHQ, line of communications and base units were accepted. When he heard the news McNaughton said that "what was now required was a re-dedication of all our energies to the training and organization of the Army to fit it for battle as soon as possible."[3]

Certainly Stuart's cable had marked the end of the first chapter in the history of the First Canadian Army. At a conference of his staff officers on 10 January McNaughton said as much. Until then the issue had been the defence of Britain and the gradual building up of Canadian strength; for that Canadian establishments had been retained. Now the strategic situation was changing. With Russian successes and the great advances in North Africa, Germany might weaken. There would be no full-scale invasion in 1943 unless there was a crack in enemy morale, and to hasten that process the Canadians were ready to co-operate with the British in smaller operations. The time allowed for planning these would probably be short and with nothing to spare for delays due to the adjustment of differences in organization and establishments. The Canadians, then, would conform to British practice which would also facilitate the close association of British and Canadian troops when they finally invaded Northwest Europe.[4]

McNaughton, at the beginning of January, had already heard from the War Office that one Canadian infantry division might be wanted in the Mediterranean for employment against Sicily or Sardinia. He discussed the proposal with Crerar on 5 January and, having been assured that the division would be returned to the Canadian Army in time for possible operations on the Continent, both men welcomed the suggestion. Crerar thought the 1st Division should be selected and McNaughton agreed.[5] On 10 February, however, General Paget told McNaughton that the tentative plan to send a small force of Canadians to the Mediterranean would not now be carried out and that the whole of the First Canadian Army would remain concentrated in Britain in readiness for operations in Northwest Europe.[6]

During this conversation with Paget, McNaughton told him he was working out the organization for the Army. What he needed to know was what the Canadian role would be in an invasion; would the Canadian Army, or a part of it, be given the task of the initial assault from the sea? Or would it be used to pass through an established bridgehead, to exploit? He pointed out that manpower was strictly limited and it would not be possible to produce the units required for both roles. If the Canadian Army were to be used in the assault, for example, dock-operating companies and beach detachments would be required; if employed in the "follow-through" role, these could be dispensed with.[7] Paget said that it had long been clear to him that the Canadians should be used to exploit from the brideghead and the organization should be based on that. He added that it had already been decided that the initial attack would also come under the command of the Canadian Army, but for the landings and the assault to secure the bridgehead he would place the I British Corps (of three divisions) at McNaughton's disposal. The 1st and 2nd Canadian Corps would then follow through and exploit.[8]

It was, however, never as simple as that. Throughout 1943 plans for future operations, on which the Canadian order of battle depended, constantly shifted ground. Instructions, in the form of urgent messages, based no doubt on the best information available at the time, flowed from the War Office, so that carefully drawn-up plans had to be amended, discarded and re-adopted in infuriating succession. McNaughton remained patient. The detail could be dealt with only in England, he informed Ottawa, and he asked for sympathetic understanding of the many problems confronting him as he requested approval for one revision after another.

Nevertheless in February, at least, the role seemed clear. SPARTAN was designed to test the Canadian Army in that role, and although the new organization would not be completed until the fall—and the exercise could hardly be a test of that—Canadian formations and units would still obtain invaluable experience from taking part in SPARTAN.

The original concept for SPARTAN, so far as the Canadians were concerned, was that the 2nd Corps should relieve the 1st in combination with Home Forces, so that the 1st Corps could prepare for the mobile role in the forthcoming exercise to which it was assigned. On 19 January, however, McNaughton recommended that Sansom's 2nd Corps, whose headquarters had come into existence only four days earlier, should take part in SPARTAN with the 5th Canadian Armoured Division and the

Guards Armoured Division under command.[9] It was his own idea, and a bold one, to throw an inexperienced corps commander and a corps that had just been organized into such an exercise. Had McNaughton been solely concerned with his own reputation—for there was no doubt that he himself would be judged as the leader of an invasion army in the light of SPARTAN—he would have made sure that Crerar's well-trained corps was left as the only major Canadian formation in the exercise; but he had a wider purpose and that was to get as much training value out of the manoeuvres for as many Canadian units as he could. He expected the 2nd Corps to make mistakes. He also confidently expected it to learn more from those mistakes, in an exercise that simulated actual battle on a large scale, than in months of routine training.[10]

By the time of the exercise in early March, Sansom's corps was still raw. Though a cable had been sent to Canada on 21 January urgently requesting the provision of signals equipment for the new corps,[11] there were still deficiencies; much of what did arrive was of a new type so that the operators of Corps Signals were only partially trained when the exercise began. There had been no preliminary staff exercise and no paper exercise (that is, without troops) in the short time available, and the corps would obviously have to "shake down" during the actual manoeuvres. The whole of the 5th Canadian Armoured Division had never before exercised together nor, it must be remembered, had Headquarters First Canadian Army operated in the field as such before SPARTAN.

For the purposes of the exercise, the First Canadian Army (1st and 2nd Canadian Corps and XII British Corps) was styled "Second Army." Its task was to break out of a bridgehead which had been established on the "Continent" (the south coast of England) by another army. The "enemy," styled the "German 6th Army," consisted of VIII and XI British Corps under Lieutenant-General J. A. H. Gammell; its task was to defend "Eastland," the eastern part of England including London, with its capital at Huntingdon. The western part of England, "Westland," was assumed to be neutral, so that McNaughton was under strict orders not to violate its territory. This he might have wished to do, to turn the flank of the "German 6th Army."

McNaughton's appreciation was this: although the "British" were to seize Huntingdon as rapidly as possible, he could not fully achieve this object without destroying the major part of the enemy forces that might endanger his occupation of the capital. He had two main courses of action open to him. First, he could sweep west, close to the Westland frontier, and then in on Huntingdon. Second, he could advance directly on Huntingdon across the Thames, west of London. The advantages of the former were obvious: movement was easier, and the ground was more open and suitable for manoeuvre, particularly of armoured forces. A direct stroke on Huntingdon, on the other hand, meant the crossing of one serious obstacle—the Thames—as well as lesser obstacles, such as the Thame and various canals, and placed more difficult country (the Chilterns) in his path.

McNaughton studied the alternatives. The first course, he concluded, was what would be expected of him, and indeed it was. The exercise director (Paget) wrote:

In view of the important factor of speed, coupled with a probable strong superiority in armour, I consider that it would have been preferable for the BRITISH to have conducted their main advance with 1 and 2 Canadian Corps through the more open country and across the smaller obstacles WEST of the THAMES, delaying the final wheel NORTH-EAST to HUNTINGDON until NORTH of OXFORD . . . thereby avoiding a direct assault across a serious obstacle.[12]

And Gammell appreciated that that was what McNaughton would do. The "enemy" commander's plan, therefore, was based on "preparing to fight on ground of his own choosing NORTH of BANBURY into which he would lure the enemy, and, having hedged him round with demolitions, seriously maul his left wing." This analysis by Gammell, Paget considered, was "detailed and sound."[13]

In the interests of surprise McNaughton decided on the second course. By means of a swift and bold move forward at the starting signal he counted on seizing a bridgehead across the Thames. For this he intended to use the 1st Corps. The 2nd Corps would advance on the left to cover the west flank of 1st Corps; and XII

Corps, which was assumed to be in process of disembarkation in "Southland," would move on the right of 1st Corps as soon as possible to protect the east flank—especially against an enemy thrust from London. Once across the river he expected to be able to bring the enemy to battle.

McNaughton started off under a handicap.[14] Though SPARTAN had been timed to start at first light on 5 March, GHQ Home Forces, which was directing the exercise, allowed the "German" army to advance one day before that; the "British," on the other hand, were not permitted to move until the "Germans" had been on their way for some hours. "He [McNaughton] was informed early on 4 March," wrote Paget, "of the GERMAN dash into SOUTHLAND, and ordered to begin his advance as soon as possible on 4 March instead of waiting until 5 March as originally planned."[15] "This," as the Canadian official historian points out, "enabled Gammell's units to make contact with McNaughton's farther south than the latter had appreciated to be probable, and incidentally they were able to 'demolish' a great number of bridges."[16]

The "British" thrust across the Thames, never easy, would be harder now and to McNaughton it seemed that the changed conditions had been imposed to force him to the west where, he had no doubt, the "Germans" would be expecting him. They would have prepared accordingly, so that, by swinging west, he would merely be conforming to the "German" plan and inviting battle in circumstances unfavourable to himself. He decided, therefore to follow his original plan which, almost certainly, would come as a complete surprise to Gammell.

"The BRITISH force," reported Paget, "was on the move in four to five hours after receipt of the order at Army Headquarters. . . . In view of the difficulties the speed with which the advance began was a most creditable effort"[17] and that, coupled with the totally unexpected direction, brought quick results. On 5 March Crerar's well-trained corps seized—intact—a bridge across the Thames at Sonning in the enemy's defensive "hinge," which was then pried open.

"This local success," wrote Paget, "had two major repercussions on the operations."

On the BRITISH side it turned the GERMAN defences at a critical point and enabled successive bridgeheads to be formed across a major water obstacle without undertaking a single assault crossing. On the GERMAN side it cracked the main pivot of the defence, and caused the successive withdrawal of forces from the WEST flank to bolster it up, leading ultimately to the scrapping of the GERMAN Commander's plan for trapping the enemy NORTH of BANBURY.[18]

In other words, McNaughton now had the initiative and the enemy was obliged to react to the "British" plan instead of the other way about.

On 6 March the XII Corps, which had now come forward, was also across the Thames and pushing forward on Crerar's right. That day a captured "German" order revealed the enemy's intention to withdraw, and on the strength of that McNaughton alerted the 2nd Corps to cross the Thames as well. Although he would then have had three corps on a narrow frontage—little more than thirty miles—McNaughton felt confident that he could harry and hustle a retreating enemy back to Huntingdon and destroy them in the process. There were not yet, however, enough bridges across the Thames to support three corps and on the 7th he went forward to the bridging sites to imbue the engineers with a sense of urgency. At 4 p.m., it was reported, the bridge situation had improved.[19]

By this time, however, McNaughton realized that Gammell was reacting to his stroke. The "German" commander was concentrating his forces to plug the gap which Crerar had punched in his defences; instead of withdrawing, the "Germans" were reinforcing steadily. McNaughton appreciated, therefore, that the "German" forces, which undoubtedly had been held to trap him in the west, were in process of being shifted to block the 1st Corps' incursions, so that he knew at once that now was the time to carry out the westward swing and he had the 2nd Corps free for this. In a hastily scribbled note to his wife, timed 5:45 p.m., he wrote: "Have had a very hard day but everything is at last sorting out and we know clearly what our plans are for tomorrow."[20]

According to the official narrative of events, put out by GHQ Home Forces, McNaughton "was receiving reports that indicated that the SIXTH ARMY was not in such a hurry to withdraw. . . . Therefore a swift and wide turning movement by 2 Canadian Corps, helped by a strong thrust NORTH and NORTH-EAST by 1 Canadian and 12 Corps, would provide a first-class opportunity for a 'pincer' movement. This might not only bring the German armour to battle. It offered a chance to trap the whole SIXTH ARMY. If he won this battle, his road to HUNTINGDON would be open and he would have destroyed the German forces. . . . SECOND [First Canadian] ARMY was now carrying out the move on which the German Commander had based his initial plan. The latter had, however, *moved his armoured formations SOUTH*."*[21]

Everything, it will be realized, now depended on the swift execution by the 2nd Corps of what McNaughton had in mind. A warning order from Army reached Sansom at 4:15 P.M. on 7 March, followed by detailed orders to each corps a little more than an hour later. "Commander 2 Canadian Corps," the official narrative continues, "decided to move with Guards Armoured Division leading on two roads, starting at 1900 hours [7 P.M.]"[22]

It must be remembered that the 2nd Corps had been alerted for a move to the east; the order to move west meant that dispositions had to be changed and it was optimistic on Sansom's part to expect to be ready to move by seven o'clock. As it was, "units and lower formations started from half to three hours late" and the move that night, and through the next day, was a fiasco. It has been described in the official narrative:

The night was a dark one. No lights were allowed and enemy patrols imposed further delays. A large part of the delay, however, was attributable to insufficient traffic control. Between 1530 [3:30 P.M.] and 1730 hours [5:30 P.M.] 2 MARCH the administrative group of Guards Armoured Division was mixed up with the fighting echelons of 5 Canadian Armoured Division, and it was this congestion that delayed the concentration of the latter formation.

---

*Italics supplied.

ANOTHER EMOTIONAL POSTER

SUPPORT OUR FORCES
and THEIR LEADERS
Honour your pledge
Buy WAR SAVINGS
CERTIFICATES-*Regularly*

Hᴇʀᴇ ɪꜱ ᴀ ᴘᴏꜱᴛᴇʀ of General A. G. L. McNaughton, Commander of the Canadian Army Overseas. Although there is no action in the picture, this poster has a tremendous emotional appeal to Canadians, just as a picture of General MacArthur would make an emotional appeal to Americans.

THIS POSTER ranked high among the Canadian posters tested. The reason it did so is made plain by these comments of people who saw it:

"McNaughton's face is so well known to all of us that this makes a personal appeal."

"He looks so serious and worried he makes you feel no sacrifice is too great."

"He is our leader and this poster makes you realize we're supporting him when we buy."

"He is a great example of a soldier. He makes you think of war, and makes you want to help."

"You just have to support him, a man like that."

"He is a good man. He has strength. We all have faith in him."

"He is our leader. A man as strong as that is a good leader,—we can trust him and follow him."

"Everyone admires McNaughton. He inspires loyalty and we must support him."

"I like the strength behind it. That's what McNaughton stands for,—strength."

An American assessment of a Canadian recruiting poster made on behalf of the U.S. National Advisory Council on Government Posters

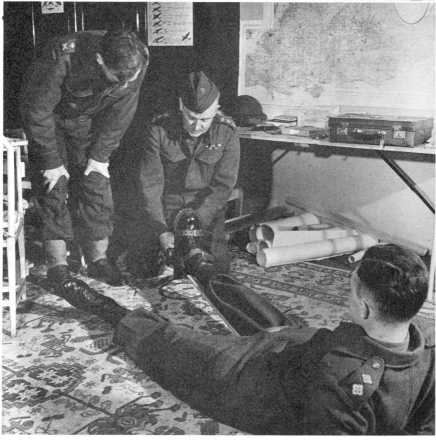

Canadian Army training, May, 1942

McNaughton was interested in everything for the good of his troops. Here
he assesses a new type of splint

EXERCISE SPARTAN
MARCH 1943

PAGET'S CONCEPT (Sketch 'A')

It was thought by GHQ Home Forces (General Paget) that Second Army (McNaughton) would make a wide sweep to the west over good "tank going" country. The commander of the "Sixth German Army" (Gammell) appreciated that McNaughton would do this, and prepared a trap accordingly.

McNAUGHTON'S ACTIONS (Sketches 'B'&'C')

First Phase: To achieve surprise, McNaughton struck boldly for the Thames. I Corps successfully established a bridgehead, XII Corps moved up on the right and McNaughton alerted II Corps to move into the bridgehead also.

Second Phase: The "Germans" were obliged to move from the trap they had prepared to counter McNaughton's thrusts.

Third Phase: The way to Huntingdon, McNaughton's objective, now lay open. McNaughton, therefore, moved II Corps to the west to form the left jaw of a British "pincer."

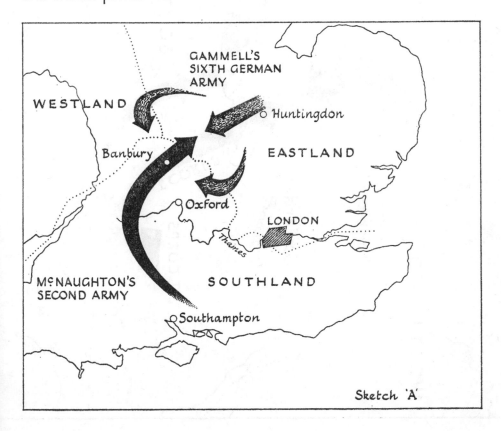

Sketch 'A'

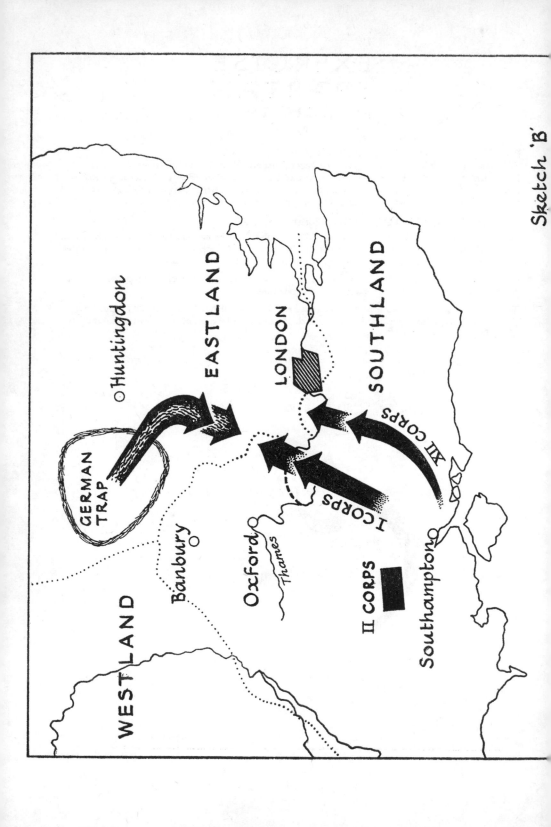

WESTLAND

Banbury

Oxford

Thames

II CORPS

Southampton

GERMAN
TRAP

Huntingdon

EASTLAND

LONDON

I CORPS

XII CORPS

SOUTHLAND

Sketch 'B'

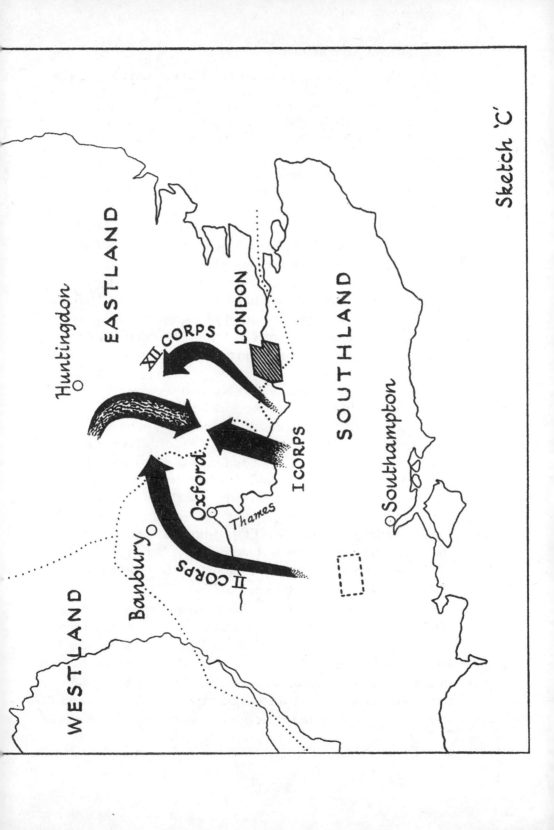

WESTLAND

EASTLAND

Huntingdon

XII CORPS

LONDON

Banbury

Oxford

Thames

II CORPS

I CORPS

SOUTHLAND

Southampton

Sketch 'C'

At 1700 hours [5 P.M.] MALMESBURY was impassable. For fifteen hours 2 Canadian Corps was out of direct wireless touch with SECOND ARMY, owing partly to difficulties caused by wireless silence and partly by the fact that personnel were handling new types of sets very recently issued to them.[23]

Any observer who saw the town of Malmesbury completely choked with military vehicles, and who watched tanks and trucks backed up for miles, grinding forward yards at a time and then halting with panting engines, would have formed a poor opinion of the move of the 2nd Corps on 7 to 8 March and, perhaps, of the Canadian leadership. But then they would not have known all the facts.

Movement on the 9th improved but it was still far too slow. That evening McNaughton issued his orders for 10 March and said that "the continued separation of 2 Canadian Corps exposed the left flank of 1 Canadian Corps and he ordered 2 Canadian Corps to act vigorously and to press on. He reinforced this," the official narrative tactfully continues, "with a personal telephone call to the Corps Commander."[24] Nevertheless, on the night of 9 March—despite the failure of the 2nd Corps to advance—"the pressure of 1 Canadian Corps and 12 Corps had prevented any major re-grouping of the German forces." An opportunity for a 'pincer' movement still seemed to exist "but only speed could make it possible."[25] This stroke, if it could now be carried out, would smash the "German" forces, but even without it the issue was no longer in doubt. As Paget says, "After 8 March the situation swung steadily in favour of the BRITISH who had begun to overcome the handicap of their lines of communication across the THAMES . . . it became only a matter of time before the concentrated BRITISH force would achieve its object."[26]

On the 11th McNaughton realized that his hopes of closing the pincers had failed. "The advance of 2 Canadian Corps had been too slow."[27] He therefore directed the 2nd Corps to advance on the left of the 1st Canadian Corps. On that day, acting on his own initiative, Sansom regrouped the 2nd Corps, placing the two armoured brigades under the Guards Armoured Division and the two infantry brigades under the 5th Canadian Armoured Division;

the infantry would be used for tank hunting while the armour swept on. "They wouldn't have got any training value out of that!" McNaughton said[28] with his consistent belief in balanced force, and so he countermanded Sansom's orders: "Army Comd directs you to re-establish normal organization armd divs forthwith. Reliable information indicates there is no enemy force on your front which you need fear and it is imperative that you push on with utmost speed. . . . Repeat utmost importance you push on vigorously and immediately."[29] By this time, however, both composite divisions had moved and their reorganization could not be completed before 6 P.M. on 11 March. Sansom's regrouping came in for criticism. General Paget stated in his report that it had been "a tactical mistake,"[30] while the chief umpire deplored "the breaking up on the eve of battle of a balanced organization which has been trained in mutual co-operation."[31]

That same evening McNaughton visited Sansom's headquarters after reconnoitring the front in a "borrowed" plane.* He gave his orders for the next day based on the intention to attack and destroy the remnants of the "German" army, using all three corps in simultaneous operations. This process was going on when the "Cease Fire" sounded at 9 A.M. on 12 March.[33]

In SPARTAN McNaughton had seized the initiative from the first, and through superior generalship had outmanoeuvred his opponent. On the whole he was satisfied with the results. His own headquarters had functioned well, as had the various arms and services. It was true that the 2nd Corps had performed badly but there were good reasons for that, and Paget was aware of them. He was shocked and surprised therefore when, three days after the conclusion of the exercise, a letter reached him from General Paget requesting that he relieve Sansom of his command.[34]

He refused to do so. But for him, Sansom would not have taken

---

*This somewhat unorthodox procedure upset the British authorities. The chief umpire (Lieutenant-General Loyd) drew attention to it in his report. "There was a desire," he said, "to get air transport for liaison purposes between British Second Army H.Q. and 2 Canadian Corps. This constituted an unauthorized use of Air O.P. [Observation Posts] but the commander evidently thought his mission important enough to justify the withdrawal of an Air O.P. from 12 Corps." Paget said: "The Air O.P.s were again most useful and as usual came in for their normal share of misuse for purposes other than those for which they are intended."[32]

part in SPARTAN at all and so *he* was responsible in good part for the unenviable position in which Sansom found himself. Mc-Naughton visited Paget at Home Forces. He again pointed out that Sansom's corps staff had been newly organized, that it was incomplete in equipment and that what had been provided had been sent at the last minute and was untried. He would warn Sansom, he said, and put him on his mettle, but more than that he would not do.[35] Though somewhat taken aback by this show of independence, Paget accepted it at the time.

Next day McNaughton sent for Sansom and placed the correspondence before him. He told him that he was confident that he could bring the 2nd Corps to the high state of fighting efficiency which he demanded. He had no doubt that the corps commander would be able to meet a future test, in another exercise. But in July, before Sansom's tactical efficiency had been tested, Paget again expressed discontent with him as a corps commander and again McNaughton rushed to his support. He would not replace Sansom unless his future conduct in an exercise justified the measure; he was now administering and building up his corps to McNaughton's satisfaction; only when his tactical efficiency had been judged would he inform Paget of his conclusion.[36] Paget then went to Brooke who, in turn, raised the matter with General Stuart during the visit of the CGS to Britain that summer.* Ralston, who heard about it from Stuart, told McNaughton that he had been surprised when Sansom had been recommended in the first place to command the 2nd Corps,[38] but nevertheless Sansom remained while McNaughton continued to command the Army.

SPARTAN had at least one useful byproduct: the development of prefabricated surfacing for temporary airfields. Throughout the

---

*This will be examined subsequently. However, by the summer Brooke had begun to shift the blame for the mistakes in SPARTAN from Sansom to McNaughton. Sir Basil Liddell Hart wrote:

As the commander of the whole army, McNaughton naturally tended to get the blame. That was natural, but in my view mistaken—a view based on subsequent examination as well as on observation at the time.[37]

exercise not a single drop of rain had fallen over southern England[39] and the clouds of dust raised by armoured columns had caused McNaughton to think about finding a way to surface friable soils. He remembered the advertisements put out in Canada for paint—"Protect the surface, and you protect everything"—and he thought that some form of reinforced tarred roofing material would be extremely useful, especially for landing strips. He turned the problem of finding the right material over to his Chief Engineer (Hertzberg) and, to advise him, obtained the services of Charles Baskin of the Imperial Oil Company of Canada, who arrived in England early in May. Prefabricated bituminous surfacing (PBS) resulted. This was a bitumenized canvas made of jute which was delivered on the site in rolls and, when laid, satisfactorily sealed the ground against weather so that it was able to support the weight of aircraft. Bomb craters could be quickly filled and sealed by PBS. On 23 June the new method was demonstrated, and various types of aircraft performed a series of landings and take-offs on a runway carefully laid by hand. The demonstration was completely successful.[40] A machine (the "stamp licker") was developed later to speed the laying process. "This machine, as it was drawn along, applied cut-back [a solvent and sticking agent to seal the overlapping layers] to the lower side of an unwinding roll of the bitumenized fabric," so that airfields could be surfaced very rapidly.[41] The new method was used extensively in various theatres of operations later in the war. There were as many as twenty-six PBS airfields in Northwest Europe by October, 1944; the British Fourteenth Army was largely supplied from airfields constructed with PBS in Burma; and the Americans made good use of it for "island-hopping."

SPARTAN had another sequel which was not so pleasant. Sir Alan Brooke attended the "Trident" Conference in Washington (12 to 25 May) and sought out Major-General Maurice Pope, who was still serving as Military Representative of the War Committee of the Canadian Cabinet. Brooke drew Pope aside and told him that McNaughton had not come up to expectations on SPARTAN, giving as an example the fact that he had on one occasion been absent from his headquarters and had become engrossed in bridging. The reasons for that have been shown: the progress of bridging on that day had been the limiting factor governing McNaughton's plan. Nevertheless, during the General's absence he had remained in constant touch with his headquarters, and it was while at the bridging sites that he had been informed of the enemy's change of plan. Out of context, however, it might seem that bridging operations were an odd thing for the army commander to be mixed up with, and Brooke knew that Pope would pass the news to Stuart, as it was his duty to do, and which he did.[42] Stuart, who was also in Washington, then obtained the story from Brooke at first hand. Surely it is singular that not one word of direct criticism had reached McNaughton either from Paget or Brooke, and yet behind his back a hint was passed to Pope and thence to Stuart and Ralston which was to be acted on later in the year.

The "Trident" Conference succeeded that at Casablanca in mid-January at which the invasion of Sicily (Operation HUSKY), which would secure the Mediterranean sea route to the Far East, had been decided upon. The strategy, briefly, was that the North African campaign would be extended into Sicily. Another important strategical decision at Casablanca was that Roosevelt and Churchill fixed the date of the cross-Channel invasion for May, 1944; in preparation for this, Lieutenant-General F. R. Morgan was appointed Chief of Staff to the Supreme Allied Commander (Designate) [COSSAC].

McNaughton received no information about the decisions taken at Casablanca except that the Canadian Army was to be kept intact for a future invasion of the Continent. He was to hear more about it in a roundabout way after Churchill had told Mackenzie King in March that the troops McNaughton required to complete his Army could not be shipped because of an urgent requirement in Britain for United States airmen. "At the Casablanca Conference," Churchill cabled:

... the President and I agreed as to the high priority to be given to the bombing of Germany. The United States Government have now requested that shipping should be made available for the ground personnel of the Air Units which they propose to send over here in the April-June quarter and I am most anxious to accede to their request. . . . I fear that the only way in which we can lift these Air Forces is by delaying the lifting of 37,000 Canadian Army personnel. . . .[43]

Roosevelt, it would seem, still thought—as he had made clear at his meeting with McNaughton—that German morale might suddenly crack under a stepped-up air offensive; and without a crack early operations against the Continent were unlikely. Nevertheless, to defer the move overseas of so many Canadian troops would postpone the completion of the army programme until about December. In Ottawa Mackenzie King noted that Ralston realized that to agree would mean "numbers of troops will be kept in Canada through summer, with continual demands that they should be employed in industry or farming. Also fears our troops in England will be very restless, hard to sustain their morale, and also the Canadian public will think our troops are being deliberately withheld from active service." The Prime Minister advised Ralston that, before making any reply to Churchill, he should "communicate with McNaughton asking his opinion on the wire from Churchill to me."[44]

And yet, influenced by Ralston, Mackenzie King did reply to Churchill before there is any record of his having heard from McNaughton: "In circumstances the strong considerations with which you are familiar in favour of Canadian troops in North Africa appear to require earnest re-examination,"[45] and the next day Stuart said much the same to McNaughton: ". . . in my opinion we should press for early representation in North Africa."[46]

McNaughton replied on 20 March:

My view remains (1) that Cdn Forces in whole or in part should be used where and when they can make the best contribution to winning the war (2) that we should continue to recognize that the strategical situation can only be brought to a focus in Chief of Staff Committee (3) that proposals for use of Cdn Forces should initiate with this Committee (4) that on receipt of these proposals

I should examine them objectively and report thereon to you with recommendations.

I do not repeat NOT recommend that we should press for employment merely to satisfy a desire for activity. . . .[47]

The same day Churchill replied to Mackenzie King:

We contemplate sending only one more Division to N. Africa from this country. This is already committed and under special training. Plans are therefore too advanced to permit of a Canadian Division being sent in its place and no further divisions are likely to be required. I fully realise and appreciate the anxiety of your fine troops to take an active part in operations and you may be sure that I am keeping this very much in mind.[48]

The Canadian Prime Minister was well pleased with the situation. By giving up shipping space to the Americans, he said, "It may well be that . . . we will be saving the lives of many of our men." McNaughton's warning against pressing for activity seemed to him to be "all right." But he could see that "both Ralston and Stuart had something else in mind and were obviously anxious to get off some message to McNaughton."[49]

Stuart said that "the morale of the troops really necessitated their being brought into action some time soon." The men "needed battle experience, some active fighting before going into a large and important engagement . . . that McNaughton had become too far removed from the troops; that Crerar was nearer to them and understood them better." Stuart was "positive" that "Crerar and the others would wish to have some action very soon in North Africa or elsewhere . . . ."[50]

Crerar did back Ralston and Stuart in their efforts to bring Canadian troops into action. "Harry Crerar to dinner," Brooke wrote on 10 February, 1943,

and a long harangue from him as to the necessity of getting some Canadian fighting soon for Imperial and political reasons. . . . This . . . was connected with the growing uneasiness amongst Canadians lest the war should finish without their having been engaged in any active operations. . . . I had to remind him that the main factor that had up to date militated against their use in Africa was the stipulation made by the Canadian Government that the Canadian Army must not be split up and must only be used as a whole—a conception that McNaughton had always held with the greatest of tenacity.* Crerar realized this concept must be broken down, but I could not get him to realize that there would still be opportunities in operations connected with the re-entry into France. He looked at such conceptions as castles in the air.[51]

It was Ralston's argument that struck Mackenzie King where he was most vulnerable, for above all else he was a politician. Ralston's thought, the Prime Minister recorded, "was of the political repercussions in Canada of our men being kept out of action so long. He feels that they do not yet believe in England that it is not due to some action on the part of the Government, and he fears that this view will grow; also that it would be very difficult to keep large numbers of troops in Canada without having a demand made that they should go back into industry. He is anxious to get reinforcements over."[52]

Mackenzie King pondered Ralston's words and made his own appraisal of the war situation. He now felt "perfectly sure that . . . there would be no invasion until next year" and that was a long time to wait. "Stuart and Ralston then said that they had both come to the conclusion themselves."[53] King knew that public opinion in Canada was clamorous to have the troops fight some-where soon; that they were not doing so, it was said, constituted "the greatest disgrace of the present war." At least "fragmentary use" should be made of the Army, for "the hand which holds the poised dagger can become palsied through lack of use." It was also said that the government was to blame for wishing to keep the Canadian Army intact. The Prime Minister, alarmed by this, in his New Year's broadcast had confidently stated that "all our armed forces" would be in action during 1943; now it seemed to him that they would not.†

---

*Once again, Brooke's version is not in accordance with the facts. We have noted McNaughton's approval of the temporary detachment of a force to Sicily.

†A good description of the state of public opinion at the time is contained in Colonel G. W. L. Nicholson's *The Canadians in Italy*, pp. 20-26. As for the morale of the troops, Nicholson points out that early in 1943 field censorship reports, "which provided a valuable sampling of the opinions held by the Canadian forces as revealed in their letters home—indicated with gratifying regularity that the morale of the Canadians in Britain was being fully maintained."

Though he felt "more convinced than ever that my duty was to back up McNaughton rather than Ralston"—that there was "a feeling between them which I think warps Ralston's judgment a bit"—nevertheless Mackenzie King decided to leave Ralston a free hand in making representations to the British authorities. He himself would remain aloof. "I intended to make very clear that the Defence Department can make its own representations to McNaughton, but that I will not let my name or office be used to further their point of view as against McNaughton's nor the civil government in Canada to interfere with the Chiefs of Staff Committee in London in the decisions upon strategy. . . . I shall insist on keeping the plane between Prime Minister and Prime Minister and the President above all department levels." His conscience bothered him a bit about what amounted to a *carte blanche* which Ralston and Stuart were to interpret very widely, for, as he said, "My mind keeps going back to McNaughton's words to me that he did not intend to allow life to be unnecessarily sacrificed."[54]

Towards the end of April Churchill had decided to include Canadian troops in the invasion of Sicily. Mackenzie King told Ralston that this was "really a decision made because of representations since made by the Defence Department," and Ralston agreed.[55] McNaughton heard the news direct from Sir Alan Brooke on 23 April.

The chance of an operation based on the United Kingdom against the Continent . . . during 1943 was now very small [Brooke said] and in view of the insistent requests made by the Minister of National Defence and C.G.S., Canada, the Prime Minister had given him a directive that Canadian participation in the next operation was to be arranged.

Brooke then asked McNaughton to agree to the sending of one Canadian division and one Canadian army tank brigade, with some ancillary units, to take part in HUSKY. A British division (the 3rd) would be displaced; it would be disappointed, and the War Office was opposed to the disruption that the change would cause.

But there it was. McNaughton said he proposed to nominate the 1st Division and the 1st Army Tank Brigade. Brooke again stressed that he was fully aware of McNaughton's need to be kept informed of operations. He was sorry that this had not been done after the Casablanca Conference. McNaughton replied that he was "not concerned with the past, but he was anxious that there should be no future difficulties."[56]

McNaughton insisted that he would have to look at the plans for HUSKY. His examination must convince him that it was a practical operation of war having a reasonable chance of success. Nye, the Vice-Chief of the Imperial General Staff, demurred. It was a matter of great urgency and he wanted an immediate decision. But McNaughton had seen only a vague plan; if the War Office produced a detailed one he would examine it at once. On 25 April, having gone into the details at the War Office, McNaughton agreed that the operation was practical and he formally requested Ottawa to approve the dispatch of troops.[57]

At the end of April McNaughton gave his reasons for recommending the participation of Canadians in HUSKY to Lieutenant-General Ismay, Chief Staff Officer to Churchill as Minister of Defence:

I said that all through our stay in England we had looked to the Chiefs of Staff to indicate our tasks. We had accepted those offered, had prepared for them with industry and despatch, and when they had not come to fruition we had expressed no discontent. In each case we knew that the decision not to proceed had been sound. We knew our importance as a general strategical reserve and that it might be fatal to dissipate it prematurely. I had made a virtue of patience and I was sure that at the present the Canadian Army was patiently waiting its opportunity. However, for some time and with growing intensity more recently, public opinion in Canada was being incited to demand action. This continued propaganda in the press would disquiet people as to whether or not we were making a proper contribution and in course of time through letters and papers would possibly have an effect on the Army here. We must be, and we were, on the alert for this, and I had told the C.I.G.S. recently that I would go to him the moment danger was in sight. This was not yet. So these considerations did not enter into my decision to recommend participation in HUSKY. These had been taken by me on purely military grounds. . . . I considered it sound and within the means available. . . .

I said that the Canadian Government's approval had been sought for this specific operation only, and that if other operations were contemplated we would have to consult again.[58]

It cannot be emphasized too strongly that the invasion of Sicily *only* had been decided upon at the Casablanca Conference. Though the invasion of Italy, which followed the seizure of Sicily, may seem to have been merely the second step in a single concept, that was not the case. Field-Marshal Alexander put it well when he termed the conquest of Sicily the end of the North African chapter of strategy; the invasion of Italy marked the opening of a European chapter.[59] There was no question at Casablanca of the troops from Sicily being automatically committed to an Italian campaign or any other. That is the reason for McNaughton's statement that Canadian approval covered only "this specific operation."

McNaughton, then, took it for granted that the Canadian force for Sicily would be returned to his command when the Sicilian campaign was over and there was every indication that this would be well before any invasion of Northwest Europe could take place. That, too, was the impression Mackenzie King and General Stuart received from Churchill at the "Trident" Conference. Churchill told the Canadian Prime Minister then that "there will be no invasion of Europe this year from Britain. I tell you that." Stuart, Mackenzie King recorded, clearly understood that after they had gained battle experience "in Italy"* the Canadian troops would be brought back to Britain "to impart . . . to the other divisions in England, the experience they had gained in actual battle." This operation, he went on, was the "one to be known as 'Husky.' " King was not certain whether Churchill had said the troops would be brought back to England after some of the fighting: "My recollection is that he did."[60]

It was essential, McNaughton considered, to have it confirmed

---

*From the later reference to HUSKY, Sicily was meant. This ambiguity raises a doubt, however, whether Stuart and Mackenzie King were clear in their own minds about the distinction between the two campaigns.

that the division and the tank brigade would, in fact, return from Sicily in good time for the cross-Channel assault. Early in May he cabled Stuart, warning him that "insofar as Cdn Army is concerned, the departure of 1 Cdn Div leaves our army out of balance"; he was anxious to get it back before "serious operations."[61] Then, having heard from the War Office that they were considering asking for another Canadian division, this time for service with the First Army in North Africa, he cabled Stuart again: "I must point out and warn you that if this request is made and accepted it will end the conception on which we have been proceeding, namely that Canada's contribution to the war can best be through her own Army."[62] A fortnight later, when discussing the probable role of the Canadians in Northwest Europe (which again was thought to be that of breaking out of the bridgehead), General Paget repeated McNaughton's point about the effect of the dispatch of Canadian troops to the Mediterranean on the balance of the First Canadian Army.[63] Then, at the end of the month, the Canadian commander received some reassurance. He was told at the War Office by the VCIGS that there was no intention of sending any more Canadian formations to the Mediterranean; on the contrary, those involved in Sicily would be "brought back at a not distant date. Canadian plans should make provision for their return before large-scale operations against North-West Europe."[64] And in mid-June Nye was even more reassuring; McNaughton must assume, the VCIGS said, that the division and the tank brigade in Sicily would be returned to the United Kingdom in the late autumn of 1943. Paget, who was aware of this, reviewed his plans with McNaughton three days later. He had now, he told McNaughton, been appointed to command the 21st Army Group in the cross-Channel invasion, the target date for which was 1 May, 1944. He would like to employ one Canadian division in the actual assault on the enemy coast and, because of its experience in Sicily, he thought the 1st Canadian Division would be best for this.[65] It will be seen that McNaughton had every right to feel confident that two of his formations would acquire battle experience in Sicily and return to disseminate their knowledge throughout the Army before the invasion from the West. He therefore heartily supported the Sicilian campaign.[66]

McNaughton's selection of the 1st Division (Major-General H. L. N. Salmon) and the 1st Army Tank Brigade (Brigadier R. A. Wyman) was guided by considerations of seniority and efficiency. Furthermore, as he told General Brooke, he had "every confidence" that Salmon, as the senior Canadian commander in the Mediterranean, would be "able to keep out of difficulties and function correctly within the constitutional arrangements for a mixed force."[67] Salmon, whose planning staff had been assembled on 24 April, energetically tackled the main problems, familiarizing himself with the operation and preparing his force for embarkation in mid-June. A flight to the Middle East on 29 April was arranged so that he could consult with British planners in Cairo. Shortly after luncheon on the 29th, when McNaughton was discussing technical development matters of common interest to the army and the air force with his old friend (now Air Vice-Marshal) Stedman, news arrived that the aircraft had crashed and Salmon was among those killed.[68]

McNaughton immediately appointed Guy Simonds to take Salmon's place. Since his arrival as a major on McNaughton's divisional staff in Ottawa during the fall of 1939, this brilliant young officer had risen rapidly. We have seen something of his work at the time of Dunkirk, at the Canadian Staff School and on the JUPITER review. It had not taken McNaughton long to single him out for advancement, and Simonds had served as Brigadier General Staff of the 1st Canadian Corps and as a supernumerary BGS in a British corps under Montgomery during a tour of duty in North Africa. On his return to England in mid-April, 1943, McNaughton had appointed him commander of the 2nd Division, a major-general at the age of thirty-nine, the youngest of the Canadian generals. On 30 April McNaughton asked Simonds to breakfast at his home, Largiebeg, and there he briefed him.[69]

He dealt mostly with a matter that would be unfamiliar to Simonds—the constitutional arrangements that had been made for the participation of a Canadian force under overall British com-

mand in operations. For Sicily, Eisenhower would be Supreme
Allied Commander, with Alexander as his deputy; indeed, Alex-
ander had a dual appointment for he would also be directly in
charge of the land forces. Montgomery commanded the British
Eighth Army and Simonds would come under British command.
Though Eisenhower was in charge of the complete operation,
Simonds would answer to the British, "the reason being that the
only legal formula we had was the Visiting Forces Act which did
not give authority to place Canadian troops under other than
British command." Simonds had the "right of reference" to the
Canadian government concerning operations which he might
judge to be unsound, but this was to be exercised only in an
extreme case. There should be no trouble with Montgomery, as
McNaughton had in the past discussed Canada's constitutional
position with him, but if there were Alexander could be counted
on to hold a "very steady hand on the throttle."[70] Simonds, as
Salmon had done, went into the plans in London; he then spent
the first ten days of May in Cairo. McNaughton, with preparations
well in hand, took four days' leave at the Royal Hotel, Winchester,
and spent it with his son Edward fishing the River Itchen.[71]
Meanwhile the Canadian troops earmarked for Sicily moved to
Scotland to complete their training. They adopted British stores
and equipment wherever possible to facilitate supply and maintenance in the theatre of operations; the Tank Brigade likewise
discarded its Canadian tanks for American Shermans, as these had
been commonly used in North Africa.*

Though the preparation of the forces for Sicily kept Mc-
Naughton busy, he never lost sight of the main role of the Army.
He remained in close touch with Morgan (COSSAC) and had

---

*Nevertheless, McNaughton never lost sight of Canadian industrial production.
Even at this time he conveyed a message to Mackenzie King that "increased
energy and drive" were still essential. The United States was rapidly filling war
requirements and Canada would be unable to obtain contracts unless she constantly evolved and developed new and better weapons. "Without this increased
drive . . . Canada might find itself with unused factories at the end of the war
and in place of entering the era of reconstruction with full facilities in being, we
might find ourselves in the category of suppliers of raw materials rather than as
skilled manufacturers. In order to make the best use of factories which had been
built . . . it was essential to increase the tempo of technical development [to provide items] so good that they would be adopted universally."[72]

already, in April, appointed Major-General Turner as Canadian Liaison Officer to COSSAC's staff, in order to kept abreast of the planning and be able to anticipate requirements intelligently and foresee (and forestall) difficulties. McNaughton was still concerned that, in the invasion role, the Canadian Army might not receive adequate air support and in February he had proposed that a Canadian Composite Group Headquarters should be set up; it was, as he told Air Marshal Edwards, a case of "now or never" if the RCAF "wished to consolidate its strength in the United Kingdom."[73] Edwards agreed and, with McNaughton, sought authority from Ottawa to form the group but before approval was given the British Army Co-operation Command was abolished on 1 June. The Royal Air Force then set up a Tactical Air Force, organized on the same lines as the Desert Air Force which had supported the ground operations in North Africa, and McNaughton was informed by Paget that the tactical air support for the Canadian Army in the invasion role would be provided from this. McNaughton's hope of a national air force to support a national army disappeared, and later in June he was informed that Number 83 Group, RAF* was to be affiliated with the First Canadian Army.[74]

Towards the end of May McNaughton began to think of a trip to the Mediterranean theatre. He had visited the formations training in Scotland, and had met Montgomery at the War Office where, on 19 May, knowing what would be closest to McNaughton's heart, Montgomery had assured him that the Canadian formations in Sicily would fight as such and would not be broken up.[75] The invasion was timed for 10 July and McNaughton had

---

*83 Group included 15 squadrons of the RCAF although its headquarters was British. It seemed appropriate that it should be assigned to support the Canadian Army. On McNaughton's return to Canada in January, 1944, however, No. 84 Group was substituted for No. 83, and this had the "regrettable effect of separating the RCAF component in North-West Europe from the Canadian Army." For further details see Stacey, *The Victory Campaign* (Ottawa: The Queen's Printer, 1960), p. 41. There was no real reason why an RCAF group could not have been incorporated in the Tactical Air Force. But it would have been very hard to find enough RCAF squadrons and the matter was not pressed.

suggested that he should visit Tunisia a month beforehand to see the arrangements for the administration of the Canadian troops. He told the VCIGS on 27 May that Montgomery was "entirely in sympathy with the proposal" but felt that he should come out "during operation HUSKY rather than before." But as Mc-Naughton "had no intention of interfering with operational matters and . . . in this regard . . . relied entirely on the good sense of General Alexander and General Montgomery," he thought that an earlier visit might be more appropriate. Nye agreed to assist in arranging transportation.[76]

It so happened that Stuart had a similar visit in mind. In the middle of May, before Montgomery had returned to England, the CGS had sent a delighted cable to him in North Africa, which was to be passed by CMHQ, and which concluded with the words, "Hope to see you soon." Here, McNaughton said, was a breach of security. Those words, from the Canadian CGS to Montgomery, could have only one meaning, should they come into enemy hands —that Canadian troops would shortly be joining Montgomery's command. Though McNaughton drew the matter to his attention by transatlantic telephone, Stuart merely resented the interference and refused to change his message, an attitude which McNaughton warned him might well endanger Canadian lives.[77] In the end, both men left for the Mediterranean together at a later date than McNaughton had at first envisaged.

The decision to change the date was taken by Sir Archibald Nye on 12 June. By then a conference had been arranged at Largs, in Scotland, to discuss combined operations, especially army-air co-operation, in the invasion of Northwest Europe. McNaughton, as the leader of one of the armies to be employed, was summoned to attend from 28 June to 3 July. He pointed out to Nye that these dates clashed with those arranged for his Mediterranean visit. It was most important, the VCIGS said, that McNaughton should be at Largs; the Mediterranean trip could start as soon as possible afterwards and he was sure that Brooke would agree with him.[78] A week later, having heard that Stuart was to come to England, McNaughton suggested to Major-General Kennedy at the War Office that Stuart too should be at Largs; he and McNaughton could then leave for the Mediterranean together on 7 July. Kennedy agreed to take it up with Alan Brooke and later that afternoon he telephoned McNaughton to say that the CGIS had "approved the arrangements for the North African visit and had cabled General Eisenhower requesting facilities and special attention."[79] On 23 June a letter from Kennedy's office informed McNaughton that a reply had been received from Eisenhower stating that "he would be very pleased to see General McNaughton and General Stuart with four staff officers for about one week on or about 8 July 1943."[80]

Stuart did not reach England in time to attend the conference at Largs. Before leaving for the Mediterranean, however, he sent Brigadier R. B. Gibson, his Deputy Chief of the General Staff (who had accompanied him from Canada), back to Ottawa with a report which Gibson delivered to Mackenzie King and Ralston at the Prime Minister's office on 10 July. Stuart's report drew attention to British doubts concerning McNaughton's judgment in Exercise SPARTAN earlier in the year[81] and to Brooke's view that McNaughton should not command the Canadian Army in active operations. Ralston wanted to leave for England at once to settle the matter—McNaughton would be removed and Crerar installed in his place—but King restrained him. Stuart was to remain in England and Ralston might join him there but not until the current session of Parliament ended. In his report, Stuart also advocated building up the Canadian force in the Mediterranean to a corps; this Ralston strongly backed. King hesitated; it had, he thought, been understood that the present division would be brought back after it had acquired battle experience. Gibson, however, indicated that McNaughton "naturally preferred to keep the Army intact 'for the final blow' but was agreeable to a second division going to the Mediterranean."[82] It would seem that the report Stuart had sent back by Gibson—that McNaughton had not objected to further troops being sent to Sicily—had removed King's hesitation. But McNaughton's views had not been properly presented. He always made clear that no additional troops should be sent *unless they returned to rejoin the army in time for the cross-Channel invasion,* as will be seen.

McNaughton had made plain to Kennedy that he had two objects in mind in requesting the visit to Sicily:

(a) to witness a combined operation in order that the lessons learned could be used to benefit the training of the Cdn. Army in the U.K., and

(b) to be available to ensure that the Cdn. contribution to the operation was completely in accordance with the requirements of the G.O.C.-in-C. 15 Army Gp [Alexander], under whose operational direction the Cdn. formations were serving.[83]

Though he saw Alexander, neither he nor Stuart were to achieve the first object of their visit.

The plane, after stops at Gibraltar and Algiers, reached Tunisia without incident, and McNaughton and Stuart were in the War Room of Headquarters 15th Army Group on 10 July while the landings in Sicily were in progress; it soon became apparent that these had been successful. Three days later General Eisenhower, who had been in Sicily, returned to Tunisia and he and Mc-Naughton had a chat. He was very glad to have Canadian troops under his command, and though he had not been able to see Simonds personally in Sicily, he hoped McNaughton would tell him so when he met him. General Carl Spaatz had been given instructions to fly McNaughton to Malta, where the Governor, Lord Gort, would put him up. That afternoon McNaughton and Stuart met Spaatz at Headquarters, Mediterranean Air Command, and General McNaughton addressed American officers at Spaatz's request. Next day, 14 July, they flew to Malta in Spaatz's private aircraft and were taken by car to the Governor's palace at Valletta, where they were quartered throughout their stay in Malta. That evening General Alexander arrived at his Tactical Headquarters in Malta and had a talk with McNaughton during which he said that he was flying to Sicily in the morning and would find out from Montgomery if he had any objection to the visit of Stuart and McNaughton; he would let McNaughton know the answer on 15 July. Later, at dinner with Gort, who was a friend from prewar days, McNaughton heard at first-hand the story of Dunkirk and what had prompted Gort to disobey the order of the British government and the French Commander-in-Chief, which had saved the BEF.[84]

During the morning of 15 July, still with Gort, McNaughton received a telephone call from a member of Alexander's staff informing him that permission would not be granted for any member of his party to visit Sicily. McNaughton was thunderstruck. For the commander of a national army to be prevented from visiting his own troops was decidedly unconstitutional, to say the least. It abrogated every principle he had fought for, and seen established, over the years and amounted to a denial of Canada's status as a separate nation. His force was merely *allied* to the British and he had a right to visit it any time he wished. Furthermore, on this occasion his visit had been cleared by both Brooke and Eisenhower. He requested an interview with Alexander, which was arranged for twelve o'clock.

McNaughton met Alexander at his headquarters as arranged and was told that "on General Montgomery's advice" he could not agree to General McNaughton or General Stuart visiting Sicily "owing to the shortage of transport" on the island. The trouble, he said, "lay with the War Office in that he had not heard of the visit in time to make arrangements." McNaughton brushed this aside. There was an important principle involved, he said, and he could not take the refusal without protest. That was why he had asked for this interview. Constitutionally he had not only the right but the duty to visit the Canadian formations fighting in Sicily. Did Alexander "confirm that his request for facilities to visit Canadian troops in Sicily was refused?" Alexander did, repeating that the visit could not be arranged then because of lack of transport. He suggested that he might wait for some days or come back two weeks later. Stuart, who was also present, said he would wait; McNaughton said that he would go back to England.[85]

McNaughton left Malta that night with Stuart, who accompanied him as far as Tunisia. On the evening of the 17th he met Eisenhower, who had arrived at the Headquarters Tunisia mess to swim, and had a long talk with him. McNaughton told him what had happened: that Alexander and Montgomery could not agree to his going to Sicily because of "a shortage of transport on the island." Eisenhower was unaware of this; he was under the impression that McNaughton had been there. According to Mc-Naughton's record, Eisenhower said that "Montgomery's reason and his action were silly."

General Eisenhower said that he was very sorry that the Canadian Army had not been associated with the U.S. Army so that he could have intervened and made General McNaughton's visit possible. He said that he was very loath to interfere in the internal administration of the British Army except by suggestion, which he had done in [this] case. . . . He said that he had assisted in the provision of air transport . . . to Malta and he thought that by doing so the completion of the journey to Sicily would be easily arranged.

McNaughton feared "dangerous repercussions" on the morale of Canadian troops and also politically, but the effective prosecution of the war was more important than a constitutional squabble and he intended, therefore, to return to Britain as quickly as he could to "forestall any ill-considered action" and to "allay trouble." Stuart said he would remain in North Africa for several days and he hoped he might be permitted to visit Sicily, as it was important that the Canadian formations should be visited by a senior Canadian officer.[86]

On returning from his swim Eisenhower told McNaughton that he had spoken to Alexander, who had been on the beach. He had pointed to "the possibilities of serious repercussions" if the visit was denied. Once again Alexander had refused to overrule Montgomery. McNaughton suggested that the matter be dropped; he would do everything possible in Britain to "minimize the unfortunate effects of the refusal."[87]

The best account of this incident in Tunisia is contained in Captain Harry C. Butcher's book, *My Three Years with Eisenhower.** In it Alexander's autocratic attitude clearly emerges: while he had "treated McNaughton politely," he told Eisenhower, "if he had been a junior officer he would have placed him under

---

*New York: Simon & Schuster, 1946; see pp. 366-7.

arrest."* The reaction of the Americans is also interesting. Eisenhower and Butcher supported McNaughton. The former "felt Alexander was not giving sufficient weight to the problem of a democracy conducting a war," while Butcher "ventured the query as to how the British had ever succeeded in holding together an empire when they treat the respected military representative of its most important Commonwealth so rudely." Another member of Eisenhower's staff, however, backed Alexander, concluding that "if McNaughton is the military figure he is supposed to be, he will understand the situation and will accept the inevitable like a soldier."

What was at the back of Montgomery's refusal (for the initiative lay with him) to allow McNaughton to visit his own troops in Sicily? Certainly, with the publicity that had surrounded his victories in North Africa, he had grown more and more insufferable. He hated visitors and in July, 1944, even tried to prevent Churchill from visiting France. Churchill did not "understand the situation"; instead, according to Brooke, he had flown into an "unholy rage." " 'What was Monty doing dictating to him; he had every right to visit France when he wanted? Who was Monty to stop him? As Defence Minister he had full right to visit any front he wanted!' "[89] A tactful letter† from Montgomery, at Brooke's instigation, removed the difficulty on that occasion; but Alexander had not thought fit to exert similar pressure from Malta on behalf of McNaughton.

Montgomery's own version of the Sicily incident is this:

I had a difficult decision to make soon after we landed [in Sicily]. General McNaughton, the G.O.C.-in-C. First Canadian Army (in England), had arrived in Malta about the middle of July with a party of staff officers and he asked to be sent over to Sicily to see the Canadian troops.

---

*Eisenhower's record, according to Alexander's biographer, reads: "He has been so persistent that if he were a junior officer I would put him under arrest."[88]

†"The C.I.G.S. has just informed me that you are under the impression that I am trying to stop you from coming to France. This is the last thing I should do and I will always welcome your visits. I shall always have a caravan available for you. . . . I only hope you will pay me a visit soon."[90]

The 1st Canadian Division had not been in action before and officers and men were just beginning to find their feet. Guy Simonds, the Divisional Commander, was young and inexperienced; it was the first time he had commanded a division in battle.

I was determined that the Canadians must be left alone and I wasn't going to have Simonds bothered with visitors when he was heavily engaged with his division in all-out operations against first-rate German troops. However, to make sure I went to see Simonds and asked him if he would like McNaughton to come to Sicily. His reply was immediate—"For God's sake keep him away."[91]

This is substantially what happened, as has been confirmed by Simonds,[92] and there was sense behind it. Moreover McNaughton, a reasonable man, would undoubtedly have appreciated that it was sensible, and postponed his visit until things had settled down. But that was not the reason given. He was told, as had been Alexander, that "shortage of transport" was behind the refusal and that, as Eisenhower so rightly said, was "silly." Montgomery did not consult Alexander nor Eisenhower nor Sir Alan Brooke. Instead he acted arbitrarily, his reaction being, as his Chief of Staff said, "very definite, and perhaps a little brusque. On no account would he allow the visit."[93] McNaughton did not forget nor forgive. As Montgomery recorded, "I have not met him since those days, although I have paid many visits to Canada since the war ended. It seemed to me that he had never forgiven me for denying him entry to Sicily in July 1943."[94] Nor, when the truth was out, did McNaughton have much time for Simonds, who could easily have suggested a short postponement. Simonds was to recall, years later, that after Sicily he detected a distinct chilliness in their relations.[95]

Up to this point the relationship between McNaughton and Montgomery had been generally good. There were small differences but not more than usually occur between strong-willed men. The record shows mutual respect and one searches it in vain for major altercations. McNaughton had followed the progress of the North African campaign with pleasure and had praised Montgomery highly for his victories. Montgomery, on his side, seems to have had some knowledge of McNaughton's far-sightedness with regard to weapons, and in January, 1943, he requested a few of his carrier-borne flame throwers for use at the Mareth Line. "Not fifty," replied McNaughton, who wanted them employed for mass effect, not in penny packets, "but I will release five hundred."*96 July of 1943 marked the parting of the ways.

The day after his return to England on 20 July McNaughton demanded an interview with Brooke. It was a stormy meeting. Though Montgomery had clearly been in the wrong the CIGS showed neither the slightest comprehension of Canada's constitutional position nor sympathy for McNaughton's championship of it. Asked about his visit to the Mediterranean, McNaughton told him what had happened and of Montgomery's refusal because "transportation was not available."

I had indicated that I considered this reason to be without adequate foundation in fact, but nevertheless, General Alexander had adhered to his position and I therefore said I would withdraw from the theatre. . . .

At first, General Brooke expressed the view, forcibly and with some passion, that I had no right to visit Canadian troops. . . .

I said that . . . as a matter of principle . . . there should be no doubt that representatives of the Canadian Army would have access to our troops at all times in [sic] their discretion—that I must maintain this principle, and that he need be under no anxiety that this right would be used to hamper the appropriate conduct of military operations as we were just as much concerned as anyone else with the effective prosecution of the war. . . . I also pointed out the special considerations relating to myself as the Commander of the Canadian Army, which included the formations in Sicily, and that I was fully aware the people of Canada would expect me to at least see something of our troops in their first battles. . . .

. . . . General Brooke [then] apologized for any lack of courtesy and consideration which might have been shown to me . . . and I replied that there was no question of apology to me personally, and that so long as the principle of my right to visit Canadian

---

*"The Ronson," said McNaughton, "will not be exposed to the enemy unless in suitable numbers and against a strategically important objective."

troops was not in doubt I was prepared to let the matter drop. . . .

General Brooke expressed great concern that I had left North Africa without waiting for an opportunity to see the Canadian troops, and he hoped I would go out again and do so later. . . .

The conversation, which lasted an hour, turned to the war situation in general, and then Brooke suddenly flashed back to the point at issue: Canada's constitutional position with regard to her Army:

General Brooke referred to the views which I had often expressed to him on the military advantage of keeping the Canadian Army together, and, with some heat, to the letter I had written to him when, in the course of an exercise when he was C.-in-C. Home Forces, he had detached a couple of our battalions from 1 Canadian Division. He said these views had influenced him against proposing operations involving only a part of our force. He spoke of Mr. Ralston's* insistence last year that battles be found for the Canadians, and he implied that this he would now do. . . .

At times, the atmosphere of the conversation became somewhat tense, and General Brooke was obviously disturbed and anxious. . . .[97]

Charles G. Power, Canada's wartime Minister of Air and Associate Minister of National Defence, referred to the fact that "the Canadian troops were a direct responsibility of the Canadian government, and not of any other Allied powers." Many senior British officers either did not, or would not, understand that. Power was incisively correct when he went on to say: "It must be said for General McNaughton that so long as he was Commander-in-Chief of the Canadian forces he very strongly upheld his own authority. I fear this did not tend to increase his popularity with the British War Office and the chiefs of staff."[98]

Stuart returned to England on 25 July without having visited Sicily and two days later he went with McNaughton to call on General Morgan at Norfolk House to hear something of COSSAC

---

*The Defence Minister, Ralston, had been a battalion commander in the First World War and was usually addressed as "Colonel."

planning. Morgan was uneasy about rival British and American aims. He had had conversations recently with Stimson* and Winant,† and with Eden and Alan Brooke. American eyes were fixed upon operations, as early as they could be mounted, against Northwest Europe. British policy favoured further and intensified operations in the Mediterranean. To carry out a successful offensive across the Channel by the target date of 1 May, Morgan warned, "would require the complete resources of both countries being placed at the disposal of those charged with the direction of the operations." If troops were dispersed from the United Kingdom to the Mediterranean, as the British seemed to want, the date for the invasion might have to be set back, perhaps as late as 1 September, 1944.

Morgan firmly stated that the detachment of additional Canadian formations to the Mediterranean would have an adverse effect on Anglo-American co-operation in the uneasy climate that existed over strategy. Suppose Canadian divisions were sent in exchange for British divisions, Stuart asked, what then? Then, said Morgan, the effect might not be so harmful. It was important, Stuart continued, for Canadian troops to gain battle experience; if further operations were to take place in the Mediterranean it was the view of the Canadian government that one additional division and a corps headquarters should be provided. And, if the target date for the invasion was to be as late as Morgan had indicated, the First Canadian Army could be reassembled in time to take place in the attack on Northwest Europe. For political reasons there must be no more inactivity on the part of the Canadian troops in Britain. He therefore wished to place on record with COSSAC that the Canadian government stressed the importance of additional Canadian formations gaining early experience in active operations.

McNaughton objected strongly to a Mediterranean strategy. The Canadian Army had been directed by the Chiefs of Staff Committee to the invasion of Northwest Europe *as an army*, where it would do most good; he opposed a desire for activity merely for

---

*Henry Stimson, United States Secretary of War.
†John G. Winant, United States Ambassador to the Court of St. James's.

activity's sake. He suggested that the occupation of Italy would bring no military advantages to the Allies; quite the reverse. The terrain favoured the defensive and the Germans could conduct successful defensive operations in Italy with fewer troops than the Allies would need. The Allies, moreover, would incur the task of feeding a starving Italian population. McNaughton thought that minor operations against Sardinia, Corsica and Southern Italy—with the increasing bombardment of strategic targets from these places—would serve the Allied purpose of holding German troops away from Northwest Europe without the actual occupation of Italy.[99]

"Military logic," wrote Ralph Allen, reviewing this period, "was overwhelmingly on his side, even if political logic was not. Far from calling for more divisions in the Mediterranean, the grand strategy of the Allies called for fewer. Seven of the divisions already there were earmarked for return to Britain and the build-up for Normandy."[100] Sir Basil Liddell Hart spells it out still more clearly:

The claims that have been made for the value of the Italian campaign as an aid to the cross-Channel attack do not stand analysis. For the distracting effect caused by the Allies' amphibious flexibility diminished when the ubiquitous threat was translated into an actual landing. By June 1944, they were employing in Italy a strength in troops double that of Kesselring. That was not a good investment proportionately, and justified the American argument for breaking off the offensive there after the strategic airfields in the south were gained. Moreover, its continuance did not draw German reserves away from Normandy, nor prevent them reinforcing Normandy, as the British hoped—and have claimed.[101]

Ralston, as Mackenzie King had promised, joined Stuart on 28 July. On the 29th Stuart and Ralston (it would be too much to believe that there had been no prior consultation) had a long talk with McNaughton at Headley Court. Not only did Stuart favour building up the force in Sicily to a corps; he now said this could be done even if there was no certainty that it could be brought back in time for the invasion of Northwest Europe. He recognized that this would destroy the Army. ("Headquarters First Canadian

Army as an operational command would be redundant.") Ralston showed a "strong predilection" for this course which would enable "important economies" to be effected. Despite more than a year's intensive work to build and equip the Army as a balanced force, despite the long hours and the frustration that had been involved, McNaughton remained patient. He spoke of the advanced state of organization and training of the Army; the close relation with 83 Group, RAF; of the long schedule of exercises that had been arranged; and of the loss of continuity and the delay that would inevitably arise if it became necessary for the War Office to set up a British army to replace the Canadian. He pointed to the improvement in the shipping situation—that early in 1944 shipping need not be considered as a factor which would prevent the return of additional formations, should they be sent for a *short* tour of duty, from the Mediterranean theatre. The dispatch of additional troops to the Mediterranean, therefore, did not mean that the Army as such should be regarded as redundant. He then talked about the Army:

They must take what he said about it as strictly impersonal and not as any special pleading, for without that assurance he would not feel inclined to make any statement whatever. He reminded Ralston and Stuart that *the Army had not been created at his suggestion;* * and every step forward had met with the approval of the British authorities. He had supported the proposals because, in the light of existing circumstances at the time, he had felt them to be right and proper as the best contribution Canada could make to the winning of the war.

McNaughton reminded Ralston and Stuart that the force at present in the Mediterranean theatre had been authorized to undertake the campaign in Sicily only. If operations were to continue in the Mediterranean he "unhesitatingly supported developing a Canadian Corps" there and widening its authority to undertake further operations but only on the assumption that the corps "would return to the United Kingdom if the decisive attack on Germany was to be launched from here."[102]

There was no assurance, McNaughton continued, that COSSAC,

---

*Italics supplied.

and the setting up of the 21st Army Group, was not just a façade. The War Office had assured him repeatedly that these measures represented "a real and firm intention" but did they amount to a mere gesture to appease the Americans while the British really intended to make Italy the major theatre?* The Canadian government should insist on participation in the political direction of the war. He referred to the generous contributions made by Canada in men and matériel which justified consultation. What Ralston should do was to go to Washington to present the Canadian case. Ralston gloomily agreed that the present position was "contribution without representation" but he was convinced that there was no hope of obtaining "entry into the Councils in Washington." Stuart said it looked as if they would have to "gamble" on the probability that the British view of continuing in the Mediterranean would prevail.

McNaughton said there was no need to do that. There was no objection to Canadian detachments being engaged in widely separated operations provided they were returned in time for an invasion when this became really firm. For that reason he had adopted British establishments; he had accepted standardized equipments; he had even relinquished a line of supply straight back to Canada for a pooling of stocks, and had not objected to global planning and a global allocation of materials. Because of this HUSKY had been possible for the Canadians with little disruption. The present difficulties could be met by setting down certain conditions under which Canadians would be employed, and he then wrote down what follows:

(i) If operations are to continue in the Mediterranean, and if additional Canadian troops are required (or in replacement of British divisions) Canada would be glad to raise its contingent in North Africa to a Corps of appropriate composition.

(ii) As regards planning and development in the U.K., we would continue to go on the basis that the Canadian contingent in North

---

*General Morgan himself had doubts that summer. "Were we really only taking part in a gigantic cover plan or hoax, with the object of hoaxing, among others, ourselves?" He could understand the feelings of Americans "that the British might, possibly not by design but quite possibly for lack of proper appreciation of American power, sell the Yanks down the Mediterranean again."[103]

Africa would return to the Canadian Army in the U.K. before the date set for a major offensive on the Continent.

"This brought forth further argument," McNaughton's Personal Assistant laconically recorded, "and it became quite clear that neither the Minister nor the C.G.S. accepted para (ii)."[104]

During the next few days Ralston saw Churchill. With Stuart, he had a long talk with Brooke. The Minister and the CGS attempted to persuade the British to accept a Canadian build-up in the Mediterranean and, to make this palatable, they imposed no conditions regarding the return of any formations from that theatre before the cross-Channel invasion. This was a course which they had obviously determined to pursue, despite McNaughton's objections, and they were anxious to have the policy settled. On 5 August they told McNaughton something of what was going on. Churchill, it appeared, had been dubious about Ralston's proposal but Brooke favoured it and had "undertaken to talk to Churchill himself." Ralston had based his request, he said, on (a) giving training to a Canadian corps headquarters; (b) obtaining battle experience for additional Canadian troops; (c) the morale of the Canadian Army in the United Kingdom; (d) the morale of the Canadian people. As for strategy, Brooke clearly supported "an extension in the Mediterranean; he said that the policy would be settled at the forthcoming conference [in Quebec]."[105]

Brooke, Ralston said, had then discussed the First Canadian Army. If one of its corps was detached to the Mediterranean he saw no need for Army Headquarters at all; "this superstructure would not be worthwhile if the Canadians were in two theatres." Ralston stated that he had then put a leading question to Brooke: if he were asked to advise the Canadian government, would he now recommend the abandonment of the Canadian Army? Yes, he would. Then, Ralston claimed to have asked him, what about his having recommended the formation of an army at the end of 1942? The situation, Brooke was said to have replied, had changed since then.[106]

McNaughton remembered Brooke's words to him after his abortive trip to Sicily; that he would, in effect, find battles for the Canadian as Ralston wished, even if that meant that the Army

Some of the publicity focused on McNaughton during the war years

The Standard

PHOTONEWS

■ FEBRUARY 24 1940

10 CENTS

THE KING AND McNAUGHTON

More publicity

would be divided. The position he had always adopted with Brooke regarding the autonomy of the Canadian force had been undermined by Ralston, who appeared quite willing to sacrifice all that McNaughton stood for. There was no need for this. Ralston, for political reasons, wanted to increase Canada's contribution in the Mediterranean to a corps. McNaughton had agreed. All he had asked for was a safeguard that the corps would return in time to take part with the Army in operations in Northwest Europe, which he deemed essential. Everyone would have been satisfied if only Ralston had had the wit to insist on the inclusion of that vital clause. McNaughton was now aroused and spoke very plainly to Ralston.

It could be taken as a foregone conclusion, he said flatly, that the Canadian Army would be dispersed. Not exactly, Ralston replied, but McNaughton interrupted him. It was so, he said. The Minister's statements, "however conditionally he had intended them, would play into the hands of individuals," including Brooke, "who desired the break-up of the Canadian Army to buttress their own positions; War Office plans might now evolve to make this result inevitable." Not at all, said Ralston; he had made it clear to Brooke that the sole purpose in sending Canadian troops was to give them battle experience. Any specific proposals would have to come before the Canadian War Cabinet on their merits. McNaughton disagreed. Having expressed the views he had, Ralston had compromised Canadian freedom of judgment. Moreover, despite the Minister's strenuous denials, he for one was convinced that Ralston was bent on the dissolution of the First Canadian Army. He based that on the stand Ralston had taken with regard to reinforcements as recently as 2 August.* Again Ralston denied that that was what was in his mind.[108]

---

*McNaughton was referring here to a request he had made for reinforcements from Canada to replace men who were unfit either medically or for other reasons (there were four thousand illiterates alone), that is, to make up normal "wastage." Ottawa promised five thousand but on 2 August Ralston told McNaughton that he regarded this number as replacements for "battle casualties" only and had made a commitment to the cabinet to that effect. Though McNaughton objected, Ralston said "the men would not be forthcoming in any event and he would not ask the Canadian Cabinet for them." McNaughton said he would not have believed that Ralston's interpretation was possible; it would make the reinforcement situation in the Canadian Army "very precarious."[107]

Then, McNaughton said, determined to make one last attempt, if there was "a real intent" to bring the troops back from the Mediterranean for the decisive cross-Channel attack the Canadian Army need not be broken up. Ralston should insist on that. But Ralston switched the talk to the lack of battle experience of the Canadian commanders, including, very pointedly, McNaughton himself.[109]

If that was bothering him, McNaughton flashed back, he would be glad "to develop Crerar," send him off to battle, and then relinquish command of the Army to him: "The important thing for Canada at the end of the war was to have her Army together under the command of a Canadian."

Not so, said Ralston. The important thing was "a voice at the Peace Table proportional to her battle contribution."

"Armies in being," McNaughton returned, "were a more real measure of the weight which would be attached to the voice of any country."[110]

What advice, Stuart interposed, would McNaughton give the Canadian War Cabinet? That could not be given, McNaughton replied, on the "as if" and "when" basis on which the discussion had so far been conducted; it could only be related specifically to the strategic plan when it was known. As a matter of principle he was opposed to the dispersion of the Canadian Army but if a corps moved to the Mediterranean on the same basis as the 1st Canadian Division had moved, that did not imply dispersion. If the Canadian government, however, decided upon real dispersion "then they would be wise to put someone in control who believed in it." He himself certainly did not. He "wanted Canada, both as a contribution to the war and for what it would mean after the war, to end up with the Army under her own control."[111]

In conclusion, he again reminded Ralston and Stuart that the approval of the Canadian force in Sicily was limited to that operation. He did not know if the Canadian government would consult him prior to an extension of operations there but he wished to be informed of their intentions. On Ralston's saying that he proposed to review the documents, McNaughton, remembering his experience in Malta, suggested that in any future instruction a "right to

visit" clause should be included but Ralston "doubted the wisdom" of inserting any such provision.[112]

During the afternoon of the following day Field-Marshal Sir John
Dill, who was over from Washington, telephoned McNaughton
and at his suggestion the General drove to the War Office to meet
him. They chatted pleasantly on personal matters for a while and
then McNaughton turned the conversation to the general strategy
of the war. Dill, one of the Combined Chiefs of Staff in Washington—a body responsible for all combined operations and for world
strategy under the final direction of the heads of governments—
would obviously have something authoritative to say. Close to the
Americans as he was, Dill favoured a Northwest Europe strategy
over a campaign in Italy. Minor operations against Sardinia or
other islands would, he said, secure the Allied objective of tying
down German troops and keeping "a show of war" going in that
theatre without committing large Allied forces to Italy. This
coincided with McNaughton's own view and in that congenial
atmosphere he told Dill of the pressure that Ralston was applying
to put the Canadians into battle. "I told him, personally and very
frankly, of my present difficulties." Dill thought about it for a
few moments and then said there would be a natural tendency on
the part of the War Office to agree, if at all possible, with any
proposal put forward by a political representative of Canada. His
own view was that "the maintenance of the Canadian Army was
a factor of great military importance," which should not be lost
unless there were overriding military requirements calling for the
use of separate divisions. The general strategy would be arrived at
very shortly. Only then could conclusions be drawn as to what best
should be done from a strictly military point of view. This was
clear-headed. Again, it coincided with McNaughton's own views
and he was greatly reassured.

The conclusions McNaughton drew from his talk with Dill
were these: the chance of a Canadian corps being really required
in the Mediterranean was remote; too much importance should
not be placed on Ralston's statement of Brooke's views, which
were probably no more than a reflection of Ralston's own; and
the important military advantage of maintaining the Canadian

Army as such was not an idea peculiar to himself but was shared by Dill, whose judgment he trusted. He returned to Headley Court greatly cheered but his optimism, as so often in his life, was unfounded.*[113]

On 7 August, 1943, at a final meeting with Ralston before the Minister's return, McNaughton told him of Dill's views. He then talked enthusiastically and at length of the organization of the Army and of its training for the invasion role. But neither Ralston nor Stuart, who was also there, made any comment. This must have struck McNaughton as ominous. Ralston merely said that the strategy to be followed would be decided at Quebec; and when McNaughton asked him if the Canadian government still favoured the sending of additional troops to the Mediterranean, he answered bluntly, "Yes."[114]

Then, on the 12th, McNaughton received a cable from General Alexander inviting him to visit Sicily. McNaughton accepted and made arrangements to leave on 18 August.

The "Quadrant" Conference, attended by Churchill, Roosevelt and Mackenzie King, was held at Quebec from 14 to 24 August. Early in this period the Sicilian campaign ended. After the "Trident" Conference in Washington during May, where Churchill had pressed strongly for an invasion of Italy after Sicily, it had been thought best to await the outcome in Sicily before concluding any firm plan. The decision reached at Quebec was made all the easier when the Badoglio government, which had taken over from Mussolini on 25 July, informed the Allies that the Italians wanted to fight on their side. Italy was the next objective, though that theatre would take second place for supplies to the projected invasion of Northwest Europe. The first landings in Italy took place nine days after the "Quadrant" Conference ended.

Ralston had reached Quebec on 10 August. It is clear at this distance that he was determined that McNaughton must go and it

_____

*It was McNaughton's last meeting with Dill who died in November, 1944. General Marshall offered a grave for him in the Arlington National Cemetery—a unique honour for a British soldier—which Lady Dill accepted.

is equally apparent from Mackenzie King's record of his discussion with Ralston, Stuart and Brooke that there had already been some consultation between these three. The upholding by Mc-Naughton of Canada's constitutional position, though troublesome to the British, obviously could not be openly stated as the grounds for his removal; nor could his attempts to keep the Army together, for there were many in Canada who would support him.

On his arrival at Quebec, Ralston at once talked with King about future strategy; he pointed to the rival American and British plans and—before any decision had been reached with regard to them—was "all for another division going to Sicily and into Italy."[115] Ralston stated that "McNaughton seemed favourable at first to the idea of another division going to Sicily and possibly to the formation of an Army Corps, but that, later, he had objected to the breaking-up of the Canadian Army." Ralston then told King "that Brooke had expressed surprise at the judgment McNaughton had shown in military exercises earlier in the year [SPARTAN]."[116]

Four days later Stuart confirmed to the Prime Minister what Ralston had told King. He went further. "Brooke and General Paget," he said, "no longer felt confidence in McNaughton's capacity to command troops in actual combat." McNaughton "had himself spoken of the possibility of resigning." Even Mc-Naughton's insistence on Canada's constitutional position and on his right as the senior Canadian commander to visit his troops in Sicily, were turned against him. And Stuart, though he had played a very shadowy part, had been there; he knew the circumstances. Nevertheless, Stuart reported "that Montgomery would not allow McNaughton to cross over to Sicily or to have any part in the operations there. That ... they had had some very sharp words and McNaughton had gone back to Britain very much annoyed...." Paget and Brooke "were particularly enthusiastic about Crerar. Felt he was an exceptionally good officer, and Crerar was very popular with the men." Both Ralston and Stuart stated that "McNaughton seemed much older and suffering a good deal from strain."[117]

Later that day Brooke, whom Mackenzie King "liked exceedingly," told the Prime Minister that McNaughton

seemed to have become more suited for planning and research than for action in the field. He said he ought to be the head of a great research institute. I [King] said: "As you know, he was head of our Research department." He replied: "Yes, and excelled himself at that kind of work. Full of inventive genius, but interested in study." His conversation rather confirmed what Stuart had said to me. When I mentioned Crerar, Brooke said he had the very highest opinion of Crerar. Could not have a better man. Would trust him in command anywhere, etc. I did not in any way ask for an opinion on either of the men. All was volunteered.

After Brooke had spoken of McNaughton, I said what he had just said I had felt a little about myself. That I had been getting out of touch with the men in the party who were in the field, concentrating more on the work in hand, and that, as one got older, one became more interested in philosophical thought and the like. He said that was it exactly.*[118]

"There is no doubt," the author of *The Mackenzie King Record* states, "that the possibility of McNaughton's retirement as Commander of the Canadian Army became an active possibility from this time on."[119] McNaughton in the past had repeatedly battled Alan Brooke and had prevailed; it was the same with Ralston. But when these two came together in a common purpose—to replace him—their combined strength was too much for him without the Prime Minister's support. And this McNaughton no longer had; already at Quebec King was reflecting that "one of the most difficult problems to settle at this . . . conference will be the command of our force, and what is to be arranged for McNaughton." He had decided that, "quite apart from any differences between Ralston and himself, and incompatibility between the temper of the two men, there may be a necessity for someone else having command of the operations on the Continent. It is really too bad as the Army is really due to McNaughton and he has lived in the hope of commanding it in action. I can understand, however, how four years of service with health not too good may have affected his judgment."[120]

---

*This, coming from Brooke who had been exposed to McNaughton's dynamism, is not devoid of humour.

The dicision to invade Italy, then, as we have seen, was taken at Quebec. What now of the Canadian force in the Mediterranean theatre which McNaughton had placed "in combination" for the invasion of Sicily only? Churchill, Mackenzie King recorded, spoke of the Canadians being "out of the fight for a time in order to be ready to invade Italy. . . . He then said that the question had been raised by McNaughton . . . as to whether our men going to Italy was to be regarded as part of the one operation. He asked me if I could say that it was." Under Churchill's blandishments, and aware of Ralston's desires, Mackenzie King gave way. "I told him I had always understood that Sicily was a simply a step to invading Italy, and to the invasion of Europe from the South. I would, however, like to confer with the Minister of Defence before giving a definite word . . . but I felt quite sure that the Government had always regarded the whole operation as one. Apparently McNaughton has questioned this."[121]

It is clear that Churchill and Ralston had won Mackenzie King completely over. (As McNaughton pointed out, "King's reply was the equivalent of 'Yes' ":[122] the invasion of Italy was an extension of the Sicilian campaign.) We have noted earlier Stuart's record of a conversation with Churchill at the "Trident" Conference, with which Mackenzie King agreed, that the Canadians were to be brought back to Britain after Sicily had been seized. This by now had been forgotten or ignored. Ralston, who was in Ottawa, is stated to have examined the record and satisfied himself that Canadian troops "had been committed for Italy and not just Sicily,"[123] but Brigadier R. J. Orde, (Judge Advocate General) disagreed. This question, he said, did not arise. He was called to Ralston's office late that night and found John Reid (Legal Adviser, Department of External Affairs) and Stuart already there. Ralston said he had had a message from Mackenzie King about "putting a bigger toe into the boot" and wished to be assured that no further Order in Council was required to enable Canadian forces to serve in combination with British troops in Italy. Reid and Orde assured Ralston that there was no need for such legislation; under the existing arrangement McNaughton had full powers to act. Ralston told Mackenzie King this and the Prime Minister gave the signal to go ahead. It was agreed that Stuart would send an appropriate message to McNaughton. No fewer than sixteen messages were successively changed by Ralston until at last one met with his approval. This *directed* McNaughton to act as the government wished—the first time that he had placed a force "in combination" by direction.*[124]

On 31 August Churchill, having so easily gained the services of Canada's HUSKY force for Italy, told Mackenzie King that "he was not at all averse . . . to Canada having an Army Corps in Italy, but he would have to bring back British divisions to London to keep faith with the Americans as to keeping a certain number of divisions in England."[125] Though there were many vicissitudes before that was accomplished, with Churchill's words Ralston had really achieved his aim of breaking up the Army over the strong protests of McNaughton.

McNaughton, as directed, had committed the Canadian troops in Sicily to the invasion of Italy when he finally managed to visit Sicily and to have a talk with Montgomery on 24 and 25 August. He had arrived in Sicily four days earlier, had met Simonds, toured units, and covered the ground which the Canadians had fought over from the coast to the final battle area. Because of their extensive training in Britain, the Canadians had conducted themselves like seasoned veterans. In Montgomery's words, "The Canadians were magnificent in the Sicilian campaign. They had done no fighting before, but they were very well trained and they soon learnt the tricks of the battlefield which count for so much and save so many lives."[126]

On 22 August Montgomery wrote: "My dear Andy, I am glad to hear you have arrived and are with your Canadians. Welcome to the Eighth Army."[127] But it was a bit late for that. McNaughton

---

*Perhaps Ralston doubted if McNaughton could be relied upon to carry out government policy in view of his decided opinion that the policy was wrong. McNaughton's own words (when interviewed by the Canadian Press, 27 December, 1943), are the best answer to that: "In the evolution of a military force and in formulating plans we seek a clash of wits. But once a decision is reached all controversy ceases and that decision is supported with the whole heart and energy of everybody and we carry on along that course until new information warrants further review."

visited Montgomery at his Tactical Headquarters in a fine villa at Taormina overlooking the blue waters of the Strait of Messina. In his record of the visit the bitterness which he now felt towards this man comes through quite clearly:

I arrived . . . on the late afternoon of 24 August. . . . I was conducted to Montgomery's bedroom and private office. I was invited to admire his canaries and their very elaborate cages which had been made by the C.E. [Chief Engineer] Eighth Army. I was particularly invited to note that the cages bore the Eighth Army sign, the Crusader's Shield. Montgomery said he liked to watch canaries. One of the hens was now nesting and the domestic life of the pair was very interesting to watch. He had also acquired a peacock which had now been trained to sit on top of his caravan and not to stray away; a fitting decoration for the Eighth Army Commander's caravan. . . . I must go and see the peacocks and the caravans, one of which had belonged to "Electric Whiskers" [Marshal Graziani] and another to another general he had captured. His BGS [Brigadier, General Staff] had secured a remarkable Italian car for his own use but he . . . had pinched it for himself. Did I not agree that he was right to take it for himself? After more of this personal and Eighth Army egotistical nonsense, to which I can claim to have listened with all courtesy and attention, we passed on to a discussion of matters related to the affairs of 1 Cdn Div. . . .[128]

They discussed Simonds, who "had done very well but he, Montgomery, had watched him closely. . . . He, Montgomery, made it his business to train generals and I could expect Simonds to be first class when he had finished with him—first class."

Montgomery referred to the Canadians who would be fighting under his command in Italy and the talk turned to the fallacy of breaking divisions or brigades in regrouping. McNaughton warned Montgomery that "if this were ever done to ours we might be expected to take strong exception on grounds of military inefficiency quite apart from constitutional propriety." Montgomery agreed that it was not the right thing to do.*

---

*Nevertheless, in May, 1944, Montgomery won control over Canadian troops to a degree that never would have been contemplated by McNaughton. At that time, during a talk with Montgomery, Mackenzie King agreed that "when battlefield conditions warranted it, Canadian units could be dispersed and placed under British command."[129]

Next morning the conversation continued. As to the set-up in England, Montgomery said, this was wrong. The 21st Army Group should be a general headquarters.* Did McNaughton not think so? McNaughton did not. He went on to sketch the present organization there and at COSSAC which "clearly did not draw Montgomery's approval." On one subject they did agree. "We spoke of the power of artillery, concentrated. He said the whole Divisional Artillery and on occasions the Corps R.A. or even the Army R.A. should fire as a single battery. I agreed and I said that for more than a quarter of a century I had been an exponent of this very doctrine." Montgomery also spoke of "the great importance of Air Burst Ranging . . . which was now being used extensively."

At the conclusion of the meeting that morning, Montgomery talked of McNaughton himself. He "referred also to my own position and the difficulties of training an Army and at the same time being Senior Officer. He advocated that I should concentrate on the latter and become a Minister. I thanked him for this (gratuitous) advice but made no comment." Montgomery then insisted on taking McNaughton over to his caravans to see his peacock. It had "strayed away and was absent" and after that McNaughton left.[130]

Nevertheless, despite what undoubtedly was to McNaughton an unpleasant meeting, he kept his antipathy towards Montgomery to himself. At a press conference later in the day he pointed to the "extraordinary efficiency of the Eighth Army":

This efficiency included the staff, the army organization and in particular the Army Commander himself. He added that he was very pleased with the sympathy and understanding with which the Canadians had been handled. . . . He pointed out that the Eighth Army had given effective direction to enable the division to drive forward. . . .

Asked if he would care to comment on the question of the use of the Canadian Army as a whole or in part, McNaughton replied that he would "state nothing that would carry comfort to the

---

*In view of subsequent developments it may be wondered if Montgomery did not already have his eye on the command of 21st Army Group.

enemy." He also declined to comment on the future of the 1st Canadian Division.[131]

There is no doubt at all what his feelings really were. His dream of an autonomous Canadian army had now been shattered. One division had already been absorbed by a British army and Montgomery was already using the first person possessive in references to Canadian troops. In future British histories* of the war the Eighth Army would feature prominently; the Canadian Division would be largely ignored. McNaughton's old fears that Canadian troops would be regarded merely as British manpower seemed well on the way to being realized. He could understand Montgomery's elation when, on visiting the 1st Canadian Division in September, Montgomery recalled that "the Canadian Corps had formed part of the army he commanded in England a year and a half ago and said":

I like to feel that I played a small part in helping that corps and your group to prepare itself for battle.

I used to feel that when the time came for it to go into battle I should like it to do so under my command, so when you came out here it was a great day for me.[132]

A brief picture of McNaughton in Sicily has survived in the memory of a gunner officer whose unit he visited:

The last time I saw him was in Sicily where he came during that short campaign to see his troops in their first real action. He visited us—the R.C.H.A., his old Regiment—and I remember his tropical uniform being something less well-tailored than those of other senior officers who were perhaps more conscious of their "image." He looked like a tired civilian in hastily assembled general's garb. No Hotspur; no "once more unto the breach" stuff; no wonderful Montgomery hokum. He seemed quiet, diffidently kindly, and genuinely interested in us and how we were getting along. I do remember the surprise with which I imagined that he seemed actually respectful to the troops—unusual among commanders that we saw. He looked as though he really wanted to get up to an observation post and stay with us.

---

*In Peter Young's *Short History, World War 1939-1945* there are twelve brief references to Canadian troops and these consist of little more than the word "Canadians." This book, according to the *Times Literary Supplement*, is a "standard work."

Among all those I knew in the gunners there was, I think, a unanimous conviction that Andy McNaughton was an officer and gentleman from the inside out, and that he could be depended upon to do the right thing, without posturing, publicity-seeking and being a "psychological" soldier.

Although he had such a long and distinguished active military career, I always thought of him in terms of Henry V—"we are but warriors for the working day. Our gayness and our gilt are all besmirched with rainy marching in the painful field. . ."[133]

Montgomery's two-division assault across the Strait of Messina went in on 3 September, with the Canadians on the right. The invasion was preceded by a mighty barrage of five hundred and thirty guns, but—there was no resistance. The Germans had left. The shells crashed down on gaily dressed Italian civilians, men, women and children, waiting to greet the liberating troops with flowers. In Montgomery's words:

The Germans evacuated Reggio before we got into the town so we had no opposition from soldiers. But there is a zoo in the town and our shelling broke open some cages; a puma and a monkey escaped and attacked some men of the H.Q. 3rd Canadian Brigade, and heavy fire was opened by the Canadians.[134]

It was mere "showmanship," McNaughton said: "In the result this operation represents a vast toll of expenditure in wasted ammunition which could have been obviated by a few patrols to contact the Italians standing around on the beaches and who knew, on the previous day, that the Germans were withdrawing. . . . . The consequence of this was an ammunition shortage which in the later actions . . . might well have cost us dear."[135]

McNaughton returned to England and on 1 September moved to Portsmouth for Exercise HARLEQUIN which was still continuing when, on 2 September, Nye sent for him from London. The Canadian government, Nye said, had now formally proposed to send an additional division to Italy and the matter had been referred to Churchill who was then in Washington. The War Office would study the implications of this and advise Churchill, who would discuss them with Roosevelt and with King. If another division were to go, Nye continued, the War Office would favour having a Canadian corps in the theatre, with basic corps troops. This corps "must be considered more or less a permanent commitment as it was highly improbable that shipping would be available in time for it to return to the United Kingdom by the target date of 1 May 1944," and it was even unlikely that it would return by 1 September of that year.

So that was that, McNaughton thought. Though he was convinced that it was folly, it was the will of his government. He asked what type of division would be required, armoured or infantry? Infantry, Nye replied, there was already more than enough armour there. That would leave the Canadian Army out of balance, McNaughton said—two out of three infantry divisions would be in Italy and he would be left with a preponderance of armour. It was probable, Nye thought, that British infantry formations would be placed under his command; it would be "most unwise" to disband the Canadian Army because of its advanced state of organization and of training. It thus appeared that McNaughton would command an Anglo-Canadian force in France and while this was not the national expedition he had counted on, something had been gained; it would fight as a Canadian army.[136]

On 14 September McNaughton had a talk with Brooke, whom he had not seen for some weeks because of the conference in Quebec. Brooke recounted his experiences in Canada, talked "of the great pleasure he had taken in the fishing provided," and seemed very cheerful. McNaughton turned the conversation to "the suggestion made by Colonel Ralston" that there should be a Canadian corps in Italy and asked about the feasibility of the project. Brooke, without hesitation, said that shipping would not be available.

McNaughton, with rising hopes, "well understood the shipping difficulties." He also appreciated "that to move an additional Canadian division and Corps troops to Italy would correspondingly reduce the total force deployed [from Britain] against the Axis in 1944. . . ." He had been afraid "that the political considerations in Canada might override the military considerations which were heavily weighted against the move."

Brooke said that McNaughton should carry on as he was doing with the First Canadian Army; he should complete its development and continue with its training. He did say, however, that the 1st Canadian Division was not one of the seven Allied divisions scheduled to return from Italy that fall. Did that hold good into the late spring of 1944? The division might be considered as the eighth division (after the three British and the four American) for return. Brooke thought that to say 1 May would be premature in any case; 1 June or even 1 July would be more realistic. He gave McNaughton the impression that he could count on it by then.[137]

Nevertheless, three weeks later, the decision was reversed. At a further meeting with Brooke on 7 October, McNaughton was told that the Canadian government's proposal had been re-examined on the basis of an exchange of divisions and "an interchange of personnel only" (each division would leave its equipment behind to be taken over by the other), and had been found feasible. This was due to Churchill's pressure after King, prompted by Ralston, had tried again.* Two British infantry divisions, one armoured division and an airborne division, as well as XXX Corps Headquarters and corps troops, had been recalled from Italy. They would leave their equipment behind and the Canadians would be supplied from that. McNaughton accepted the inevitable. What type of division, then, would be sent? He again referred to the further imbalance that would result from the dispatch of more infantry. Brooke said he preferred an armoured division, in any case, and McNaughton agreed to that. He nominated the 1st Corps under Crerar and the 5th Armoured Division.

Brooke then digressed to talk of Churchill, of his wish for "adventures in the Adriatic"† and neighbouring waters. "He spoke passionately of his difficulties in keeping Mr. Churchill from

---

*Massey had seen Churchill at the end of September, asking that "the negative reply to the Canadian Government's request" be reconsidered.[138]

†At a future meeting with Mackenzie King at Quebec on 12 September, 1944, Churchill had conducted the Canadian Prime Minister to the map room and pointed to Italy: "What he is particularly interested in," King wrote, "is the movement of British and other troops across the Adriatic over to the mainland and up the route that Napoleon took with a view to making a drive in through the Balkan States."[139]

... fanciful objectives at the expense of existing commitments ... always looking for some small place with a magnifying glass and exaggerating its importance." McNaughton agreed that his experience had been similar: "he read only the parts of a memorandum which suited his fancy."

What then, asked McNaughton, turning back to business, of the First Canadian Army? Its headquarters was well organized and he thought it should be used as such. Brooke referred to recent invasion planning, which called for one British army of three corps in the assault instead of two armies. No final decision could be taken until a supreme commander had been appointed which would be very soon. McNaughton pointed to the high quality of his own staff and stressed the importance of an early decision. "General Brooke made no reply," McNaughton recorded, "and during a long pause did not raise his eyes from his desk."[140] The decision of the British Chiefs of Staff reached Canada on 8 October where, King noted, "Stuart was much elated. Said it was a great compliment to Crerar. Spoke of what it would mean to have a Canadian Armoured Division in Italy. That they were as fine an armoured division as there was in the world—splendid looking Canadians. All young Canadians of the very best type and training. They might be expected to give a magnificent account of themselves."[141]

Ralston, unaware of McNaughton's discussion with Brooke and that he had accepted the position philosophically, exercised himself with the question of how McNaughton should be notified. In King's words:

The telegram had been telephoned to Ralston who had made three suggestions for a wire to McNaughton—one was that he could count on our Government giving immediate approval. The second, he should proceed at once to get on with the movement. ... Thirdly—that if he wished to make any comments, they would be received. In referring to this third suggestion, Stuart said he was sure Ralston would be just as well pleased if that were left out altogether. There was no need to send it. I immediately said I thought what he was going to say was that the third statement should be made the first in the wire. That I felt that was McNaughton's due; that as long as we continued him as Chief of the Army, we should have confidence in him. Stuart said that he was not at all sure that McNaughton would like the course now suggested by Brooke and the Chiefs of Staff. That it would, of course, mean [the] breaking-up of the Canadian Army in England.[142]

Mackenzie King, characteristically, "stressed the importance of the record being such as to make clear that McNaughton had not been 'ignored or walked over,' " as in fact he had. "If we ignored him he might well resign, and there would be great feeling throughout the country that he had done the right thing. . . ."[143] But the break-up of the Army had not yet been decided upon, as we have seen, and while that issue was still open McNaughton would remain to fight it. On 12 October Ralston notified King of a message from McNaughton which, in King's words, "as I had expected, accepted the situation, with as little in the way of demurring as could have been expected, if he McNaughton were to do justice to his own position and view."[144]

Nevertheless, McNaughton was deeply hurt. Having put in hand the Order of Detail for the corps in Italy and completed arrangements with Lieutenant-General Weeks at the War Office for the first lift of twenty-five thousand men from 14 to 17 October, overcome by disappointment, he was "ill in quarters."[145] The sailing of the 1st Division for Sicily, which he had watched with Morgan and Mountbatten on a June day at Largs, had caused him no misgivings. Their training completed by experience in battle, those men would be back to give the army the stiffening it needed. Then the "dagger pointed at Berlin" would be driven home, "right in the belly," as he had promised American correspondents in Washington in 1942. With the departure of the corps to Italy, his "famous dagger had become more handle than blade"; his army, no longer a spearhead, little more than a corps itself. Those brave words were now "a hollow laugh." Well might it be said that his "illness was not of the body. He suffered from a broken heart."[146]

And then—crowning irony—he heard by cable on 21 October that Eisenhower did not want the corps, not yet, at any rate. "The arrival of these troops at this time is likely to cause us considerable embarrassment." Only because he appreciated "the political con-

A thoughtful commander

Clement Attlee at Dunsfold for the opening of the Canadian-constructed aerodrome, 1942

siderations which may be involved," did he agree to accept the Canadian Corps Headquarters. Nor could he promise an immediate active role: "The aspect which causes me most concern is the pressure I anticipate will be put upon me to get these troops into action at an early date. I cannot guarantee to do this. . . ."[147]

Nor did he. The convoy, carrying the bulk of Corps Headquarters, the 5th Armoured Division, and army and corps troops, left the Clyde on 27 October. Corps Headquarters was established temporarily at Taormina, Sicily, while the Armoured Division went on to Naples where it arrived on 8 November. Having left its own equipment behind (McNaughton handed over 3,350 vehicles to the returning British units), the Canadians took over the stocks which the British had left behind. In the case of vehicles, these turned out to be no more than junk. Two-wheeled drive to begin with, thousands of miles over the Western Desert had not improved them. "To make matters worse, it appears that a natural spirit of camaraderie among the veterans of the desert fighting had led to extensive 'swapping' of the 7th Armoured Division's better vehicles for the worst in other units and formations of the Eighth Army, these latter finishing up in the hands of the Canadians." Replacement vehicles would have to come from England*; suitable tanks would not be available, and then only in small quantities, before January.[149] It was the end of January before the incoming troops received vehicles, tanks and guns, and even then not up to the full scale.

Three months were wasted while Canadian troops undertook tasks which, in the words of the Canadian official historian, "neither added to their standard of training nor brought them nearer to contact with the enemy." They operated transit camps for the British, and controlled refugees.[150]

McNaughton referred to all this as a phase in "the deliberate break-up of the Canadian Army." He was obviously smarting when he wrote on the draft of the official Canadian account:

A solemn undertaking was given me by Brooke and other officers in connection with the despatch of 5th Canadian Armoured Division that proper equipment would be made available immediately

---

*McNaughton provided these; he sent out 3,200 Canadian vehicles.[148]

on arrival. These promises, made by the highest military authorities in the United Kingdom, were dishonoured and Ralston and Stuart became consenting partners in this iniquitous situation which, for example, left the Signals of the 5th Canadian Armoured Division for months without even radio sets on which to keep up their training. As another example some of our best-trained artillery regiments were relegated to the role of stevedores at one of the ports. This . . . cannot properly be left out of this *History*.[151]

It was not until early in 1945, when he was Minister of Defence, that McNaughton fully discussed with Mackenzie King this splitting of the Army to send a corps to Italy. King claimed ignorance of many of the facts. He was amazed to learn, he wrote in his record of his conversation with McNaughton, of "the position of Ralston and Stuart [which] had all been directed to fighting even against the will at the time of the British authorities as well as Eisenhower, the head of the American command. [McNaughton] gave me other information which he had cabled to Canada at the time of taking away the Canadian forces which I know never came before the War Committee. I recall Ralston saying repeatedly Canada would have no real voice in peace if we did not do more fighting. I kept telling him the Chiefs of Staff knew what they were about, were holding the Canadian army intact for the best of reasons. . . . I have no doubt that McNaughton has been completely vindicated on the stand he took."[152]

As for the "rump" of the Canadian Army left in Britain, there was now some doubt that its Canadian entity would be retained. With a corps destined for Italy, it was obvious that it would have to include a British corps if it were to remain as an army; but General Paget made proposals that were of wider significance, and far more dangerous to Canadian aspirations, than that. On 18 October, even before the corps had sailed, Paget came to Headley Court to discuss "the consequential effects" of its move to Italy. The XII British Corps, he said, would come under McNaughton's command in time for the invasion; that was satisfactory. But he proposed to take away from him the 3rd Division and the 2nd

Armoured Brigade and place both these formations in I British Corps, which in turn would come under the command of an American army for the assault role. As the 3rd Canadian Division would have under its command a British beach group and other ancillaries, Paget insisted that a proportion of the staff officers at the headquarters of the division must be British. He also stated his intention of taking some corps troops away from McNaughton for use by I British Corps. McNaughton asked if his division and the armoured brigade would return to him after the assault. "Possibly," Paget replied, "but it was more likely that they would continue in I British Corps." Moreover, Paget continued, after McNaughton had received XII British Corps, his command would comprise more British than Canadian troops; it would therefore be necessary for him to replace a due proportion of his army staff with British officers. None of this was firm as yet, and, as McNaughton told Stuart, Paget said "he was merely indicating his views as to what should be done."[153]

There is no doubt, however, that Paget's views reflected COSSAC planning. Morgan, writing of this period, says:

It was . . . stipulated that, under direction of Commander-in-Chief 21 Army Group the initial assault would be carried out by a *composite army** consisting of approximately two British or Canadian Corps and two United States Corps under the unified control of the Commanding General, First United States Army. The Commanding General, First United States Army would then remain in immediate charge of land operations until such time as, in the opinion of Commander-in-Chief, 21 Army Group, number and composition of the forces ashore in France warranted the introduction into the line of battle of another Army Headquarters which would be British or Canadian.[154]

The consternation caused in Ottawa by the message from McNaughton, in which he warned of "the implications of these proposals," can be imagined. Was the much vaunted First Canadian Army to be broken down still further and possibly merged piecemeal without identity in British and American formations? There was this danger and if it happened the political repercussions could

---
*Italics supplied.

be disastrous. Ralston, through his insistence on having a corps in Italy, over the resistance of McNaughton, would be blamed for this final break-up of the Army. And should McNaughton resign, and give the facts, what then? But surely he would resist. After six days of nail-biting suspense further word came from London in the form of a chilly message from McNaughton:

After most careful and impersonal review I have come to the conclusion that under the conditions which have come into existence no other course is now open but to accept Paget's proposals for the present and until the progress of the war makes possible a re-collection of Canadian units and formations in a homogeneous Canadian Army.

You will realize that profound changes in our system of organization will be necessary and in particular, since the commander of the proposed Anglo-Canadian Army will be a subordinate of C.-in-C. 21 Army Group with large numbers of British troops in command, it will not be practicable for him to discharge also the functions of Senior Combatant Officer in this theatre.

I would appreciate early instructions for general guidance as to policy to be followed.[155]

By this time McNaughton's stand on constitutional rights where the employment of his force was concerned had completely antagonized Brooke whose relations with McNaughton, in any case, had never been good. That, combined with McNaughton's hostility towards Ralston, who had pushed political considerations at the expense of the military so that the army had finally been split, had made his removal inevitable; but it was that message, beyond doubt, which made it urgent.

Its significance, partly perhaps because he was not a soldier, escaped Mackenzie King. He seemed to care nothing whether the Army survived in name or not. "There will remain a Canadian Army Corps in Britain," he wrote. "Then, when the main assault comes, instead of our men bearing the brunt of this assault, it will be divided between British, Americans, and ourselves." McNaughton's message "would indicate that he more or less sees the situation as it has developed with respect to the Canadian Army." That same day, however, Ralston, who appreciated that the disappearance of the Army would reflect upon himself, told Mackenzie King that "he felt he must go overseas to deal with the Army situation." And then the Prime Minister must have come alive to what was about to happen for, with the unity of Canada, as always, his first consideration, he cautioned Ralston that he was anxious to keep McNaughton "in control as long as possible as I know he will make no demand for conscription."[156]

Ralston left, taking Stuart with him, but before they arrived in England the picture with regard to the Army proved to be not so dark as Paget had predicted. At a meeting with Brooke at the beginning of November McNaughton requested a clear-cut decision on the Army's future; the headquarters was now fit to control and direct troops in battle and there was anxiety among the staff which was bad for morale and which must be set at rest. Brooke said the 21st Army Group would require two armies as a minimum; that there were available the Second British under Anderson and the First Canadian under McNaughton. "Neither time nor material were available to create another British Army" and in consequence, and unless the supreme commander, when appointed, had other ideas, there would be a definite role for the headquarters of the Canadian Army. A British corps would be added to complete the Army's strength.[157] There was no hint that McNaughton would not command it.

Three days later General Paget confirmed what Brooke had said. No Canadian formations now would be taken away; instead XII British Corps and another British division would be added, making a total for the Army of seven divisions. He asked McNaughton to accept the British corps as soon as possible.[158] Again on this occasion—difficult to deal with as McNaughton had always been because of his unyielding championship of Canadian rights —nothing was said about his not being the man to lead the Army.

After his visit to Paget McNaughton spent the rest of the afternoon in his office; then he went home and had tea. About an hour after dark the telephone rang and McNaughton picked it up to hear Ralston's voice. He had just arrived in London with Stuart, he said, and would like to see him. It was arranged that they should lunch at Army Headquarters next day.[159]

On 5 November, after luncheon, McNaughton asked Ralston if he would like to go to his office for a talk. Ralston agreed. Would he like Price Montague, who had lunched with them, to be present? "No," the Minister replied, "just Stuart and myself." There was no doubt about what was bothering him. In McNaughton's office, Ralston immediately mentioned the two messages which McNaughton had dispatched and asked if he had any supplemental information. McNaughton said he had, and described the changed situation as described by Brooke and Paget.[160] Although this must have relieved Ralston's mind, McNaughton did not give him time to speak; instead he swept on to attack Ralston's "Mediterranean" policy.

He made no bones about the fact that he violently disagreed with the dispatch of the corps. It had been "forced against the views of the military authorities"; he was convinced that Allied Force Headquarters, Algeria (on which the force had been "imposed . . . without their prior consent"), the CIGS and Morgan were all against the move. He pointed to Eisenhower's cable, a copy of which he had sent to Ottawa. Ralston "demurred" and Stuart said "he did not think this statement was correct."[161]

McNaughton swept that aside and returned to the attack. For Sicily there had been an understanding that the Canadians would return in time for the target date in Northwest Europe. A measure of operational control had been retained, in that he had asked for, and been given, access to all plans, including those for the return of the force in the late autumn of 1943, and it was only after consideration of these that he had recommended that the Canadian government approve. Now, "as a result of subsequent actions and our insistence on sending out additional forces against the views of the CIGS, all operational control had evaporated." Ralston disagreed. The Canadian commander's right of reference to the Canadian government had been preserved. "A very slim safeguard," retorted McNaughton, "and not to be compared with the right to look into proposed campaigns in advance!" However that might be, Ralston interposed, McNaughton himself had signified his agreement to increasing the Canadian force in the Mediterranean. Yes, said McNaughton, under certain conditions* and under certain safeguards but these had been swept away in the method used to obtain the concurrence of the British government to the build-up to corps strength in Italy. Brooke had been against it all along. He had been very favourable at the Quebec Conference, Ralston said. McNaughton had no knowledge of that; he could only judge from what Brooke had said to him.[162]

Ralston had no wish to pursue this argument and he shifted ground. How were McNaughton's relations with Brooke—and with Paget? McNaughton reminded him of what he had told him on his last visit, that he had "some doubts of General Brooke's attitude to myself." The recent meeting, however, had been cordial. As for Paget, "apart from some differences of view over SPARTAN and the Commander of 2 Cdn Corps there was no occasion that I knew of when we had had the least difficulty." Ralston then said that he and Stuart would see Brooke and Paget, after which they would have another talk with McNaughton. Ralston and Stuart stayed to have tea with Mrs. McNaughton at Largiebeg, while McNaughton left to attend an artillery demonstration at Larkhill.[163]

The angry exchange with McNaughton merely confirmed for Ralston and Stuart what they already must have known: that the army commander was unalterably opposed to their policy, a policy which they had brought Mackenzie King to accept and which was now the policy of the government. McNaughton had stated during their previous visit that if they were determined to proceed with "real dispersion" they would be wise to put "someone in control who believed in it." After this last clash they had no other course, but because of the prestige which McNaughton still enjoyed in Canada they needed the help of Brooke and Paget. Three days later, one can deduce, the latter had promised their support. It is possible that Brooke had another reason by then for wanting to

---

*Provided the corps returned in time for the invasion of Northwest Europe in 1944.

be rid of McNaughton. Paget was a doubtful starter as the commander of the 21st Army Group* and Brooke was casting around
for a replacement for him. Montgomery, the most successful
British commander, would be very much in his mind and, in fact,
a month later Brooke formally recommended Montgomery *vice*
Paget as the Commander-in-Chief 21st Army Group.[165] If, in fact,
Brooke had Montgomery singled out in November, as seems likely,
here was a heaven-sent opportunity to remove McNaughton who,
after Sicily, could never have served under Montgomery's command. There is some evidence that this was the real reason for
McNaughton's removal. In conversation with Mackenzie King,
early in February of 1945, McNaughton accused Montgomery
of "determination to get control of the army." "He feels bitter
toward Montgomery whom he thinks deliberately sought to usurp
his position," the Prime Minister recorded. "I am inclined to
think it was more the High Command. *They were anxious to get
Montgomery into the post he is now in. . . .*";†[166] (Montgomery was
commanding the 21st Army Group at the time of this discussion.)
Time Magazine, speculating on the reasons for McNaughton's
return to Canada in January, 1944, correctly reported that Mc-
Naughton "drew back from Montgomery's well-known arrogance,
his maddening habit of lecturing other generals as if they were
backward children"; that "sparks flew whenever their flinty wills
clashed."[167] And Montgomery had some say in replacing unsuit-
able senior commanders. He had not had the 21st Army Group
long when he replaced Anderson, who was commanding the
Second Army, and brought in Dempsey who had been one of his
corps commanders in Italy.[168]

On Monday, 8 November, Ralston and Stuart visited Mc-
Naughton's headquarters again. There was a show of interest in
the artillery demonstration which McNaughton had attended and
then the real purpose of Ralston's visit emerged. He told Mc-
Naughton bluntly, and without preamble save that he expressed
sympathy for his position, "that both Brooke and Paget had indicated that McNaughton was no longer acceptable to them to com-

---

*McNaughton had first heard of this from Morgan in May.[164]
†Italics supplied.

mand the Canadian Army in the field."* McNaughton did not reply. "Brooke had said," Ralston went on, "that Crerar might be acceptable as the result of further experience in Italy." Then "there was some more sympathy," McNaughton recorded, "and a statement from the Minister that he and his colleagues would like to do anything possible for me I might wish."

It seemed, McNaughton said after a pause, that he was "out of harmony" with the British authorities; if so, he would "feel it necessary to get out of the way." No lack of harmony had been mentioned, Ralston hastened to say, and in fact both Brooke and Paget had been very complimentary about McNaughton's service and had especially praised his airburst-ranging. What then, Mc-Naughton asked, had inspired this turn of events? His insistence on keeping the Canadians together and the unpleasant interviews he had had with Brooke? And Paget—was it because of SPARTAN and the disagreement over the command of the 2nd Corps? SPARTAN was not a fair test for the corps commander. In later exercises the corps had done not too badly; the headquarters had shown itself to be well organized though McNaughton was still "under some anxiety concerning the tactical handling of the Corps and its formations."[171]

Stuart thought it might be well for McNaughton to hear at first hand from Paget why he did not want him, and McNaughton agreed to call on Paget. Ralston and Stuart then questioned the accuracy of the statements contained in his cable to Ottawa at the end of October in which he had "indicated the possibility *that 3 Canadian Division, 3 British Division and an American Division would be under an American Army in the assault."*† McNaughton replied that his text reflected precisely what Paget had said, but

---

*What this was based on was never clearly stated. Sir Basil Liddell Hart wrote: "Whether McNaughton would have proved an effective commander in the field may be questionable, and is a matter that can never be settled, but he was certainly a soldier of outstanding vision and ability who grasped the conditions of modern war earlier and more fully than most others."[169] While Churchill's attitude did not emerge at that time, it is clear from a conversation with Mackenzie King recorded in mid-September, 1944, at Quebec that he sided with Brooke: "[McNaughton] was a fine fellow, a good engineer, etc." but "Churchill said he of course would not have done as commander of the forces on the Continent."[170]

†Italics supplied.

this was only one of many possibilities. The "whole set up was like mercury, very shifting and difficult to grasp." Ralston said that in his conversations with Brooke and Paget the name "Anglo-Canadian Army" had been proposed as the name of the combined army, but he had insisted that the name "First Canadian Army" should be retained.*[172]

Next day McNaughton saw Paget alone at his headquarters at St. Paul's School and the account which follows is his record of what passed between them. He did not offer to shake hands but merely said: "You know why I am here." Paget hastened to assure McNaughton that his conversation with Ralston and Stuart had been without "premeditation" on his part; the question as to whether McNaughton was fit to take the First Canadian Army overseas had been "sprung on him." *Ralston had made much of the message about the 3rd Canadian Division coming under an American Army in the assault†* and had read extracts from it. Paget then told McNaughton that what he had said in October was only a possible course; it might well be that the Canadian Army would have the assault corps under its command. McNaughton agreed that it had been a tentative proposal; he had made that clear in his cable.[173]

The Minister had gone on to express doubt concerning Mc-Naughton's fitness to command an army. Paget said he had felt the "unfairness of the suggestion." He had agreed that there was some doubt whether McNaughton "would stand up to the strain"; he had had "an unfair load" to carry over the past four years and now he might be made "Head of a Military Heaquarters" in London or be given "a big job" co-ordinating Allied supply. Paget admitted that he had been in a very difficult position. Some of his replies had not been clear and definite. He repeated that the last four years had been tough and that on occasions McNaughton had

---

*When Parliament met Ralston was able to announce on 11 February, 1944, that "we are going to use that army headquarters and these army troops as a Canadian organization . . . we will have an army headquarters which we expect will have the distinction of having under its control, not only our own corps and army troops but such other formations and units of the allied countries as may be allotted to it."

†Italics supplied.

shown signs of strain. He had had much more to bear than any other army commander. He had told Ralston also that "Mc-Naughton's interest in the technical side [of the Army] might possibly be absorbing more than could properly be given without detriment to training and command."[174]

Ralston had then said that McNaughton would continue to command the First Canadian Army but there was "no guarantee" that he would take it overseas. Stuart had asked about SPARTAN: how had McNaughton handled the Canadian Army in that exercise? Paget said he had told him sharply that that had nothing to do with the matter. The Canadians had had "less criticism" than the "other British Army." Paget told McNaughton that he had then turned to Ralston and expressed regret at the "unfair suggestions" that had been made and chagrin that a person could be "ground between the stones of criticism given in conversation."[175]

McNaughton, after hearing that, discussed business. He spoke to Paget "as the Commander of the First Canadian Army," which he still was. "We had operations in prospect and I wanted to know what we had to do to organize for them. Later on someone else might take over from me but for the moment I had to get on with the work." Paget, much relieved, turned to the organization for the assault but could give little definite information save that the 3rd Canadian Division should train with I British Corps. XII Corps would come under McNaughton's command about the middle of December.[176]

With that out of the way, McNaughton returned to Paget's discussion with Ralston and Stuart. He was disturbed, he said, to think that Paget might have taken exception to something of which he himself was unaware. Quite the contrary, Paget replied: everything had always been very clear between them. If Mc-Naughton remained in command of the Army (it was not his business whether he did or not and he resented being brought into the matter), he "had not the least reserve that they could work together in operations." He would welcome his continuing to command the Army while it was in the United Kingdom and, if he himself were to remain in command of the 21st Army Group, in war. "He repeated, with emphasis, that it was Ralston and Stuart who had suggested doubts about my fitness to command, not he, and had felt it was unfair to have pressed him for any opinion." McNaughton and Paget shook hands in parting.[177]

On the 10th Stuart came to see McNaughton. He asked "what had transpired" at the meeting with Paget. By now McNaughton recognized Stuart for the enemy he was and he refused to say. "I told him that this was my personal business which I did not intend to discuss with him." Nevertheless, he gave Stuart an indication that he intended to fight. "I said I was reviewing my personal position and when my mind was clear I might see Ralston once more . . . his proposals, in my view, were contrary to the public interest and . . . I would have to oppose them." Stuart asked if he would see Brooke and suggested that he should do so. But McNaughton could expect no support from that quarter. "I replied that I had been through the agonizing performance with Paget and I did not wish to repeat it."[178]

That same day McNaughton sent a message to Mackenzie King outlining his discussions with Ralston and Stuart, and with Paget. He had "lost all confidence in Ralston" and could "no longer remain in comd of First Cdn Army responsible to any government of which he is a member":

(1) Ralston following his arrival in the UK last week went to see Paget (2) He then with Stuart came to my headquarters and expressed great regret at the news he had to impart to me and sympathy for me in my position (3) He then told me that Paget had said I was unfit to command an army in the field (4) Today I called on Paget and discussed the whole matter with him (5) Paget stated in the most emphatic terms that Ralston opened his conversation with him by expressing doubts as to my fitness to comd First Cdn Army (6) Paget also said that Stuart had put some questions likewise implying doubt in my military abilities (7) Paget said he had felt in a very difficult position and perhaps had not been definite in his replies to Ralston and Stuart (8) He expressed great resentment at the position in which he felt he had been placed (9) Paget then gave me his most categorical assurance that everything had always been clear between us and he had not the least reserve that we could continue to work together both in UK and in operations in the field; he said he welcomed my remaining in comd Cdn Army both now and later on in NW Europe.

The situation we have to face is that a Minister of the Crown on whom I have every right to reply for support comes here and by suggestions and suppositions casts doubts in the minds of senior officers of another country with whom I have to work as to my fitness then takes their silence or partial replies as assent to the view he has implied. Then comes to me and no doubt to others also and imputes his suggestions to them as a positive statement of their opinion.

I would say Mr. Prime Minister that quite apart from the question of the support which a Minister of National Defence owes I think to a Cdn Army Comd I regard Ralston's action as one of the meanest and most despicable of my whole experience and this is not the first time he has acted in this way to cause me very great anxiety for the welfare of the Cdn Army.

I have given a copy of this telegram to the Hon. Mr. Ralston and with the greatest regret for any trouble it may cause you I place my resignation in your hands.[179]

Here was a pretty mess and the Prime Minister was "deeply concerned"; as usual, he looked at the political implications:

McNaughton has many more friends than Ralston in the Army and in the country. It may be that McNaughton is not physically equal to the task, but there can be no doubt that Ralston and General Stuart have been a little over-anxious to get a change made instead of allowing time to help bring this about. I have been afraid of this right along. I think they have been most anxious to get Crerar in McNaughton's place. One danger there is that Crerar may seek to bring about conscription. McNaughton would never admit it. However, I feel now the absence of any need of conscription can be made very apparent and will not be attempted at this stage.[180]

King's position was an extraordinarily powerful one had he been able to exploit it at that time.

It was "ludicrous," he noted, "that Ralston has never yet withdrawn his resignation as Minister, but left it in abeyance, I having refused to accept it, so that literally I have, at the moment, both McNaughton's and Ralston's resignations in my possession." It was important to prevent "the situation becoming known"; he felt "the whole business had grown out of weariness on Mc-Naughton's part which had led to exasperation in the end."[181] He therefore notified McNaughton of his "distress" and counselled caution. He hoped he would "not find it necessary to take any further step until I have heard from Ralston and have had a chance to communicate with you again."[182]

McNaughton assured King "that no further step of any sort in the matter will be taken by me until I know your wishes,"[183] and thus Mackenzie King had succeeded in averting precipate action by McNaughton which he feared would stir up feeling on the army commander's behalf. "McNaughton was highly regarded by the people of Canada and by the fighting men. Would become more so once it was known that he had become what might be termed 'a martyr'. . . . That I certainly did not wish to allow anyone to say this had been due to the callous and indifferent action of the Government in not recognizing his state of mind and his life service to our country as well as particularly his service through the trying period of the past four years."[184]

On the 13th Mackenzie King received a cable from Ralston which pleased him greatly. It contained a memorandum prepared by Stuart "of the sequence of events and representations made regarding doubts as to McNaughton's capacity to command in the field," which purported to show that the initiative had come from the British. This summary, McNaughton commented later, was Stuart's version of the events in defence of his own actions; he, McNaughton, had not been given the opportunity to see it, let alone rebut it.[185] Nevertheless, Mackenzie King "felt sure Mc-Naughton's feelings would change once he came to realize what the sequence of events had really been," and "If it should prove that I have been able to get these difficulties bridged in a manner which will prevent their disclosure at least until after the war, I will have done the war effort a greater service than many armies could render, and Canada and the British Empire, a service beyond calculation."[186] The salient parts of Stuart's summary read as follows:

1. It is quite obvious from McNaughton's cable to the Prime Minister that he believes that the Minister by suggestion and

implication initiated the chain of events that has culminated in the present situation.

2. I was intimately connected with this chain of events and am anxious to make the record quite clear as to what actually did take place.

3. In June, 1943, Sir Alan Brooke, then C.I.G.S., in the course of a casual conversation at the White House in Washington, made certain remarks on his own volition about McNaughton to the Minister and myself. This was the first time that any doubts were in my mind as to McNaughton's fitness to command the Canadian Army in the field.

4. A few weeks after this, I received a copy of Paget's report on "Spartan" exercise. This report was highly critical of action taken by Headquarters First Canadian Army during the exercise. It came as a great shock to me.

5. I proceeded to the United Kingdom early in July, 1943, for the purpose of proceeding to North Africa, and before leaving the United Kingdom for Africa was told in no uncertain terms by Brooke and later by Paget that, in their opinion, McNaughton was not suited to command an army in the field. Brig. Gibson, one of my staff officers, was then in the United Kingdom. I told him what had taken place and instructed him to return to Canada at once. ... I was particularly anxious that the Minister should hear personally from Brooke and Paget just what each had to say to me about McNaughton. . . .

6. The Minister arrived in the United Kingdom and Brooke repeated to him just what he had said to me. . . .

7. The Minister reported to War Committee in my presence exactly what had taken place in our various meetings with Mc-Naughton and Brooke.

8. My understanding of the result of our conversation with Brooke was that in Brooke's view:

(a) McNaughton should be relieved of his command of the Canadian Army before it took the field in active operations.

(b) The task of informing McNaughton to this effect was, in the circumstances, not his responsibility but was that of the Canadian Government.

(c) Every effort should be made to find other suitable employment for McNaughton. He (Brooke) had canvassed this situation thoroughly and had to admit that he had nothing helpful to offer.

9. I was very conscious of my own responsibilities to the Canadian Army in this connection. My own feeling was that a military situation had arisen and that it had to be faced and action taken. I had been advised that those responsible for the conduct of military operations based on the United Kingdom had no confidence in McNaughton's suitability to command in the field. The main issue involved was not that of McNaughton's future or his feelings; it was that over 200,000 young Canadian lives were at stake. In spite of any political or any other ramifications, I was convinced that no individual and no Government should, in this instance, neglect to face the issue and take action. I expressed my opinion in these terms to the Minister, to the War Committee and to the Prime Minister during the Quebec Conference.

10. The Minister was reluctant to act. He felt that McNaughton's condition might improve and that Brooke and Paget might, in the course of time, change their minds. . . .

11. The receipt from McNaughton of a cable outlining General Paget's proposal concerning the future disposition of the Canadian Army in the United Kingdom brought matters to a head. . . . The Minister and myself left for the United Kingdom. . . .

12. After arrival in the United Kingdom, the Minister and myself saw McNaughton, Brooke and Paget. The details of these conversations are covered in other memoranda.

13. I have written this memorandum to make it quite clear that the whole basis of McNaughton's cable to the Prime Minister rests upon a completely false premise. Brooke on his own volition initiated the whole chain of events by his remarks in Washington. Paget, at about the same time, did likewise through his publication of his report on "Spartan." I cannot remember whether, in my subsequent talks with Brooke and Paget, the topic was opened by them or whether I asked them to elaborate on their former and initial observations. I cannot see that it matters one way or the other. . . .[187]

Stuart's summary raises two main questions: first, if McNaughton's ability to command was in doubt during March (as seems most unlikely), why did Brooke wait for more than two months before doing anything about it, and then no more than a hint dropped in Washington? During those two months, it may be remembered, Sansom was blamed, not McNaughton. Second, if it

A carrier-borne flame thrower in action

Sicily, August, 1943

Lieutenant-General A. G. L. McNaughton, 1942

really was a question of military ability, this is hardly a condition (as mentioned in Stuart's paragraph 10) "that might improve"; in fact, by this time, the excuse for removing McNaughton seems to have shifted to his state of health. This Stuart admitted later. When referring to McNaughton's bitter stand against splitting the Army, he told Ralston that he had concluded "throughout the period of our discussions" that "McNaughton was not physically or temperamentally fit to command an army in the field. . . . I feel so strongly on this point," he went on, "that I would have placed my resignation in your hands if my recommendation to you had not been acted upon."[188]

Meanwhile, in England, Ralston and Stuart had immediately gone to Paget with the copy of McNaughton's cable to the Prime Minister in which he had submitted his resignation. What went on at that meeting is not known but next day, in a letter to McNaughton, Paget challenged McNaughton's summary of their conversation.[189] McNaughton passed a copy of Paget's letter to King. On the 13th McNaughton and Stuart visited General Paget at his request. He read from a statement, copies of which he then handed over, and this is what he said:

We three know each other well and there should be no need for us to finesse against each other. What we are here for now is to speak frankly and to do our best to clear up misunderstandings which have arisen.

(a) I have two frank statements to make:
the first is that I do not consider you (McNaughton) fitted to command the 1st Canadian Army in active operations. I gave you my reasons for this opinion at our last meeting, namely that you have had four very strenuous years in command and in addition a great deal else to do which is outside the sphere of an Army Commander, and the strain has told on you.
Also your enthusiasm and ability in research and development work has led to your becoming too much absorbed on the technical side at the expense of training and command.

(b) And the other frank statement I have to make is that it was not General Stuart nor Mr. Ralston who inspired this opinion: it is one to which the C.I.G.S. and I have been coming for some time, though I had not intended to speak to you about it until I knew what other employment there might be for you, and that does not rest with me. I did not know when I met Mr. Ralston and General Stuart that the C.I.G.S. had already given his opinion to them, nor did I know that I was going to be asked for mine: but that is why I was asked for my opinion: it was not because either Mr. Ralston or Stuart were trying to make suggestions to me that you were not fit to Command an Army in the field. I hope that from what I have now said it is clear that Mr. Ralston and Stuart have played straight in this matter, and that if anyone is to blame it is myself for not having told you (McNaughton) earlier of my doubts about your fitness for command—in the field. As I have said, I did not wish to do so until I knew what other employment there was for you.

I am very sorry for the misunderstandings which have arisen and led to so much trouble, and I hope it is not too late to get the matter put right.[190]

"At the close of the interview," McNaughton recorded, "Paget stated the change of Comd of First Cdn Army should take place as early as possible, and that the setting up of the combined British-Canadian Army was the appropriate occasion (indicating possibly that he proposed to nominate a British officer)." Stuart had the same impression, for he stated "that there was no question the Cdn Government would insist on appointing a Canadian and the discussion stopped at that."[191]

McNaughton did not believe Paget and certainly Paget's "second frank statement" smacks of special pleading. Immediately after the meeting was over McNaughton returned to Canadian Army Headquarters and gave Major-General Turner a resumé of what had taken place. "Among other things, I said it was quite evident Paget had not been truthful; that my account of our first interview was absolutely correct; that I thought that Paget was probably acting under instructions of higher authority."[192] (In February, 1944, Ralston told Stuart of a conversation McNaughton had had with the Prime Minister in which he mentioned a letter "written to him by Paget from Cairo which letter, McNaughton intimates, confirms McNaughton's notes of first conversation between Paget and him and also infers that the line subsequently taken by Paget with McNaughton was under orders.")[193]

However, it was now quite clear to McNaughton that he must go and in his manner of going he had no wish to embarrass the Canadian government. He told Turner that "my future action had to derive from the Prime Minister's appeal and Paget's two statements which, while I did not believe them, I must accept."[194] He therefore drafted a cable to Mackenzie King which went off that day, with a copy to Ralston:

... you may be quite sure that I will make every endeavour to find a solution for the difficulties of the existing situation which will in no way rebound to the disadvantage of Canada and the Canadian Army.

... Paget stated (A) that he and Brooke had come to the conclusion independently that I was not fit to command the Canadian Army in the field and (B) that it was neither Ralston nor Stuart who had inspired this opinion. ... I have accepted these statements.

... As a consequence of (A) I request that you accept my resignation to take effect at the earliest date which is possible without detriment to the public interest or trouble to yourself.

... As a consequence of (B) I relieved Ralston and Stuart of the charge I made against them that they had inspired this adverse opinion against myself. ...[195]

Next day Ralston and Stuart, heartened by McNaughton's cable, came to Army Headquarters. McNaughton first had a private conversation with the Minister.

[Ralston] spoke of the difficulties we had had in getting on together. He said that he knew that officially I had worked with him but he was sincerely desirous of feeling that he had my personal esteem. I said I had known him on and off for more than 25 years and that I had always credited him with the best and proper motives, but his methods were not mine, nor his conclusions. We were both very strong-willed and perhaps naturally clashed. I would do my best to get on with him in the interim, but then we would probably clash again.[196]

They spoke of the affairs of the Army (Ralston had insisted on a Canadian commander), of Crerar and of Simonds. McNaughton told Ralston of his "endeavour to develop" Crerar "and to shield him from the controversy in which I had necessarily been involved." Simonds would probably take over the 1st Corps and McNaughton had already discussed that with Montgomery. As for Montgomery, "We did not like one another, but nevertheless our conversations had been objective."

McNaughton told Ralston that, now he could no longer look after the Canadian Army, "he and Stuart would have a more direct responsibility." He appealed to him "to reverse the trend to dispersion he had started, namely to insist that the Canadian Army should be reintegrated at the earliest opportunity, which he should constantly seek; also that he should work towards the re-establishment of Canadian control in operations which had now evaporated. . . ."

Later, after Stuart had been sent for, McNaughton repeated his views of their responsibilities:

(i) Canadian action at any time should be such as to make the greatest possible contribution to the successful prosecution of the war, having regard to the actual situation which exists and the particular requirements of the moment.

(ii) Subject to the above, and as a longer term policy, Canada's greatest contribution will be given through the integration of her forces in a balanced homogeneous Army under Canadian command, with the most direct channels possible to the Canadian Government.

Stuart claimed to have followed the first principle with regard to the division in the Mediterranean and, later on, the corps "but as further talk on this," said McNaughton wryly, "seemed likely to raise the whole contentious issue, I did not pursue the point."

Ralston spoke of Paget's reference to McNaughton's work in the technical sphere. McNaughton said that his part in this "had been largely the business of organization which was a proper function." He "expressed the view that the provision of the best in weapons and equipment was very much the concern of an Army Commander." The Minister then spoke of "himself and his colleagues wishing to do whatever they could" to provide McNaughton with a job. McNaughton replied that he was not interested in having a job made for him. "Perhaps a call to some useful service might come." This was not the first time he had "clashed with those in authority and had had to move on."[197]

It was agreed that McNaughton should stay on until a successor could be appointed; that was the wish of the Prime Minister.[198] But towards the end of the month reports began to appear in newspapers both in Britain and in Canada that the retirement of McNaughton was imminent, alleging that his health was not robust. A statement would be required and Stuart asked if McNaughton would be willing to have it said that he was to retire shortly on grounds of health? If that would be least embarrassing for King, McNaughton replied, he was willing but it was for the Prime Minister to decide. However, he insisted on being medically examined, which was done on 26 November. The report stated that he was "below par" and strongly recommended that he should be "given leave of absence and freed from all military responsibility for three months, at which time he should be re-examined. Provided he is not exposed to undue hardships it is our opinion that General McNaughton could carry on his present duties for a limited period."[199]

Stuart's approach to McNaughton about his retirement gave McNaughton the opportunity of questioning Stuart closely on the part he had played in his removal. Stuart stated that he had heard casually from Brooke in Washington that McNaughton was not suitable to command an army in the field. At about this time he had seen a report on SPARTAN which had contained some criticism of McNaughton; that this was "in a way, tied in." He had come to London in July to go to North Africa and again seen Brooke who had elaborated on his view of McNaughton: he was "temperamental" and devoted too much time to matters other than the Army. As a result of that, Stuart had sent a wire to Ralston asking him to come to London so that Brooke could repeat his opinion to the Minister direct. Stuart said that, having formed views against McNaughton, he had felt he must report them. McNaughton replied:

... that I had no objection to him advising the Canadian Government ... as he saw fit, but I thought it most unfortunate that he had not been frank with me. He must remember that I was not in the position of being a subordinate of Brooke. I was, in fact, in certain military matters, representing the Government of Canada, and as such I had to deal both with Brooke and with Paget as representatives of another Government. I had never had any idea that this interchange of adverse views on myself was taking place behind my back.

I think that Stuart then, perhaps for the first time, realized the wrongness and unethical character of his action, for he again said, very defensively, that having these views, he had felt it was his duty as CGS to press them on the Canadian Government. . . .

This record, McNaughton noted at the foot of his memorandum, "is a complete admission of the basic charge I make against the Minister of National Defence and the C.G.S. Canada, namely, that they have by conversations, some of which were 'casual,' with representatives of another government with whom I have had to deal directly as a representative of Canada, and without any advice to me, progressively placed me in a position where these representatives would know—but not myself—that in discussing matters with them I did not rest on the support and confidence of the Canadian authorities. If the Minister and/or C.G.S. had been frank with me when they first heard Brooke's opinion in casual conversation, then we would have been in a position to consult, and to stand together in maintaining Canada's interest in matters in which Brooke was representing other interests, which were not necessarily, and indeed probably not, the same as ours."[200]

During the first week of December McNaughton felt unwell— occasioned by fatigue and worry—and he stayed at home in bed. On the 10th he asked to be relieved of his command as soon as possible. Ralston decided to appoint Stuart Acting Army Commander as well as Chief of Staff at Canadian Military Headquarters in London—a new appointment designed to replace Montague as senior officer—which, as the *Manchester Guardian* observed, would have the effect of bringing Canadian troops overseas "under the direct control of the Minister." This, according to the Canadian official historian, was an "acute comment."[201] Stuart, however, was to seize his moments of independence in the future and, in words reminiscent of those of Cassius to Brutus before Philippi, Ralston chided him gently: "We have recently gone through a pretty diffi- cult time together, and, as I told you in London, I cannot express adequately the full measure of your counsel and help," but then: "I am afraid that the telegrams that have passed within the last week or two have appeared more like those emanating from parti- sans on opposite sides than from co-workers in a common cause."[202] Later, when Crerar took over the Army from Stuart, "these two officers shared the duties formerly carried out by McNaughton as Senior Combatant Officer of the Canadian Army Overseas."[203]

The day appointed for McNaughton to turn over the command of the Army to Stuart was 27 December. On the 26th McNaughton addressed a final message to all ranks in his command, which reads in part:

Tomorrow, with the deepest and most heartfelt regret, I leave the Command of First Canadian Army, and in consequence, this is the last occasion when I have the privilege of addressing myself to you.

I do so, to thank you for the support you have given, in over- flowing measure, in building the First Canadian Army into the complete, well-balanced, effective, battleworthy organization it is to-day.

I do so, to thank you for the confidence and for the cheerfulness with which you have accepted all tasks as they arose; for the energy and the determination you have given to their discharge; and for the patience and discipline with which you have borne the many changes and disappointments of the last four hard years. . . .

I pray there will come an early and triumphant end to this present strife and that soon you may return once more to Canada, your kith and kin—

May Divine Providence bless you one and all.[204]

On the 27th Stuart was too sick to attend. He finally arrived at Army Headquarters at 11 A.M. on the 28th and took over Mc- Naughton's office. McNaughton then sent a message off to Canada to the effect that Stuart had assumed acting command "pending the appointment of my successor."[205] He then drove to Largiebeg, where his wife was waiting.

Early in January, they left by car on the first stage of their return to Canada. For half a mile from Largiebeg to the end of Tyrrell's Wood, both sides of the narrow country road were lined with troops. All the officers from headquarters were there, as well as hundreds of other officers and thousands of men. McNaughton stopped the car, got out and walked the whole length of the impromptu parade, crossing the road from one side to the other, shaking hands. This spontaneous show of affection made Stuart's report to the Prime Minister—that McNaughton was not close to the troops—a mockery. Mrs. McNaughton, following in the car, heard their shouts to her, "Mom,* bring him back to us soon!"

Thus the "restless and incisive intelligence and the singularly compelling personality that had dominated the Canadian field army so long . . . passed from the overseas stage."[206] McNaughton climbed back into the car and, for the first time on any journey with his wife, drove the twenty miles to London in silence; he could not speak a single word.

---

*As well as having been Home Sister at Number 15 Canadian General Hospital, she had worked in a soldiers canteen, started by the Honourable Mrs. Northgate, whose family owned Headley Court. Mrs. Northgate, who was responsible for counting the rations, was known affectionately as "Meany"; Mrs. McNaughton as "Mom."

Notes

PART FOUR

CHAPTER 1

1. Colonel C. P. Stacey, *Six Years of War* (Ottawa: The Queen's Printer, 1956), p. 36.
2. J. W. Pickersgill, *The Mackenzie King Record*, Vol. I (Toronto: University of Toronto Press, 1960), p. 37.
3. *Ibid.*, p. 38.
4. *Ibid.*
5. Interviews for CBC Archives, December, 1965.
6. *The Mackenzie King Record*, p. 38.
7. Interview with General Mc-Naughton, 14 July, 1965; CBC interviews.
8. McNaughton interview.
9. Wilfrid Eggleston, *Scientists at War* (Toronto: Oxford University Press, 1950), p. 13.
10. *Six Years of War*, p. 64.
11. McNaughton interview.
12. CBC interviews, December, 1965.
13. War Diary, General Staff 1 Div., October, 1939.
14. *Ibid.*
15. *Ibid.*, Appx. X-4.
16. CBC interviews.
17. W.D., G.S. 1 Div., October, 1939, Appx. X-4.
18. Address of 4 November, 1939, McNaughton Papers.
19. W.D., G.S. 1 Cdn Div., Appx. XI-1.
20. *Ibid.*
21. *Ibid.*, Appx. XI-2.
22. *Ibid.*, Appx. XI-3, Pt. 1.
23. W.D., G.S. 1 Div., 7 November, 1939.
24. *Ibid.*, 8 November, 1939.
25. *Ibid.*, 9-14 November, 1939.
26. *Ibid.*, November, 1939, Appx. XI-2.
27. *Ibid.*
28. *Ibid.*, Appx. XI-4.
29. *Ibid.*
30. *Ibid.*
31. CBC interviews.
32. W.D., G.S. 1 Div., November, 1939, Appx. XI-4.
33. "Scrapbook, 1939," McNaughton Papers (newspaper unknown).
34. W.D., G.S. 1 Div., 1 December, 1939.
35. *Ibid.*, 16 November, 1939.
36. *Six Years of War*, pp. 64-8.
37. CBC interviews.
38. Captain B. H. Liddell Hart, *Memoirs*, Vol. I (London: Cassell, 1965), p. 90.
39. W.D., G.S. 1 Div., 20 November, 1939.
40. *Ibid.*, 28 November, 1939.
41. H. Duncan Hall and G. C. Wrigley, *Studies of Overseas Supply* (London: H.M. Stationery Office, 1956), p. 58.
42. J. de N. Kennedy, *History of the Department of Munitions and Supply: Canada in the Second World War* (Ottawa: The King's Printer, 1950), Vol. II, p. 150.
43. W.D., G.S. 1 Div., 22 November, 1939.
44. Major-General A. G. L. Mc-Naughton, address to Canadian Military Institute, "Machines and Weapons of War," Toronto, 15 December, 1932.
45. W.D., G.S. 1 Div., November, 1939, Appx. XI-17.
46. *Ibid.*
47. *Ibid.*
48. McNaughton interview.
49. CBC interviews.
50. *Ibid.*
51. File, "Hon. R. J. Manion," McNaughton Papers.
52. *The Mackenzie King Record*, p. 38.
53. *Ibid.*, p. 39.
54. W.D., G.S. 1 Div., 8 December, 1939.
55. *The Mackenzie King Record*, p. 39.
56. W.D., G.S. 1 Div., 8-9 December, 1939.
57. *Ibid.*, 10 December, 1939.
58. *Ibid.*, December, 1939, Appx. XII-15.
59. *Ibid.*, Appx. XII-15(a).
60. McNaughton interview.
61. The Earl of Avon, *The Eden Memoirs: The Reckoning* (London: Cassell, 1965), p. 83.

62. Vincent Massey, *What's Past Is Prologue* (Toronto: Macmillan, 1963), pp. 317-8.
63. *Bulletin and Scots Pictorial,* 19 December, 1939.
64. *Daily Express,* 19 December, 1939.
65. W.D., G.S. 1 Div., 17 December, 1939.
66. *Daily Express,* 19 December, 1939.
67. *Ibid.*
68. W.D., G.S. 1 Div., 17 December, 1939.
69. *Daily Telegraph,* 20 December, 1939.
70. *Daily Express,* 20 December, 1939.

CHAPTER 2

1. W.D., G.S. 1 Div., December, 1939, Appx. XII-17(b).
2. Stacey, *Six Years of War,* p. 195.
3. *Ibid.,* p. 213.
4. *Ibid.,* p. 214.
5. CBC interviews.
6. *Ibid.*
7. *Ibid.*
8. Avon, *The Eden Memoirs: The Reckoning,* p. 91.
9. CBC interviews.
10. Eggleston, *Scientists at War,* p. 15.
11. CBC interviews.
12. *Ibid.*
13. Interview with General Mc-Naughton, 22 July, 1965.
14. Pearson to McNaughton, W.D., G.S. 1 Div., January, 1940, Appx. I-1.
15. W.D., G.S. 1 Div., 22 December, 1939.
16. *Six Years of War,* p. 232.
17. Colonel C. P. Stacey, *The Canadian Army 1939-1945* (Ottawa: The King's Printer, 1948), p. 7.
18. W.D., G.S. 1 Div., February, 1940, Appx. LVII.
19. *Six Years of War,* p. 233.
20. *Ibid.*
21. W.D., G.S. 1 Div., 14 March, 1940.
22. *Six Years of War,* p. 232.
23. W.D., G.S. 1 Div., March, 1940, Appx. IV.
24. *Ibid.,* Appx. XLIII.
25. CBC interviews.
26. W.D., G.S. 1 Div., March, 1940, Appx. XLIII.

27. *Ibid.*
28. *Ibid.*
29. *Ibid.*
30. *Ibid.*
31. *Ibid.*
32. McNaughton, cited by Lloyd Stevenson, *Sir Frederick Banting* (Toronto: The Ryerson Press, 1946), p. 379.
33. Banting, cited *ibid.,* p. 384.
34. Toronto *Daily Star,* 30 January, 1945.
35. Information supplied by Mrs. McNaughton.
36. W.D., G.S. 1 Div., December, 1939, Appx. XII-25(a).
37. *Ibid.,* 30 December, 1939.
38. W.D., G.S. 1 Div., 31 December, 1939.
39. *Ibid.,* February, 1940, Appx. XLIII.
40. *Ibid.,* January, 1940, Appx. I-26.
41. *Ibid.,* Appx. I-34.
42. *Ibid.,* February, 1940.

CHAPTER 3

1. W.D., G.S. 1 Div., 8 January, 1940.
2. *Ibid.,* 9 January, 1940.
3. *Ibid.,* February, 1940, Appx. XXII.
4. *Ibid.,* 10 January, 1940.
5. "Notes of a Conference held at G.H.Q., France," McNaughton Papers.
6. W.D., G.S. 1 Div., 12 January, 1940.
7. *Ibid.,* 13 January, 1940.
8. CBC interviews.
9. *Ibid.*
10. W.D., G.S. 1 Div., January, 1940, Appx. I-30.
11. *Ibid.,* Appx. I-29.
12. *Ibid.,* Appx. I-21.
13. *Ibid.*
14. *Ibid.,* Appx. I-8.
15. *Ibid.,* Appx. I-6.
16. *Ibid.,* Appx. I-24.
17. W.D., G.S. 1 Div., 12 February, 1940.
18. *Ibid.,* April, 1940, Appx. XXIII.
19. *Ibid.,* 6-7 February, 1940.
20. Interview with General Mc-Naughton, 4 August, 1965.
21. W.D., G.S. 1 Div., March, 1940, Appx. IV.
22. *Debates, House of Commons,* 9 September, 1939.
23. W.D., G.S. 1 Div., March, 1940, Appx. IV.

24. *Ibid.*
25. CBC interviews, December, 1965.
26. Stacey, *Six Years of War*, p. 68.
27. W.D., G.S. 1 Div., March, 1940, Appx. LIV.
28. *Ibid.*, Appx. XXXVIII.
29. W.D., G.S. 1 Div., 29 March, 1940.
30. *Ibid.*, April, 1940, Appx. III.
31. *Ibid.*, Appx. XIII.
32. *Ibid.*, Appx. VIII.
33. *Ibid.*, Appx. XXXV.
34. *Ibid.*

CHAPTER 4
1. CBC interviews, January, 1966.
2. *Ibid.*
3. *Ibid.*
4. W.D., G.S. 1 Div., April, 1940, Appx. XXXV.
5. CBC interviews, January, 1966.
6. W.D., G.S. 1 Div., April, 1940, Appx. XXXV.
7. *Ibid.*, 17 April, 1940.
8. CBC interviews.
9. Stacey, *Six Years of War*, p. 232, f.n.
10. W.D., G.S. 1 Div., April, 1940, Appendices, Message GS 327 dated 17 April.
11. CBC interviews.
12. *Six Years of War*, p. 261.
13. *See* reference 7.
14. External to Dominion, 17 April, 1940, in appendices to W.D., G.S. 1 Div.
15. Massey to External, 18 April, 1940, *ibid.*
16. *Six Years of War*, p. 256.
17. External to Dominion, 19 April, 1940, W.D., G.S. 1 Div.
18. Rogers to External, 22 April, 1940, *ibid.*
19. CBC interviews; McNaughton interview, 25 August, 1965.
20. *Six Years of War*, pp. 262-3.
21. CBC interviews.
22. Ironside to McNaughton, 25 April, 1940, W.D., G.S. 1 Div.
23. Stanley to McNaughton, 23 April, 1940, *ibid.*
24. W.D., G.S. 1 Div., 19 April, 1940.
25. *Ibid.*, May, 1940, Appx. XXVI.

CHAPTER 5
1. W.D., G.S. 1 Div., May, 1940, Appx. XII.
2. *Ibid.*, Appx. XLII.
3. John Swettenham, *To Seize the Victory* (Toronto: The Ryerson Press, 1965), p. 113 f.n.
4. W.D., G.S. 1 Div., May, 1940, Appx. XLIV.
5. *Ibid.*
6. W.D., G.S. 1 Div., 17 May, 1940.
7. CBC interviews, December, 1965.
8. W.D., G.S. 1 Div., 20 May, 1940.
9. *Ibid.*, Appx. LXV.
10. CBC interviews, January, 1966.
11. *Ibid.*
12. W.D., G.S. 1 Div., May, 1940, Appx. LXV.
13. Stacey, *Six Years of War*, pp. 266-7.
14. CBC interviews, January, 1966.
15. *Ibid.*
16. *Ibid.*
17. *Ibid.*
18. *Ibid.*
19. W.D., G.S. 1 Div., May, 1940, Appx. LXV.
20. CBC interviews.
21. W.D., G.S. 1 Div., Appx. LXV, "F," G.S.O.2's Diary of Events, 23-24 May, 1940.
22. *Ibid.*
23. Winston S. Churchill, *Their Finest Hour* (London: Cassell, 1949), p. 72.
24. *Ibid.*, p. 73.
25. *Ibid.*
26. British Official History, *The War in France and Flanders, 1939-1940*, p. 168.
27. Comment by Major-General G. R. Turner, 16 February, 1945, on prelimenary narrative, "History of Canadian Military Forces Overseas, 1940-42," McNaughton Papers.
28. CBC interviews.
29. *Ibid.*
30. *Ibid.*
31. *Ibid.*
32. *Ibid.*
33. W.D., G.S. 1 Div., May, 1940, Appx. LXV-10.
34. *Their Finest Hour*, pp. 71-2.
35. *Ibid.*, pp. 70-71.
36. *Ibid.*, p. 70.
37. McNaughton interview, 28 July, 1965.
38. British Official History, *op. cit.*, p. 165.
39. W.D., G.S. 1 Div., May, 1940, Appx. LXV, "E."
40. *Ibid.*, 11.
41. External to Dominion, 23 May, 1940, MS Papers, Vol. 1.

42. David Devine, *The Nine Days of Dunkirk* (London: Faber & Faber, 1959), p. 50.
43. British Official History, *op. cit.* p. 147.
44. Lord Ismay, *Memoirs* (London: Heinemann, 1960), p. 130.
45. *Ibid.*, pp. 130-1. Interview with General McNaughton, 15 December, 1965.
46. *The Nine Days of Dunkirk*, p. 54.
47. British Official History, *op. cit.*, pp. 148-9.
48. *Ibid.*, p. 149.
49. W.D., G.S. 1 Div., May, 1940, Appx. LXXIV.
50. *Ibid.*
51. *Ibid.*
52. *Ibid.*
53. *Ibid.*
54. *Ibid.*
55. *Ibid.*
56. McNaughton interview, 28 July, 1965.
57. W.D., G.S. 1 Div., May, 1940, Appx. LXXIV.
58. *Ibid.*
59. *Their Finest Hour*, p. 65.
60. CBC interviews, January, 1966.
61. *Ibid.*
62. Appx. LXXXI.
63. *Ibid.*
64. *Six Years of War*, p. 272.
65. W.D., G.S. 1 Div., May, 1940, Appx. LXV.
66. *Ibid.*

CHAPTER 6

1. CBC interviews.
2. Churchill, *Their Finest Hour*, p. 155.
3. W.D., G.S. 1 Div., June, 1940, Appx. XIV.
4. *Ibid.*, Appx. X.
5. *Ibid.*
6. *Ibid.*
7. *Ibid.*, Appx. XVIII A.
8. *Ibid.*
9. CBC interviews.
10. *Ibid.*
11. *Their Finest Hour*, pp. 123-4.
12. W.D., G.S. 1 Div., 5-8 June, 1940.
13. *Ibid.*, 10 June, 1940.
14. *Ibid.*, Appx. XLVII.
15. Major-General Sir Edward Spears, *Assignment to Catastrophe*, Vol. I (London: Heinemann, 1954), p. 205.
16. *Their Finest Hour*, p. 98.
17. Stacey, *Six Years of War*, p. 277.

18. *Their Finest Hour*, p. 169.
19. Arthur Bryant, *The Turn of the Tide* (London: Collins, 1957), p. 170.
20. *Ibid.*, p. 160.
21. *Six Years of War*, p. 275.
22. Interview with General McNaughton, 17 June, 1965.
23. *Ibid.*
24. *Six Years of War*, p. 276.
25. McNaughton interview.
26. W.D., G.S. 1 Div., June, 1940, XLI, XLIX.
27. Interview.
28. W.D., G.S. 1 Div., June, 1940, Appx. LXI.
29. *Ibid.*
30. *Ibid.*
31. McNaughton interview.
32. W.D., G.S. 1 Div., June, 1940.
33. Interview.
34. *Ibid.*
35. *Ibid.*
36. *The Turn of the Tide*, p. 162.
37. *Ibid.*, p. 166.
38. W.D., G.S. 1 Div., June, 1940, Appx. LXI.
39. *Their Finest Hour*, p. 161.
40. *The Turn of the Tide*, pp. 168-9.
41. Brooke's comments on his own diary entry, cited *ibid.*, pp. 169-70.
42. *The Turn of the Tide*, p. 170.
43. *Ibid.*, pp. 170-1.
44. *Ibid.*, pp. 172-4.
45. McNaughton interview.
46. W.D., G.S. 1 Div., June, 1940, Appx. LVIII.
47. Interview.
48. W.D., G.S. 1 Div., Appx. LXIX.
49. *Six Years of War*, p. 279.
50. Interview.
51. *Six Years of War*, p. 281.
52. W.D., G.S. 1 Div., June, 1940, Appx. LXV C.
53. Interview.
54. W.D., G.S. 1 Div., June, 1940, Appx. LXIX C.
55. Interview.
56. W.D., G.S. 1 Div., June, 1940, Appx. LXIX.
57. *Their Finest Hour*, p. 189.
58. W.D., G.S. 1 Div., June, 1940, Appx. LXIX.
59. *Ibid.*
60. *Six Years of War*, p. 283.
61. W.D., G.S. 1 Div., June, 1940, Appx. LXIX.
62. *Ibid.*, Appx. CXLIV.
63. Interview.

64. *Six Years of War,* p. 282.
65. *Ibid.*
66. Interview.
67. *Six Years of War,* p. 282.
68. *The Turn of the Tide,* p. 185.
69. Interview.
70. *Ibid.*
71. W.D., G.S. 1 Div., June, 1940, Appx. CXLV.
72. Interview.
73. *Their Finest Hour,* p. 234.
74. Interview.
75. *Ibid.*

CHAPTER 7

1. *Churchill, Their Finest Hour,* p. 226.
2. "Financial Programme for Canada's Participation in the War," Minister of National Defence, 24 September, 1939.
3. Historical Section, G.S., *The Canadians in Britain, 1939-1944,* (Ottawa: The King's Printer, n.d.), p. 28.
4. W.D., G.S. 1 Div., June, 1940, Appx. LXXXVII.
5. *Ibid.,* Appx. LXXXII.
6. *Ibid.*
7. CBC interviews, June, 1966.
8. W.D., G.S. 1 Div., June, 1940, Appx. CIV.
9. *Ibid.,* Appx. CXVIII.
10. CBC interviews.
11. W.D., G.S. 1 Div., June, 1940, Appx. CXXV.
12. *Ibid.*
13. CBC interviews.
14. W.D., G.S. 1 Div., June, 1940, Appx. CXXV.
15. CBC interviews.
16. W.D., G.S. 1 Div., June, 1940, Appx. CLI.
17. CBC interviews.
18. W.D., G.S. 1 Div., July, 1940, Appx. XVIII.
19. *Ibid.,* Appx. XXXV.
20. *Ibid.,* Appx. LXXXIX.
21. CBC interviews.
22. W.D., G.S. 1 Div., June, 1940, Appx. CLXVII.
23. W.D., G.S. VII Corps, July, 1940, Appx. XII.
24. W.D., G.S. 1 Div., July, 1940, Appx. LXVII.
25. CBC interviews.
26. W.D., G.S. VII Corps, July 1940, Appx. VII.
27. *Ibid.*
28. *Ibid.,* Appx. LI.

29. W.D., G.S. 1 Div., 18 June, 1940.
30. CBC interviews.
31. *Ibid.*
32. W.D., G.S. 1 Div., June 1940, Appx. XCIII.
33. *Ibid.,* Appx. LXXXII.
34. *Ibid.,* Appx. CXXXV.
35. W.D., VII Corps, August, 1940, Appx. CI.
36. *Ibid.,* September, 1940, Appx. CXIV.
37. W.D., G.S. 1 Div., 24 June, 1940.
38. *Ibid.,* Appx. CXIV.
39. *Ibid.,* Appx. CXXV.
40. *Ibid.,* Appx. CLI.
41. McNaughton, "Canada's Part in the Inception, Development and Promotion of the Newest Land Battle Weapons," *Industrial Canada,* November, 1945.
42. W.D., G.S. 1 Div., 4 July, 1940.
43. W.D., G.S. VII Corps, 1 August, 1940.
44. *Ibid.,* Appx. XLIV.
45. *Ibid.,* October, 1940, Appx. XLV.
46. *Ibid.,* Appx. XLVI.
47. *Ibid.,* Appx. I.
48. Information supplied by Brigadier R. J. Leach, 20 April, 1967.
49. Ross Munro, "Canada's McNaughton," *Liberty,* 27 February, 1943.
50. Wallace Reyburn, "General in Battle Dress," *Maclean's Magazine,* 15 February, 1943.
51. W.D., G.S. VII Corps, September, 1940, Appx. XVIII.
52. *Ibid.,* December, 1940, Appx. LXXVIII.
53. *Ibid.,* October, 1940, Appx. IIA.
54. *Ibid.,* November, 1940, Appx. XXXIV.
55. *The Canadian Mirror,* 20 July, 1940.
56. W.D., G.S. VII Corps, July 1940, Appx. XV.
57. *Ibid.,* October, 1940, Appx. LXXXVI.
58. Ibid., November, 1940, Appx. XXIIIA.
59. *Their Finest Hour,* p. 348.
60. McNaughton interview, June, 1966.
61. General Sir Frederick Pile, *Ack-Ack* (London: Harrap, 1949), p. 182.
62. *Ibid.*
63. W.D., G.S. VII Corps, November 1940, Appx. XXIIIA.
64. *Ibid.,* September, 1940, Appx. LXXXII.

65. *Ibid.*, Appx. CXXII.
66. *Ibid.*, November, 1940, Appx. LI.
67. CBC interviews, June, 1966.
68. W.D., G.S. 1 Div., July, 1940, Appx. XIV.
69. *Ibid.*, 18 June, 1940.
70. CBC interviews.
71. W.D., G.S. 1 Div., June, 1940, Appx. CXLIII.
72. W.D., VII Corps, 9 August, 1940.
73. *Ibid.*, August, 1940, Appx. XXXVII.
74. W.D., G.S. 1 Div., July, 1940, Appx. LXIII.
75. W.D., G.S. VII Corps, August, 1940, Appx. XLIV.
76. CBC interviews.
77. W.D., G.S. VII Corps, August, 1940, Appx. XLIV.
78. *Ibid.*, September, 1940, Appx. XCI.
79. *Ibid.*, Appx. CXXVII.
80. *Ibid.*, Appx. XCI.
81. *Ibid.*, October, 1940, Appx. XXIV.
82. *Ibid.*, September, 1940, Appx. CVI.
83. *Ibid.*, October, 1940, Appx. C.
84. *Ibid.*
85. *Ibid.*, Appx. CX.
86. W.D., G.S. 1 Div., July, 1940, Appx. I.
87. CBC interviews.
88. W.D., G.S. 1 Div., June, 1940, Appx. CXVII.
89. *Ibid.*, July, 1940, Appx. XVIII.
90. CBC interviews.
91. W.D., G.S. 1 Div., July, 1940, Appx. XVIII.
92. Information supplied by Colonel Harold Hemming, May, 1966.
93. *Their Finest Hour*, p. 236.
94. W.D., G.S. 1 Div., 17 July, 1940.
95. CBC interviews.
96. W.D., G.S. VII Corps, August, 1940, Appx. IX.
97. *Ibid.*, Appx. LIX.
98. CBC interviews.
99. W.D., G.S. 1 Div., June, 1940, Appx. CXXIV.
100. *Ibid.*
101. CBC interviews.
102. *Ibid.*
103. W.D., G.S., VII Corps, August, 1940, Appx. VI.
104. W.D., G.S. VII Corps, September, 1940, Appx. XLII.
105. CBC interviews.
106. Appx. XLII.

107. W.D., G.S. VII Corps, October, 1940, Appx. XV.
108. CBC interviews.
109. W.D., G.S. VII Corps, October, 1940, Appx. XXVIII.
110. Statement by Colonel E. M. D. Leslie, 20 March, 1966.
111. W.D., G.S. VII Corps, September, 1940, Appx. XIII.
112. *Ibid.*, August, 1940, Appendices VI, XI.
113. Letter, Major-General C. Churchill Mann to General McNaughton, 14 April, 1965.
114. W.D., G.S. VII Corps, September, 1940, Appx. VIII.
115. *Ibid.*, October, 1940, Appx. II.
116. W.D., G.S. VII Corps, 23 November, 1940.
117. *Ibid.*, September, 1940, Appx. XV.
118. *Ibid.*
119. CBC interviews.
120. W.D., G.S. VII Corps, 4 September, 1940; October, 1940, Appx. XXVII.
121. *Ibid.*, August, 1940, Appx. XCIII.
122. *Ibid.*, 1 September, 1940.
123. *Ibid.*, September, 1940, Appx. XX.
124. *Ibid.*, Appx. LVI.
125. *Ibid.*, Appx. LXXX.
126. *Ibid.*, Appx. I.
127. *Ibid.*
128. CBC interviews.
129. W.D., G.S. VII Corps, September, 1940, Appx. V.
130. *Ibid.*, November, 1940, Appx. XXV.
131. *Ibid.*, September, 1940, Appx. LVII.
132. *Ibid.*
133. *Ibid.*, Appx. LXVI.
134. Interview with General McNaughton, 27 October, 1965.
135. W.D., G.S. VII Corps, September, 1940, Appx. CX.
136. *Ibid.*, October, 1940, Appx. LI.
137. *Ibid.*, Appendices XIX. XX.
138. *Ibid.*, 13 November, 1940.
139. *Ibid.*, October, 1940, Appx. CIII.
140. *Ibid.*, August, 1940, Appx. XXIX.
141. Ibid., November, 1940, Appx. XCVIII.
142. *Ibid.*, August, 1940, Appx. XCVIII.
143. *Ibid.*, September, 1940, Appx. III.
144. *Ibid.*, 29 November, 1940.
145. *Ibid.*, December, 1940, Appx. XIV.

146. *Ibid.*, Appx. LXXII.
147. "Canada's McNaughton."
148. W.D., G.S. VII Corps, December, 1940, Appx. LXXIIA.
149. *Ibid.*
150. *Debates, House of Commons,* Session 1941, Vol. II, March, 1941, pp. 1424-5.

CHAPTER 8

1. W.D., G.S. Cdn. Corps, January, 1941, Appx. LA.
2. *Ibid.*, Appx. LI.
3. *Ibid.*, Appx. VI.
4. File/1/Formations/4/S, Memorandum of meeting at War Office, 17 January, 1941, McNaughton Papers.
5. McNaughton interview, 30 June, 1965.
6. W.D., G.S. Cdn. Corps, March, 1941, Appx. LXXXVIII.
7. File 1/Railway/1, 5 July, 1941; Cdn. Corps File 1/Conf/8, "Minutes . . . 22 Jul 41."
8. W.D., G.S. Cdn. Corps, January, 1941, Appx. LVII.
9. The Earl of Bessborough, *Return to the Forest* (London: Weidenfeld & Nicolson, 1962), pp. 73-6.
10. *Ibid.*, pp. 71, 76.
11. *Ibid.*, p. 74.
12. Munro, "Canada's McNaughton."
13. *Return to the Forest*, p. 74.
14. W.D., G.S. Cdn. Corps, 11-13, 26-28 February, 1941.
15. Information supplied by Lt.-Colonel George Alleyne Browne, 31 January, 1966.
16. *Return to the Forest*, pp. 77-8.
17. McNaughton interview.
18. W.D., G.S. Cdn. Corps, January, 1941, Appx. XC.
19. *Ibid.*
20. General McNaughton, Personal War Diary, July, 1943, Appx. M.
21. *Return to the Forest*, p. 75.
22. W.D., G.S. Cdn. Corps, January, 1941, Appx. LXXXII.
23. *Ibid.*
24. *Ibid.*, February, 1941, Appx. LXVI. Pile, *Ack-Ack*, p. 198.
25. W.D., G.S. Cdn. Corps, February, 1941, Appendices XIVA, LXVI.
26. *Ack-Ack*, p. 248.
27. Sir Donald Banks, *Flame Over Britain* (London: Samson, Low, Marston & Co. Ltd., 1946), p. 70.

28. *Ibid.*
29. *Ibid.*, pp. 70-1.
30. McNaughton, Comments on Official Historical Sketch.
31. Flame Over Britain, p. 71.
32. *Ibid.*, p. 108.
33. *Ibid.*, p. 136.
34. *Ibid.*, p. 109.
35. W.D., G.S. Cdn. Corps, March, 1941, Appx. XXIV.
36. *Ibid.*, June, 1941, Appx. LV.
37. *Ibid.*, August, 1941, Appx. XX.
38. *Ibid.*, July, 1941, Appx. XXXIII.
39. *Ibid.*, August, 1941, Appx. XLIII.
40. Address to be broadcast to McGill Graduates' Society meetings . . . 6 October, 1941, *ibid.*, October, 1941, Appx. L.
41. *Return to the Forest*, p. 75.
42. W.D., G.S. Cdn. Corps, January, 1941, Appx. XIV.
43. *Ibid.*, Appx, XXXII.
44. *Ibid.*, Appx. XC.
45. *Ibid.*, 14 February, 1941; November, 1941, Appx. XXXVI.
46. W.D., G.S. Cdn. Corps, March, 1941, Appendices XVIII, XLIII.
47. *Ibid.*, July, 1941, Appx. XLIV.
48. "Canada's McNaughton"; Reyburn, "General in Battle Dress."
49. *Ibid.*
50. L.S.B. Shapiro, report from Washington, 26 January, 1942.
51. "General in Battle Dress."
52. *Ibid.*
53. Lieutenant-Commander P. K. Kemp, *Victory at Sea 1939-1945* (London: F. Muller Ltd. 1958), p. 172.
54. Letter d. 13 June, 1966, Naval Historical Branch, Ministry of Defence, London, to Directorate of History, CFHQ, Ottawa.
55. *Victory at Sea*, p. 177.
56. *Eden Memoirs: The Reckoning*, p. 270.
57. Interview with General McNaughton, March, 1965.
58. W.D., G.S. Cdn. Corps, June, 1941, Appx. LVII.
59. *Ibid.*
60. *Ibid.*, Appx. LVII (2).
61. *Ibid.*, Appx. XXXIV.
62. *Debates, House of Commons,* 1 April, 1941.
63. File 3/Cdn. Corps/4/, Cable, Defensor to Canmiltry, 31 July, 1941, McNaughton Papers.

64. W.D., G.S. Cdn. Corps, September, 1941, Appx. XXVI.
65. File 3/Cdn Corps/4, Defensor to Canmiltry, 31 October, 1941.
66. Interview with General McNaughton, 20 June, 1965.
67. Pickersgill, *The Mackenzie King Record*, Vol. I, pp. 261-2.
68. *Ibid.*, pp. 262-5.
69. London *Times*, 27 August, 1941.
70. Cdn. Corps File PA 5-3-1 "Minutes . . . 15 Oct 41."
71. W.D., G.S. Cdn. Corps, October, 1941, Appx. XXVI.
72. Historical Section, G.S., *The Canadians in Britain*, p. 35.
73. McNaughton interview, 17 June, 1965.
74. "Canada's McNaughton."
75. W.D., G.S. Cdn. Corps, August, 1941, Appx. XXXVI.
76. *Ibid.*, November, 1941, Appx. X.

CHAPTER 9

1. Crerar to McNaughton, 11 August, 1941, File CC7/Crerar/6.
2. McNaughton to Crerar, 11 September, 1941, *ibid.*
3. "Memorandum on Conference . . . 27 Dec 41," File 1/Cdn Army/1.
4. Brooke to McNaughton, 7 January, 1942, File PA 5-3-2, McNaughton Papers.
5. *Debates, House of Commons*, 24 March, 1942.
6. *Ibid.*
7. Pickersgill, *The Mackenzie King Record*, Vol. I, p. 357.
8. Stacey, *Six Years of War*, p. 122.
9. *The Mackenzie King Record*, p. 360.
10. *Ibid.*
11. *Ibid.*, pp. 357, 359-60.
12. McNaughton, Personal War Diary, 10 February, 1942.
13. Memorandum by McNaughton, 5 September, 1941, file CC 7/105, McNaughton Papers.
14. *The Mackenzie King Record*, pp. 358-9.
15. *Ibid.*, p. 359.
16. *Canadian Military Gazette*, August, 1941.
17. Toronto *Globe and Mail*, 21 June, 1940.
18. Sherbrooke *Daily Record*, 7 June, 1940.
19. *Debates, House of Commons*, 24 March, 1942.

20. *The Mackenzie King Record*, p. 359.
21. *Ibid.*, p. 358.
22. *Ibid.*, pp. 357-8.
23. Hamilton *Spectator*, 19 December, 1942.
24. "Visit of Lieut.-Gen. A. G. L. McNaughton . . . to Washington, 11 Mar 42," File PA 3-6.
25. *Ibid.*
26. Pile, *Ack-Ack*, p. 1.
27. Personal War Diary, 26 February-3 March, 1942.
28. *Ibid.*, 27 February, 6 March, 1942.
29. "Visit of Lieut.-Gen. A. G. L. McNaughton . . . to Washington."
30. *Ibid.*
31. *Ibid.*
32. *Ibid.*
33. *Ibid.*
34. *Ibid.*
35. W.D., G.S. Cdn. Corps, 18 March, 1942.
36. *Ibid.*, 7, 12 March, 1942.
37. *Ibid.*, 17-18 March, 1942.
38. *Ibid.*, 17 March, 1942.
39. *Ibid.*, 19 March, 1942.
40. *Ibid.*, 20-28 March, 1942.
41. P.W.D., G.S. First Cdn. Army, 15 April, 1942.
42. *Ibid.*, 6 April, 1942.
43. Major H.S.M. Carver, "Personnel Selection in the Canadian Army" (Ottawa: National Defence Headquarters, 1945), pp. 30, 32.
44. *Ibid.*, p. 2.
45. Letter, Blair to Swettenham, 11 October, 1966.
46. File PA 3-6, attached to W.D., G.S. First Cdn. Army, April, 1942.
47. *Ibid.*
48. *The Mackenzie King Record*, p. 394.
49. Historical Section, G.S., *The Canadians in Britain*, p. 65.
50. P.W.D., G.S. First Cdn. Army, 3 November, 1942.
51. *Ibid.*, December, 1942, Appx. "F."
52. *Ibid.*, 24 April, 1942.
53. *Ibid.*, 27 April, 1942.
54. *Ibid.*, 21 April, 1942.
55. *Ibid.*, 10 May, 1942.
56. Interview with General McNaughton, 9 June, 1965.
57. Memo of a meeting held 11 April, 1942, File PA 3-6.

58. File PA 9-1-9, McNaughton Papers.
59. Information supplied by L.W.C.S. Barnes, Head, Proof and Ballistics Section, Department of National Defence.
60. L.W.C.S. Barnes, writing in *Discovery*, January, 1965.
61. Personal W. D., 7 May, 1942; December, 1942. Appx. "G."
62. *Ibid.*, 11 May, 1942.
63. *Ibid.*, 26 May, 1942.
64. *Ibid.*, 15 May, 1942.
65. *Ibid.*, 16 June, 1942.
66. *Ibid.*, June, 1942, Appx. "L."
67. *Ibid.*, October, 1942, Appx. "A."
68. *Ibid.*, 17 December, 1942.
69. McNaughton to press correspondents, 27 August, 1942. Personal W.D., August, 1942, Appx. "F."
70. W.D., 11 April, 1942; File PA 9-1-11 (Vol. 1), McNaughton Papers.
71. Churchill, *The Hinge of Fate* (Boston: Houghton Mifflin, 1951), pp. 383-4.
72. *Ibid.*, p. 396.
73. Interview with General McNaughton, 24 May, 1965.
74. *Debates, House of Commons,* 1941-42, V, pp. 224-8.
75. Associated Press report, 21 June, 1942.
76. *Debates, House of Commons,* pp. 427-8, 431, 434.
77. *Ibid.*, p. 296.
78. *Ibid.*, pp. 529-30.
79. *Ibid.*, p. 385.
80. *Ibid.*, p. 467.
81. *Ibid.*, p. 325.
82. *Ibid.*, p. 331.
83. *Ibid.*, p. 459.
84. *Ibid.*, pp. 448-9.
85. *Ibid.*, p. 443.
86. *Ibid.*, p. 345.
87. London *Times*, 2 July, 1942.
88. *Debates, House of Commons,* 1941-42, V, pp. 608-9.
89. London *Times*, 26 July, 1942.
90. *Debates, House of Commons,* 1941-42, V, p. 1148.
91. London *Times*, 17 July, 1942.
92. *Ibid.*, 30 July, 1942.
93. *Ibid.*, 25 July, 6 August, 1942.
94. *Debates, House of Commons,* 1941-42, V, pp. 1125-8.
95. J. W. Pickersgill and D. F. Forster, *The Mackenzie King Record,* Vol. II (Toronto: University of Toronto Press, 1968), p. 462.
96. P.W.D., 9 July, 1942.
97. *Ibid.*, August, 1942, Appendices, draft message McNaughton to Ralston, n.d.
98. McNaughton, "Machines and Weapons of War."
99. "Scrapbook, 1945," McNaughton Papers.
100. P.W.D., June, 1942, Appx. "H."
101. *Ibid.*
102. *Ibid.*
103. "Basis for discussion with the High Commissioner," n.d., CMHQ file PA 5-4-3.
104. *Ibid.*
105. McNaughton interview, 9 June, 1965.
106. *Ibid.*
107. Massey, *What's Past is Prologue,* p. 321.
108. Massey to External, 7 July, 1942, PA 5-4-3.
109. *Ibid.*, 1 August, 1942.
110. Attlee to Massey, 3 September, 1942, *ibid.*
111. *Six Years of War,* p. 317.
112. *The Hinge of Fate,* pp. 348-9.
113. *Ibid.*, p. 349.
114. Ismay, *Memoirs,* p. 164.
115. *Ibid.*, pp. 164-5.
116. *The Hinge of Fate,* p. 436.
117. Bryant, *The Turn of the Tide,* p. 420, f.n.
118. *Ibid.*
119. Gist of conversation Portal-McNaughton, 14 September, 1942. Memorandum dated 16 September, 1942, CMHQ file PA 1-7-1.
120. *The Turn of the Tide,* p. 319.
121. P.W.D., July, 1942, Appendix "I."
122. Interview with General McNaughton, 28 April, 1965.
123. P.W.D., July, 1942, Appendix "I."
124. McNaughton interview, 28 April, 1965.
125. P.W.D., July, 1942, Appendix "I."
126. *Ibid.*
127. *Ibid.*
128. *Ibid.*
129. *Ibid.*

130. *Ibid.*
131. *Six Years of War,* p. 323.
132. McNaughton interview, 9 June, 1965.
133. McNaughton to Ralston, 23 September, 1944, "Retirement from Cdn. Army," McNaughton Papers.
134. P.W.D., August, 1942, Appendices.
135. Notes on a conference held 10 August, 1942, CMHQ file PA 5-3-8, copy on PA 3-6.
136. *Six Years of War,* p. 335.
137. *Ibid.*
138. *Ibid.*
139. *Ibid.*
140. Lt.-General Sir Frederick Morgan, *Overture to Overlord* (London: Hodder & Stoughton, 1950), p. 282.
141. *Ibid.,* pp. 358-9.
142. Interview with General McNaughton, 6 July, 1966.
143. P.W.D., August, 1942, Appx. "F."
144. *Ibid.*
145. *Six Years of War,* p. 337.
146. *Ibid.,* pp. 395-6.
147. P.W.D., September, 1942, Appx. "H."
148. *Six Years of War,* p. 409.
149. P.W.D., September, 1942, Appx. "I."
150. *Ibid.*
151. Interview with General McNaughton, 23 February, 1965.
152. P.W.D., September, 1942, Appx. "I."
153. *Ibid.*
154. Alan Brooke, cited by Bryant, *The Turn of the Tide,* pp. 501-2.
155. London *Times,* 19 February, 1957.
156. P.W.D., 21 September, 1942.
157. *Ibid.,* September, 1942, Appx. "I."
158. *Ibid.*
159. *The Mackenzie King Record,* Vol. I, p. 418.
160. *Ibid.,* p. 419.
161. P.W.D., September, 1942, Appx. "I."
162. *The Mackenzie King Record,* Vol. 1, p. 420.
163. P.W.D., Appx. "H."
164. Memorandum dated 2 November, 1942, on meeting of McNaughton and Smuts, PA 5-3-11, McNaughton Papers.
165. *Ibid.*
166. *Ibid.*
167. P.W.D., November, 1942, Appx. "T."
168. *Ibid.,* October, 1942, Appx. "I."
169. *Ibid.*
170. *Ibid.,* Appx. "E."
171. *Ibid.,* Appx. "H."
172. *Ibid.,* Appx. "I."
173. *Ibid.*
174. *Ibid.*
175. *Ibid.,* December, 1942, Appx. "P."
176. *Ibid.,* November, 1942, Appx. "G."
177. *Ibid.,* December, 1942, Appx. "N."
178. *Ibid.,* Appx. "K."
179. *Six Years of War,* p. 101.
180. "Memorandum of a meeting . . . 19 Nov 42," P.W.D., November, 1942, Appx. "P."
181. *Ibid.*
182. *Ibid.*
183. P.W.D., December, 1942, Appx. "P."
184. *Ibid.,* 29 July, 1942.
185. *Ibid.,* December, 1942, Appx. "C."
186. *Ibid.,* Appx. "P."

CHAPTER 10

1. Personal War Diary, December, 1942, Appx. "N."
2. *Ibid.,* January, 1943, Appx. "A."
3. *Ibid.,* 9 January, 1943.
4. *Ibid.,* January, 1943, Appx. "M."
5. *Ibid.,* 5 January, 1943, Appx. "F."
6. *Ibid.,* February, 1942, Appx. "I."
7. *Ibid.*
8. *Ibid.*
9. *Ibid.,* 19 January, 1942.
10. Interview with General McNaughton, 11 May, 1966.
11. P.W.D., 21 January, 1943.
12. GHQ. *Exercise "Spartan": Comments by C-in-C Home Forces,* McNaughton Papers.
13. *Ibid.*
14. McNaughton interview, 11 May, 1966.
15. *Comments by C-in-C Home Forces.*
16. Stacey, *Six Years of War,* p. 250.
17. *Comments by C-in-C Home Forces.*
18. *Ibid.*

19. GHQ *Exercise "Spartan": Narrative of Events* (GHQ Home Forces), McNaughton Papers.
20. Letter dated 7 March, 1943, in possession of Mrs. McNaughton.
21. *"Spartan": Narrative of Events.*
22. *Ibid.*
23. *Ibid.*
24. *Ibid.*
25. *Ibid.*
26. *Comments by C-in-C Home Forces.*
27. *"Spartan": Narrative of Events.*
28. McNaughton interview.
29. *"Spartan": Narrative of Events.*
30. *Comments by C-in-C Home Forces.*
31. "Report by Chief Umpire," McNaughton Papers.
32. *Ibid. Comments by C-in-C Home Forces.*
33. *"Spartan": Narrative of Events.*
34. File PA 6-9-2, McNaughton Papers.
35. *Ibid.*
36. *Ibid.*
37. CBC interview, "Andrew McNaughton-Canadian."
38. P.W.D., July, 1942, Appx. "X."
39. *"Spartan": Narrative of Events.*
40. P.W.D., 23 June, 1943.
41. A. J. Kerry and W. A. McDill, *The History of the Corps of Canadian Engineers,* Vol. II (Ottawa: Military Engineers Association of Canada, 1966), p. 122.
42. Interview with Lt.-General Maurice Pope, October, 1966.
43. Churchill to Mackenzie King, 14 March, 1943, File PA 5-0-33, Vol. II, McNaughton Papers.
44. Pickersgill, *The Mackenzie King Record,* Vol. I, p. 496.
45. Mackenzie King to Churchill, 17 March, 1943, PA 5-0-33, Vol. II.
46. Stuart to McNaughton, 18 March, 1943, *ibid.*
47. McNaughton to Stuart, 20 March, 1943, *ibid.*
48. Churchill to Mackenzie King, 20 March, 1943, *ibid.*
49. *The Mackenzie King Record,* Vol. I, p. 497.
50. *Ibid.,* pp. 497-8.
51. Brooke, cited by Bryant, *The Turn of the Tide,* p. 576.
52. *The Mackenzie King Record,* Vol. I, p. 498.
53. *Ibid.,* p. 499.
54. *Ibid.,* pp. 499-500.
55. *Ibid.,* p. 501.
56. P.W.D., April, 1943, Appx. "PP."
57. *Ibid.,* Appx. "AAA."
58. *Ibid.,* Appx. "GGG."
59. Lt.-Colonel G. W. L. Nicholson, *The Canadians in Italy* (Ottawa: The Queen's Printer, 1956), p. 180.
60. *The Mackenzie King Record,* Vol. I, p. 504.
61. McNaughton to Stuart, 6 May, 1943, Appx. "N" to W.D., May, 1943.
62. Second message, McNaughton to Stuart, 6 May, 1943, Appx. "R."
63. P.W.D., May, 1943, Appx. "JJ."
64. *Ibid.,* Appx. "WW."
65. *Ibid.,* June, 1943, Appx. "V."
66. Interview with General McNaughton, 16 May, 1966.
67. P.W.D., June, 1943, Appx. "G."
68. *Ibid.,* 29 April, 1943.
69. *Ibid.,* April, 1943, Appx. "NNN."
70. *Ibid.,* Apps. "GGG." "NNN."
71. *Ibid.,* 9-13 May, 1943.
72. *Ibid.,* June, 1943, Appx. "M."
73. File PA 5-0-35, memo dated 18 March, 1943.
74. P.W.D., June, 1943, Appx. "B."
75. *Ibid.,* May, 1943, Appx. "III."
76. *Ibid.,* Appx. "WW."
77. *Ibid.,* Appx. "U."
78. *Ibid.,* June, 1943, Appx. "R."
79. *Ibid.,* Appx. "Z."
80. *Ibid.,* July, 1943, Appx. "J."
81. *The Mackenzie King Record,* Vol. I, p. 605.
82. *Ibid.,* pp. 604-5.
83. W.D., July, 1943, Appx. "J."
84. *Ibid.*
85. *Ibid.*
86. *Ibid.*
87. *Ibid.*
88. Norman Hillson, *Alexander of Tunis* (Toronto: W. H. Allen, 1952), p. 190.
89. Arthur Bryant, *Triumph in the West* (London: Collins, 1959), p. 234.
90. *Ibid.,* p. 236.
91. Field-Marshal The Viscount Montgomery, *Memoirs* (London: Collins, 1958), pp. 184-5.
92. Recorded interview with Lt.-General Simonds for "Andrew McNaughton-Canadian."
93. Sir Francis de Guingand, *Operation Victory* (London: Hodder & Stoughton, 1947), p. 184.

94. Montgomery, *Memoirs*, p. 185.
95. CBC interview for "Andrew McNaughton—Canadian."
96. File PA 1-0, Folio 72, McNaughton Papers.
97. W.D., July, 1943, Appx. "M."
98. Norman Ward (ed.), *A Party Politician: The Memoirs of Chubby Power* (Toronto: Macmillan, 1966), pp. 248-9.
99. W.D., July, 1943, Appx. "U."
100. Ralph Allen, *Ordeal by Fire* (New York: Doubleday, 1961), p. 433.
101. B. H. Liddell Hart, "Churchill in War: a Study of his Capacity and Performance in the Military Sphere," *Encounter*, April, 1966.
102. P.W.D., July, 1943, Appx. "X."
103. Morgan, *Overture to Overlord*, pp. 154, 167.
104. P.W.D., July, 1943, Appx. "X."
105. *Ibid.*, August, 1943, Appx. "F."
106. *Ibid.*
107. *Ibid.*, Appx. "C."
108. *Ibid.*, Appx. "F."
109. *Ibid.*
110. *Ibid.*
111. *Ibid.*
112. *Ibid.*
113. *Ibid.*, Appx. "H."
114. *Ibid.*, Appx. "J."
115. *The Mackenzie King Record*, Vol. I, p. 533.
116. *Ibid.*, p. 605.
117. *Ibid.*, p. 606.
118. *Ibid.*, pp. 606-7.
119. *Ibid.*, p. 605.
120. *Ibid.*, p. 606.
121. *Ibid.*, p. 545.
122. McNaughton comment on draft MS.
123. *The Mackenzie King Record*, Vol. I, p. 545.
124. Interview with Brigadier Orde, 27 April, 1966.
125. *The Mackenzie King Record*, Vol. I, p. 558.
126. Montgomery, *Memoirs*, pp. 184-5.
127. File PA 6-9-M-4, McNaughton Papers.
128. P.W.D., August, 1943, Appx. "R."
129. Pickersgill and Forster, *The Mackenzie King Record*, Vol. II, pp. 13-14.
130. P.W.D., August, 1943, Appx. "R."
131. *Ibid.*
132. *Evening Standard*, 16 September, 1943.

133. Letter from Lt.-Colonel George Alleyne Browne, 13 January, 1966.
134. Montgomery, cited by Bryant, *Triumph in the West*, p. 27, f.n.
135. Comments by General McNaughton on draft, "Canadian Official Historical Sketch," McNaughton Papers.
136. P.W.D., September, 1943, Appx. "A."
137. *Ibid.*, Appx. "G."
138. File PA 18-1, McNaughton Papers.
139. *The Mackenzie King Record*, Vol. II, p. 71.
140. P.W.D., October, 1943, Appx. "E."
141. *The Mackenzie King Record*, Vol. I, p. 607.
142. *Ibid.*, pp. 607-8.
143. *Ibid.*, p. 609.
144. *Ibid.*
145. P.W.D., 14-17 October, 1943, and Appx. "N."
146. Release by Lionel Shapiro, North American Newspaper Alliance, 15 February, 1944.
147. File PA 18-1, McNaughton Papers.
148. File PA 5-0-3-2, memo dated 4 November, 1943, McNaughton Papers.
149. *The Canadians in Italy*, pp. 356, 359.
150. *Ibid.*, pp. 362-3.
151. Comments on Official Historical Sketch, McNaughton Papers.
152. *The Mackenzie King Record*, Vol. II, pp. 298-9.
153. McNaughton to Stuart, 19 October, 1943, file PA 5-0-3-2.
154. *Overture to Overlord*, p. 254.
155. McNaughton to Stuart, 25 October, 1943.
156. *The Mackenzie King Record*, Vol. I, pp. 610-11.
157. P.W.D., November, 1943, Appx. "B."
158. *Ibid.*, Appx. "C."
159. P.W.D., November, 1943, sealed envelope.
160. *Ibid.*
161. *Ibid.*
162. *Ibid.*
163. *Ibid.*
164. P.W.D., May, 1943, Appx. "EE."
165. *Triumph in the West*, p. 105.
166. *The Mackenzie King Record*, Vol. II, pp. 298, 307.

167. *Time,* 3 January, 1944.
168. Montgomery, *Memoirs,* p. 218.
169. CBC interview, "Andrew McNaughton—Canadian."
170. *The Mackenzie King Record,* Vol. II, p. 91.
171. See reference 159.
172. *Ibid.*
173. P.W.D., November, 1943, Appx. "F."
174. *Ibid.*
175. *Ibid.*
176. *Ibid.*
177. *Ibid.*
178. Memo dated 10 November, 1943, File PA 5-0-3-2, McNaughton Papers.
179. McNaughton to Mackenzie King, 10 November, 1943, *ibid.*
180. *The Mackenzie King Record,* Vol. I, p. 611.
181. *Ibid.,* pp. 612-13.
182. Mackenzie King to McNaughton, 10 November, 1943, PA 5-0-3-2.
183. McNaughton to King, 11 November, 1943.
184. *The Mackenzie King Record,* Vol. I, p. 614.
185. McNaughton's comments on *The Mackenzie King Record.*
186. *The Mackenzie King Record,* Vol. I, p. 615.
187. Summary by Stuart, 12 November, 1943, D. Hist. file 312-009 (D60).

188. Message, Stuart to Ralston, 6 February, 1944, *ibid.*
189. Paget to McNaughton, 11 November, 1943, PA 5-0-3-2.
190. "Interview with Generals McNaughton and Stuart 13/11/43," *ibid.*
191. Memorandum of discussions with General Paget, 15 November, 1943, *ibid.*
192. *Ibid.*
193. Ralston to Stuart, 9 February, 1944, D. Hist. file 312-009(D60).
194. Memorandum of discussion with General Paget.
195. McNaughton to Mackenzie King, 13 November, 1943, file 312-009 (D60).
196. Memorandum dated 15 November, 1943, *ibid.*
197. *Ibid.*
198. Mackenzie King to McNaughton, 15 November, 1943, PA 5-0-3-2.
199. Report dated 26 November, 1943, PA 5-0-3-2.
200. Memo dated 29 November, 1943, File PA 5-0-3-2.
201. *Six Years of War,* p. 223.
202. *Ibid.,* p. 224.
203. *Ibid.,* p. 225.
204. Message, 26 December, 1943, PA 5-0-3-2.
205. McNaughton to C.G.S., 28 December, 1943, *ibid.*
206. Stacey, *The Canadian Army 1939-1945,* p. 93.

Index

PUBLISHER'S ACKNOWLEDGMENTS

Grateful acknowledgment is made to the following for permission to quote from copyrighted material:

COLLINS PUBLISHERS, *The Turn of the Tide* and *Triumph in the West* by Sir Arthur Bryant, and for *The Memoirs of Field-Marshal Viscount Montgomery*.

CURTIS BROWN LTD., *Flame Over Britain* by Sir Donald Banks.

GEORGE HARRAP & COMPANY LIMITED, *Ack-Ack* by Sir Frederick Pile.

HOUGHTON MIFFLIN COMPANY, *Their Finest Hour* and *The Hinge of Fate* by Sir Winston Churchill.

THE LITERARY EXECUTORS OF THE LATE MACKENZIE KING and THE UNIVERSITY OF TORONTO PRESS, *The Mackenzie King Record*, Volume I, by J. W. Pickersgill; *The Mackenzie King Record*, Volume II, by J. W. Pickersgill and D. F. Forster.

THE MACMILLAN COMPANY OF CANADA LIMITED, *A Party Politician: The Memoirs of Chubby Power*, edited by Norman Ward.

A. D. PETERS & CO., LITERARY AGENTS, *Overture to Overlord* by Sir Frederick Morgan.

GEORGE WEIDENFELD & NICOLSON LTD., *Return to the Forest* by the Earl of Bessborough.

Every reasonable care has been taken to trace ownership of copyrighted material used in this book. The author and publisher will welcome information that will enable them to rectify any errors or omissions.

THE TEXT OF THIS BOOK WAS SET IN 11 POINT BASKERVILLE TYPE WITH THE DISPLAY MATERIAL SET IN OPTIMA.